PICTURING IMPERIAL POWER

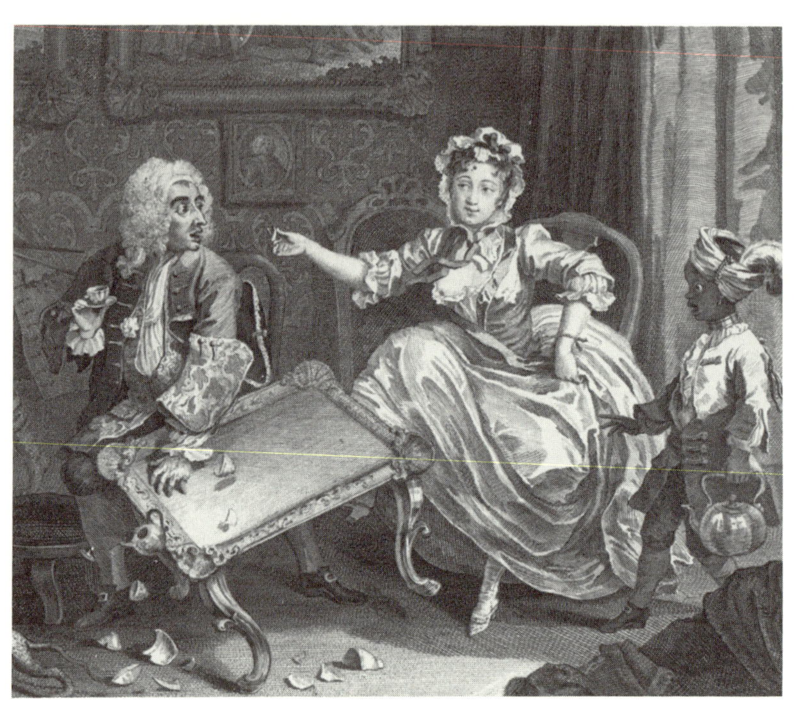

BETH FOWKES TOBIN

Picturing Imperial Power

COLONIAL SUBJECTS IN EIGHTEENTH-CENTURY

BRITISH PAINTING

DUKE UNIVERSITY PRESS DURHAM AND LONDON

1999

Frontispiece art: Detail from William Hogarth's
plate 2, *A Harlot's Progress,* 1732, engraving. Courtesy of
the Print Collection, Lewis Walpole Library,
Yale University.

FOR MY MOTHER

Contents

List of Illustrations   ix

Acknowledgments   xiii

Introduction: Toward a Cultural History
of Colonialism   1

1. Bringing the Empire Home:
The Black Servant in Domestic Portraiture   27

2. Native Land and Foreign Desires:
William Penn's Treaty with the Indians   56

3. Cultural Cross-Dressing in British America:
Portraits of British Officers and Mohawk Warriors   81

4. Accommodating India: Domestic Arrangements
in Anglo-Indian Family Portraiture   110

5. Taxonomy and Agency in Brunias's West
Indian Paintings   139

6. Imperial Designs: Botanical Illustration and
the British Botanic Empire   174

7. The Imperial Politics of the Local and
the Universal   202

Notes   227

Selected Bibliography   279

Index   301

List of Illustrations

1. William Hogarth, plate 2, *A Harlot's Progress*, 1732.   28

2. British School, *Elihu Yale, the 2nd Duke of Devonshire, Lord James Cavendish, Mr Tunstal, and a Page*, c. 1708.   29

3. William Hogarth, *The Countess's Morning Levee, Marriage à la Mode*, 1743–45.   38

4. Johan Zoffany, *The Family of Sir William Young, Baronet*, 1770.   40

5. William Redmore Bigg, *A Lady and Her Children Relieving a Cottager*, 1781.   47

6. Benjamin West, *William Penn's Treaty with the Indians*, 1771–72.   58

7. Benjamin West, *Colonel Guy Johnson and Karonghyontye (Captain David Hill)*. 1776.   82

8. Nineteenth-century copy of John Francis Rigaud, *Joseph Brant*, 1786.   83

9. Anonymous, *Sir John Caldwell*, c. 1780.   83

10. David Allan, *Thomas Graham, Baron Lynedoch*, 1769.   88

11. John Raphael Smith after Benjamin West, *Joseph Banks*, c. 1771–73.   89

12. Johan Zoffany, *Sir Elijah Impey, Chief Justice, Supreme Court of Judicature, Fort William, Calcutta*, 1783.   92

13. George Romney, *Joseph Brant (Thayendanegea)*, 1776.   98

14. Gilbert Stuart, *Joseph Brant*, 1786.   100

15. Ezra Ames, *Joseph Brant*, 1806.   104

16. Francesco Renaldi, *A European with his Family*, c. 1794–95.   112

17. Francesco Renaldi, *The Palmer Family*, 1786.   113

18. Thomas Hickey, *An Indian Girl*, 1787.   116

19. Johan Zoffany, *The Morse and Cator Families*, 1784.   120

20. Johan Zoffany, *Colonel Blair with his Family and an Ayah*, 1786.   124

21. Johan Zoffany, *The Impey Family Listening to Strolling Musicians*,
    c. 1783–84.   126

22. Arthur William Devis, *The Honorable William Monson and His Wife,
    Ann Debonnaire*, c. 1786.   130

23. Arthur William Devis, *Louisa Dent and her Children*, 1790.   131

24. Arthur William Devis, *William Dent with his brother John and an
    Indian Landlord, Anand Narain*, 1790.   132

25. Thomas Gainsborough, *The Morning Walk*, 1785.   134

26. T. Chambers after Sydney Parkinson, *A New Zealand Warrior in
    his Proper Dress, & Compleatly Armed, According to their Manner*,
    engraving, plate 15 in Sydney Parkinson, *A Journal of a Voyage to
    the South Seas, In his Majesty's Ship, the Endeavour* (London,
    1773).   141

27. Francis Wheatley, *Cries of London: New Mackrel, New Mackrel*,
    1795.   142

28. Agostino Brunias, *A West Indian Flower Girl*, c. 1769.   143

29. Agostino Brunias, *French Mulatresses and Negro Woman Bathing*,
    c. 1770.   150

30. Agostino Brunias, *Free West Indian Dominicans*, c. 1770.   154

31. Agostino Brunias, *Linen Day, Roseau, Dominica—A Market Scene*,
    c. 1780.   155

32. Agostino Brunias, *The Linen Market, Dominica*, c. 1780.   155

33. Agostino Brunias, *French Mulatress Purchasing Fruit from a Negro
    Wench*, c. 1770.   159

34. Maria Sibylla Merian, *Dissertation sur la Génération et Les
    Transformation des Insectes de Surinam*, 1726, engraved by Jan
    Pieter Sluyter, *Capsicum annuum*.   181

35. Sydney Parkinson, *Xylomelum pyriforme* 1770, plate 275 from
    Banks' Florilegium (1980–), engraved by J. F. Miller (1773).   193

36. After an anonymous artist employed by the Calcutta Botanic
    Gardens, *Caesalpinia sappan*, plate 16 from William Roxburgh,
    Plants of the Coast of Coromandel, vol. 1 (London, 1795).   197

37. Anonymous, Royal Botanic Gardens, Kew, William Roxburgh
    Collection, no. 414, watercolor, *Cylista scariosa*, n.d.   198

38. Anonymous, Royal Botanic Gardens, Kew, William Roxburgh
    Collection, no. 1841, watercolor, *Casalpinea simora Buch*, n.d.   200

39. John Singleton Copley, *Hugh Montgomerie, Twelfth Earl of Eglinton,* 1780.   204

40. Benjamin West, *The Death of General Wolfe,* 1770.   206

41. Sir Joshua Reynolds, *Lady Sarah Bunbury Sacrificing to the Graces,* 1765.   210

42. Benjamin West, drawing of the *Apollo Belvedere,* c. 1760–62.   219

Acknowledgments

I am grateful to the staffs of several research libraries and art museums for their assistance on many aspects of this project, in particular Nicholas Martland of the Library and Herbarium of the Royal Botanic Gardens, Kew; Patricia Kattenhorn of the British Library's Oriental and India Office Collections; Malcolm Beasley of the Botany Library of the Natural History Museum; Sallie D. Sanders of the National Museum of American Art (Smithsonian Institution); Gloria Greis of the Peabody Museum of Archaeology and Ethnology; Kai Kin Yung of the National Portrait Gallery; and Susan P. Casteras, Marilyn Hunt, Eric M. Lee, and Anne-Marie Logan of the Yale Center for British Art, as well as the staffs of the Aberdeen Art Gallery, the Art Institute of Chicago, Asiatic Society of Bengal, British Library, Christie's, Cortauld Institute, Eastern National Park and Monument Association, Fogg Museum, India Office Library and Records, Johnson Hall State Historic Site, Lewis Walpole Library, Los Angeles County Museum of Art, National Gallery of Art (Washington, DC), The National Gallery (London), National Gallery of Canada, National Gallery of Ireland, National Maritime Museum, National Museums and Galleries on Merseyside, the National Park Service, National Portrait Gallery, Newberry Library, New York Public Library, New York State Historical Association, New York State Office of Parks, Recreation and Historic Preservation, New York State Public Library, Pennsylvania Academy of Fine Arts, Philadelphia Museum of Art, Sotheby's, Spink-Leger Pictures, Yale Center for British Art, and the staff of the Special Collections, Tom Brown of the Photography Department, and the Interlibrary Loan Office at Hamilton Library of the University of Hawai'i. For permission to quote from manuscript material, I am grateful to the British Museum and the Bishop Museum, Honolulu, Hawai'i.

Thanks are due also to those who have read and commented on various versions and portions of this manuscript: Daniel A. Baugh, Piya Chatterjee, Candace Clements, Dian Kris, Roderick M. McDonald, Marta Savigliano, Kristina Straub, Jeff Tobin, Maria Trumpler, Gauri Viswanathan, the anonymous readers at *American Indian Culture and Research Journal*, *Studies in Eighteenth-Century Culture*, and Duke University Press. I am also grateful to audiences who attended panel sessions at the North American Conference on British Studies, the American Society for Eighteenth-Century Studies, and the International Congress on the Enlightenment for their helpful questions and comments. To my colleagues at the University of Hawai'i, David Baker, Andrea Feeser, Candace Fujikane, Ruth Hsu, Kathy Phillips, Mimi Sharma, and especially to Cindy Franklin and Laura Lyons, whose criticism and support have been invaluable, I am grateful. Thanks go to my sons, Sam and Isaac, cultural critics and artists in their own right, who, as my companions on trips to museums in North America and Great Britain, shared their insights and knowledge with me. I owe much more than can be expressed here in the way of support and encouragement to Joe, my husband, my first reader, and my best critic. This book is dedicated to my mother, Royce Elizabeth Fowkes, who, with her artist's eye and love of art museums, taught me my first and best lessons about art.

Chapter 2, "Native Land and Foreign Desires: *William Penn's Treaty with the Indians*," was published in the *American Indian Culture and Research Journal*, and an earlier version of chapter 6, "Imperial Designs: Botanical Illustration and the British Botanic Empire," was published in *Studies in Eighteenth-Century Culture*.

❧

Introduction: Toward a Cultural

History of Colonialism

This book is about art and colonialism. I focus on the representation of cultural encounters that occurred in British colonies during the late eighteenth century, in particular in northern India, the British West Indies, and the northern provinces of British America. The study of British colonialism of this period traditionally has been approached as political history. More recently, social historians have tried to account for the lived experience of colonial subjects. Though both of these approaches are crucial to our understanding of colonialism and its impact on native peoples, this book offers another approach: an examination of art produced for and by colonial subjects. Through careful analyses of paintings of colonial officials and colonized places, plants, and peoples, combined with archival work, we can come to better appreciate colonialist practices and ideologies. Because art simultaneously reflects and shapes social, economic, and political practices, paintings can be invaluable to those seeking to understand the past, particularly the politics of a specific cultural landscape. Drawings and paintings are sites where the tensions and contradictions of colonialist doctrines and practices were negotiated, more or less successfully, on an aesthetic level. Paintings, as is the case with all cultural production, are not merely reflections of larger social and economic forces; they participate in the production of meaning, in the dynamic construction of identities, and in the structuring within discursive fields of particular positionalities.

The paintings that I examine in this book perform ideological work, in part, by portraying imperialism in such a way that the appropriation of land, resources, labor, and culture is transformed into something that is aesthetically pleasing and morally satisfying. The exercise of imperial power resides, for instance, in the images of tropical flowers; botanical illustration, an extension of Linnaean botany, participated in a cultural and scientific imperialism that sought to exert control over the globe's natural resources. Images of West Indian servants and slaves testify to the power of British merchants and planters to expropriate and enslave Africans for the purpose of generating profits in the sugar trade. And portraits of culturally cross-dressed Britons in North America and northern India participate symbolically in the appropriation of native cultures, native land, and resources. Paintings of colonial officials reveal much about the strategies of appropriation and domination that were available to colonists; on the other hand, paintings of colonial subjects, the native peoples who were subjected to colonial state apparatuses, both ideological and repressive, can elucidate the strategies of accommodation, resistance, and subversion that subject peoples employ in their attempts to negotiate their status.

Imperial power was asserted, redeployed, and negotiated in what seem to be relatively benign, even mundane paintings. The paintings I have chosen to examine in this book lack the glamour, glory, and guts of the more histrionic history paintings. The paintings I discuss range from the domestic to the exotic in subject matter: portraits of colonial officials, conversation pieces of British families and their servants, portraits of Native Americans and Anglo-Indians, and natural history illustrations of people from the West Indies and of tropical flowers from India and Polynesia. Most of the paintings, drawings, and engravings discussed in this book have received scant attention from art historians. They have gone unnoticed because they have seemed to lack importance either as cultural artifacts or as objects productive of aesthetic pleasure. Because they fall below the threshold of art history conceptions of "great art," most of the paintings discussed in *Picturing Imperial Power* are today rarely exhibited. In Britain and North America, they lie crated in the basements of fine arts museums, or they reside quite comfortably in obscurity, hung in country houses, in the offices and hallways of libraries and cultural institutions, and in small regional museums and local historical societies. In some settings, like the country house and the office, they function as decor, as curios, mementos of the past, and family memorabilia; when housed in the vaults of libraries and museums, they function as archives. Other than West's painting of William Penn, which has achieved iconographic status in the United States, Anglo-Indian portraiture, which has been meticulously catalogued by Mildred Archer, and the art of the Pacific voyages of discovery, which has received the serious attention of Bernard Smith, most of the paintings I discuss in this book I happened upon in a rather haphazard manner. For instance, I owe my knowledge of the anonymous painting of John Caldwell to my sons' interests in painting miniature lead figures, a hobby that took me as their chauffeur into war-gaming shops, where I discovered extensive collections of booklets describing British military uniforms. It was in an Osprey publication on the American Revolutionary War in the Men-at-Arms series that I first saw the image of Sir John Caldwell dressed as an Indian chief.[1] This painting is one of those crated, rarely exhibited pieces.

Most of the paintings discussed in this book, which, I must say, I find fascinating and sometimes endearing, would most likely be perceived by modern viewers as bad art, as not meriting close scrutiny. What Linda Nochlin has said of nineteenth-century orientalist art can be applied to eighteenth-century colonial art: when we employ art historical categories that focus on "the aesthetic values of great art," "we inevitably miss their significance as political documents."[2] Nochlin suggests that the "fresh visual territory" presented by orientalist art can be accessed by "scholars armed with historical and political awareness."[3] By reconstructing the social, cultural, and political contexts that inform the manner and the subject matter of these paintings, this book will make visible to us today the relations of power that structure these paintings. By excavating their cultural and political engagement with imperialism, I aim to account for their ideological power and visual effect as well as to argue for their significance as agents in the colonial project.

Colonialism

My analysis of colonial art stresses the complexity, fluidity, and multivalency of cultural encounters and political interactions between colonizers and the colonized.⁴ British colonialism has too often been portrayed as a static, unchanging, monolithic structure of domination and exploitation. Too often, it is the high imperialism of the late-nineteenth-century British Raj that stands in for the whole four-hundred-year history of the British colonialist project. In her critique of the scholarship on colonialism, Ann Laura Stoler suggests that historians and anthropologists have neglected to analyze the specific workings of particular colonial practices and colonial relations: "Anthropologists have taken the politically constructed dichotomy of colonizer and colonized as a given, rather than as a historically shifting pair of social categories that needs to be explained. . . . As a result, colonizers and their communities are frequently treated as diverse but unproblematic, viewed as unified in a fashion that would disturb our ethnographic sensibilities if applied to ruling elites of the colonized. Finally, the assumption that colonial political agendas are self-evident precludes our examination of the cultural politics of the communities in which colonizers lived."⁵ This book seeks to complicate this undifferentiated notion of colonialism by providing close analyses of site- and time-specific colonial encounters.⁶

My discussions of British colonialism center on its operations in the late eighteenth century in three different locations: the northern provinces of British America, primarily Pennsylvania and New York; the British West Indian island of St. Vincent; and northern India, primarily Calcutta. Each of these sites represents a different kind of colonizing operation: the settler colonies of North America and their troubled frontier; the Caribbean slave society governed by absentee plantocrats; and the company-dominated towns of Calcutta and Lucknow, filled with British sojourners, military men, and company officials.

Most of the paintings and illustrations that I discuss were produced between 1770 and 1795, with the majority of them falling in the decade of the seventies. The last third of the eighteenth century is a significant era in the history of British imperialism, as it was a time of momentous change in the scope and tenor of the colonial project. With the loss of the American colonies, the abolitionist attack on the slave trade, and the East India Company's accumulation of wealth and power under Warren Hastings's regime in India, Britain shifted its focus from the North American continent and Caribbean Islands to the Indian subcontinent. This realignment of the colonial project, which involved the redeployment of military forces, bureaucrats, and capital investment, marks what Vincent Harlow has termed the shift from the first to the second empire.[7] The geographic shift of British colonialism from the New World to Asia was accompanied by a corresponding ideological shift. In India, colonialism, no longer simply a matter of domination, was wedded to notions of duty, honor, Christian zeal, cultural superiority, and imperial magnanimity.

In keeping with my attention to difference within the colonialist paradigm, I trace in paintings of colonial subjects three distinct but often intertwined kinds of engagement within the colonial project: the colonizers' strategies of appropriation and domination; the colonized's resistance to colonial domination; and practices of accommodation that these groups deployed. Chapter 1, which is concerned with the black servant in domestic portraiture, chapter 2, which examines in detail Benjamin West's *William Penn's Treaty with the Indians,* and the last chapter deal with colonialist strategies of incorporation and domination of colonial resources. Chapters 3 and 4, which focus on cultural cross-dressing in North America and India, respectively, trace the complicated "middle ground" between two cultures created by asymmetrical power differentials and practices of cultural and economic exchange. And chapters 5 and 6, both of which focus on natural history illustrations, examine the potential for colonial subjects to resist and subvert colonial authority.

I use the words "colonial subject" ambiguously in my title to capture the two senses of the word "subject": those who regard themselves as the subjects of history, the actors who perform on the colonial stage—the colonels in the king's army and the Jamaican sugar planters, for instance—and those who are subjected to colonial state apparatuses, specifically the Iroquois of lower Canada and New York, the slaves of Jamaica and St. Vincent, and Muslim "wives" of colonial officials in India. These subject positions were constantly in flux and continuously negotiated as colonists and their "subjects" struggled to consolidate or resist colonial power amid changing political and material landscapes. British military officers stationed in the wilds of the Canadian frontier, for instance, had continually to reinvent themselves as the "fathers" of their Algonquian allies, renegotiating their own masculinity in native terms and their role as paternalists in the material and cultural economy of the northern tribes. To maintain their tenuous authority and position of dominance on the frontier, British officials needed to (but often did not) learn Indian cultural practices so that they could be recognized, or hailed in the Althusserian sense, by Indians as their fathers. Portraits of colonial officials who were stationed on the frontier not only reflect these tensions but are actual sites where British officials constructed identities that they hoped would be recognized by Britons, Euro-Americans, and Native Americans as invested with authority.

In tracing articulations between colonial state power and cultural production, I have made an effort to attend to the specific operations of colonialism, focusing on particular places, eras, and people, as, for example, Joseph Brant's movements in upper New York State during the Revolutionary War years. However, in the course of studying local contexts, I have uncovered patterns of colonial practice and ideology that appear to operate independently of any particular colonial site and to reflect the general operations of the colonial order. The work of eighteenth-century British colonialism was extraction. Raw materials, including timber, fish, and fur from North America, sugar from the West Indies, and cotton from India, were taken from colonies and transported to England where they were transformed into commodities for domestic consumption. For colonialism to have functioned successfully as a form of extraction, Britain had to incorporate colonies—their resources, in particular, but also their people—into a British economic and political framework with Britain at the center. The British gradually discovered that they would have to practice some form of accommodation to local conditions and realities to achieve this incorporation.[8] To ensure the movement of commodities from the peripheries to the core, colonial officials, company employees, military men, planters, and entrepreneurs had to accomplish some degree, however slight, of accommodation to the colony's political, social, and geographic landscape. Not simply a matter of domination with superior weapons and numbers, British colonizers needed to learn more than a little about the lands and cultures they had conquered. In North America, for instance, British authorities, such as Sir William Johnson, superintendent of Indian Affairs, and his agents, had to learn Indian diplomatic practices in order to achieve their goal of appropriating vast tracts of native land. Accommodating themselves to native decorum surrounding treaty negotiations, Johnson and his associates conducted themselves at treaty conferences in a manner that would signal to their Indian audience that they were emissaries from their king, important men to be reckoned with. They had to adopt native patterns of speech, assume a grave and serious manner, speak in honorifics, provide gifts, and pass wampum belts to punctuate their promises and demands. These gestures, acts of cultural accommodation, were crucial to maintaining British power on the North American frontier.

The meaning of an act of accommodation is dependent on the context in which it occurs. For instance, consider what appears to be a form of cultural accommodation, cultural cross-dressing, as practiced by British officials in a variety of locations, including North America and India. Choosing to have his portrait painted wearing the clothing of subject peoples, John Caldwell, who was stationed at Fort Niagara in the early 1770s, is depicted in the leggings, loincloth, moccasins, headdress, and nose and ear rings of the Algonquian peoples he encountered in the Old Northwest (Fig. 8). Meanwhile, halfway around the world, a European man (his identity now lost) had his portrait painted wearing the clothing—pantaloons and loose jacket—of the Mughal court (Fig. 16). These men are participating in some form of cultural accommodation and perhaps some form of cultural cannibalism that functions as an act of empowerment, and on this level, they are engaged in similar practices; however, when this cultural cross-dressing is placed within its particular historical context, the meanings that are attached to such behaviors are very different depending on the location in which they occur. A comparative approach allows us to classify the various discursive and material practices of colonialism, yet it is also important that we attend to the specific coordinates of time and place to achieve a nuanced reading of those practices.

My approach to analyzing the visual culture of colonialism is relational: I move from one geographical site to another to encourage implicit comparisons between various colonial cultures. Somewhat analogous to my relational methodology is what George Marcus has called "multi-sited ethnography": "In projects of multi-sited ethnographic research, de facto comparative dimensions develop instead as a function of the fractured, discontinuous plane of movement and discovery among sites as one maps an object of study and needs to posit logics of relationship, translation, and association among these sites. . . . The object of study is ultimately mobile and multiply situated, so any ethnography of such an object will have a comparative dimension that is integral to it, in the form of juxtapositions of phenomena that conventionally have appeared to be (or conceptually have been kept) 'worlds apart.' "[9] In placing a chapter on British theft of African labor next to a chapter on British theft of Native American land, I have employed a relational methodology based on a logic of juxtaposition. Though not strictly comparative, my multisited cultural history of colonialism allows for the discovery of difference — the variety of subject positions within the colonialist paradigm, for instance — as well as the revelation of the linked practices and discourses of British colonialism. In juxtaposing specific operations of colonialism in particular places and times, my method uncovers similarities between practices and the circulation of ideologies and agents within the formal structures of the empire. In my conclusion I trace out the larger patterns that made British imperialism so flexible and thus sustainable, in particular the fluid interaction of centers where information was accumulated and then dispersed along with agents and institutional practices across a global network of colonial sites.

I see this book as participating in the ongoing work of postcolonial studies, which seeks, in part, to reconfigure modes of cultural analysis and even academic disciplines to accommodate questions concerning the operations of imperial power, particularly its deployment within state repressive and ideological apparatuses, and questions concerning the constitution of the subjectivities of both colonizer and colonized. Because postcolonial studies pose a series of threats to traditional fields of literary, visual, social, and historical study, it is not hard to understand why it has been attacked by those defending traditional methodologies; however, it is also a field that is marked by internal dissension over the terms of analysis and the perceived failure of theory to attend to the specificities of colonialism.[10] While theorists of colonial discourse have provided crucial categories of analysis — Edward Said's groundbreaking analysis and critique of orientalism, Homi Bhabha's theorizing of hybridity and ambivalence, and Gayatri Chakravorty Spivak's interrogation of representation — they have also been criticized for producing analyses that reinscribe the hegemonic discourses of the metropolitan centers.[11] Benita Parry has noted that postcolonial theory tends to ignore "imperialism's many and mutable states" while allegorizing colonialism as "a notion applicable to all situations of structural domination"; Ranajit Guha has suggested that even radical critiques of colonialism are "a prisoner of empty abstractions"; and Nicholas Thomas has argued that colonial discourse is too often analyzed in terms that are "unitary and essentialist" and that tend to "recapitulate" rather than "subvert the privileged status and presumed dominance" of colonialist discourses.[12]

Bhabha has often been singled out and criticized for his "homogenizing and transhistorical model of mutual (mis)recognitions of all cultures."[13] Bhabha has tried not "to reduce a complex and diverse historical moment, with varied national genealogies and different institutional practices, into a singular shibboleth," but Bart Moore-Gilbert argues that "homogenization is precisely what sometimes results from the way that Bhabha interrogates complex and multiform realities such as (neo-)colonialism through the narrow and ahistorical analytic models of affective ambivalence and the discursive disturbance which accompanies it."[14] Although Moore-Gilbert's critique of Bhabha seems apt, we must not forget that Bhabha's work, or for that matter the work of Said or Spivak, does not stand in for all of postcolonial studies. Postcolonial critics, such as McClintock, Shohat, Chrisman, Grewal, and Spivak herself, have gone a long way toward addressing such critiques by focusing on historical and geographical specificities, by attending to the deployment of power within the colonizer-colonized dyadic relation, and by examining "the interdependence of cultural terrains in which colonizer and colonized coexisted and battled each other," as Said has suggested.[15] In addition to the work of these postcolonial literary and cultural critics, anthropologists and historians have worked to refocus attention on intricate and mutable relationships between colonizers and colonized, such as Thomas's treatment of particular dynamics of the colonial encounter in various Pacific settings; Guha's recovery of subaltern resistance in the prose of counterinsurgency; and Stoler's work on the articulations of gender, race, and class in the late-nineteenth-century Dutch colonies in Indonesia. Site-specific work on colonialism that is exemplary in attending to the particular operations of colonial discourse are Gauri Viswanathan's *Masks of Conquest,* Mary Louise Pratt's *Imperial Eyes,* the work of the Subaltern Studies collective, and the interdisciplinary essays in the collection *Colonialism and Culture* edited by Nicholas B. Dirks.[16]

The impact of postcolonial studies on the disciplines of anthropology, history, and literary studies has been invigorating, producing such exciting work as Jean and John Comaroff's *Of Revelation and Revolution*, Gananath Obeyesekere's *The Apotheosis of Captain Cook*, and Jenny Sharpe's *Allegories of Empire*. However, when practitioners working within disciplinary boundaries begin to apply colonial discourse analysis to their traditionally defined fields, there is a danger that the full complexity of the insights and methodology of postcolonial studies is lost in undigested applications of Bhabha, for instance, to canonical or metropolitan texts, readings that, in stressing the colonizer's ambivalence and the hybridity of colonial relations, reinscribe the primacy of Europe and its dominant discourses. By insisting that work on the peripheries always be placed in relation to the metropole, a position that has been espoused in the journals of my own field of eighteenth-century studies, the cultural history of colonialism runs the danger of becoming what Frantz Fanon called "colonialist historiography."

In attempting to reimagine a colonial past, my project tries to avoid Fanon's colonialist historiography, which he defines as when the historian writes "not the history of the country which he [the settler] plunders but the history of his own nation in regard to all that she skims off, all that she violates and starves."[17] An example of colonialist historiography is the old "imperial history" of the West Indies, which, according to Orlando Patterson, had relegated the West Indies to the category of object of imperial conquest and struggle. However, beginning in the 1970s, scholars, including Sidney Mintz, Michael Craton, and James Walvin, focusing on social and labor history have created a large body of literature that has interrogated the institution of West Indian slavery, detailing the slave trade and recounting the history of individual plantations. The work of these economic and social historians has gone a long way toward redressing Fanon's critique of imperial history, as has the work of the Subaltern Studies Group, which has begun to fill the void left in the Raj's historical account. Ethnohistorians such as James Axtell, Francis Jennings, and David Richter have been credited for recovering a Native American past that a generation ago was invisible to historians of colonial America. However, this tendency that Fanon identifies with colonialist historiography—whereby the historian retells the history of the colonizers, not the colonized nation—has reemerged today in literary, cultural, and historical studies. By stressing the importance of the metropole in relation to the colonial periphery, cultural critics, in the name of postcolonial theory, have refocused attention on the metropolitan centers of Europe and are thereby instrumental in demoting studies of local resistances to the academic margins of area specialties. Too often the colonial peripheries are seen as significant only in relation to the urban centers of Europe; as a result, old imperialist hierarchies between core and periphery are reinstated in the name of "radical" intellectual work, and it is business as usual within departments of literature, history, and art. These tensions appear, of course, in my own work, which, in using colonialist visual and verbal texts to write my historical account of art and colonialism, can be accused of reinscribing Britain's primacy. But in pointing out the complexity, variety, and contradiction within the dominant position, I am working to denaturalize the power of colonialist regimes and, as such, to contribute to an understanding of colonialism as a collection of social, economic, political, and epistemological practices that were not monolithic and inevitable but conflicted and historically contingent.

Recognizing the dangers of reinscribing the dominant discourses of the metropole, Stuart Hall has been a key figure in developing approaches that resist the cultural imperialism of the dominant regimes. Recently, he has argued that a "cultural politics of the local" is one way, and perhaps the only way available for now, to resist the forces of global domination, whether by imperialism, market capitalism, or postmodern postindustrial capitalism: "The subjects of the local, of the margin, can only come into representation by, as it were, recovering their own hidden histories. They have to try to retell the story from the bottom up, instead of from the top down."[18] However, to write an alternative history, one that describes not the activities of the colonizers but the lived experience of the colonized, requires, as Hilary Beckles argues, the exercise of one's historical imagination because there is, regrettably, a dearth of eighteenth-century narratives written by West Indian slaves, Native Americans, and subaltern South Asians.[19] To recover the lives of these subaltern peoples, one has to rely on the journals, private papers, official reports, and natural histories as well as paintings and drawings of British travelers, sojourners, planters, settlers, bureaucrats, and military officers.[20] These sources are, of course, problematic because their authors were biased observers whose texts served multiple purposes, including the desire to inform and entertain their readers and viewers, to justify to themselves and others their position as colonists and/or slave owners, and to persuade the British public that colonial practices, including slavery in North America, were not just profitable but also humane institutions.[21]

Despite these problems inherent in the use of colonialist representations to reconstruct the lives of colonized peoples, these visual and verbal texts are rich sources, full of rhetorical strategies that reveal much about both colonizers and colonized. One way to recover subaltern subjectivity from an elite text is to read the imperialist text symptomatically—that is, reading what is not there but is implied and called into existence by a series of oppositions. This is a method that Ranajit Guha recommends in his "The Prose of Counter-Insurgency," as does Edward Said in his *Culture and Imperialism:* "contrapuntal reading . . . must take account of both processes, that of imperialism and that of resistance to it, which can be done by extending our reading of texts to include what was once forcibly excluded."[22] Similarly, Richard Leppert uses the notion of a "semiotic 'present absence'" to describe the way in which India is displaced in Anglo-Indian conversation pieces.[23] Adopting Said's, Guha's, and Leppert's reading tactics, I hope to give, in Said's words, "emphasis and voice to what . . . was once forcibly excluded" in the visual and verbal texts of empire, to recover not only the processes of imperialism but resistances to it.[24] My chapters on the black servant in domestic portraiture and on West's painting of Penn's treaty with the Delaware trace the impact of imperial power on the peripheries, charting the twin colonizing strategies of expropriation and incorporation of labor and land in the New World; my chapters on cultural cross-dressing in North America, India, and the West Indies attempt to gain access to the resistance at the local level to the pressures of the homogenizing effect of the British imperial agenda. Joseph Brant's manipulation of military costume, West Indian slaves' mimicry of their masters' attire, and the Calcutta artists' ability to inject their Mughal idioms into British designs are eloquent gestures that register various levels of negotiation of and resistance to imperial power.[25]

Colonial Art

A word is in order here about my approach to visual culture, which could be characterized somewhat vulgarly as cultural studies meets colonial discourse analysis. Eclectic in its use of theory and interdisciplinary in its approach to history and art, *Picturing Imperial Power* does not "cover" areas of inquiry or provide a comprehensive view of specific subject matter, but seeks to further the conversation about the relations between culture and colonialism, to encourage cultural critics to think about the historical specificity of cultural production, and to raise questions about art and power that I hope are, in W. J. T. Mitchell's words, "provocative rather than merely provoking."[26] What makes *Picturing Imperial Power* a cultural studies project is its commitment to an interdisciplinary approach, which in this case brings together colonial history and the semiotics of visual culture. This book's indebtedness to cultural studies can also be felt in its focus on representation and its insistence that cultural production, which includes "high" art as well as more popular, mundane, or "trivial" forms of visual and verbal expression, is crucial to the process of meaning-making and is, as such, a form of social practice. In the words of the editors of *Visual Culture*, art is "actively engaged in organizing and structuring the social and cultural environment."[27] I would add "political" to this list. Like the objects of many cultural studies analyses, most of the paintings discussed in this book have been overlooked as aesthetically inferior and culturally insignificant. By placing these ignored and forgotten images in tandem with colonial discourse theory, I hope to jog them out of the realm of trivia, memorabilia, and collectibles and into the realm of significant cultural production.[28]

I read these paintings as colonial discourse, for they participate in specific practices and ideologies that circulated in and about the late-eighteenth-century colonial encounter. Although images in paintings do not, strictly speaking, constitute a language, they do function representationally, as a symbolic system of meaning-making that has its own conventions and rules and as such operates discursively. Both words and images function by representing what we perceive to be the world around us, and, as poststructuralists are eager to remind us, words and images do not merely reflect the world but mediate, even create, what we believe to be reality. As Susan Wolff has argued, "art always encodes values and ideology" and as such offers the cultural critic a vantage point from which to interrogate the sociocultural forces at work in any given society.[29] Cultural criticism that views art semiotically can be found in John Barrell's *Painting and the Politics of Culture: New Essays on British Art, 1700–1850,* which contains essays by historians, art historians, and literary critics on the political and social effects of visual culture. Examples of full-length and richly textured treatments of the semiotic and ideological content of visual images include Richard Leppert's *Music and Image,* a study of the role of musical life in the shaping of gender and class identities and in the construction of privatized space and domesticity; David H. Solkin's *Painting for Money,* which locates painting at the intersection of contending discourses over commerce, luxury, and virtue; and Marcia Pointon's *Hanging the Head,* which examines portraiture's participation in the ideological construction of masculinity, femininity, and bourgeois subjectivity. These books offer exciting and powerful analyses of British culture, but they tend to ignore Britain's colonial relations and exhibit symptoms of what Paul Gilroy has identified as the "little England syndrome."[30] This focus on England as if it were a self-contained entity, impervious to foreign influence and untouched by colonial influx, is derived, as Gauri Viswanathan has pointed out, from Raymond Williams's "critical approach that consistently and exclusively studies the formation of metropolitan culture from within its own boundaries."[31] Only Marcia Pointon, in her chapter "Going Turkish in Eighteenth-Century London: Lady Mary Wortley Montagu and Her Portraits," and Harriet Guest in Barrell's volume explore the intricate interrelations between eighteenth-century constructions of upper-class gender formations and the exoticism figured respectively by the Ottoman court and the tattooing practices of Polynesians.[32] In another article, "The Great Distinction: Figures of the Exotic in the Work of William Hodges," Guest links exoticism with late-eighteenth-century ideas about upper-class masculinity by examining the images that Hodges created as draughtsman for Captain Cook's second voyage into the Pacific.[33] Though Leppert's book on music in eighteenth-century Britain focuses on the construction of class and gender boundaries within English society, he has published separately an essay entitled "Music, Domestic Life and Cultural

Chauvinism: Images of British Subjects at Home in India," which brilliantly traces the way British ideas of cultural superiority were deployed in the imperial setting. Leppert's and Guest's work on India and Polynesia, respectively, are exemplary in their examination of the relationship between visual representation and the complexities of colonial practice and imperial ideology.[34]

Drawing on a range of theoretical perspectives from cultural studies, postcolonial theory, and cultural anthropology, I use a battery of theories to access the significance of these paintings and their role in generating, maintaining, and resisting imperial ideologies. Michel Foucault's equation of knowledge with power undergirds my treatment of botanical illustration as an appendage of British imperialism. The Marxist notion of mystification is implicit in my explanation of how imperial magnanimity masks the theft of native land and how domesticity elides labor in the representation of servants. Susan Stewart's and Harriet Guest's discussions of the exotic and Michael Taussig's discussion of mimesis inform my treatment of the representation of Native Americans. My discussion of Anglo-Indians is indebted to Michael Leppert's tracing of the links among music, visual art, and colonial policies. In the chapters on cultural cross-dressing and ethnographic art, I borrow Stuart Hall's and Dick Hebdige's ideas about the semiotics of clothing and style as a form of resistance to explore the hybrid clothing of Indians and colonial officials in North America as well as the gala dress of slaves in the Caribbean. I have also found useful feminist, queer, and postcolonial theories of performance, in particular Judith Butler's discussion of drag, Peggy Phelan's notion of performing identities, and Homi Bhabha's analysis of colonial discourse, to explore masquerade and mimicry as forms of subversion and empowerment.

In my discussions of portraits of colonial subjects, I focus on performance as a strategy of appropriation and resistance. Sitters for portraits can to some degree perform their identities by manipulating their dress, accoutrements, countenance, and pose. Joseph Brant, famous Mohawk warrior, loyalist, and leader of the Grand River Mohawks, was very aware of the importance of costume and manner in shaping viewers' responses to him. He would always have his portrait painted in what he called his Indian clothes, which in actuality he wore only on occasion. An anecdote captures his self-consciousness about costume and manner in the presentation of self and how he could play with his audience's fear and curiosity by performing the role of a "wild Indian." While on a visit to London to negotiate with the king's ministers compensation for lost Mohawk lands, Brant attended a masquerade dressed in "native" attire—loincloth with leggings, ruffled shirt, a draped blanket, a tomahawk, and a painted face—nothing like what he wore to his delicate negotiations with the Crown. At the masquerade, another guest, dressed as an Ottoman, pulled Brant's nose, testing to see if he were wearing a mask. Brant responded with a war whoop and brandished his tomahawk, acting as if he had been mortally offended by this affront, terrifying the Ottoman greatly, and scattering other guests, various gypsies and milkmaids, who ran off shrieking.[35] Brant's friends assured onlookers that he was acting in jest, but perhaps Brant was doing something else. In fulfilling his audience's expectations about Indians, their stereotypes about their haughty and violent behavior, Brant was performing their fantasies, even parodying them, and in doing so established his position as someone who, in knowing both Iroquois and British cultural practices and beliefs, was in this instance in the superior position. Able to see himself from the dominant culture's position and to step outside of his beliefs and practices, he was, in performing an Indian, asserting his superiority to those of the dominant culture who surrounded him.

As Peggy Phelan describes in *The Unmarked,* posing for a portrait is a process whereby one performs an identity that one believes others expect to see. Uncertain about what the body looks like or how substantial it is, we perform, Phelan says, "an image of it by imitating what we think we look like. We imagine what people might see when they look at us, and then we try to perform (and conform to) those images. . . . The imitative reproduction of the self-image always involves a detour through the eye of the other."[36] Ideally, artist and sitter collaborate to produce an image that reflects what the sitter hoped to project to the world.[37] However, in some cases, as in Brant's, the sitter has less control over the artist's rendering of an image, as he or she is not the patron, the one, because paying for the portrait, whom the artist must ultimately please. Brant sat for portraits by Peale, Romney, Stuart, Ames, Berczy, and Rigaud, but he paid for only the one painted by Rigaud. The Duke of Northumberland commissioned Stuart to paint a portrait of Brant, whom he had known and fought beside during the American Revolution; it still hangs in the current duke's residence, Syon House, near London. Of all the portraits of Brant, Rigaud's was the one Brant liked best. He persuaded General Haldimand, who arranged to have Rigaud paint Brant's portrait, to let him buy it (Fig. 9). Eventually it was shipped to Canada and hung in his home on the Grand River, where it remained until it was destroyed by a fire in the mid-nineteenth century. In approving of the Rigaud portrait, Brant authorized this image out of the number of his likenesses that circulated in British imperial culture.

Whoever pays for them, portraits imply an empowered subject. However delicate and complex the negotiations among sitter, artist, and patron, portraits are of somebody: an individual with a name, a family, and a home. Even though the identity of the figures in a portrait are often lost over time, they are still somebodies who for various ideological and material reasons have achieved the status of subject. In addition to portraits, this book also deals with paintings of people who are not named or otherwise presented as individuals. The ethnographic art of Agostino Brunias does not portray the countenances of individuals; rather, he painted types of people—slaves, servants, street hawkers, and higglers—none of them named (Figs. 28–33). He sketched them on his visit to Dominica and St. Vincent in the 1770s. Some of his sketches Brunias turned into oil paintings while in the Caribbean and some he waited until he returned to London to transform into paintings and engravings. The African and Afro-Caribbean men and women, whose activities of dancing, bathing, selling, and buying are figured in his paintings, struggle for that subject position that is denied to them as objects of ethnographic study. Painting a wide array of African Caribbean figures, Brunias carefully recorded the customs, manners, and clothing of his subjects, which contributed to their status as objects of a natural history inquiry. However, these paintings of African Caribbean activities, such as the higgling and hawking of the Sunday markets, contain a narrative element about slaves' abilities as agriculturalists and entrepreneurs; such narratives, by documenting the slaves' agency, work to disturb and disrupt the natural history conventions that Brunias employed in his pictures of West Indian life. Even when the artist and patron, in this case Brunias and Sir William Young, worked together to erase a subject's personhood, they did not succeed entirely, as the objects recorded contain within themselves powerful narratives that cannot be completely suppressed.

The following chapters sketch out the various colonialist strategies of domination as they manifest themselves in paintings, strategies that include appropriation of native culture, labor, and natural resources as well as strategies of elision and mystification that serve to rewrite the conditions of domination and expropriation. For instance, the chapters on West's history painting *William Penn's Treaty with the Indians* deals with one form of colonialist expropriation, the theft of Indian land in North America. Another chapter foregrounds the extraction of slave labor in the West Indies. I began this book with an interest in how colonial state power was deployed in various drawings and paintings of the 1770s and 1780s, but as I pursued this topic, it became clear to me that colonialism was not a fixed monolithic entity of state power, but a continually shifting and self-contradictory set of practices and ideologies that offered its agents various positions within these structures. As I mentioned before, the colonial officials, who tried to impose imperial will on Native Americans and Euro-American settlers in the backwoods of the frontier, could not merely assert their military might to achieve their end; they had to reconstruct their authority so that it would be recognizable to those over whom they had hoped to dominate. Colonial officials, expecting to hail Indians as subjects of the Crown, found that Indians would not comply with imperial dictates. Colonial officials learned that to be successful in their mission, they had to allow themselves to be interpellated by their native allies into Indian discursive and social practices, learning to speak, for instance, the formal, decorous rhetoric of the great Iroquois and Algonquian orators as well as adopting the ritual exchange of wampum during the lengthy process of treating with the Algonquian and Iroquoian peoples. British colonial agents could not merely assert their authority as officials of the Crown; they had to earn the respect of their "subjects," in this case, the tribes of the Great Lakes and Ohio River Valley, before they could presume to lead them against George III's enemies.

The work of domination is multiplicitous and complex, as is the work of resistance to that domination. Strategies of resistance that are deployed in the various paintings and drawings I discuss exploit the contradictions inherent in colonialist ideologies and practices. For instance, in the chapter on botanical illustration and tropical plants I tease out the ideological contradictions that inform botanical illustration as a genre and as a practice of cultural imperialism. Botanical illustration's Platonic claim to represent a timeless ideal conflicts with its inherited legacy, derived from Netherlandish still life, of mortality and decay. The ideological and generic instability of botanical illustration makes it a form that could be easily appropriated by native artists who were employed by the Calcutta Botanic Garden and who recast their illustrations in the syntax of their own cultural tradition (Mughal) of flower painting. In the case of the botanical drawings of the Calcutta Botanic Garden, the Indian draughtsmen created images that subtly undermined Western scientific systems of thought by evoking indigenous ways of seeing and knowing (Figs. 34–36).

The cultural and political structures of colonialist domination are subtly destabilized by the contradictions captured in Brunias's ethnographic art. The nature of property comes into question in Brunias's pictures of West Indians, which are filled with images of slaves who are wearing elaborate European clothing and jewelry. These items, on which Brunias has lavished great attention, approach the category of fetish in his paintings' glistening surfaces and brilliant colors. His concern with rendering slaves' dress mirrored plantocratic preoccupation with slaves' clothing and jewelry. Planters and their visitors found slaves' use of clothing unsettling and perturbing. Slaves purchasing elegant cloth and gold jewelry called into question the relationship between property and personhood. Can property own property? Were slaves property, their masters' chattel, or were they persons whose subjectivity was established by their possession of property? Brunias's images of West Indians also capture the parody implicit in the slaves' elaborate costumes and their mimicry of their masters' cultural deployment of clothing.

In the chapters on cultural cross-dressing and ethnographic art, I explore mimicry as a form of resistance to colonial power. Mimicry that borders on parody is also implicit in Joseph Brant's portrait painted by Rigaud. In this portrait, the one Brant liked and eventually purchased, he wears a hybrid costume consisting of a British military jacket complete with shoulder straps and epaulets, plus an Indian blanket thrown over his shoulder and a feathered headdress. Brant's appropriation of the accoutrements of the privileged—the military jacket—is his attempt to establish himself as a subject in the eyes of the British, the Iroquois, and himself. His blending of Indian and British costume calls attention to the constructedness of power and interrogates the innate authority that British officials claimed to possess. However, when depicted in the hybrid costume of the Indian Department, complete with red military jacket, moccasins, leggings, beaded sash, and blanket thrown over his shoulder, Guy Johnson is engaged in another form of hybridity related to and yet distinct from Brant's. Although both men employ hybrid practices to figure themselves as leaders on the Old Northwest's frontier, they operate from different positions of power within the formal structures of colonialism—Brant in the subordinate position, Johnson in the dominant. As a Briton and a colonial official, Johnson is invested with the authority of his post as superintendent of the Indian Department; Brant, on the other hand, occupies a more precarious position as he traverses the unstable middle ground between his people and British colonial authority.

Several of the paintings that depict cultural encounters within colonial structures not only represent hybrid subject matter such as Joseph Brant's or Guy Johnson's uniforms but are hybrids themselves in terms of their conflation of distinct genres such as the state portrait with the family conversation piece, or the combining of natural history illustration with genre or "fancy" pictures. Hybrid forms also arose out of the convergence of English painting's visual codes and the colonial subjects that British artists sought to portray. When English forms of painting—domestic portraiture, the garden conversation piece, genre or fancy pictures, and the country house portrait—were exported to the colonies, subtle generic and ideological shifts occurred when these quintessential English genres incorporated alien subject matter. An oak tree in a traditional garden conversation piece carries a specific set of connotations having to do with English national identity, sturdy independence, military vigilance, and moral integrity. When a British gentleman in India poses beneath a banyan tree, the formula that links the owner of the property with the noble oak does not work at all or at least not in the same way (Fig. 24). In effect, when a painting, such as a garden conversation piece, includes tropical plant life, native servants, or "exotic" landscape, such additions to the generic formula call attention to the artificiality of the genre, questioning its ideological foundations. A conversation piece set in an English garden might pass as natural and normal, but a conversation piece set in the Indian countryside might disturb the casual and easy acceptance of the link between land and power, an equation that was, as Mark Girouard has demonstrated, foundational to British society.[38] Such tensions and contradictions arose out of combining a colonial setting with formal principles and visual idioms that grew out of British institutions and reflect British social and economic relations.

Each of my chapters focuses on a particular problem presented by the representation of the Other (Native American, African Caribbean, Indian people, plants, and landscapes), problems having to do with negotiating difference and domesticating the alien. Colonial relations between the British and their West Indian colonies are explored in chapter 1, "Bringing the Empire Home: The Black Servant in Domestic Portraiture," which focuses on the figure of the African Caribbean servant in eighteenth-century British conversation pieces. Of the various ideological uses that the figure of the black servant was put to in the earlier part of the century, most frequent was its use in conjunction with foreign luxury goods such as sugar, tea, and coffee, all commodities associated with the dark "others" of the world. Toward the last quarter of the century, however, the figure of the black servant often appeared in domestic conversation pieces. Most of chapter 1 concerns itself with the context and significance of two such paintings, Johan Zoffany's *The Family of Sir William Young, Baronet* (Fig. 4) and William R. Bigg's *A Lady and Her Children Relieving a Cottager* (Fig. 5), and the ideological shift that signals the demise of the old empire and its brutal colonial system fueled by desire for profit, and the anticipation of the birth of the new empire—perhaps ultimately no less brutal—that sought its legitimacy in moral superiority.

The imperial underpinning of the benevolent gesture is explored in chapter 2, "Native Land and Foreign Desires: *William Penn's Treaty with the Indians.*" This chapter focuses on the colonial politics surrounding the production of Benjamin West's *William Penn's Treaty with the Indians* as well as the historical basis for the subject of this myth-making painting (Fig. 6). Thomas Penn commissioned West's painting of his father's famous but mythical treaty with the Indians to rewrite the history of the Penns' less-than-upright dealings with the

Delaware. By placing trade goods in the emotional and visual center of the painting, West rewrote conquest as commerce and elided from this transaction the British appropriation of Indian lands. The trade goods simultaneously erased the Delawares' right to their lands while bringing them into the world economic system as consumers of commodities manufactured in England. Commerce implies exchange of commodities, and native land in this instance is reduced to an exchangeable commodity.

The politics of British-Iroquois relations is also explored in chapter 3, "Cultural Cross-Dressing in British America: Portraits of British Officers and Mohawk Warriors." This chapter explores the significance of cultural cross-dressing—the wearing of another culture's clothes—as it is manifested in eighteenth-century portraits of British officers wearing Native American clothing and in portraits of Mohawk warriors wearing British military dress. Benjamin West's portrait of Colonel Guy Johnson (Fig. 7) and an anonymous portrait of Sir John Caldwell (Fig. 8) figure Britons dressed in native clothing, while Rigaud's portrait of Brant portrays the Mohawk dressed in British military uniform plus his Iroquoian headdress. These images of hybridity—a mingling of British and Iroquoian cultures—suggest that appropriation was a strategy not limited to colonizers. However, subordinated deployment of hybridity, like Brant's, must be understood as resistant to domination, while Johnson's and Caldwell's reinscribe hierarchies that ensure colonial systems of extraction and expropriation. In examining the way in which displaying oneself dressed in another culture's clothing can be a form of empowerment as well as appropriation, this chapter marks a shift in the focus of this book away from representations that worked to mystify the relations of exploitation of labor and appropriation of land, toward images that complicated, even subverted, British imperial aspirations and objectives. The other portraits of Brant, who was routinely portrayed in a mixture of British and Indian dress by West, Romney, and Stuart, play out the complexities of British-Indian relations in the last quarter of the eighteenth century and attest to the hybridity of what was British America.

Hybridity in India was a more explosive and threatening phenomenon. Chapter 4, "Accommodating India: Domestic Arrangements in Anglo-Indian Family Portraiture," begins by focusing on Francesco

Renaldi's unusual conversation pieces that feature British employees of the East India Company surrounded by their Indian wives and children (e.g., Fig. 17). These paintings represent a remarkable moment in the history of the British and Indian relations when British officers and company employees lived with Indian women as domestic and sexual partners, adopting the clothing, customs, and familial arrangements of the Indian society in which they participated. Some of the paintings of bibis, the common-law wives of British men, belong to the genre of portraits of favorite mistresses, and other paintings of bibis, husbands, their children, and extended families are family conversation pieces, much like Zoffany's *The Family of Sir William Young.* This chapter argues that Renaldi's paintings of a racially and culturally hybrid domesticity represented a threat to an emerging British nationalism that, along with self-sacrificing heroism in the service of empire, posited a domestic femininity and a domestic morality as the distinguishing characteristics of a superior culture. Whereas Renaldi's portraits of hybrid Anglo-Indian households can be seen as undermining British imperial ideals, other portraits of Britons in India, by Johan Zoffany for instance, display a complete confidence in British moral and cultural superiority. Some portraits by Zoffany and most of Arthur William Devis's portraits include India in the form of servants, details of house interiors, and plants and outdoor settings. The India that is represented in these portraits is one that is relegated to the margins—a servant standing behind his master or a banyan tree seen through a window. British domestic order seems to be maintained in the midst of the alien presence of Indian servants, plants, or objects. The way Indian servants and Indian settings are incorporated into the composition of these domestic portraits reveals much about the varying degrees of tolerance and appreciation with which the British sojourners viewed India and suggests ways in which India resisted being banished to the margins.

Chapter 5, "Taxonomy and Agency in Brunias's West Indian Paintings," and chapter 6, "Imperial Designs: Botanical Illustration and the British Botanic Empire," explore the genre of the natural history illustration and its inherent contradictions between the static, idealized image of the "typical" and the narrative elements contained within these images that, in suggesting change over time, undermine the stasis and typicality of the illustration. Agostino Brunias, an Italian painter, was employed by Sir William Young in the 1770s to document West Indian life, in particular the customs and manners of African Caribbean slaves and freedmen. Brunias's careful rendering of the surface detail of African Caribbean dress, while conforming to the dictates of natural history illustration, also reflects the inordinate interest manifested by plantocrats about slaves' use of clothing. Despite the rigors of their lives as workers on sugar plantations, slaves managed to accumulate enough wealth through gardening and the selling of vegetables and fruits to purchase or trade for cloth. Out of this cloth they created sumptuous outfits, which they wore on special occasions such as the Christmas ball. Brunias's depictions of slaves' clothing, while in keeping with the dictates of ethnographic art, contain narrative elements that refer to slaves' agronomic and merchandizing skills, which ultimately were disturbing to planters, as these narratives implied slaves' ingenuity, hard work, and commitment to self-actualization. Brunias's paintings, therefore, contain elements that work against the natural history frame; narratives that speak of the slaves' creativity and moral worth ultimately position the African Caribbeans as subjects rather than objects of the natural history inquiry and thereby undercut the aims of illustration.

Chapter 6 examines botanical illustration's participation in the construction of the British botanic empire, focusing primarily on those illustrations that were commissioned by the British East India Company and published under the direction of Sir Joseph Banks, director of Kew Gardens and president of the Royal Society. Botanical illustrations were employed by a British botanical establishment keen on asserting European systems of control, namely a Linnaean system of classification. The conventions of botanical illustration worked to decontextualize plant life and assisted in the worldwide traffic in plants orchestrated by Kew Gardens. Despite botanical art's complicity with Linnaean botany's attempt to decontextualize plant life, some botanical artists managed to resist the totalizing discourse of Enlightenment universality. Sydney Parkinson's illustrations of Polynesian flora—produced literally right under Banks's supervising eye—contain elements that resist Linnaean botany's search for ideal types that fit into an abstract and static hierarchical system (Fig. 35). Also subtly subversive of the aims of Linnaean botany are the illustrations produced by Indian artists employed by the botanists who worked for the British

East India Company in Calcutta (Figs. 36–38). While conforming to the demands of their botanizing patrons, the Indian artists did not completely erase the plants' ecological and cultural contexts. Parkinson's and the anonymous Indian artists' images suggest that plants have an existence that lies outside the British system's control and management.

In my last chapter I conclude with a discussion of the role of representation in the exercise of colonial power. Borrowing the terminology that Bruno Latour has developed to analyze technoscience, this chapter explores the localizing epistemology of abstraction by linking two pairs of terms: the universal and the particular and the core and the periphery of colonial relations. This chapter uses Latour's ideas about the processes of inscription to analyze the way eighteenth-century aesthetic categories of the universal and the particular participated in the formation of colonial power and the construction of colonial subjects. Inscription, mirroring the mechanical processes of extraction, is a form of abstraction whereby an absence is rendered present. Representation in the colonial setting—a map, a report, or a drawing—was used to carry traces from the peripheries of the empire to the metropolitan center, where a particular kind of power, crucial to colonialism, was consolidated, a power possessing the ability "to act at a distance on unfamiliar events, places, and people."[39] Focusing on a portrait by John Singleton Copley, *Hugh Montgomerie* (Fig. 39), I argue that colonial power as represented in art was figured as operating in a universal register, whereas colonies and the colonized were localized in representations that figured them as simultaneously singular and typical.

Paintings of colonial officials, their families, servants, and surroundings, however mundane or innocuous they may now seem, participated in the production and circulation of several powerful ideologies that helped to create and maintain British imperial order. While eighteenth- and nineteenth-century British imperialist domination of much of the globe was dependent on military might, technical superiority, and shrewd mercantilism, Britain's hegemonic control also relied on the ideologies of racial superiority, domestic femininity, Christian charity, paternal benevolence, intellectual curiosity, scientific observation, and good taste to make sense of imperial activity and to bolster the individual agent's commitment to maintaining that hegemony. As Raymond Williams has pointed out, hegemony is not static, unchanging, and monolithic. It is a fluid construct that changes in response to resistance and challenge, shifts to absorb dissonance, and renews itself as old forms fail to be productive of power.[40] This book aims to catch some of these ideologies at work, ideologies that were employed in the last quarter of the eighteenth century when Britain was evolving from the first empire to the second, shifting its focus from the Western Hemisphere to the Eastern, and reinventing its imperial project as a civilizing mission. In tracing the negotiation of various forms of imperial power in the paintings I have examined, I have been surprised by the flexibility of eighteenth-century British imperial authority and have come to marvel at the variety of ideological positions that were available to Britons who constructed and maintained their imperial presence in the far-flung corners of the globe. And I have been impressed by the complexity of colonial interactions, in particular, the variety of positions, ranging from assimilation to open protest, that colonial subjects took to cope with as well as to resist the ideologies and mechanisms of colonial domination.

1

Bringing the Empire Home

THE BLACK SERVANT IN DOMESTIC

PORTRAITURE

I am the sugar in the bottom of the English cup of tea. STUART HALL, "Old and New Identities, Old and New Ethnicities"[1]

Several eighteenth-century portraits and conversation pieces contain the figure of the black servant. Most frequently a boy or an adolescent male, the servant is dressed in livery and wears either a turban or a skullcap. Both head coverings are exotic and allude to the Turkish, Moslem, and Mughal cultures of the Levant, northern Africa, and the Indian subcontinent. This conflation of Arabic, African, and Indian origins is typical of many eighteenth-century representations of black servants. What seems to matter is not that these servants are African, Muslim, or Indian, but that they are exotic, that they originate in tropical, fertile, and remote lands. Their status as exotics is reinforced by the frequency with which they are associated in prints and paintings with the consumption of foreign luxury goods such as sugar, tea, tobacco, and coffee, all commodities associated with the dark others of the world. In Hogarth's *A Harlot's Progress* (1732), for instance, the liveried, turbaned black child is carrying a pot of hot water, and the overturned table is spilling tea cups and tea accessories onto the floor (Fig. 1). In the conversation piece portraying Elihu Yale and his friends

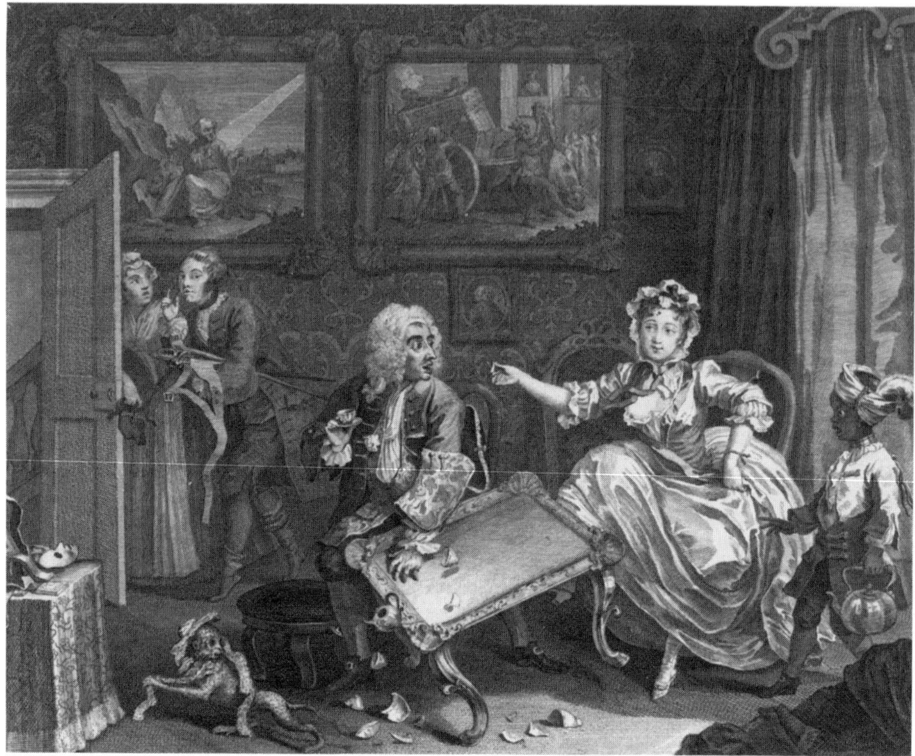

1. William Hogarth, plate 2, *A Harlot's Progress*, 1732, engraving. Courtesy of the Print Collection, Lewis Walpole Library, Yale University.

(1708), a black boy, also liveried and turbaned, is serving the four tobacco-smoking gentlemen (Fig. 2). The black figure exoticizes the activities of these English subjects, calling attention to the foreignness of their activities.

Closely associated with the consumption of exotic commodities, the figure of the black servant in domestic portraiture is emblematic of overseas trade and colonialism. As David Dabydeen argues, images of Africans and African Caribbeans were included in portraits of British aristocratic men and women as a way to indicate the colonial connections of these wealthy and powerful people. Images of black people were also placed on signs, advertisements, and business cards of sugar and tobacco merchants; in this way, the black figure came to be associated with New World colonies and the production

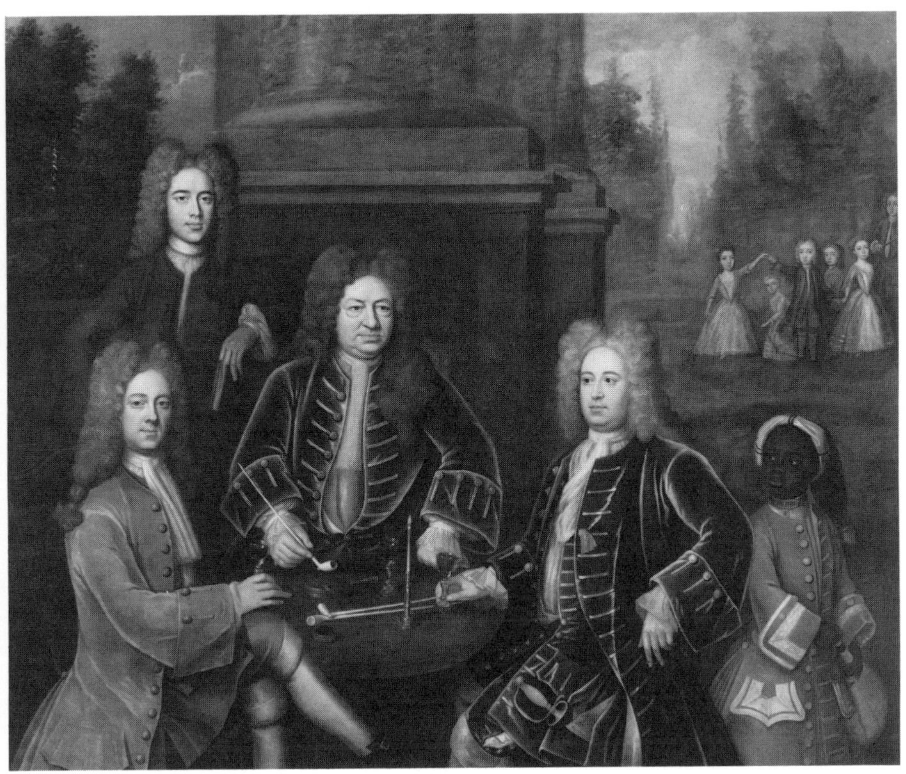

2. British School, *Elihu Yale, the 2nd Duke of Devonshire, Lord James Cavendish, Mr Tunstal, and a Page*, c. 1708, oil on canvas. Yale Center for British Art, Gift of the 11th Duke of Devonshire.

of commodities such as sugar and tobacco.[2] As attitudes toward the consumption of exotic commodities shifted over the course of the century from intense feelings of anxiety and/or excitement to a complacent acceptance of coffee, tea, and sugar as naturally belonging to the English domestic scene, so did attitudes change toward the figure of the black servant. In the early part of the century, the black page is often portrayed as naughty or disruptive and is frequently placed in scenes that contain innuendoes of sexuality or moral laxity. However, as the century progressed, the figure of the black servant was placed in closer proximity to children and mothers, signaling the incorporation of the exotic into the everydayness of the domestic scene. In this chapter I explore the figure of the black servant as an emblem of the exotic, tracing the eventual incorporation of the exotic into domestic life, and I suggest that the black servant in eighteenth-century English painting is best understood in the context of the eighteenth-century response to Britain's mercantile and imperialist activities.[3]

The Exotic

Frances Burney's play *A Busy Day* (1801) opens on a scene of confusion, with the entrance of the heroine, a rich heiress, who has just arrived in London after a long voyage from Calcutta. Her coach has overturned, her baggage is scattered, and her black servant, Mongo, is in need of assistance. Anxious about Mongo's welfare, Eliza says, "Poor Mongo! my care of you shall be trebled for the little kindness you seem likely to meet with here."[4] Mongo, who never materializes on the stage, serves as a device, as Tara Ghoshal Wallace argues, to display Eliza's "moral superiority" to those who surround her in this London setting (2). The English servants cannot believe Eliza is in earnest when she asks them to help Mongo; they keep repeating in disbelief and disgust, "What, the Black?" Even Eliza's English maid cannot understand why Eliza lavishes so much concern on him: "after all, a Black's but a Black; and let him hurt himself never so much, it won't shew" (32–33). Mongo, "a semiotic present absence,"[5] confers on Eliza the role of responsible imperialist; her enormous wealth— £80,000—is purified of the taint of corruption and rapacity often associated with returning nabobs by the workings of her sympathetic heart and her benevolent regard for Mongo.

What is interesting about Mongo aside from his blackness and his absence is his name. As Wallace points out, Mungo was a common name for African slaves, and Burney may have had in mind Isaac Bickerstaff's *The Padlock* (1768) and his "Negro servant called Mungo" (32). The name Mongo implies that the servant is African, and yet, this servant is described by the hero of the play as "an inexperienced black servant just imported from Calcutta" as part of Eliza's legacy from her adoptive father, a rich merchant. This Mongo seems to be both Indian and African, and it does not seem to matter whether he is from Africa or India, for "a Black's but a Black," as Eliza's servant says.[6] Mungo stands in for Britain's colonial possessions in the West and East Indies and acts as a reminder that colonies create wealth for Britons while also creating responsibilities associated with governing subject peoples and with stewardship of the colonial resources.

Wealth, like Eliza's inheritance, derived from colonial possessions and overseas trade, was regarded by many as morally suspect and as potentially destabilizing of England's social, economic, and political order. Oliver Goldsmith, for instance, in his poem "The Deserted Village" blames the devastation of the rural economy and peasant communities on the infiltration of the old society by merchants, "trade's unfeeling train," who, in Goldsmith's estimation, lack civic virtue, valuing "unwieldy wealth and cumbrous pomp" above all else. Angered by the "devastation" of "rural virtues," Goldsmith points the finger of blame at "Luxury."[7] He argues that the city, with its dazzling commodities and garish entertainments, had seduced the gentry from their rural responsibilities, making room for a new class of owners associated with "trade" to take their place. The word "luxury" was associated with money generated by speculation and with the consumption of expensive and useless commodities produced by overseas trade, colonial ventures, and the slave trade, commodities such as tea, china, silk, coffee, chocolate, mahogany, ivory, and sugar. Condemning London for its corruption, materialism, and avariciousness, Goldsmith is particularly upset by the city's production of new men, who invade the countryside and pollute its rustic beauty by building ornate palaces and artificial gardens, destroying the economic and social fabric of the old agrarian society. Attacking luxury and the corroding effect of money on the morals of the nation was a favorite theme of eighteenth-century writers.[8]

This discourse on luxury provided a useful and persuasive explanation for the social and economic changes that were occurring in the countryside: the enclosure of common property, the pauperization of the small farmer, the disenfranchisement of the laborer, and the depopulation of rural communities. Historians argue over whether Goldsmith and others were right to blame the erosion of the paternal order on the destabilizing effect of mercantile capital, yet it is clear that such formulations about the unsettling effect on the old society of new money derived from the colonies and overseas trade were commonplace in eighteenth-century art, drama, poetry, prose nonfiction, and fiction. Nabobs, or the recently returned and enriched servants of the East India Company, and their West Indian counterparts were regularly ridiculed on stage and in cartoons. The landed upper classes looked askance when ordinary men of the middle and lower classes, the sons of curates, lawyers, estate managers, and tradesmen, who had made fortunes as sugar planters in the West Indies or as factors of the East India Company, returned to England, bought country estates, and moved into their set. Sons of the upper class married the daughters of this class of *nouveaux riches* to help ease the pinched cash flow that plagued many landed families. This is the plot not only of Burney's *A Busy Day* but also of Richard Cumberland's *The West Indian* (1771). Both plays open with a chaotic scene depicting the bustle and commotion surrounding the arrival in London from the colonies of the wealthy children of such nabob figures. In *The West Indian* the heir of a sugar magnate arrives with an entourage of black servants carrying boxes, parrots, and monkeys; in *A Busy Day*, Eliza, the adoptive heiress of an East Indian merchant, arrives at an inn with her baggage, her black servant, and £80,000 with which to buy a husband, preferably the eldest son of a baronet, which she does succeed in doing over the course of the play. Even though Eliza and her West Indian counterpart, Belcour, make disruptive entrances and contribute to the confusion typical of comic plots of mistaken identities, both protagonists possess warmth, charm, and charitable dispositions that mitigate against the chaos they bring with them. Eliza's and Belcour's sympathetic hearts are meant to sweep away the reservations an audience might have about the origins of their wealth and to make a place for these colonial subjects in the upper tiers of British society.

The processes whereby colonial wealth, products, and peoples were absorbed into British society aroused anxiety in some late-eighteenth-century observers. However, in comparison with the earlier part of the century, such anxieties were mild, for overseas trade and colonialism had been a volatile issue in the first third of the century, provoking a range of responses from righteous condemnation to eager acceptance. With the expansion of colonial domains, the exploitation of colonial resources, and the global circulation of merchant capital, early-eighteenth-century critics and admirers of empire focused their attention on the impact of the consumption of foreign commodities on the English character and domestic economy. Some delighted in the acquisition of wondrous exotic objects—sugar, chocolate, tea, coffee, tobacco, china, and silk—while others were less enthusiastic about what they perceived as dangerous substances destructive of native English virtues. As Louis Landa, J. G. A. Pocock, Laura Brown, and David Solkin have demonstrated, the consumption of exotic luxury goods was not an ideologically neutral activity in the early eighteenth century.[9] Some writers saw the exotic as insidious, sapping native enterprise and ingenuity and spreading the seeds of moral and economic decay; others argued that the conspicuous consumption of luxury goods was not necessarily antithetical to virtuous conduct; and still others celebrated England as the center of a global system of exchange. Pope, for instance, in the "The Rape of the Lock," registers ambivalence toward the beau monde's consumption of exotic commodities with his portrait of Belinda, who sits at her dressing table admiring not only her own image in the mirror, but the trinkets and perfumes, culled from around the globe, that are arranged on the table:

> This Casket *India*'s glowing Gems unlocks,
> And all *Arabia* breath from yonder Box.
> The Tortoise here and Elephant unite,
> Transform'd to *Combs,* the speckled and the white.[10]

Pope's catalogue extends from the contents of Belinda's dressing table to Hampton Court's social gatherings, where the queen "Doth sometimes counsel take—and sometimes tea" (3:8) and her guests play cards, take snuff, and drink hot chocolate and coffee. The sensory language that Pope uses to describe Belinda, her attendants, and her activities conveys the seductive beauty of the exotic, and yet Pope registers with his ironic linking of oppositions—"stain her honor or her new brocade" (2:107)—his concern that the social rituals of the beau monde are at best merely beautiful and at worst empty, trivial, even immoral.

Less ambivalent about the consumption of luxury goods, Pope's contemporaries Joseph Addison and Richard Steele praised the new merchant class for their efforts in transforming London into the center of global exchange. Addison wrote in *The Spectator* that the overseas merchant was a "Citizen of the World" and that London was "a kind of *Emporium* for the whole Earth":

Our Ships are laden with the Harvest of every Climate: Our Tables are stored with Spices, and Oils, and Wines: Our Rooms are filled with Pyramids of *China,* and adorned with the Workmanship of *Japan:* Our Morning's-Draught comes to us from the remotest Corners of the Earth: We repair our Bodies by the Drugs of *America,* and repose our selves under *Indian* Canopies. My Friend Sir Andrew calls the Vineyards of *France* our Gardens: the Spice-Islands our Hot-Beds; the *Persians* our Silk-weavers, and the *Chinese* our Potters. Nature indeed furnishes us with bare Necessaries of Life, but Traffick gives us a great Variety of what is Useful, and at the same time supplies us with every thing that is Convenient and Ornamental.[11]

Addison and Steele assured their audiences that "there are not more useful Members in a Commonwealth than Merchants"[12]; as Mr. Sealand says in Steele's *The Conscious Lovers* (1722), "we merchants are a species of gentry that have grown into the world this last century, and are as honorable, and almost as useful, as you landed folks."[13] An even more aggressive promoter of the idea that merchants were useful, nay exemplary, citizens of the nation was George Lillo in his tragedy *The London Merchant* (1731). The great merchant Thorowgood, whose generosity and hospitality rivals that of the aristocracy, remarks that "honest merchants" such as himself "contribute to the safety of their country." Echoing Addison's panegyric on the merchant who knits "Mankind together in mutual Intercourse of Good Offices,"[14] Thorowgood instructs his apprentices in the "science" of trade. It is not "merely . . . a means of getting wealth," he says; "it is founded on reason and the nature of things": "I have observed those countries where trade is promoted and encouraged do not make discoveries to destroy, but to improve, mankind; by love and friendship to tame the fierce and polish the most savage; to teach them the advantages of honest traffic by taking from them, with their own consent, their useless superfluities, and giving back to them in return what, from their ignorance in manual arts, their situation, or some other accident, they stand in need of."[15]

While Addison, Steele, and Lillo praised mercantile capitalism, other writers, such as Jonathan Swift, were highly suspicious of England's consumption of foreign luxury items. Swift's hostility to the importation of luxury goods—"those detestable Extravagancies of . . . Tea, Coffee, Chocolate, China-ware"[16]—emerges in Gulliver's description of the Yahoo (English) economy. Gulliver explains to his Houyhnhnm master that "this whole Globe of Earth must be at least three Times gone round, before one of our better Female Yahoos could get her Breakfast, or a Cup to put it in. . . . In order to feed the Luxury and Intemperance of the Males, and the Vanity of the Females, we sent away the greatest Part of our necessary Things to other Countries, from whence in Return we brought the Materials of Diseases, Folly, and Vice, to spend among ourselves."[17] The link between imported luxury goods and moral decay is made explicit in Mandeville's controversial *The Fable of the Bees* (1714) and its lengthy explication of his thesis that prosperity is contingent upon vice:

> Luxury
> Employ'd a Million of the Poor,
> And odious Pride a Million more.
> Envy it self, and Vanity
> Were Ministers of Industry;
> Their darling Folly, Fickleness
> In Diet, Furniture, and Dress,
> That strange ridic'lous Vice, was made
> The very Wheel, that turn'd the Trade.[18]

Mandeville enraged his readers by insisting that England's prosperity, which was derived from trade, was driven by people's immoderate passions and illicit desires: "I own it is my Sense that no Society can be rais'd into such a rich and mighty Kingdom, or so rais'd, subsist in their Wealth and Power for any considerable Time without the Vices of Man." Women's appetites for the exotic are linked with political corruption and imperial rapine: "The haughty Chloe, to live Great, / Had made her Husband rob the State: / But now she sells her Furniture, / Which th' *Indies* had been ransack'd for." Mandeville contends that the "prosperity of London and Trade in general" and consequently the health and well-being of the "Nation . . . depends entirely on the Deceit and vile Stratagems of Women."[19] Countless other literary productions, moral tracts, and economic treatises register an anxiety and alarm over the deleterious effects of consuming foreign luxury items, "Things of no real Use, but . . . detrimental, and injurious." According to John Woodward in his *State of Physick, and of Diseases* (1718), "the Use of Chocolate, of Coffee, Limonade, Punch: but more especially Tea" promotes ill health and moral decline: "the Consequence of this great Increase in the Arts of Luxury and Intemperance, are Vice and Immorality: Irreligion, Impiety, Passion, Animosity, Contention, Factions: Neglect of Thought, Studyes, and Business, Misspending of Time, Ignorance, Stupidity, Poverty, Discontent, Sickness, Disease."[20] Writers like Woodward and Swift blame what they see as a decline in the morality of the nation on the consumption of exotic commodities as well as the overseas trade and colonial ventures that were responsible for this supply of foreign luxury goods.

Hogarth participated in this morally and politically charged discourse on the consumption of the exotic with his portrayal of Moll Hackabout and her decline into a life of harlotry, disease, and death.[21] In the second plate of *A Harlot's Progress* (1732) Hogarth places the figure of the black servant, a turbaned boy carrying a pot of hot water, at the far right side of the picture (Fig. 1). His body is in motion, as if he is walking into the scene, and his face has a look of surprise, his eyebrows arched in shock and his eyes wide open. His gaze directs our gaze across the room to the monkey (a sign of exotic and deviant sexuality) and the upset tea table. This print is full of movement—the Jew's wig is falling off; Moll Hackabout's gown is sliding off, exposing her right breast; her lover is gliding out the door; the teapot and cups are falling off the table; the monkey is running away; the servant is entering the room—and the direction of all this movement is right to left. Because our gaze moves across the print from right to left, as if directed by the boy's gaze, it is almost as if his gaze initiates the movement and sets in motion all the disorder we see. The right-to-left movement mimics the movement of the eye when reading Arabic, Hebrew, and Chinese and therefore is associated with foreign practices that can be quite destabilizing for a Western viewer. This right-to-left movement associates disorder with the foreign in much the same way as the boy's turban (Arabic), the Jewish patron (Hebrew), and the china and tea (Chinese), as exotic items, are all linked to moral dissolution.[22] The disruptive energy of the black servant's entrance into the scene and the moral disorder associated with his presence are not limited to what is depicted in this second plate but spill over into the next several plates, moving Moll through several more scenes in a downward spiral that ends in her moral and physical destruction. In detailing the corruption of a native English country girl, *A Harlot's Progress* functions as a critique of London, the trading capital of the world, a place polluted by foreign interpenetration and made a site of moral instability.

As David Dabydeen and other critics have pointed out, Hogarth shares with Swift a fear of the foreign and associates the exotic with moral decay.[23] In the fourth scene of *Marriage à la Mode* (1743–45), Hogarth uses two black servants, one a turbaned boy playing with horned statues and the other a man serving a lady a beverage, chocolate perhaps, to underscore the immoral atmosphere of the countess's boudoir (Fig. 3). Filled with foreigners and freaks—an Italian castrato, a German musician, a French dancing master—the room, hung with Italian paintings of mythical and biblical sexual transgressions, is given over to foreign amusements and dangerous flirtations. The lawyer is making an assignation with the countess to meet at a masquerade, a popular form of amusement introduced to London society by John Jacob Heidigger, a Swiss; under the cover of disguise, these masquerades offered freedom from usual social restraints, enabling all sorts of transgressions to take place.[24] The countess, a rich merchant's daughter, sits at her toilet immersed in the lifestyle of the degenerate aristocracy, who have turned their back on English ways and English values and are busy imitating French manners and consuming European fashions and culture. Through the gestures of the black servants, particularly the childlike figure who sits in the lower right corner of the painting playing with figurines of horned mythical beasts, Hogarth links foreign bodies with sexual transgression and moral decline. The horns on the figurines, emblems of cuckoldry, refer to the countess's disastrous assignation with her lover in a bagnio, a scene depicted in the next painting in the series. As in *A Harlot's Progress*, the black servant is associated with morally corrosive practices: his play with the horned beasts foretells the adulterous liaison between the countess and the lawyer; in foretelling this event, the page's play seems to precipitate his mistress's immoral conduct. Hogarth uses the bodies of the black servants to perform the ideological work of attaching the stigma of moral transgression to overseas trade. Ironically, this stigma is attached not only to overseas trade but to colonial ventures, including the slave trade, which brought these black servants into the English domestic enclosure.[25]

Hogarth's use of black servants in his *Progresses*, his visual equivalents of cautionary tales, is a departure from the tone and visual

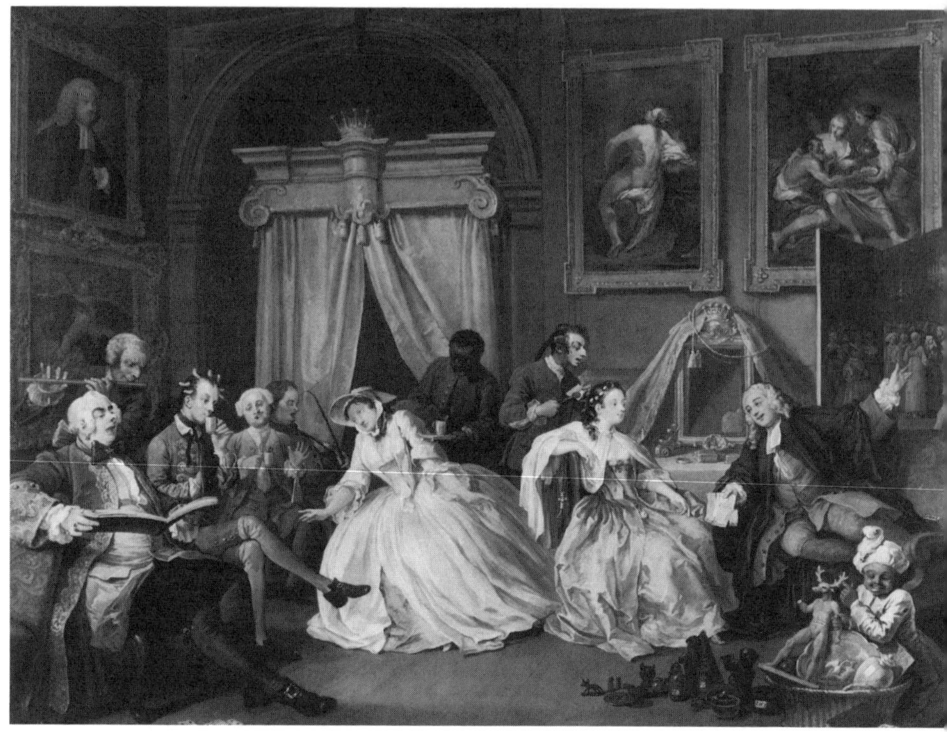

3. William Hogarth, *The Countess's Morning Levee, Marriage à la Mode,*
1743–45, oil on canvas. National Gallery of Art, London.

idioms of the dozens of portraits of aristocratic men and women that
contain the figure of a black servant. For example, two paintings, a
conversation piece and a portrait of a lady, convey none of Hogarth's
xenophobia and moral panic over the exoticism associated with black
bodies. The conversation piece *Elihu Yale, 2nd Duke of Devonshire, Lord
Cavendish, Mr Tunstal, and a Page* (1708), attributed to the British
School, contains a child-sized black servant waiting upon these four
distinguished and powerful gentlemen, who are smoking tobacco and
drinking wine (Fig. 2). Like the Hogarth *Progresses,* the black servant
is associated with the consumption of exotic luxury items, but unlike
Hogarth's pages, the black servant in the Yale conversation piece is
not a disruptive force. Despite his mischievous grin and the curious
expression on his face, this figure's energy is contained by the arrangement of the men. Together they make up a triangle, the black servant
making the tail point of the triangle in the bottom right corner. The

boy is part of a configuration that is dominated by the Englishmen. They are in control; they look at us directly, undisturbed by the boy's grin, while he looks at them. The servant's exotic turban and impish expression, like the tobacco smoking, provide variety and entertainment, which is absorbed and contained by the arrangement of figures in the painting's composition.

Likewise, spacial relations between the black servant and the aristocratic figure in Godfrey Kneller's portrait of the Duchess of Ormond contain and delimit whatever sexual innuendo the page's presence may convey. He is there to serve her. His crouching body and boyish face emphasize her height; his round black face offers contrast to her white skin and elegantly long face, arms, and torso. She dominates him and takes the upper position on every binary opposition that his presence creates—white/black, tall/short, long/round, adult/child— with the exception of female/male. Her dominating presence is intensified by this reversal; her whiteness and aristocratic bearing overturn the "natural" hierarchy of male over female. The page's potential for disruption is contained by the vertical hierarchy established and the binary oppositions put into play in this portrait. He is there, as Sander Gilman would say, to sexualize her, to make her exotic, but it is an exoticism she is in control of as she confronts us with her cool and haughty gaze, challenging us to admire her.[26] In creating spacial hierarchies, both these paintings reiterate racial hierarchies and communicate the justness and orderliness of white people dominating and controlling black people. Both paintings participate in seventeenth- and eighteenth-century discourses that represented Africans as intellectually, culturally, and morally inferior to Europeans. The spacial hierarchies employed in the Yale and Ormond portraits refer to this discourse to justify the imposition of white power over black and the exploitation of Africa and Africans for England's benefit, asserting with confidence Britain's ability to master the exotic and incorporate it into the domestic moral and political economy.

Colonial Relations

Whereas the Hogarth prints, the Yale conversation piece, and Kneller's portrait stress the exoticism of the black page, Johan Zoffany's depiction of a black servant domesticates the servant's exotic origins

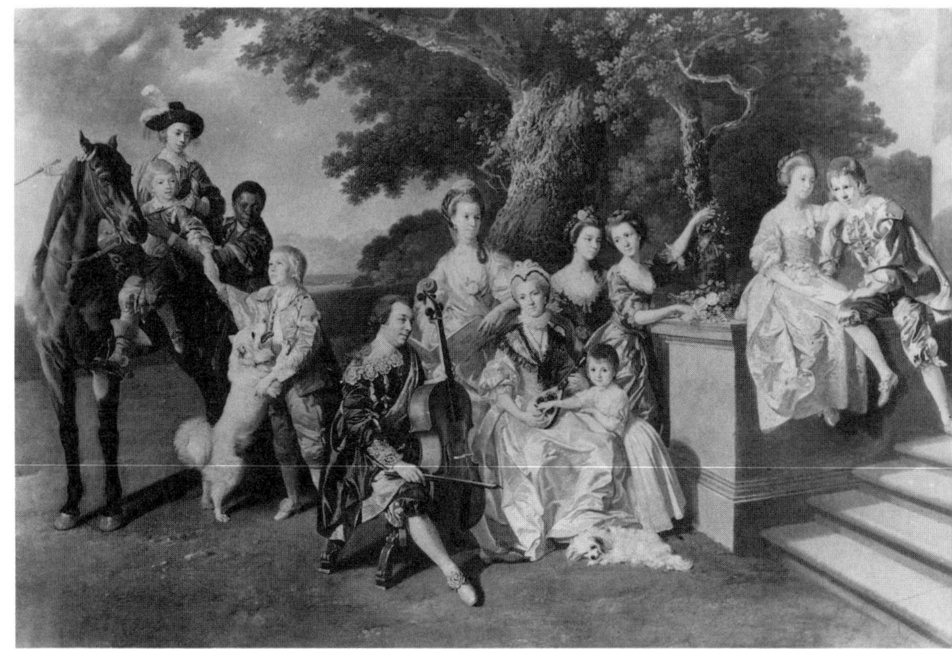

4. Johan Zoffany, *The Family of Sir William Young, Baronet,* 1770, oil on canvas. The Walker Art Gallery. Courtesy of the Board of Trustees of the National Museums and Galleries on Merseyside.

by firmly locating him within the bosom of an English family.[27] Zoffany's *The Family of Sir William Young, Baronet* (1770) is a portrait of a large family group of eleven members arranged in three groups (Fig. 4). The center of the painting is occupied by Sir William, who was governor of the Caribbean island of Dominica and commissioner of St. Vincent, and his wife, both playing musical instruments. Also sharing the center of the picture is a small child, a lap dog, an older woman holding a portfolio of music, and two young women reaching for the blossoms on a flowering tree. On the right side of the painting an older boy and girl sit on a stone pedestal, one of her arms bent and resting on his shoulder. This boy, according to G. C. Williamson, is William Young, the second baronet, who was to become a proslavery MP and eventually governor of Tobago. On the left side of the painting astride a horse is another son, Brook, wearing a cavalier hat and holding a riding crop.[28] Seated in front of him is a little boy, John, who is being supported by a young black male servant standing next to the horse. This boy is reaching down to hold hands with another boy, Harry, who seems to be a bit older than he.[29]

The arrangement of the figures lends them a lovely sense of intimacy, harmony, and family unity. Everyone in this picture is joined to someone else. Hands touch, bodies overlap, and gazes intersect. The girl lounges against the boy on the pedestal, her hand and arm draped over his shoulder. The mother embraces a child while sitting in front of the three standing women, their bodies fused in an oval configuration. The young man on the horse and the servant are looking at the standing boy, who is also being gazed upon by an eager, upright dog; at the same time, the young boy on the horse looks at the standing boy, but his sight line passes through that face and rests upon his father's. In this way the left side of the painting is linked to the center scene.[30] The left and right groupings are linked to each other by gazes as well. The young man on the stone pedestal is gazing at the little boy on the horse; their faces mirror each other with a three-quarter turn, both looking in from the edges of the scene. Each figure, either through sight or touch, is put in relation to the others; each is embedded in this domestic scene. Sir William dominates this large gathering; he is the largest and the closest figure, but he is the most separate of the members of this group. He is separated from his wife by the cello (his toe is touching the rim of her gown), and yet he is joined to her by the cello's sexual symbolism, its feminine shape and his prominent bow.

The other element that unites these figures is their dress. With the exception of the black servant, each is dressed in Van Dyck–style costumes, as if for a party, a masquerade, or a family performance. The Van Dyck dress adds an unusual note to this domestic scene; the lavish and elaborate clothes, replete with lace collars, feathered hats, satin capes, and swashbuckling boots, are highly artificial, and though popular in portraits of women and children (Gainsborough's *Blue Boy*, for instance), are perhaps a bit excessive for this large group. There is a whiff of arbitrary power about these costumes, as they allude to Van Dyck's portraits of Charles I; other political referents that might adhere to these costumes are the absence of natural rights, with its inverse, the divine right of kings, and the authoritarian power and patriarchal hierarchies of this Stuart monarchy. These political ideas were not antithetical to the sentiments of a slave owner and a planto-crat apologist for the slave trade; in fact, Sir William might wear these ideas as comfortably as he does the Van Dyck costume. Despite the formality of the elaborate costuming, the family looks as if it is in the midst of rehearsing or getting ready for some musical performance, bringing a sense of informality, ease, and spontaneity to the scene.[31]

The black servant participates in this domestic scene, sharing in its gay and warm family life. A gentle smile and fond look grace his face as he holds one child and looks at another. He is an integral part of the scene: his arm is criss-crossed by the arms of the two boys holding hands. But he is also a support, like the horse, and, like the dog, gazes on the standing boy's face. He is included in the family portrait, like the animals, as an accoutrement or prop to help communicate this family's qualities. His pleasant face conveys the feeling that he seems to care about the family and to be particularly fond of Sir William's children. His attachment to the family speaks well of him but even more so of the family, as worthy of his loyalty. His well-being reflects well on them.

Zoffany has so skillfully woven this group together with affection-ate gazes and gracefully linked arms and hands that we almost forget the material relations that undergird this family's social, economic, and political position. As Sacheverell Sitwell coolly remarks, "Sir Wil-liam was a West Indian magnate, being Governor of the islands of St. Vincent and Dominica. For this reason a negro servant occurs in the picture."[32] The glint of gold (or brass, perhaps) that shines from beneath the black servant's neckcloth is a metal collar that slaves wore much the same way dogs wear collars. This black servant, a slave, is emblematic of more than Sir William's colonial post; he stands in for the hundreds of slaves that the Youngs owned on their several West Indian sugar plantations, two in Tobago, three in St. Vincent, one in Dominica, and two in Antigua, one of which his son refers to as the "old mansion of my ancestors" in his *Tour through the Several Islands*.[33] As a plantocrat and colonial official, Sir William profited economi-cally, politically, and socially from his West Indian connections; in 1769 he was made a baronet, and at the time of his death his estates' com-bined worth was estimated to be over £200,000.[34] Perhaps this con-versation piece, painted in 1770, is a celebration of the family's newly acquired status. The lavish and almost excessive costumes allude to an aristocratic heritage this family did not possess, for, as Robin Simon suggests, the Van Dyck costumes were popular with "families without ancestors of the right kind to have been portrayed by Van Dyck himself."[35] The Young portrait is, Sitwell concludes, "an alternative to the group of Anglo Indian nabobs and their families," nabobs being infamous for their extravagant display of newfound wealth.[36]

As governor of Dominica and commissioner of St. Vincent, Sir William Young reaped financial and social rewards in the exercise of his power. As commissioner, he was instrumental in appropriating land from French occupants and the Black Caribs, who dominated the windward and northern parts of the islands. The Black Caribs regarded these lands as their own, having arranged a treaty with the French in the early part of the century that guaranteed these lands for their use. When the English, under Sir William's leadership, tried to penetrate Black Carib territory and to claim it as forfeited to the English Crown by the French capitulation of the island in the Treaty of Paris in 1763, the Black Caribs regarded the English as invaders and usurpers of their lands. In the early 1770s the commissioners, having surveyed and sold off the leeward and southern coastal lands, sent surveying parties to the windward side of the island in preparation for parceling and selling these lands. The Black Caribs harassed the surveying parties; eventually the commissioners persuaded Lord Hillsborough of the Treasury to send troops to enforce British rule on the Black Caribs and to make them relinquish their valuable lands to the Crown. The result was the First Black Carib War, which ended in a stalemate and was heavily criticized in London as "a violation of the natural rights of mankind, and totally subversive of that liberty it gloried to defend."[37]

As a member of the ruling elite of Antigua, St. Vincent, and Dominica, Sir William was responsible for dispossessing the Black Caribs of their land and for enforcing the systematic economic exploitation of African labor that the institution of slavery entailed. The horrors of slavery are too well-known to be retold here, and the history of the slave trade and its connection with the sugar plantations of the Caribbean have been well documented in recent years.[38] But a brief examination of the nature of the institution Sir William profited from and was required to maintain as a colonial administrator will help us to appreciate how effectively Zoffany and his sitters conspired to rewrite the foundation of their artful ease.[39]

The Slave Trade: "A Fund of Wealth"

The development of the sugar plantations in the West Indies began slowly in the seventeenth century, but sugar production increased rapidly and steadily throughout the eighteenth century, particularly in the third quarter of the century, along with the increasing demand for sugar in the British domestic economy. According to David Richardson, "sugar consumption per head in Britain rose from 6.5 lbs around 1710 to 23.2 lbs in the early 1770s," and the time of greatest growth was between 1750 and 1775.[40] Because sugar production requires an enormous labor force—as Eric Williams put it, "sugar meant labor"—increasing numbers of African slaves were brought to the Caribbean to work in the sugar plantations.[41] The increased productivity of the plantations and high demand for sugar made these West Indian plantations very profitable.

The West Indies' sugar production not only provided planters with profits ranging from 8 percent to 20 percent on capital invested in the purchase of slaves but also increased the wealth of Britain by stimulating industry within Britain and trade throughout Britain's imperial domain. Eric Williams asserts in his seminal *Capitalism and Slavery:* "The West Indian islands became the hub of the British Empire, of immense importance to the grandeur and prosperity of England. It was the Negro slaves who made these sugar colonies the most precious colonies ever recorded in the whole annals of imperialism."[42] Michael Craton writes that William Pitt figured that the West Indian plantations "made four times as much profit for their owners as all other overseas holdings put together, and that the triangular trade [Britain–West Africa–West Indies] produced a quarter of the profits of all overseas English trade."[43] Williams goes on to argue that the profits obtained by the sugar planters "provided one of the main streams of that accumulation of capital in England which financed the Industrial Revolution."[44]

Although Williams may have exaggerated the importance of the West Indies' trade in slaves and sugar in the accumulation of capital and its investment in the Industrial Revolution, most historians agree that the slavery-sugar trade did contribute greatly to England's national wealth. The slave trade stimulated the manufacturing of textile and metallurgical goods, which were in turn sold to markets in Africa in exchange for slaves, and it stimulated trade in agricultural commodities with New England to feed the slaves on the ships and those on the plantations. With the profits from this trade with the West Indies and the refining of West Indian molasses, New England merchants, manufacturers, and farmers bought commodities manufactured in Britain. As one contemporary apologist for the slave trade argued, "The *Negroe-Trade* therefore, and the natural Consequences resulting from it, may be justly esteemed an inexhaustible Fund of Wealth and Naval Power to this Nation."[45] Another spokesperson for the plantocracy extolled the economic benefits of the slave trade by claiming that "the artificers and mechanics employed at Liverpool alone, receive one hundred thousand pounds annually for labor and materials employed in equipping the ships engaged in it."[46] The sugar-slavery nexus not only promoted British manufacturing and trade but also stimulated the burgeoning banking and insurance industries in England.[47]

While a significant portion (8 percent to 50 percent, depending on the historian) of Britain's economic growth can be attributed to the sugar-slavery system, individuals also profited. Michael Craton describes this process: "Acting as yeast, profits from the sugar plantations enabled penniless adventurers to found rich dynasties, created a powerful class of wealthy absentees and, ultimately, provided one of the most transformative transfers of capital in England's history."[48] The planters returned to England, "bought land and entered English politics, many of them 'buying' into titles by political patronage or marriage," and, unlike the North Americans, the West Indian planters "became English again."[49] The topic of buying titles and reinvesting in England recalls us to our task at hand: Sir William Young. Profiting both monetarily and politically from his position as a slave owner, a planter, and a colonial official in sugar-producing colonies, he petitioned the government to return "home" in 1773, where he did, indeed, buy an estate.[50]

In Zoffany's portrait of the Young family, the only reminder of this system that brutalized Africans for profit is the figure of the servant.[51] His presence is eclipsed by the warmth of domestic affection and the casual intimacy that this family's musical performance generates. The family's elegance and grace rewrite the origins of their social position, locating their socially and economically privileged position in their genteel artistic and musical accomplishments. The Van Dyck costumes lend to Sir William and his family an aristocratic and cultured past, and the musical instruments and sheet music imply domestic harmony and this family's ease with their European cultural heritage.[52] Well-known for his musical parties and hospitality, Sir William "drew people about him from every quarter in the West Indies." Describing his opulent and elegant manner of entertaining, his son praises his father for possessing "that vivacity in conversation, that freedom, and that refinement in manners, that 'curiosa felicitas,' which Petronius, I think, attributes to Horace, and which, so united the fine gentleman, and the open-hearted man. . . . With the voice of music, and the fine arts, he made jovial parties of colonization."[53]

The art (in the form of Van Dyck portraiture) and music alluded to in this conversation piece declare this family's cultural superiority, a superiority reinforced by the presence of their black servant. He represents the ignorant slave and unenlightened African who has benefited by his association with this family, sharing in the warmth of its domestic harmony. What Macauley would say of the Indians in the nineteenth century could be said by Sir William of this black slave: "I see the morality, the philosophy, the taste of Europe, beginning to produce a salutary effect on the hearts and understandings of our subjects."[54] The warmth of the Youngs' domestic ties and their pleasure in their participation in the arts work to justify not only their black servant's servitude but slavery as well. The servant's affectionate look and gentle smile erase the material conditions of his own exploitation and the egregious abuses of power that marked Britain's colonial rule of the West Indies. The black servant's presence reminds us of Sir William's West Indian legacy but immediately transforms that brutal colonial power into an elegant, graceful, and refined celebration of English art, music, and domestic life.[55]

Imperial Magnanimity

A black servant is also placed within a family setting in William Redmore Bigg's *A Lady and Her Children Relieving a Cottager* (1781; Fig. 5), but this servant functions very differently from Zoffany's. Not a por-

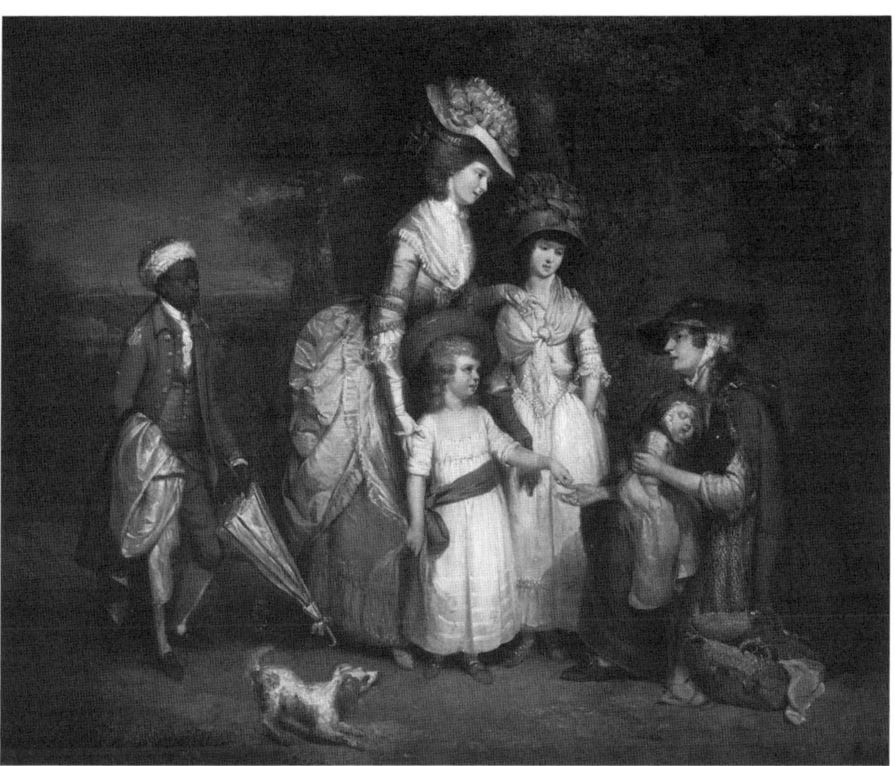

5. William Redmore Bigg, *A Lady and Her Children Relieving a Cottager*, 1781, oil on canvas. Philadelphia Museum of Art: Given by Mr. and Mrs. Herald Paumgarten.

trait of a family group like Zoffany's *Sir William Young, A Lady and Her Children Relieving a Cottager*, sometimes referred to as *The Charitable Lady*, is a genre painting, which, true to type, is "fraught with narrative or anecdotal interest" and, like Hogarth's *Progresses*, is also "imbued with strongly moralistic presuppositions."[56] Placed within the domestic orbit of a charitable gentlewoman, Bigg's servant marks the intersection of several late-eighteenth-century discourses on class, race, and gender. The charitable activity depicted in this painting is more complicated than its title implies. Not simply about the sentimental pleasures of almsgiving, this painting depicts a mother teaching her youngest child, a son, about class relations and social responsibility.[57] This son, a child still dressed in the nongendered clothing of infancy, stands at the center of the picture. His older sister stands behind and to the right of him while his mother stands to the left of him. She has her hand firmly on his shoulder, urging him forward and steering him toward the object of his charity: a poor woman and her baby. He holds a coin in his hand to give to the woman, who cradles her sleeping baby against her body while holding out her hand to receive the boy's gift. The poor woman is seated by the side of the road and in front of what looks to be an abandoned cottage. She is wearing traveling clothes, and a nearly empty basket lies beside her. The roadside and her cloak, hat, and basket suggest that she may have been displaced and may even be a member of the growing population of the vagrant poor. This act of charity seems to be spontaneous, as though the charitable lady, her daughter, her son, and her black servant had been out walking on their estate (a manor house lies off in the distance) and had come across the distressed woman and her baby. The gentlewoman sees this as an opportunity to teach her younger child, her son and heir, about his responsibilities as a member of the gentry, which include the duty to supervise and care for the poor within his estate community. The boy is reluctant to perform this act of charity; he hangs back and has to be urged forward as if he were afraid of the poor woman, but his mother perseveres, teaching him his Christian duty to dispense charity. The boy's white robe with blue sash, his golden curls, his round straw hat that looks like a halo, and his outstretched hand, all reminders of innumerable portrayals of Jesus, underscore the Christian nature of this charitable act.

A Lady and Her Children Relieving a Cottager is filled with topical material, new ideas that were much debated and discussed during the last quarter of the eighteenth century. One such topic is women's roles as mothers and particularly their duties as moral guides for their children.[58] In the next few years Mary Wollstonecraft and Hannah More would address the need for women to receive a proper education so that they might be better mothers and teachers of their own children.[59] Throughout the 1780s and 1790s women's magazines, particularly the *Lady's Magazine,* published stories and essays extolling the lives of exemplary mothers who would not leave the education and care of their children to servants and tutors, but who took an active role in the moral education of their children.[60] Mothers became instrumental "in sowing the seeds of those virtues" that were important to the proper functioning of society: "a wise and judicious mother, attentive to the religion and education of her children, appears moving in a high and splendid orbit, shedding the beneficial and extensive influence of her instructions, through the different ranks of society, and through the various departments of public and private life."[61] Late-eighteenth-century portrayals of women as tender mothers devoted to their children's moral improvement were the beginnings of what was to become the Victorian cult of motherhood. By 1816 Ann Taylor, an evangelical author, could write that the role of "mistress and mother of a family occupies one of the most important stations in the community"; as one Victorian magazine proclaimed, woman was "given to man as his better angel, to dissuade him from vice, to stimulate him to virtue, to make home delightful and life joyous. . . . [I]n the exercise of these gentle and holy charities, she fulfils her high vocation. But great as is the influence of the maiden and the wife, it seems to fade away when placed by that of the mother. It is the mother who is to make the citizen for earth . . . and happy are they who thus fulfil the sacred and dignified vocation allotted to them by Providence."[62] Bigg's depiction of the mother in *A Lady and Her Children* echoes these contemporary concerns. By portraying a woman actively engaged in the moral instruction of her offspring, the painting aligns itself with new ideas about domestic femininity and women performing useful instead of merely decorative functions in the family unit.[63]

It is significant that Bigg's gentlewoman is teaching her children their charitable duties as members of the upper classes, for charity had become a fashionable avocation for the middle and upper classes. Solkin traces the "blossoming culture of sentiment" in his discussion of midcentury visual representations of sympathy, in particular those paintings in Thomas Corum's Foundling Hospital by Hogarth, Highmore, and Hayman that were representations of acts of kindness to children. In keeping with the fashionable taste for sympathy, midcentury portraits of great military leaders, such as the Marquis of Granby, General Amherst, and Lord Clive, feature gestures of friendship and benevolence, ensuring viewers that, as Solkin suggests, even Britain's imperial victors were tempered by a natural magnanimity.[64] However, it was with the publication of Henry Mackenzie's tremendously popular *The Man of Feeling* (1771) that a sympathetic heart revealed in a gesture of kindness became the most powerful model

for charitable action in the late eighteenth century. Harley, the hero
of the book, is a man of extreme sensibilities: he sighs and cries his
way through the narrative, stopping along the way to offer his sympathy, his help, and what little money he has to bestow on various
victims of betrayal and bad luck. One such victim is an old soldier
who has returned from India penniless and broken in health. Harley
finds him seated by the roadside clutching his ragged bundle; he stops
to hear the old man's story, sheds tears at his tale of woe, and offers
him aid. The roadside, the bundle, the sad tale told, the spontaneous
feelings of benevolence, and the gift of a coin, all represented visually
in Bigg's painting, are standard features of novels of sensibility that
encouraged readers not only to respond with tears to tales of distress
but to perform benevolent actions for the victims of real distress.[65]

While Henry Mackenzie detailed the pleasures of benevolence,
other writers, including moralists, politicians, and economists, were
concerned with determining how and to whom charity should be
distributed. During the last quarter of the century the population of
the poor increased so that 1 million out of 9 million were vagrants in
1801.[66] Contemporaries fought, and historians are still fighting, over
why there was an increase in the number of destitute people; some
argue the cause lies in enclosure and the resulting displacement of
agricultural laborers, and others argue that better nutrition or less
disease reduced the death rate among the poor and so swelled their
ranks.[67] The increase in the number of people dependent on the parish
system of welfare stirred the resentment and anger of poor-tax-paying
landowners and farmers, and the number of homeless adrift in the
rural scene and in the cities alarmed officials concerned with public
safety.[68] Countless tracts were produced offering various solutions to
the problems caused by the increase in indigence and the resulting increase in the poor rate. Some writers, like David Davies in his *A Case
for Husbandry* (1795), urged the gentry to live on their estates and to
resume their traditional roles as superintendents of the poor. Some,
like Joseph Townsend in *A Dissertation on the Poor Laws* (1786), urged
the abolition of the poor laws, which, in guaranteeing the poor of the
parish minimal food and housing, gave "encouragement to idleness
and vice."[69] In "Pauper Management Improved" (1798), Jeremy Bentham went so far as to propose the imprisonment of people who were
unable to feed, clothe, and house themselves.

Bigg's treatment of the woman receiving alms does not reflect

Bentham's criminalization of poverty, nor does it radiate any of Townsend's hysteria about the "clamours . . . of the incessant demands of the most improvident and lazy of the surrounding poor."[70] This woman is decently clothed, her face appears appropriately grateful, and her body posture and lowered position are properly humble. Her gender is also important; a man begging might appear too menacing and not the proper object of charity for a woman and children. The two mothers, the pauper and the gentlewoman, mirror each other: just as the upper-class woman teaches her children their charitable duties, the poor woman will teach her child to be grateful and deferential. Both mothers are responsible for reproducing this society's hierarchical social and economic relations.

In addition to the topical issues of charity and domesticity, this painting with its inclusion of the black servant alludes to contemporary debates surrounding slavery and its abolition. To paint a picture depicting Christian charity and to include in it the representation of an African servant was to participate in the new and powerful abolitionist discourse that had emerged in the 1770s. The movement to abolish the slave trade began in earnest in the late 1760s with Granville Sharp's attack on slavery in England and his legal battle to protect slaves in Britain from being forced against their will to return to the West Indies. John Wesley's *Thoughts Upon Slavery* (1774), "the first really penetrating attack upon the system," shaped the opposition to slavery that became "inextricably tied up with religious revivalism that swept through all classes of Englishmen after 1770."[71] In 1783 the Quakers petitioned Parliament to abolish the slave trade, and in 1784 the Society of Friends published and distributed 12,000 pamphlets entitled *The Case of Our Fellow-creatures, the oppressed African, respectfully recommended to the serious Consideration of the Legislature of Great Britain by the People called Quakers.* In 1784 James Ramsay published a description of the conditions under which slaves lived based on his experience as a clergyman in St. Kitts, *An Essay on the Treatment and Conversion of African Slaves in the British Sugar Colonies,* and in 1786 Thomas Clarkson published his prize-winning essay, *On Slavery and Commerce of the Human Species.* Roger Anstey argues that by the 1780s it was commonplace to argue that slavery was incommensurate with notions of Christian benevolence and that slavery was regarded as morally indefensible and antithetical to Christian doctrine.[72]

By placing the figure of the black servant in the context of Christian charity, Bigg was underscoring the link between abolition, charity, and Christian duty.[73] His painting shares with eighteenth-century religious revivalism of both Wesleyan and Evangelical Anglican varieties a concern with "the duty of Christian charity"—doing good works based in a desire to imitate Jesus' acts of charity.[74] As many abolitionists and philanthropists were motivated by religious zeal, several of the most prominent leaders of the abolitionist movement had experienced a moment of conversion, a moment of "spiritual rebirth" that was "accompanied by a flooding love of all men and by a sense of mission, so that converts . . . became abolitionists in the selfsame instant."[75] Clarkson experienced conversion in 1785 and Wilberforce in 1787. Several prominent evangelicals, Hannah More and William Wilberforce particularly, were famous for their concern for the souls of both black slaves and the English poor.

Not only does Bigg's painting reflect current concerns surrounding poverty, charity, religion, and abolition, but his choice of a woman performing these Christian duties and what had been traditionally paternal caretaking roles also reflects the growing involvement of women in organized charitable, abolitionist, and ultimately political activities. As Moira Ferguson most convincingly demonstrates, by the 1780s middle- and upper-class women were actively engaged in the antislavery campaign, albeit within the context of religious duty and sentimental "feminine" feeling.[76] Bigg's portrayal of a charitable gentlewoman has much in common with Hannah More and her legacy as a philanthropist and an abolitionist. Throughout the 1780s More wrote tracts admonishing fashionable people to turn away from the frivolity and emptiness of the "gay world" and to seek real happiness in what she called "practical Christianity," a combination of doing good works and taming one's own selfish desires by constant soul watching and "Christian vigilance." More espoused an evangelicalism that promoted strict regulation of self and others that, despite its doctrine of Christian love and philanthropy, was socially very conservative. Her charitable endeavors, notably her Sunday schools, sought to control the poor, teaching them gratitude and deference to their betters and cheerful compliance with a system that ultimately oppressed them. More taught Christian doctrine as a way to teach self-discipline to the poor and to inculcate in them a respect for social and economic hierarchies.[77] Likewise, More's treatment of the African slave in her poem "Slavery, a Poem" (1788) stresses the African's place in the hier-archy of humanity: "Tho' dark and savage, ignorant and blind, / They claim the common privilege of kind." As Moira Ferguson argues, em-bedded in More's depiction of the African is a colonialism without slavery that ensures the subject position of the ex-slave and posits the African as in need of civilizing Christian enlightenment: "Under the guise of benevolence, she implicitly validates the great chain of being in conjunction with class and colonial dominance: the 'poor' African is a destined social inferior who deserves help." [78]

Bigg's *A Lady and Her Children* demonstrates a similar kind of pater-nalistic treatment of the poor and the African. The poor woman's posture is humble and duly deferential, reinforcing her position in the social hierarchy that places her near the bottom; her gratitude reinforces the upper-class family's charity and reassures us that she is not one of Townsend's "clamourous" poor who think they have a right to their master's wealth. Bigg's portrait of the charity is senti-mental; it reassures us, as John Barrell says of rural genre paintings in general, "that the act of relieving the miseries of the poor is an act of economic exchange: our gift of alms is an *ex gratia* payment, but one given in return for the cheerful obedience of the poor in the past, as it is calculated to purchase more of the same in the future." [79] This act of charity is therefore ultimately conservative; its aim is to idealize and promote the old society's paternalistic and hierarchical social order.

And where does the black servant fit into this ideological frame-work? I think we can assume that he is not a slave. Unlike the Young family's black servant, the young man wearing livery in Bigg's paint-ing does not wear a gold collar around his neck. The combination of Christian imagery—the child's halo in particular—with the act of charity implies that this upper-class family in performing their Chris-tian duties would extend such charity not only to the poor in the form of pecuniary assistance but also to their "black brethren" in the form of liberty, albeit a liberty that is constrained by paternalistic bonds. The livery, small stature, and respectful distance of the black figure, like the poor woman's deference, reassure us that the social order that privileges property, both real and mobile, will prevail de-spite the potentially disruptive desires of the disenfranchised and the transformation of property that the emancipation of slaves entailed. The composition of the painting, an overlapping of four triangles, reinforces the poor woman's and the black servant's dependence on the upper-class woman's benevolence and reinforces their position in the class hierarchy. The vertex of all four triangles is the gentlewoman's head; a small triangle is made up of the gentlewoman's face and the two faces of her children; a second triangle, a right angle, consists of the gentlewoman's face, her son's face, and the poor woman's face; a third triangle is composed of the gentlewoman's face, her son's face, and the servant's face; and the fourth triangle encompasses the whole group of figures—the gentlewoman's head is the apex, the poor woman's figure forms the right side of the triangle, and the black servant's figure forms the left, while the bottom of the triangle is made up of the feet of the figures and the hems of their dresses. A small dog plays outside these triangular configurations of human ties.

In Bigg's *A Lady and Her Children* social, economic, and racial hierarchies are maintained spatially and ideologically. The gentlewoman dominates her children, the poor, and the African, but she dominates with magnanimity, signaling the demise of the old empire and its brutal colonial system fueled by desire for profit and anticipating the birth of the new empire that sought its legitimacy in moral superiority. Philanthropic gestures to the poor and to the dark others of the world enabled Britain to establish itself in the nineteenth century as the agent of civilization and moral order, performing imperial acts not out of greed but out of altruism, carrying out for the sake of others "the white man's burden." Linda Colley argues that the abolition of the slave trade was crucial to the construction of Britain's sense of moral superiority: "Successful abolitionism became one of the vital underpinnings of British supremacy in the Victorian era, offering— as it seemed to do—irrefutable proof that British power was founded on religion, on freedom, and on moral calibre, not just on a superior stock of armaments and capital." Colley goes on to say that "the anti-slavery movement had an overwhelmingly conservative impact . . . because it supplied the British with a powerful legitimation for their claims to be the arbiters of the civilised and the uncivilised world."[80]

Associated with the exotic, the figure of the black servant can reveal artists' and their patrons' attitudes toward mercantile capitalism and colonialism. The shift in attitudes toward the exotic, its potential to disrupt English cultural practices, and its eventual domestication can be traced in paintings and prints that feature the black servant, in particular Hogarth's *Progresses,* Zoffany's *The Family of Sir William Young, Baronet,* and Bigg's *A Lady and Her Children Relieving a Cottager.*[81] Hogarth's orientalized African page is linked to the consumption of exotic commodities, revealing Hogarth's deep distrust of things foreign and his fear of their potential to destabilize the tenuous moral order of commercialized London and its new role as the emporium of the world. The black pages in the Duchess of Ormond and Yale portraits also exude exoticism, but unlike in Hogarth's prints, these pages do not threaten the social order because their powerful masters exert control over the African domain. The black servant in Zoffany's family portrait is not exoticized; instead, he is absorbed into an affable, elegant English domesticity just as the profits from sugar plantations were absorbed into Britain's national economy. While in Zoffany's family portrait we can see Britain's pride in dominating and exploiting the world for its aggrandizement, in Bigg's painting we can see a different kind of power at work: a feminized, Christianized, benevolent power that was to become one of the dominant discourses of nineteenth-century British imperialism. In Bigg's painting we see the emergence of this new imperial order, one that rewrote exploitation and self-interest as altruism and exercised its benevolent power not only on its own working classes but on its colonial subjects as well.

Returning to Fanny Burney's Mongo after viewing these paintings and prints, we can now see that implicit in her black servant are these various versions of the black servant: the orientalized African page, the (West) Indian subject of colonial rule and rapine, and the free servant, object of female benevolence. The fact that Mongo never appears on stage does not lessen the power of his presence. The object of Britain's imperial might and imperial magnanimity, Mongo exists in the mind's eye of the audience, put there by artists such as Hogarth, Zoffany, and Bigg.

2

❧

Native Land and Foreign Desires

WILLIAM PENN'S TREATY WITH THE INDIANS

> It seems natural to Whites, to look on lands in the possession of Indians with an aching heart, and never to rest 'till they have planned them out of them.
> JOSEPH BRANT[1]

Like Bigg's *A Lady and Her Children*, Benjamin West's painting *William Penn's Treaty with the Indians* portrays a scene dominated by a benevolent gesture (Fig. 6). While Bigg depicts a gentlewoman overseeing her child's charitable gift of a coin to an impoverished mother and child, West portrays Penn and his associates dispensing gifts to Indians. In both paintings political and economic power is disguised as the workings of a highly developed moral sensibility; in West's painting conquest is presented as an act of magnanimity. *Penn's Treaty* has assumed legendary status in American popular culture, making its way into high school history textbooks as an example of the nobility of Penn and his power to effect peaceful relations between Europeans and Indians. West's presentation of Penn's "justice and benevolence" toward the Indians is a masterpiece, not only aesthetically as an engaging painting but politically as a powerful piece of propaganda that continues to work its magic on viewers today.[2]

West's masterpiece functions on two narrative levels. The first level is the story depicted—William Penn's mythical treaty with the Indians; the second, not represented explicitly but lying buried beneath the surface, is the story of Thomas Penn, William Penn's son, and his effort to negotiate several other and equally ambitious land deals with Indians. Commissioned by Thomas Penn and painted in 1771 and 1772, *Penn's Treaty* celebrates simultaneously both Penns' successful acquisition of enormous tracts of Indian land. This chapter will examine West's painting in the context of the land speculations of William and Thomas Penn. More attention will be given to Thomas Penn's efforts to acquire Indian land because his speculation in Indian land can help to explain why he commissioned the painting and why he felt the need to have his family's relations with Native Americans depicted in such an amicable light.[3]

Peaceful Exchange

Before turning to the context in which the painting was produced, we need to take a look at the painting itself and the dramatic scene it portrays. At the center of *Penn's Treaty* is a bolt of cloth painted an eye-catching white in this rather dark composition. Quakers and Indians stand around this source of light as if it were a campfire. West has, in fact, substituted the cloth for the council fire around which such treaties usually took place. For Algonquian and Iroquoian peoples, particularly the Six Nation Confederacy and its allies, the fire symbolized peace and was always to be kept burning as long as peaceful relations existed between the treating parties. The bolt of cloth, like the fire it displaces, is a part of the peaceful negotiations that are under way in this scene. The cloth's placement in the composition and its color stress its power to effect this peaceful exchange of Indian land for European manufactured goods.

West uses light and color to move our eyes around the semicircle of men. The white cloth grabs our attention, and then our eyes oscillate between the cloth and the Indians who are adorned in reds, whites, and greens. The shape, color, and texture of the arm of the muscular Indian sitting in a cluster of Delawares and the sheen on his shaved head capture our attention and direct our eyes around the semicircle of exotic men with red-feathered headdresses, beaded head and arm bands, and elaborate earrings hung in ears that have been slit to accommodate them. The brightly clothed, feathered, and heavily

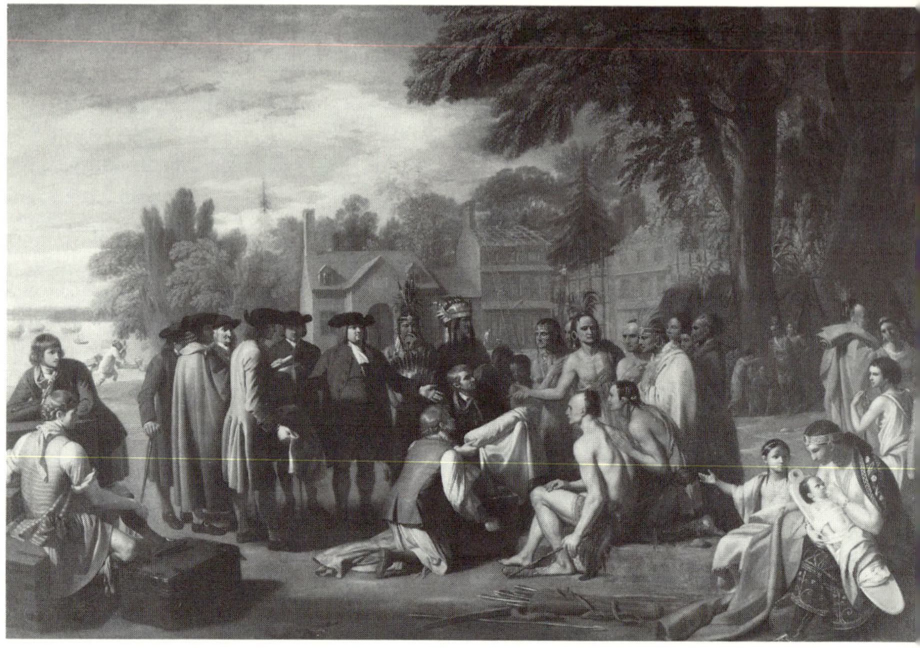

6. Benjamin West, *William Penn's Treaty with the Indians*, 1771–72, oil on canvas. Courtesy of the Pennsylvania Academy of Fine Arts, Philadelphia. Gift of Mrs. Sarah Harrison (The Joseph Harrison Jr. Collection).

decorated men absorb our attention; we linger over the detail in their dress, hair, and ornamentation. Light shines on the Indians' faces, illuminating their excited features which express mingled surprise, awe, and envy. In contrast to these gaily decorated Indians, William Penn is hardly visible at first glance. He stands half-obscured by shadows, dressed in brown, and would escape our notice if it were not for his white neck cloth. The Quakers' faces are obscured by shadows; they are distant, unemotional, calm. Soberly and discreetly dressed, their clothing reflects their subdued emotional state.

The details of dress and the use of color work to obscure the true nature of the exchange that is taking place. Penn and his fellow Quakers are capitalists, traders, dealers who profit from their investments and exchanges in commodities. They are motivated by the desire for gain. In this painting the Europeans' acquisitiveness is displaced onto Indians, for it is on the Indians' faces that greed flickers. West has arranged the figures so that the posture of the Indians—their necks outstretched and their bodies leaning forward—indicates their excitement and eagerness over the prospect of possessing this lustrous cloth. It is as if these Indians can barely restrain their emotions and their desire to consume these commodities. West has made the Indians into the desiring/consuming subjects while the Quakers are represented as the bestowers of gifts. To effect this reversal, which makes the Indians the greedy ones and erases the Quakers' desire for native land, West has employed not only light and color but gendered codes as well to shape the moral stature of the parties.[4]

Portraying the Delawares dressed in brightly colored clothing and elaborate jewelry and the Quakers in anachronistically drab garb, West has used gender to differentiate the desires of these men. West's choice of a bolt of cloth to represent trade goods marks the Indians' desires as distinctly feminine. Instead of a bolt of cloth, he could have chosen to paint a hatchet, a rifle, or a barrel of rum, but these items were too heavily associated with frontier violence and would not have served his purpose of showing a treaty that would ensure peaceful relations between Indians and colonists. West could have painted cast iron pots, hoes, and blankets to represent trade items, but instead of these useful and ordinary objects, which may have had the effect of humanizing the Indians, he chose to portray the Delawares coveting a bolt of cloth, not unlike the cloth that women in London would gather around to purchase in a linen draper's shop. West has cleverly reduced the Indians' desire for trade goods to a desire for cloth, which was (and still is) a heavily gendered item.

West's Indians are depicted as emotional, gaudily dressed, and feminine in their desire for cloth and trinkets. In the minds of Europeans this love of finery was associated with women; eighteenth-century British moralists were forever chastising women for their fondness for "frippery." Addressing a female audience in *A Father's Legacy to His Daughters* (1774), Dr. John Gregory wrote that "the love of dress is natural to you, and therefore it is proper and reasonable." Jonathan Swift comments, "how naturally do women apply their hands to each others lappets and ruffles and mantua's, as if the whole business of your lives, and the publick concern of the world, depended on the cut or colour of your dresses."[5] It was also an eighteenth-century commonplace that women and "savages" shared a love of finery and bodily decoration as well as a consequent mental and moral weakness: "A strong inclination for external ornaments ever appears in barbarous states. . . . An immoderate fondness for dress, for pleasure, and for sway, are the passions of savages; the passions that occupy those uncivilized beings who have not yet extended the dominion of the mind, or even learned to think with the energy necessary to concatenate that abstract train of thought which produces principles. And that women from their education . . . are in the same condition, cannot, I think, be controverted."[6] For this moral philosopher, European women and New World savages were less rational and self-disciplined than European men; in short, they were less civilized and occupied a lower rung on the ladder of cultural evolution. Even though the decorated bodies of women and savages were admired by European men, these bodies were also believed to be morally suspect because they were thought to exude a debased sensuality associated with an intellectual inferiority.

West purposely highlights the Indian figures' bright clothing, feathers, and jewelry to feminize and debase them, while his use of browns and blacks for the Quaker garb underscores their moral superiority and the absence of frivolous desires. Reinforcing the feminine qualities of these Indians is the foregrounded madonnalike figure of the nursing Indian mother and child. The Quakers, all men, are plainly dressed, their masculinity and rational powers stressed by their attire. West chose to paint them wearing not what these men would have worn in the late seventeenth century—satin waistcoats, silk stockings, brocaded jackets, laced cuffs, and elaborate wigs—but what Friends wore in the mid-eighteenth century, the now famous "plain" Quaker costume. If West had painted Penn wearing what he had really worn, Penn would have been far more decorated and finely dressed than any of the Indians.[7] Genteel and fashionable attire on William Penn would have blurred the binary opposition that West has put into play between the feminized, desiring, and morally inferior Indians and the rational, self-disciplined, and beneficent Quakers. If West had painted Penn in historically accurate attire, he would have blurred the ideological subtext of this painting, which goes something like this: Unable to restrain their emotions and their desires to consume these commodities, the Indians, like women, are easily seduced into parting with their only valuable commodity for gaudy trinkets, and they deserve what they get: the loss of their land (and honor) and the erasure of their presence in this place. West stresses the inevitability of this erasure of Indian ways and the inexorable "progress" of civilization by eclipsing the Indian town in darkness. The Indian houses stand in the shadows as if already disappearing while the houses of the Europeans rise up in full light and the sun dances on the river and the distant ships holding cargo. West uses light and color as well as the details of dress to reinforce binary oppositions between the feminized, savage, and immoral Indians and the masculine, civilized, and liberal Quakers.

West's portrayal of Penn's peaceful exchange of goods for land simultaneously represents and masks the true nature of the encounter between the real William Penn (and his heirs) and the Lenni Lenape (and their heirs). What looks like some kind of gift giving or exchange of commodities for land is in reality an act of conquest. Penn had been granted Pennsylvania by the Crown, in whose name the land had been claimed by right of "first discovery." As Native American activist Menno Boldt argues, the Crown's claim to land in North America violated seventeenth- and eighteenth-century international law: "'First discovery' entitled a state to declare sovereignty over and to claim title to only *unoccupied* territory. The British Crown knew North America was not unoccupied. Thus, the Crown knowingly violated two of the prevailing European principles of international justice: it declared sovereignty over Indians and claimed title to their lands."[8] As historian Urs Bitterli observes, Penn labored to legitimate the Crown's dubious grant by having his agents visit each band of Delawares living along the rivers that fed into the Chesapeake Bay and by purchasing quitclaims from them, thus indicating Bitterli contends, that he did not accept the Crown's claim of sovereignty and the idea that this land was empty, unencumbered, and there for the taking. In fact, Penn recognized the Indians as the original owners of the land, and before he would sell any part of his huge grant, he insisted on having the legal title to it. In exchange for their land, the Delawares accepted his offer of peace, gifts, and reserves, land on which they were to live unmolested.[9]

The contradiction that stems from Penn's having to buy Indian land he supposedly already owned lies submerged in West's painting, surfacing in the striking ideological reversals that drive the narrative depicted there. Penn's desire for Native American land fueled his actions, particularly his seeking of quitclaims, and yet Penn and the Quakers surrounding him are not represented as people driven by desire. They are the calm, rational, and deliberate "Friends," whose actions are inspired by radical Christian beliefs and governed by the tenets of political economy. Penn and his investors in this new colony stand aloof from the exchange of merchandise, thereby erasing their link with the profit motive. A member of the group holds a map or deed that establishes Penn's proprietary status and legal control of the land. The play of light and shade as well as the contrast of lively reds and greens and somber browns and grays assist in creating the impression that William Penn is someone who acts not out of self-interest, but out of enlightened and dispassionate altruism.

The other contradiction that haunts this painting concerns the representation of Penn as a man of peace and as someone whose fair and sound business practice ensures peaceful relations with Indians. Although Penn was careful to conduct himself honorably and peaceably vis-à-vis Indians, he was able to finesse his deals with them because the threat of violence was implicit in the European colonization of America.[10] Violent confrontation had occurred between Europeans and Native Americans in the mid-Atlantic region in the fifty years previous to Penn's arrival. Penn's insistence on peaceful relations with the Indians distinguished him from his predecessors, the Dutch, for instance, in the Hudson River Valley and the New England Puritans who had nearly exterminated the Pequots and were in the midst of conducting total war against the Wampanoags and the Narragansetts. Penn's construction of himself as a man of peace implicitly contained its opposite, the violent, greedy, genocidal European. His successful exchange of "land for peace" benefited enormously from the very real threat of European warfare.[11] The Delawares knew that this was the best deal they were going to get, and they took it.[12]

By portraying Penn and his fellow Quakers as thoughtful, serious, and somber men, West was stressing the Quakers' peaceful tactics in getting what they wanted. He wrote in his commentary on this painting, "The great object I had in forming that composition was to express savages brought into harmony and peace by justice and benevolence, by not withholding from them what was their reight [sic], and giving to them what they were in want of, as well as a wish to give by that art a conquest made over native people without sward or Dagder [*sic*]."[13] What West means by "not withholding" is that Penn, unlike many of his colonizing entrepreneurial contemporaries, paid something for lands he took, and by "giving to them what they were in want of," Penn gave Indians manufactured goods that they did not possess. West sees commerce as pacifying and civilizing the savages, as giving them what they lacked and bringing them into peaceful relations with the white man.[14] This painting celebrates the moment when the Delaware Indians were brought into the rational, enlightened, and mechanistic workings of global mercantile capitalism. The bolt of cloth, simultaneously a payment, a gift, a commodity, and a promise of peace, masks under the guise of trade an act of conquest.[15]

Colonial Politics

By commissioning West to paint *William Penn's Treaty with the Indians* Thomas Penn asserted the legality of his father's royal grant and stressed the peacefulness of his father's dealings with the Indians of the Delaware and Susquehanna River region. However, his reasons for portraying his father's negotiations with Indians arguably had less to do with re-creating the historical past and more to do with putting in a good light his own dealings with Indians. As Ann Uhry Abrams points out, the iconography of this painting has much more to do with contemporary politics than with representing an actual historical moment. Abrams argues quite convincingly that Thomas Penn commissioned West "to celebrate the return of peace to Pennsylvania" after years of conflict between Quakers and Penn's agents as well as between Indians and backwoods settlers.[16]

As Abrams notes, West's painting draws upon Pennsylvania legend to comment on contemporary politics to promote Thomas Penn's position as proprietor of the colony of Pennsylvania. His role as proprietor had been attacked in the 1750s by the Assembly of Pennsylvania led by Benjamin Franklin, who sought to do away with the proprietary form of government and to substitute in its place a charter from the king, which was the form of government of several other colonies. West's painting underscores the Penns' hereditary interest in Pennsylvania, reminding viewers that Thomas Penn's father was a peaceful man whose interests were paternal and benevolent, who encouraged merchants in their commerce, who provided them with trade and land on which to build a thriving community, and who protected the colonists from the hostility of Indians. This painting seeks to smooth out difficulties between Penn and the colonists by representing William Penn, and Thomas Penn by association, as the benevolent protectors of colonists, their commerce, their communities, and their well-being. The open, outstretched hand of the figure of William Penn signifies not only his gift to the Indians of goods in exchange for land, but also his creation of the colony and economic opportunity for generations of colonists. This double act of benevolence highlights the Penn family's role as guardians of trade and keepers of peace, issues that were of utmost importance in the 1750s and 1760s in colonial Pennsylvania.

Abrams has explored in detail the painting's colonial context and the battle between Thomas Penn, as absentee proprietor, and the Quaker-dominated Pennsylvania Assembly; however, more needs to be said about the politics implicit in this painting, in particular those politics surrounding the acquisition of Indian land. The image of William Penn treating with the Indians was a powerful icon for colonists and those concerned with colonial life. West tapped into an already existing tradition — the iconographic representation of a European and a Native American treating peacefully together. As Abrams has demonstrated, this image appeared in peace medals given by colonists to Indians as tokens of their peaceful relations. What is celebrated in the peace medals and in the West painting is the non-violent transfer of Indian lands to white colonists. Vivien Green Fryd has called this transaction "land for peace," implying that the Europeans would have gotten the land they desired one way or another, either through the Indians relinquishing it peacefully or through the Europeans waging war. West's use of the peace medal configuration reinforces the image of the Penns as peacemakers. This image needed bolstering, especially after the turbulence arising out of the Walking Purchase of 1737 and the treaty with the Six Nations in 1754.

West's painting successfully disguises the political and economic turmoil involved with the Penn family's dealings with the Eastern and Western Delawares; instead, it describes Penns as clever negotiators with the natives, as promoters of commerce, and as the beneficent founders of a thriving colony. Thomas Penn was especially interested in promoting this image of himself and his family, as he had been accused of fraud in his dealings with the Indians and was held responsible for the violence that occurred on the frontier during the 1750s and 1760s. One of the ideological goals of this painting was to present the Penns as capable leaders, peacekeepers, and knowledgeable negotiators with Indians to counter the mounting critiques of the proprietary system in general and the Penns' speculation in Indian land in particular, speculation that some thought benefited only the Penns at the expense of the safety of those living in the western reaches of the colony.

Purchasing Indian Land

In its use of Pennsylvania legend to rewrite the recent past, West's image of William Penn's treating with the Delawares functions much like a palimpsest. Scratch its ideological surface, and beneath this image lie layers of other treaties, all involving Thomas Penn and all productive of dissension, not the peace commemorated in the painting. From the late 1720s until the late 1760s and the ratification of the Treaty of Fort Stanwix, Thomas Penn eagerly and aggressively pursued the acquisition of Indian land on which to expand his empire in the New World. Penn's acquisition of land was often criticized by natives who insisted that they had never agreed to sell the land, that they were never fully compensated for the land, and/or that the negotiators of treaties and surveyors of deeds always took more land than the Indians intended to give away. During these decades, Penn and his representatives met frequently with the headmen of various bands of Delawares and Iroquois, simultaneously purchasing lands and dealing with complaints about those purchases. For instance, at a conference in 1728 the Tulpehocken Delawares complained they had never been recompensed for land settled on by German immigrants; in 1732, on one of his trips to America, Penn personally met with Delawares who also complained about being displaced by his father's acquisitions; in 1737 Penn's representatives conducted the infamous Walking Purchase for lands along the northern reaches of the Delaware River and in the Lehigh Valley; in 1742 and 1744 Penn's representations treated with the bands of Delawares who had refused to vacate this land; in 1754 at the Albany Congress, John Penn, Thomas's nephew, persuaded the Six Nations to sign away their authority not only over lands along the northern branch of the Susquehanna River but also along the western branch, thereby extending Penn's holdings to the Ohio River in what is now western Pennsylvania; and in 1756 Penn's people had to defend the Walking Purchase against the accusation of fraud by the Delaware chief Teedyuscung. Penn's aggressive land acquisition policy aroused the hostility of the displaced Indians, especially those bands of Delawares who had lived along the Delaware, Lehigh, and Susquehanna Rivers, as well as members of the Six Nations who regarded the Wyoming Valley as their hunting lands and the Susquehanna as their western road into the Ohio region and their southern route to the Shenandoah Valley.

While William Penn tried to maintain an air of legitimacy in his dealings with the Delaware, his son was guilty of making fraudulent land claims. To illustrate the extent to which West's painting was a bold attempt by Thomas Penn to rewrite history through the body of his father, we need to examine Thomas Penn's relations with the Indians living in western Pennsylvania, the Province of New York, and the Ohio River Valley. Two of Penn's many questionable land deals are particularly significant for their role in creating friction on the frontier: the Walking Purchase of 1737 and the "sale" of lands along two branches of the Susquehanna River at the Albany Congress of 1754. The Walking Purchase has received a great amount of attention from historians as an example of the kind of deception that land speculators like Thomas Penn engaged in to acquire Indian land. What makes this land swindle particularly outrageous is the hypocrisy of Penn and his agents and the pretense to legality that Penn's lawyers promulgated. What outraged Delawares then and irritates contemporary historians now is Penn's blatant lying and his claims to have been pursuing a legal course of action as well as fulfilling his father's wishes. Penn pretended to have a draft of a deed from his father that stipulated that the Penns owned a tract of land that stretched from the banks of the Delaware River as far as a man could walk in a day and a half. Francis Jennings points out that in a British court of law a draft of a deed or a copy of a deed would not have given anyone legal possession, but that in Pennsylvania Penn could get away with this kind of legal charade. Not only did the Penns use a dubious deed, they employed runners to "walk" the distance; they covered over sixty miles and thereby extended the bounds of the purchase to include far more than the original disputed lands.[17]

The Walking Purchase was an attempt on Thomas Penn's part to get lands beyond the boundary of what his father had obtained so that he might sell the land to get out of debt. Penn was so desperate to generate money from Indian land that he sold the lands belonging to Delawares above the Tohickon Creek before he had "legally" secured the Walking Purchase. Even before the Walking Purchase, Nutimus, a Delaware sachem, repeatedly protested Penn's maneuvers to get his people's land, saying of Penn, "He keep begging and plagueing us to Give him some Land and never gives us leave to treat upon any thing till he Wearies us Out of Our Lives." After the Walking Purchase, the land that Penn had sold secretly to speculators could then be sold "legally" to settlers who thought they were buying with clear titles. However, Nutimus continued to protest the Walking Purchase, despite threats from colonial settlers who believed they were in the right. Nutimus wrote to the Bucks County chief justice: "We dare not Speak for our Rights but there is an Uproar and [we are] in danger of being Cut to pieces. . . . [I]f this practice must hold why then we are no more Brothers and Friends but much more like Open Enemies." Jennings states that with the total sales of Pennsylvania lands amounting to over £200,000, the Penn family "rose from the shabby gentility of perpetual debt to a status of substantial riches and power."[18]

Complaints by Delawares continued into the 1740s and were dealt with at two conferences, one in Philadelphia in 1742 and another at Lancaster in 1744. The Iroquois—sachems from the western and southern nations, mostly Senecas and Onondagas, not Mohawks— were invited to attend to help settle the disputes between the Penns and Delawares, who were sometimes referred to as the Iroquois' cousins or nephews. Essentially what transpired at these meetings was that the Iroquois told the Delawares to stop complaining and to vacate the land. In Philadelphia on July 12, 1742, Canasatego, an Onondaga sachem, delivered a dramatic speech in which he chastised the Delawares for their unruliness, accusing them of being "in the wrong in their Dealings" with Penn's agents, and promised to "remove them, and oblige them to go over the River Delaware, and quit all Claim to any Lands on this side." Canasatego directed the follow-ing comments to those Delawares present, which included Nutimus and Sassoonan:

Let this Belt of Wampum serve to chastise you. You ought to be taken by the Hair of the Head and shaken severely, till you recover your Senses and become sober. You don't know what Ground you stand on, nor what you are doing. . . . But how can you to take upon you to sell Land at all? We conquered you; we made Women of you; you know you are Women, and can no more sell Land than Women; nor is it fit you should have the Power of selling Lands, since you would abuse it. This Land that you claim is gone thro' your Guts; you have been furnished with Cloaths, Meat, and Drink, by the Goods paid you for it, and now you want it again, like Children as you are. . . . You act dishonest Part, not only in this, but in other Matters: Your Ears are ever open to slanderous Reports about our Brethen; you receive them with as much Greediness as lewd Women receive the Embraces of bad Men. And for all these Reasons we charge you to remove instantly; we don't give you the Liberty to think about it.[19]

This speech and the part played by the Iroquois in the enforcement of the Walking Purchase have troubled those historians who admire the Six Nations for the way they held onto their land and their identity despite the proximity of colonial governments. Historians have ac-cused the Iroquois of failing to protect their dependencies from colo-nial greed and encroachment, of gaining from the loss of Delaware lands, and of acting as if they were agents of the Penn proprietary government.[20] The cultural and historical gap may be too great to understand fully and therefore judge the Iroquois for their actions concerning Delaware land, but we can analyze the way British and Euro-American contemporaries and historians alike have interpreted the Iroquois sachem's gendered language.

The language that the Iroquois sachem Canasatego used to describe the relations between the Delawares and the Six Nations is interesting for many reasons. The terms "cousin," "nephew," and "grandson" are commonly used to express various relations between the Six Nations and their Algonquian neighbors to the south and west. What strikes historians as puzzling is his use of "women" to describe the eastern Delawares. Many historians assume that this is a derogatory term meant to chastise and humiliate the Delawares and to remind them of their dependent status vis-à-vis the Six Nations.[21] Others have pointed out that the Iroquois did not think of women as inferior or as dependent, but rather as vital to the survival of the community and complementary to men in their social, economic, and political functions. David Richter has suggested that women had their sphere of activity involving food production and internal government, and men had their sphere of activity involving hunting and war. Women's work was crucial to the band's well-being, and their opinions were respected; for instance, the women's council would choose the leaders, and men would not go to war without the consent of the women's council. In general, women were concerned with intratribal affairs, and men were occupied with extratribal affairs.[22] That Canasatego called the Delawares women was not necessarily an attack on their integrity as a people; rather, it can be interpreted as reminding the Delawares that the Iroquois were to act as their mediators in any dealings with the colonists. Perhaps Canasatego was reminding them that the various Delaware bands, acting as single entities, had failed in the past to protect themselves from the depredations of colonial governments and the Euro-American greed for land, and that they should have relied on their more astute uncles, the Iroquois, to negotiate with foreigners. Whether or not the Iroquois could have protected or even wanted to protect the Delaware and Susquehanna Indians from the Penn family's desire for native land is another question, too complex to be dealt with adequately here.

Canasatego's use of a gendered language is reflected in West's painting, which, as I have argued, is heavily gendered in its representation of the Delawares and Quakers. Perhaps West knew of this famous speech; he spent his youth in Philadelphia, where this council convened, and his early adulthood in Lancaster, the site of the 1744 Treaty, and the Iroquois delegation's treatment of the Delawares may have been a part of local legend. West employs gender to discredit and trivialize the treating Indians in his painting, and this attitude parallels the way most British and Euro-American observers have interpreted Canasatego's speech, which, of course, reveals much more about them than about the Iroquois sachem.

The Penn Purchase and the Albany Congress

Tensions over the Penns' acquisitive land policies reached a crisis point at the Albany Congress in 1754. Some historians have suggested that the Penns were adroit in using the Iroquois to effect purchases of land in Pennsylvania and that it was their work at Lancaster that, according to Francis Jennings, "opened a gate to the trans-Appalachian west for British colonization, and it guaranteed a violent French response."[23] At Albany the Penns were able to wring even greater land concessions from the Iroquois than at Lancaster. At the Albany Congress Thomas Penn's nephew, John, treated with the sachems representing the Six Nations (Mohawks, Senecas, Onondagas, Oneidas, Cayugas, Tuscaroras) with the goal of purchasing land that extended westward beyond the Allegheny Mountains, in what is now western Pennsylvania. The purchase of this enormous tract of land soon caused severe difficulties for the Penn family, as it occasioned the resentment of the Indians living in that area, primarily the western Delawares and Shawnees. This resentment grew as forts were built along the Ohio River and as settlers, encouraged by the security these forts provided, moved into what had been Indian territory. This movement of colonists into western Pennsylvania and the northern Ohio River Valley was in violation of the treaty of 1726 between Great Britain and the Six Nation Confederacy. The Confederacy ceded all their lands, including the lands of the Delawares, to the king for him to hold in trust and for the government to guard from French incursions and to protect for Indian use only. In what was known as the Deed of 1726, the Iroquois ceded lands to the Crown with the understanding that these lands were being surrendered "for Protection, and not Settlement," "to be protected and defended for their Use as hunting Lands." This territory was regarded by the Six Nation Confederacy and its allies as hunting grounds vital to the maintenance of their way of life and, more important perhaps in the minds of the English, as vital to the continuance of the fur trade. The Board of Trade described this Deed of 1726 as a "measure . . . most wise and prudent with regard to their own interests, and the most advantageous with regard to Ours."[24]

By 1756 the resentment felt by Indians living in western Pennsylvania as well as by some of the members of the Six Nation Confederacy over colonial invasion into western lands had grown so great that British authorities feared that the Iroquois and their allies, which included the Delawares and Shawnees, would not support the British in the impending war with France. Sir William Johnson, superintendent of Indian Affairs in the Northern District of North America, worried that the colonists' invasion of Indian lands might alienate the affections of the Confederacy and drive them into the arms of the French. He was concerned by the colonists having "claimed large Tracts of Country & attempted settlements thereon. . . . Our indiscriminate avidity alarms them with Jealousy, and raises Prejudice against us wch are improved by the French." In contrast to the English and colonists, the French had told the Indians that they did not want to possess their lands but only wanted to trade with them. After conquering Oswego, the French told the Onondagas that they had driven the "English from their Lands & would not like them [the English], keep possession, but leave 'em free to them and their Posterity forever." [25]

In a series of letters to the Lords of Trade and Plantations, Sir William Johnson suggested that the Penn purchase was alienating their Indian allies: "The Great Patents of Lands wch had been purchased & taken up in those parts & our extended scattered Settlements beginning to crowd upon the Indians, had been a long Eye sore to them, infected them with Jealousy & disgust towards the English." He repeats his accusation a few months later: "I think I have before now hinted to your Lordships my opinion, that the Hostilities wch Pensilvania in particular had suffered from some of the Indians living on the Susquahanna did, in some measure, arise from the large Purchase made by that Govt. two years ago at Albany. . . . The Province of Pensilvania, whose raising Forces and building Forts on the Susquahanna River, tho' it hath very plausible Pretences, is at the Bottom bad policy & really intended to secure Lands wch it would more for the true Interest of the community to give up, at least for the present." He implies that not only was the Penn claim to the western lands causing bloodshed on the frontier, but that the disaffection aroused by this claim could threaten the ability of the British to protect their North American colonies from French expansion in the New World. Linking Penn acquisitiveness with bloodshed, Johnson suggested that "the most effectual method of producing Tranquility to that Province would be, a voluntary & open Surrender of that Deed of Sale." [26]

Johnson urged the Board of Trade to use its power to make Thomas Penn relinquish the deed of sale for the lands along the Susquehanna and beyond the Alleghenies, even if the Penns were legally the owner of these vast tracts of land.

Complaints by the Iroquois, Delawares, and Shawnees about white settlers moving into their lands were taken seriously by the Board of Trade. Acting as the Board's agent, Sir William Johnson was especially aware of the dangers of alienating the Iroquois. At the Albany Conference of 1754 he and the commissioners from the six northern colonies met with the sachems of the Six Nations to discuss the French threat, to persuade the Confederacy to align itself with the English, and to listen to Indian complaints about fraudulent land claims as a way to appease their resentment. The commissioners recognized that "purchases of Land from the Indians by private persons for small Trifling Considerations have been the cause of great uneasiness and discontents. And if the Indians are not in Fact imposed upon and injured, Yet they are apt to think that they have been." The colonial commissioners urged that "the Complaints of the Indians relative to any Grants or possessions of their Lands fraudulently obtained be enquired into, and all injuries addressed." The commissioners also set up guidelines for purchasing Indian lands, stressing that "all future Purchases of Lands from the Indians be void unless made by the Government where such Lands lye, and from the Indians in a Body in their Public Councils." [27]

While such resolutions were being passed at the Albany conference, John Penn made the deal with the sachems of the Six Nations to purchase the Delaware land west of the existing boundaries of Pennsylvania. The purchase conformed to the guidelines, in that Penn was authorized by his government and the exchange took place in a public council. Problems arose, however, when the Delawares complained that they had not authorized the sale of their lands; the Six Nations had acted for them, and the Delawares and some members of the Six Nation Confederacy felt that this was not right. The Penns' agents had taken advantage of the Iroquois myth of Delaware dependency to effect the purchase. The notion that the Delawares were dependent on the authority of the Six Nations and could not act for themselves in council stems from Iroquois claims that they had defeated the Delawares in the seventeenth century and had extended over them their political and military power, making the Delawares dependent on the Six Nations for military protection and acting for the Delawares in council, making treaties and, in this case, selling their land. The Delawares protested their status as Iroquois dependents, but the British continued to support the idea that the Six Nations could dominate the western Indians living beyond the pale of Iroquoia.[28]

The Penn purchase also was questioned by the Six Nations. A year after the Albany Conference, several members of the Six Nations complained to George Croghan, an Indian agent for the government of Pennsylvania, that the deed was never a deed of purchase but rather "a Deed of Trust." Croghan reported that the Pennsylvania delegates revealed to him that the lands west of the Alleghenies "was neither Purchased nor Paid for."[29] The distinction between a deed of trust and a deed of sale was enormous in the minds of the Indians, but in the colonial courts their differences were all too often elided. Land held in trust was not supposed to be for sale; the Crown or, in the case of Pennsylvania (not a Crown colony), colonial officials were supposed to exert exclusive control over the land and protect it from alienation. This protective mechanism rarely functioned, as the pressure from land speculators was too great and the rewards of selling Indian land were too tempting.[30]

Conflicts between Indians and colonists over land had many causes, some having to do with basic cultural, economic, and philosophical differences. The Iroquoian and Algonquian peoples of northeastern America did not think of land as a commodity to be possessed exclusively by one individual. Because they held land communally and because their form of government was not hierarchical but consensual, no one person could claim ownership and the right to alienate the land from the people who used the land.[31] Europeans and Euro-Americans, obsessed with the idea of private property and insistent on exclusive access to land, sought the "owners" of Indian lands so that they could purchase them. Land speculators, Indian traders, and colonists would approach an Indian in private and persuade him with gifts of rum, cloth, and metalwork to put his mark on a deed and "sell" his land, thereby circumventing the consent of the larger group and the uncertainties of a public council. For instance, Conochquiesie, an Oneida sachem, complained to Johnson about the methods that Connecticut's agent, John Henry Lydius, used to obtain Indian land:

"Brother. You promised us that you would keep this fire place clean from all filth and that no snake should come into this Council Room. That Man sitting there (pointing to Coll: Lyddius) is a Devil and has stole our Lands. He takes Indians slyly by the Blanket one at a time, and when they are drunk, puts some money in their Bosoms, and perswades them to sign deeds for our lands upon the Susquehanna which we will not ratify nor suffer to be settled by any means."[32] Confusion between Indians and Europeans over land tenure also arose when Indians would "sell" land thinking they were giving whites permission to use the land temporarily, for a lifetime or less, not realizing that selling was a permanent form of alienation. One of the most common complaints by Indians was that when they had agreed on a sale of a certain tract of land, surveyors acting for the new owners would enlarge upon the tract of land, doubling, trebling, even increasing its size a hundredfold, something that Thomas Penn had tried to do with the Walking Purchase.[33]

The Penn Purchase and Frontier Violence

In their quest for more land on which to expand westward, the Penns had angered the Delawares and irritated the Iroquois. A delegate from the Six Nations explained the Indians' grievances at a public meeting with Sir William Johnson: "The Governor of Pennsylvania bought a whole Track and only Paid for half, and desire you will let him know, that we will not Part with the other half, but keep it. These things makes us Constantly uneasie in our Minds, and we desire you will take care that we may keep, our lands for our selves."[34] The Delawares' and Iroquois' grievances over the Penn purchase aroused anxiety on the frontier and concern on the Board of Trade. Recognizing the danger that the Penn purchase had occasioned on the frontier, the Board of Trade worried that the Penn's appropriation of western lands would threaten Britain's alliance with the Iroquois and the Ohio Indians against the French. The Board of Trade argued: "The extensive Purchases of Land made not only by the Proprietaries of Pennsylvania, but in other Governments bordering on the Indian Country, have long since occasioned Disgusts and Suspicions of Injury in the minds of the Indians; And that these Jealousies have been one principal Cause of their Defection from the British Interest, and of the Hostilities which they have committed on the Frontiers of His Majesty's Provinces." [35]

The Penns were outraged by the suggestion that the Delawares were upset about the purchase of lands in Wyoming Valley and lands west of the Susquchanna River; they even demanded proof that the Delawares felt betrayed by the treaty of Albany. As the proprietaries of Pennsylvania, they challenged Sir William and "all the World to shew any one Instance of their Conduct, that has given Dissatisfaction to the Six Nations." Thomas Penn was most upset that his reputation as an honorable man had been besmudged by Sir William's insinuations. His reputation as a fair dealer with the Indians was important to him; he was "extremely desirous" that "Rectitude of all our Proceedings with the Indians shoud appear in the most publick Light." Even more important, he certainly did not want to be held responsible for Indian attacks on frontier settlements.[36]

It was during this crisis over the Penn purchase of 1754 and its role in promoting frontier violence that the Pennsylvania Assembly under the leadership of Benjamin Franklin sought to undermine the Penns, their agents, and the governor of the province by treating with the Indians themselves.[37] Concerned about the "Desolation and Terror" of a "cruel War" that the Delawares, Shawnees, and Mingos had been waging "against Your Majesty's Subjects in . . . Provinces of Virginia, Maryland, Pensylvania, and New Jersey," Benjamin Franklin and representatives from the Assembly usurped William Penn's legacy and cast themselves in the role of peacemakers.[38] The Quakers believed that the Indians who were participants in the frontier warfare were acting in response to the unfair dealing of the Penns and the proprietary government. They met twice with the Delawares in 1756 and 1757 and heard their complaints against Penn not only for the recent purchase of Susquehanna lands but old grievances stemming from the Walking Purchase of 1737. Those Delawares who had been cheated of their lands in the Lehigh Valley region and had been evicted with the help of the Iroquois had moved west to the Susquehanna and beyond, where they joined the western Delawares and Shawnees in attacking Pennsylvania frontier settlements. The Quakers were right that the frontier violence grew out of recent and old grievances, for when asked by the new governor William Denney if the people or the government of Pennsylvania had done injury to the Delawares, Teedyuscung, a Delaware chief treating at Easton in 1756 with the colonial government, responded: "this very ground that is under me (striking it with his Foot) was my Land and Inheritance, and is taken from me by fraud." Detailing the various forms of frauds, Teedyuscung explained how the sons of William Penn "forge[d] a Deed like the true one," how they bought land from one sachem that "belongs to the other," and how they "took in double the Quantity intended to be sold."[39] Franklin and his Quaker associates were convinced by Teedyuscung's assertion "that the Indians had been unjustly dispossessed and defrauded of large Quantities of Land," and they promised Teedyuscung's people that they would bring these matters before the king. However, Franklin was outmaneuvered by Johnson, who resented Franklin's interference in what he regarded as his business. Johnson persuaded the Board of Trade to reject Franklin's petition to lay the documents of the Penn purchase before the king and to refer the Indians' complaints and the negotiation for settlement back to Johnson. Unfortunately, Teedyuscung would not meet with Johnson because of Johnson's association with "the Indian Nations . . . who had been instrumental to the misunderstanding in selling the Lands in Question."[40] Despite these internal struggles for power and influence, Franklin and Johnson, though pitted against each other, succeeded in bringing before the Board of Trade the Penns' questionable land dealings.

After much discussion with the Board of Trade, on December 11, 1756, the proprietaries decided to relinquish the lands west of the Alleghenies, but they insisted that if the Iroquois decided to sell these disputed lands, they must sell to the Penn family. This decision to relinquish a legal claim on Indian land is rather remarkable as it does not conform to the usual chain of events involving European and colonial desires for Indian land. The Penns' returning the land to the Iroquois and the western Delawares and Shawnees can be interpreted as a gracious and benevolent act, but it can also be seen as prudent. The Penns were clearly acting in their own interests, for if the Iroquois and their dependents had refused to align themselves with the British, then France could have won the French and Indian War (the Seven Years' War) and the Penns would have lost a lot more than the lands contiguous to the Susquehanna, Monongahela, and Allegheny Rivers.[41] This return of native land was, however, only a minor setback in the Penns' plans, for in the late 1760s after the French and Indian War, the Penns finally succeeded in acquiring vast tracts of western lands.

Boundaries

Benjamin West's painting conveys a sense of the inevitable movement of Europeans onto Indian lands and the resulting retreat of the natives to lands beyond the frontier. Toward the right margin of the painting, the figure of a Delaware man is walking out of the picture, headed into the dark, primeval forest, carrying a rolled blanket over his shoulder. He looks as if he has received his goods in exchange for his land and is moving on to lands beyond the Delaware River. His movement out of the picture is in a left-to-right line. This movement is reiterated by a figure in the background on the left margin of the painting, which appears to be a man with a dark complexion, possibly an African servant or seaman, who looks as if he is unloading a boat, for he is carrying bundles from the shore in the direction of the buildings. Ships lie in wait in the harbor, ready to unload their cargo and passengers, and this anticipated movement, also left to right, is echoed by the way the Europeans have already transformed the landscape, clearing the forest and building houses. The European landscape has pushed back the Indian village to the far right of the painting so that it occupies only a fraction of the picture's space.

Despite representations such as West's, this movement of colonists onto Indian land was not necessarily inevitable, nor was it seen as inevitable in 1770. After winning the war with France, the British Crown reasserted its desire to protect the western lands from white settlers and land speculators. The British government tried to create a viable border between its colonies and Indian territory with the Proclamation Line of 1763; reiterating the treaty of 1726, it declared the Allegheny Mountains the border between Euro-American settlements and native lands.[42] This kept Penn from reasserting his claims, but it did not stem the flow of whites into the lands beyond the Alleghenies. The Crown had very little control over the movement of whites into Indian lands. As Georgiana Nammack points out, "despite

the continued efforts of the Crown to regulate and control the grant-
ing of lands in the colonies, it seemed that the home government had
genuine difficulty in enforcing its authority, and the problem of curb-
ing speculation in huge grants persisted." [43] Distressed by the influx
of white settlers and dissatisfied with the implementation of British
policy, the Western tribes, primarily the western Delawares and Shawnees of Ohio and the Senecas of the Great Lakes region as well as
some Chippewas, Hurons, and Miamis, inspired by the example of
Pontiac, an Ottawa war chief, conducted raids on the forts and settlements in the Ohio River Valley. After two years of frontier warfare,
Johnson finally persuaded the Senecas to bury the hatchet and quit
harassing frontier settlements. In 1766 Pontiac made peace with the
British. [44]

In 1768 Johnson negotiated the Treaty of Fort Stanwix. By this
time Johnson and Thomas Penn were on the same side, Penn having
appointed Johnson to act as leader of the Pennsylvania delegation.
Johnson succeeded in fixing the boundary between Indian lands and
colonial provinces not along the Allegheny Mountains but along the
Ohio River. The Board of Trade had wanted the boundary to be the
mountains so that colonial settlements would be restricted to within
300 miles of the Atlantic, an area fairly reachable by His Majesty's
troops. Johnson ignored the Board of Trade's advice and the orders
of the Earl of Hillsborough, secretary of state, and drew the line to
the Tennessee River, thereby alienating lands — what was to become
Tennessee, Kentucky, and part of Alabama — on which the Cherokees lived and hunted. [45] This boundary displeased the Cherokees,
the Board of Trade, and the Delawares, Shawnees, and Mingos who
occupied what was to become western Pennsylvania, Ohio, and Indiana. Johnson was criticized by both London and the Ohio Indians for
giving away too much land to the colonists. But as some historians
have suggested, Johnson was realistic in his estimations of the seriousness of the white incursion into Indian territory and felt it was
impossible for the Indians to hold onto land that they had already
lost to backwoods settlers, traders, and speculators. Johnson may have
reasoned that it was pointless to attempt to create a frontier line along
the Allegheny Mountains when it had already broken down as a real
border. In general, his policy on Indian land was to encourage Indians
to sell their lands that had been squatted on by colonists so that they

could at least get something for land that they were in the process of losing control over.[46]

Sir William Johnson also disobeyed orders from the Board of Trade when he drew the boundary to exclude from Indian territory a large tract of land along the Susquehanna River known as the Wyoming Valley. He arranged for this land to be sold to Thomas Penn, who gave the Iroquois 10,000 Spanish dollars. Johnson's reasoning was that the Wyoming Valley had been under dispute for several years; fighting over it were Delawares, Iroquois, white settlers from Connecticut who claimed it as part of their province, and the Pennsylvania colonial government, which thought Connecticut's claims absurd. Johnson may have thought a clear title under the Penns would prevent further hostilities in this area.[47] Penn was probably delighted with this purchase, as the valley was part of what he had thought he was buying in Albany in 1754 when his agents treated with the Iroquois for western lands. After fourteen years, Penn finally got what he wanted: land on which to expand westward.

Painted a year after the ratification of the Treaty of Fort Stanwix, West's painting is a celebration of Thomas Penn's "peaceful" acquisition of Indian land, marking Penn's successful resolution of violent conflict over westward expansion. It is also a vindication of his character and an assertion of his own standing as a gentleman and a plain dealer. Through the figure of his father, Thomas Penn rewrote the history of his own troubled relations with the Delawares and asserted his peaceful intentions and goodwill toward colonists. As Ann Uhry Abrams has noted, Thomas Penn had suffered greatly under Franklin's attacks in the late 1750s, and after the Treaty of Fort Stanwix he was also plagued by accusations that he had obtained large tracts of land for speculation and personal gain. Abrams suggests that West's painting, in reiterating "the images of peace in Pennsylvania," was "a visual resolution of the many conflicts that had divided the Colony for over two decades."[48] West achieved this visual resolution not only by employing the iconography of the peace medal but also by using color, light, movement, and gender to reinforce the ideological projections and displacements that lie at the heart of this painting.

The Penns' troubles over acquiring Indian land were never really resolved—only postponed until the American Revolution transformed their relationship to North America. The troubles caused by land speculation and Indian resistance to backcountry settlement shifted from the Penns' shoulders to the new American federal government, which feebly struggled to contain individual, corporate, and state desire for Indian land, insisting that it had assumed from the British Crown sovereignty over Indian land, and with sovereignty, stewardship over Indians and their lands.[49] But that is another story, one that involves issues of land, identity, and sovereignty, issues that will be addressed in the next chapter, on cultural cross-dressing.

3

Cultural Cross-Dressing in British America

Among the hundreds of eighteenth-century British portraits of gentle-men in military dress, one of Colonel Guy Johnson, Sir William Johnson's nephew, and another of Sir John Caldwell are remarkable for their display of Native American dress. Johnson's uniform is a combination of British military and Iroquois clothing (Fig. 7), whereas Caldwell is almost entirely dressed as an Indian chief complete with feathered headdress, tomahawk-pipe, and wampum belt (Fig. 8). Equally remarkable for its representation of cultural cross-dressing is a portrait by John Francis Rigaud of Joseph Brant, or Thayendanegea, the famous Mohawk warrior and leader, who is depicted wearing a British military uniform and a modest Iroquoian headdress (Fig. 9). The aim of this chapter is to explore the political significance of the hybrid dress worn by Caldwell, Johnson, and Brant within the context of British-Iroquois relations during the last quarter of the eighteenth century.[1]

Given the colonial context of the British officers' cultural cross-dressing, we must consider whether the Britons are engaged in a form of appropriation of native culture that parallels other kinds of European appropriations of native resources — of land and labor, for instance. If these culturally cross-dressed Britons are engaged in some

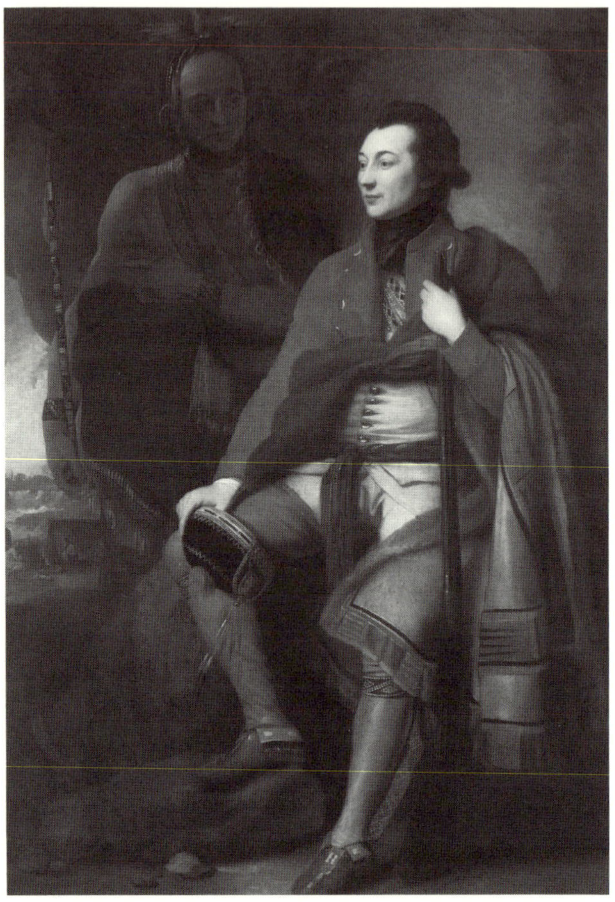

7. Benjamin West, *Colonel Guy Johnson and Karonghyontye
(Captain David Hill)*, 1776, oil on canvas. © Board of
Trustees, National Gallery of Art, Washington, DC,
Andrew W. Mellon Collection.

form of appropriation, what does it mean when an American Indian
dresses in British military garb? Is he, like the Britons, appropriating
the power of the Other, or is he reproducing on his body a partial and
therefore debased version of colonial power? I view these portraits
of cultural cross-dressers in the context of colonial discourses that
deployed the rhetorical strategies of accommodation, appropriation,
exoticization, and decontextualization to manage colonial subjects,

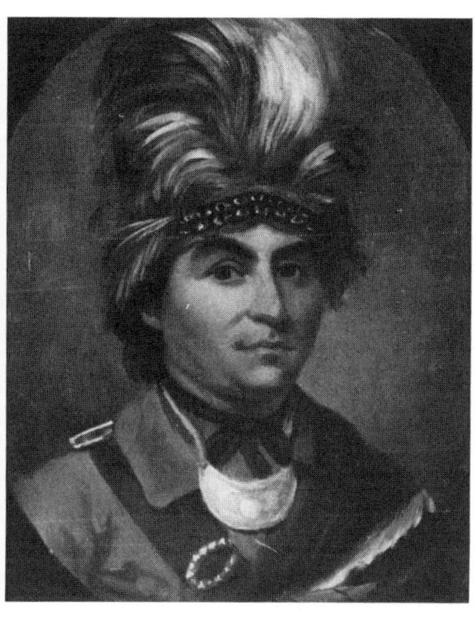

8. Nineteenth-century copy of John Francis Rigaud, *Joseph Brant*, 1786, oil on canvas. The New York State Office of Parks, Recreation and Historic Preservation at Johnson Hall Historic Site.

(*Below*) 9. Anonymous, *Sir John Caldwell*, c. 1780, oil on canvas. King's Regiment Collection. Courtesy of the Board of Trustees of the National Museums and Galleries on Merseyside.

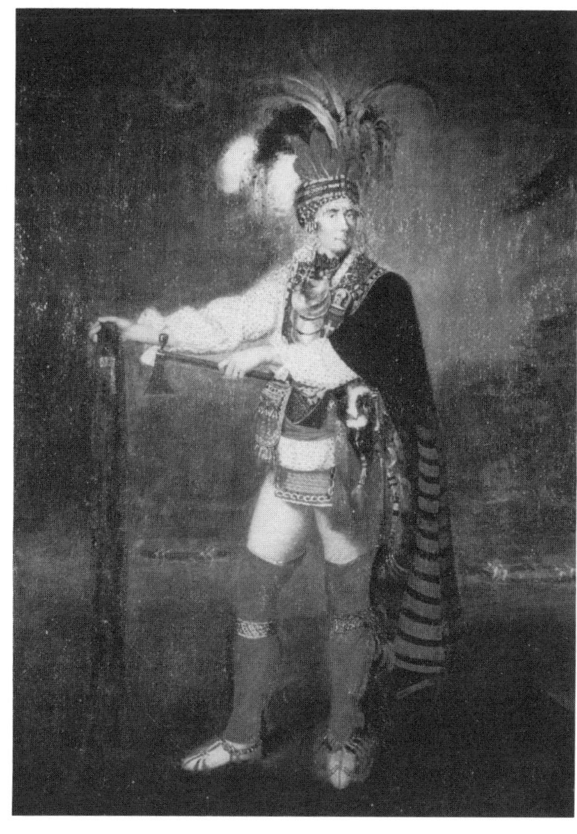

and I explore the ways in which Brant's display of hybrid dress works to resist these colonizing strategies.[2]

Souvenirs

We do not know the identity of the artist who painted the portrait of John Caldwell, but Paul L. Stevens argues persuasively that the man represented in this painting is Sir John Caldwell, 5th Baronet, of Castle Caldwell in County Fermanagh, Ireland, nephew of Lieutenant Colonel John Caldwell, who was the commander of Fort Niagara, near Detroit, from 1774–76.[3] Young Ensign Caldwell came to America to join his uncle, who served with the King's Regiment of Foot and was stationed at Fort Niagara. Stevens suggests that the nephew was sent out to the uncle by his parents to break up an improper match with the "wrong" young woman. While the identity of the figure in this painting has traditionally been designated as that of Lieutenant Colonel Caldwell, Stevens contends that because Lieutenant Colonel Caldwell died in 1776 at Fort Niagara after a cold winter on the Great Lakes, the young man in the painting was most probably his nephew, who returned to Britain after his uncle's death.[4] I think we can assume that the clothing and ornaments he is wearing are not the trophies of war but gifts from the various Indian tribes that he encountered or, even more likely, gifts his uncle received while assigned the duties of negotiator with the various bands of Algonquians and Great Lakes Indians.[5]

In his desire to display his (uncle's?) Indian souvenirs, John Caldwell assumes a pose mimicking the Vatican's *Apollo Belvedere* (see Fig. 42), that masterpiece of classical statuary frequently used as a source for poses in eighteenth-century portraiture.[6] His arms are arranged to exhibit the wampum belt and the tomahawk-pipe; his head is turned to show off the heavy Indian earrings and nose ring and to bring into full view the glory of the elaborately feathered headdress. Every detail of Indian dress is carefully delineated—the beaded pouch, the polka-dot Indian shirt, the fringed moccasins—all at the expense of considerations of composition. Without line or color to give order to this proliferation of detail, the painting is rendered less than coherent. There is too much to take in, and one does not know where to look first or how to look at the painting as a whole.

Paralleling this lack of formal coherence in the painting is the cultural dissonance created by the costume Caldwell wears. A close examination of his moccasins, headdress, pipe, tomahawk, and a belt of wampum reveals that he is wearing not an "authentic" chief's costume, but a pastiche concocted from the clothing and accoutrements of various Indian tribes. According to the historian Colin Calloway, "the pipe is eastern Sioux, the garters are Chippewa, and the pouch, knife, and sheath are from the eastern Great Lakes."[7] This taking of bits and pieces of clothing from various Indian tribes thoroughly decontextualizes the items, divorcing them from their original owners, the Chippewa or Anishinabeg in the case of the garters, for instance. Separating the items from those who created and wore them has the effect of reducing their power to signify, to be a part of an elaborate sign system that constitutes being Anishinabeg. Harriet Guest argues that the exotic is created by just such decontextualizing acts; Caldwell's garters become exotic because they are dislocated, as Guest would say, "from any signs of the personal estate or cultural context that might produce legible or potent significance."[8]

What Caldwell achieves with this pastiche of decontextualized objects is an illusion of Indianness, but it is an Indianness rendered powerless by its incoherence. Caldwell, meanwhile, is made more powerful by his manipulation of the Indian artifacts. American Indian scholar and activist Ward Churchill argues that just such a dislocation of an artifact from the people who made it and the presentation of various artifacts and cultural practices of different native peoples as if they were all produced by undifferentiated generic Indians are classic strategies employed by those trying to deny authority to Indian cultures and peoples. Churchill argues that the process by which native traditions are "lumped together into a single homogeneous and consistent whole, regardless of actual variances and distinctions," creates the effect of rendering the "distinctions between cultural groupings of indigenous people . . . either nonexistent (ignorance) or irrelevant (arrogant)."[9] Caldwell's pastiche of Indian objects reduces the complexity of Indian-British and Indian-Indian relations with the illusion that there is a generic Indian and that tribal affiliations do not matter but exist only on the superficial level of dress and design, not on the level of the real politics of military might. Sir John's pastiche functions as a kind of denial, for in the 1770s and 1780s, tribal distinctions were very important. A British officer had better know the difference between a Mohawk and an Oneida warrior if he wanted to find an ally against the American rebels. Presumably, Ensign Caldwell's uncle knew the difference between tribes, as he had been posted to the Detroit area, living among the Seneca and the Chippewa and recruiting them as allies; it is not certain, however, that the nephew understood the significance of the various ornaments and items of clothing he wore for this portrait.

Caldwell's wearing of Indian clothing empowers him in a variety of ways. By decontextualizing the Indian artifacts, Caldwell denies to them the power to speak of Indian culture and Indian political power. He emerges from the clutter on his body as the only true subject of a narrative that relegates Indians to the realm of local color. His Indian outfit functions as a souvenir, carrying within it his narratives of having lived in Indian territory. As Susan Stewart suggests in her book *On Longing,* souvenirs function "to generate narratives"— not narratives of the originators of the artifacts, which in this case would have been the Chippewa who made the garters, but narratives of Caldwell's experiences among the Chippewa. Stewart writes: "Removed from its context, the exotic souvenir is a sign of survival— not its own survival, but the survival of the possessor outside his or her own context of familiarity. Its otherness speaks to the possessor's capacity for otherness: it is the possessor, not the souvenir, which is ultimately the curiosity."[10] His costume is a souvenir of his sojourn and an emblem of his ability to master the experience of a radically foreign environment.

As the only true subject of the narratives that his souvenirs in their state of disorientation can speak of, Caldwell remains strangely untouched by the exoticism he wears. The excess of his finery alerts us to the masquerade and reveals his true identity as a British gentleman, who, in playing at being an Indian chief, reminds us of his ability to appropriate the unfamiliar without being transformed by it. Though wearing native dress, he has not gone native. The portrait of Caldwell dressed as an Indian chief could almost be taken for a fancy dress portrait. With the popularity of the masquerade, it became fashionable, especcially for women, to have their portraits painted wearing fancy dress or masquerade costumes.[11] Some aristocratic ladies had their portraits painted dressed as shepherdesses, milkmaids, and cottagers' wives in what could be described as class cross-dressing. Men who attended masquerades dressed not only as priests and Sufis but also as African slaves described in the newspaper reports as Mungos, and as Indian chiefs.[12] There is, I believe, an element of frivolity that plays about Caldwell's portrait, and perhaps that tone can be attributed to the masquerade quality of his clothing.

While traces of the masquerade inhabit Caldwell's cultural cross-dressing, his portrait is informed by another kind of portraiture that also features aspects of cultural cross-dressing: the portrait of the tourist.[13] Young Englishmen on the Grand Tour would frequently have their portraits painted in Italy wearing their new, elegant, European-style clothing and standing in front of some moldering monument of bygone Roman glory. David Allan's *Thomas Graham, Baron Lynedoch* (1769) is an example of the tourist portrait; he holds in his hand the new Italian-made gun and lounges rather smugly in front of the Temple of Vesta (Fig. 10). The painting proudly declares "I was there!" and smacks of a special kind of arrogance mingled with ignorance that only a tourist can have. Caldwell's portrait, probably painted in Britain, re-creates the setting of North America, albeit dimly, with two canoes filled with Indians voyaging in a dark river. More than the setting, Caldwell's clothing, or rather his souvenirs, mark him as a tourist. His presentation of himself as a tourist, someone who has toured, in this case not merely Europe, but the wilds of North America, resembles another portrait of a famous tourist, Sir Joseph Banks, who accompanied Cook on his first voyage around the world. Banks remarked that, while other young men were touring France and Italy, he was touring the whole globe. On his return to England, Banks had his portrait painted by Benjamin West to commemorate this momentous occasion (Fig. 11). In the portrait Banks stands upright in the midst of the objects he had collected on his voyage: spears, bowls, plants, and a tapa cloth that hangs cloaklike around his shoulders. West captures Banks's confident air, proud manner, and sheer delight in having completed his mission successfully and in having accumulated so many marvelous possessions.[14] Caldwell's presentation of himself as an Indian chief owes much to the genres of fancy dress portraiture and tourist portraiture, for in both genres cultural cross-dressing, though mildly transgressive and ultimately playful, represents an attempt to master and appropriate for oneself the power of an alien culture.

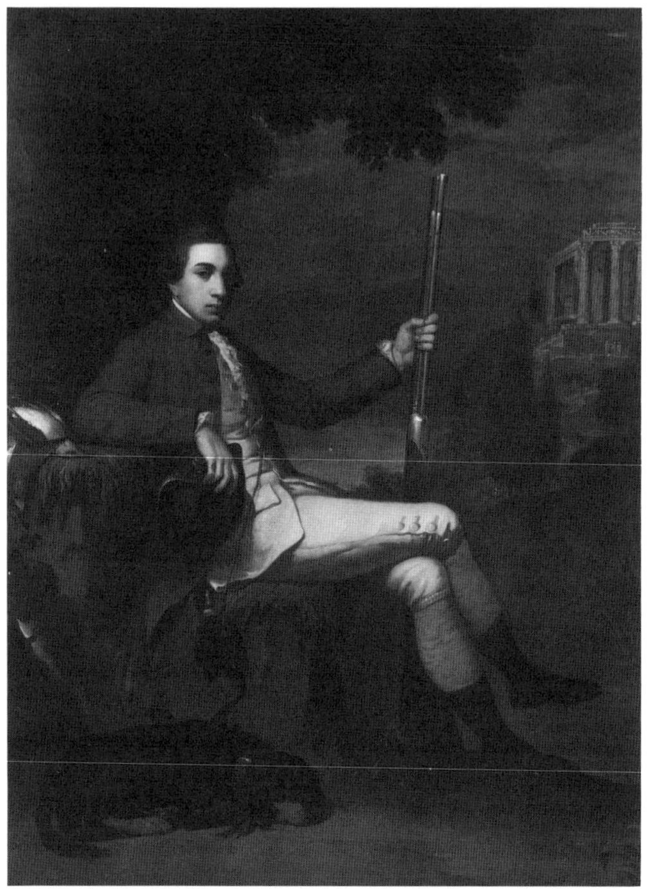

10. David Allan, *Thomas Graham, Baron Lynedoch,* 1769, oil on
canvas. Yale Center for British Art.

I have borrowed the term cross-dressing from the discourse on
gender identity, finding it useful in analyzing the representation of
cultural identities and affinities. It implies that identity is a matter
of performance rather than something that emanates from within
our bodies. Cross-dressing—drag, for instance—simultaneously performs and parodies gendered identity, and as such has been interpreted by queer theorists as a radical critique of our society's notion of
gendered identities, pointing out the social construction of femininity
and masculinity and calling into question our society's heteronorma-

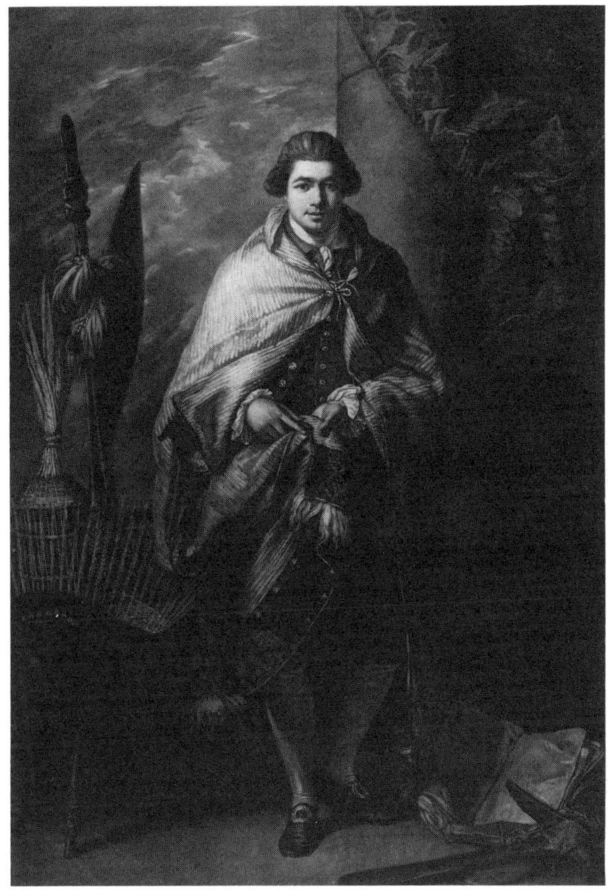

11. John Raphael Smith after Benjamin West,
Joseph Banks, c. 1771–73, mezzotint. By permission
of The British Library.

tivity. Diana Fuss sees drag as a performed critique of heteronormativity, as it works to "unmask all identity as drag." [15] Drag's excessive
mimicry and its parodic performance of gendered identity are for Fuss
a source of subversion of and resistance to the dominant culture's
compulsory heterosexuality. Judith Butler suggests that "the notion
of an original or primary gender identity is often parodied within the
cultural practices of drag, cross-dressing, and the sexual stylization of
butch/femme identities." In parodying social codes that dictate iden-

tity, cross-dressing denaturalizes gender categories and opens up the possibility of "a fluidity of identities."[16]

However, cross-dressing, with its mimicry and potential for parody, is not always subversive or counterhegemonic. As Butler notes in her discussion of drag as a form of gender parody, "parody by itself is not subversive," and as Bakhtin has argued, parody allows for venting of subversive energies while reinscribing the existing power structures.[17] Much of the theoretical discussion of mimicry, masquerade, and parody in Homi Bhabha's formulations and in the work of feminist and queer theorists assumes that the one who engages in mimicry or parody is in the oppressed position and is trying to subvert the dominant discourse. But when we apply these notions of mimicry and parody to Sir John Caldwell's cross-dressing, we have to consider the power differentials at work in his adoption of native dress. Does not his status as a British gentleman and officer in His Majesty's imperial forces affect how we read his cultural cross-dressing? Marjorie Garber characterizes the cross-dresser as the "figure that disrupts," but Anne McClintock points out that cross-dressing, despite its status as the "embodiment of ambiguity," is not always transgressive and can, in fact, be reactionary. Garber's book is perhaps the fullest discussion of cross-dressing, and yet, because her analysis is dependent on a Lacanian reading of fetishistic behavior, she is unable, as McClintock argues, to "do theoretical justice to the rich diversity of cultural cross-dressers and historical fetishes that she herself reveals." The sexual, racial, ethnic, and class positions of the cross-dresser shape the performance so that cross-dressing can subvert or reinscribe the dominant codes or do a little of both. Positionality is crucial, therefore, in determining the political effect of cross-dressing.[18]

The question, then, becomes: What is the effect of Caldwell's "deliberate and playful" putting on of native garb?[19] In displaying the trophies of his (or his uncle's) sojourn in Indian territory, is Caldwell mimicking, even parodying Indians?[20] And in mimicking or parodying Indians, is he trying to reduce the potential of these artifacts to convey the power that lies latent in them? Caldwell's pastiche could be seen as parody, assuming he felt being British made him automatically superior to the Chippewa; on the other hand, there are countless narratives of "white Indians," Europeans who deserted their own cultures for Indian communities and ways of life. In *The Invasion Within:*

The Contest of Cultures in Colonial North America, James Axtell states that "the Indians, despite all odds, succeeded in seducing French and English colonists in numbers so alarming to European sensibilities that the natives were conceded to be, in effect, the best cultural missionaries and educators on the continent."[21] Caldwell, as a member of his king's imperial forces, is positioned as a powerful subject, and yet his masquerade as an Indian chief may indicate that he felt threatened or envious of the people whose clothes he wore for his portrait.

Caldwell's pastiche denies to Indians and their cultural productions the power to signify, but in denying them this power, is he acting out of fear? He may be overcompensating, admitting on some level his own inadequacy and their potency. It is as if Caldwell and his Indian souvenirs are engaged in a struggle over who will get to speak, whose narrative will win and drown out its rival. In his efforts to display all his souvenirs, Caldwell is excessive; instead of impressing his viewers with the tales of his sojourn in America, he reveals himself as overeager and, as Ward Churchill might say, arrogant and ignorant.

Appropriating the Power of the Primitive

The portrait of Colonel Guy Johnson presents a totally different colonizing dynamic at work: Johnson is not a tourist, nor is he dressed for a masquerade (Fig. 7). This portrait belongs to the category of state portraiture: portraits depicting men in their official capacity, surrounded by the paraphernalia of their official function. In the same way that portraits of judges, Johan Zoffany's of Sir Elijah Impey, for instance, depict the judge surrounded by his law books, holding the sword of justice and wearing his grand wig and long red robes (Fig. 12), this portrait of Colonel Guy Johnson depicts him in his official capacity, that of acting superintendent of Indian Affairs of the Northern Colonies, a position he inherited from his uncle Sir William. The setting, his clothing, and the Indian standing deferentially behind him are emblems of his office. This painting conveys a seriousness and earnestness that are typical of such official portraiture, a quality that clearly is absent from Caldwell's playful representation of himself as an Indian chief.[22]

The style and tone of Benjamin West's official portrait indicate that

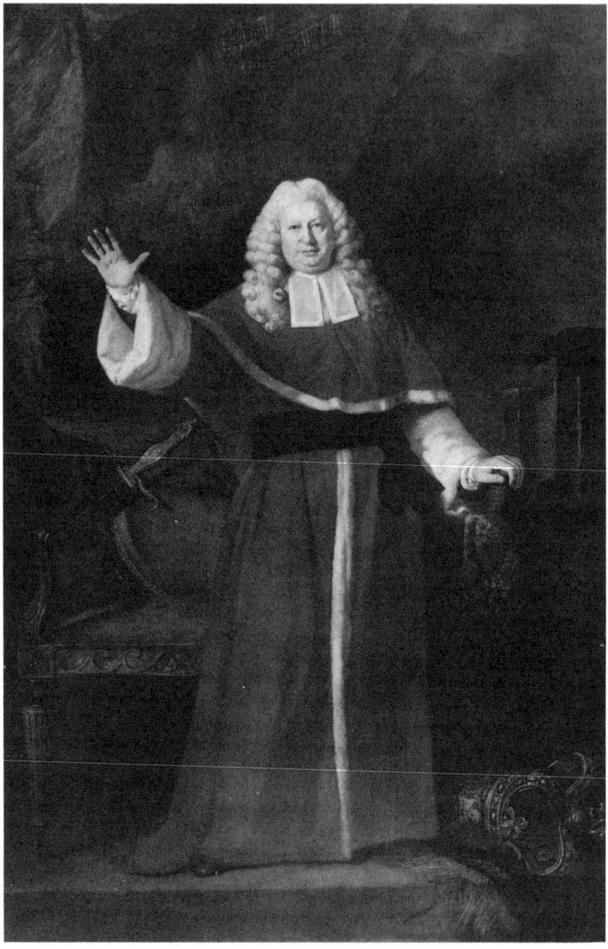

12. Johan Zoffany, *Sir Elijah Impey, Chief Justice, Supreme Court of Judicature, Fort William, Calcutta,* 1783, engraving. Oriental and India Office Collections, shelfmark P694. By permission of The British Library.

Guy Johnson had a very different attitude toward the North American native population than did Caldwell with his posture of smug mimicry. Johnson had much more respect for Indians than did Caldwell, for he had grafted onto his identity that of the Native American and had found tremendous power in appropriating the ways of the "primitive."[23] This mingling of British and Indian identity is present in this painting on an ideological and aesthetic level. Unlike the incoherent pastiche of decontextualized Indian artifacts in the Caldwell portrait, Benjamin West's treatment of Johnson's Indian clothing is integrated into the painting's use of color, light, and line. The vibrant red of the military jacket is echoed in the beaded sash and moccasins, the colorful borders on the blanket, and the red feathers of the hat unique to the Indian service. The bits of red create a pleasing and harmonious whole: our eyes are caught by Johnson's lit face and his bright red jacket and then follow the trail of red around an oval shaped by his right arm on one side and the folds of the blanket on the other, circling around the bright buttons on his slightly protruding belly. The moccasions, leggings, sash, and blanket do not stand out as separate from the man; they are integral to him, a part of who he is. West's incorporation of native detail into the design of the whole indicates a sensitivity to his sitter's personal history as well as to the implications of Johnson's political ties to the Iroquois.

Guy Johnson was the nephew and son-in-law of Sir William Johnson, who, as the ranking colonial official in charge of Indian affairs, had figured so prominently in the Pennsylvania land deals featured in the previous chapter. The elder Johnson occupied the position of superintendent of Indian Affairs of the Northern Indian Department from 1755 until his death in 1774, when Colonel Guy Johnson assumed the position as acting superintendent—after going to London to persuade the powers that be, the colonial secretary and the Board of Trade, that he was the man for the job. While in London, he had his portrait painted by West.[24] Painted four or five years after *William Penn's Treaty with the Indians,* this official portrait also confronts the specter of colonial warfare. Whereas the Penn history painting works to smooth over old grievances and to silence current acts of violence, the Johnson portrait evokes the idea of borderland violence by portraying the hovering Mohawk figure in warrior's dress and by depicting Johnson's rifle and military uniform. Comparing the composition of these two paintings, particularly West's arrangement of figures, important aesthetic differences emerge that reflect the different relations that the Penn family had with the Delawares and the Johnson family had with the Iroquois. Even though the Penn painting is supposedly about peace, very clear divisions exist between colonists and Indians, with the Quakers occupying the left side of the painting and the Delawares the right side; tension is conveyed through this spacial confrontation and oppositional placement of bodies. On the other hand, the Johnson portrait conveys a strong message about potential warfare through the carefully constructed union of Briton and Mohawk, the outline of their bodies creating an oval shape emblematic of harmonized difference.

To be portrayed as an ally of the Mohawks was of strategic importance to Johnson. Wearing the hybrid Indian Department uniform for his portrait, Johnson positioned himself as someone who was adept in dealing with both British and Native American cultural practices. His desire to be seen as a negotiator and facilitator between the British and the Iroquois is supported by the spacial relations in the portrait. Behind Johnson stretches North America, its people and natural resources. Johnson is placed between us and the northwest frontier, as if to say that if one wanted access to the Iroquois and their land, one had to go through Johnson, the gatekeeper who patrols the borderlands of North America.[25] The proprietary nature of Johnson's relationship with the Iroquois that this portrait succeeds in conveying is communicated in a letter from General Gage to the acting commander of Fort Niagara, in which he stresses the younger Johnson's need to be kept apprised of Indian affairs: "You will therefore be pleased to correspond with him as heretofore with Sir William Johnson, and give him every necessary information of the apparent temper and disposition of the Indians that visit your Post."[26] In assuming his uncle's position, Johnson had to place himself in the center of the colonial web, a site where information was accumulated, cultural knowledge was dispersed, and political power was exercised.[27]

An important part of this portrait's representation of Johnson's intermediary role in colonial-Indian affairs is the figure who stands behind him. Some art historians have argued that the Indian figure is Joseph Brant, a Mohawk warrior of great renown, who had accompanied Johnson on this trip to London. Johnson and Brant were related. Molly Brant, Joseph's sister and a very powerful person in her own right, was Sir William Johnson's common-law wife for over twenty years, from when they met until he died.[28] Joseph Brant accompanied Guy Johnson to London for two reasons: to signal his approval of Johnson as an adequate replacement for his brother-in-law and to act

as a spokesman for the Six Nations in their attempt to get the British
government to follow up on their promises to protect Indian lands
from the encroachment of white settlers. Brant's mission was to remind the British government of its promises of friendship to the Six
Nations and to argue for the strengthening of their relations as allies.
Whether the shadowy figure in the Johnson painting is indeed Brant
or John Hill, as some have argued, does not really matter in terms of
the overall effect. Including the figure of a Mohawk warrior dressed
in battle costume conveys the very intimate and complicated relations
that existed between the Johnson dynasty and the Iroquois, and also
underscores the political and military alliance between Britain and the
Six Nations in the impending war with the American rebels.

These political and military relations are played out in Guy Johnson's clothing. West has carefully contextualized the Indian moccasins, leggings, and blanket by locating them in a specific place—the
rapids in the background are most probably Niagara Falls—which allude to the Mohawk lands in what was to become New York State.
And, of course, the figure of the Mohawk warrior acts to contextual-
ize Johnson's Indian clothing, suggesting that he is wearing Mohawk
moccasins, leggings, and garters. Unlike Caldwell's trinkets, Johnson's
clothing has not lost its power to signify and speaks clearly of his
alliance with a powerful people whom his government and the government of the American rebels were desperately courting as military
allies.[29] Johnson is empowered by his Indian costume, but not in the
same manner as Caldwell. Johnson locates his power in his relations
with a specific group of people, the Mohawks of New York, whose
military prowess was legendary. Lord George Germaine, colonial secretary, said of the Iroquois: "The Dread the People of New England
&c have of a War with the Savages, proves the Expediency of our
holding that Scourge over them."[30] The Mohawks were famed for
their fierce fighting, and most colonials, who grew up on stories of
Indian atrocities, torture, and scalping, feared the very thought of
Mohawks as enemies. In wearing Mohawk clothing Guy Johnson puts
into play these fears of Indian violence and appropriates the power
of the so-called primitive to enhance his image as a powerful man
who is at ease in both Indian and British worlds. Johnson's wearing
of Mohawk clothing is the visual analogue, albeit a far more subtle
and sophisticated one, to Ethan Allen's description of himself as a

fierce fighter. Writing to the Iroquois to persuade them to join the rebel cause, Allen says, "I know how to shute and ambush just like Indian and want your Warriors to come and see me and help me fight Regulars you know they Stand all along close together Rank and file and my men fight so as Indians Do and Ambush the Regulars."[31] To fight "like [an] Indian" is to be a fearsome and effective warrior. Johnson's relaxed pose underscores the ease he feels in the company of the threatening figure of the Mohawk warrior, whose naked upper body indicates his readiness for warfare. Johnson's adoption of Mohawk ways and warfare heightens his military stature as well as presenting a powerful and threatening image of British-Iroquois unity.[32]

In figuring British-Iroquois unity within the context of impending war, West demonstrates his political acuity and sensitivity to his patrons' social and political needs. Comparing his treatment of *Penn's Treaty* with his handling of the Johnson portrait reveals that each painting, though both structured around contradictions, presents Indian-British relations in a very different light. The Penn picture looks backward in time in its attempt to represent peace and to celebrate the end of frontier violence. The Johnson painting, on the other hand, looks forward to the impending war between loyalists and colonists. The Penn history painting, obstensibly about peace, stresses division in the arrangement of figures, whereas the Johnson portrait, portending war, conveys an intimacy between Britons and Indians through the proximity of overlapping bodies.

Hybridity

Unlike Caldwell's full-scale masquerade, Johnson's outfit, an amalgam of Indian and British clothing, is typical of the Indian Department and such provincial units as Roger's Royal Rangers and Sir John Johnson's Royal Greens (Sir William's son and heir).[33] His hybrid uniform is characteristic of a world that was in flux, occupied simultaneously by Indians of different tribes and affiliations, English, Scots, Irish, Germans, Euro-Americans, and African Americans. The Johnson-Brant household, typical of frontier life, was a mixture of nationalities, cultures, and races. Sir William Johnson, an Irishman, who early in his life saw that being a member of the Church of England would be expedient, had recanted his Catholicism and moved to the province of New York, where he became a major landowner. His first "wife" was his German American housekeeper; his second, Molly (Wari) Brant, a Mohawk from Canajoharie Castle on the Mohawk River. His tenants were a mixture of German and Scottish farmers. Both he and his Indian brother-in-law, Joseph Brant, who was a Mason and a devout Anglican, owned slaves of African descent.

The hybridity of this world can be seen not only in the beaded, feathered cap of the Indian Department that Johnson holds in his hand but in the blanket draped over his arm. Clearly Indian in design and function, the blanket is also clearly British in manufacture. It is the product of a mingling of cultures, a mingling that occurred in what historian Richard White calls the middle ground. White argues that together, Indians and Europeans constructed over the course of tens of generations "a common, mutually comprehensible world" and forged "new systems of meaning and of exchange." [34] Johnson's blanket can be seen as an emblem of this middle ground, a sign that has meaning in this world of shared experience.[35] Other "Indian" clothing that is dependent on British manufacture appears in both the Caldwell and Johnson portraits. The plumes in Caldwell's headdress are ostrich and were obtained as a trade item, as is all the jewelry, including the earrings, armbands, and chains. Other trade items are the calico cloth from which "Indian" shirts were made, and the beads from which the very important wampum belts were made. Caldwell wears a polka-dot Indian shirt and holds a string of wampum, which was used to convey messages intertribally and to record important deeds and agreements within tribes and villages. Caldwell and Johnson both sport bead-embroidered garters and sashes. Although the Indians in the northeast woodlands did not possess metallurgical technology to manufacture iron and other metals, nor did they know in the eighteenth century how to weave cloth and to make glass beads, they refashioned British-made cloth, metal, and beads to suit their own purposes and incorporated these foreign materials into their own cultural sign systems and everyday physical world.[36]

In *Mimesis and Alterity,* Michael Taussig describes the hybridity of the modern world where Cuna Indians in Colombia sew the image of the RCA logo of a dog listening to a gramophone into their elaborately embroidered appliquéd blouses, which they have been making

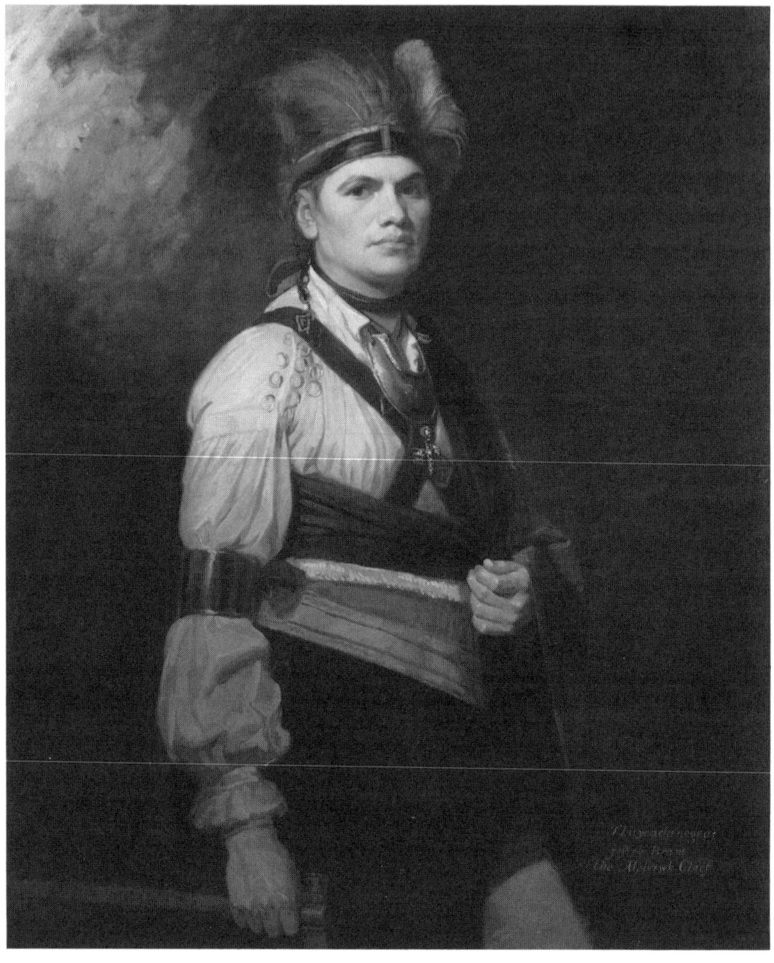

13. George Romney, *Joseph Brant (Thayendanegea)*, 1776, oil on canvas. National Gallery of Canada, Ottawa. Transfer from the Canadian War Memorials, 1921.

for over a century and now sell worldwide. Taussig marvels at the dizzying displacements that abound in this era of "second contact," when the circuits of the world capitalist system have permeated the globe, dissolving boundaries and identities in its wake. However, he is mistaken in limiting this era of the second contact to the twentieth century and postcolonial moment: eighteenth-century British

America bears all the marks of Taussig's "borderland where 'us' and 'them' lose their polarity and swim in and out of focus."[37]

This borderland's mingling of us and them is noticeable in the clothing worn by Joseph Brant in a portrait painted by George Romney in 1776 during his visit to London with Guy Johnson (Fig. 13). The silver gorget around his neck is the only purely British item of clothing that he wears, and his leggings, obscured in the shadows, are the only purely Indian item. Everything else is hybrid. Of British manufacture and Indian design is his shirt, blanket, tomahawk, jewelry, ribbon around his neck, armband, and headdress. Brant's hybrid dress reflects his role in the Revolutionary War. As a leader of a band of loyalists, he captained a unit of men, mostly white residents of his homelands in the Province of New York, who all wore a bit of yellow lace on their hats to identify themselves as Brant's Volunteers.[38] These men, resistant to traditional military authority, were described by a Major Gray as refusing to "be under any command"; he complained, "I have been thirty years a soldier, but never had so much trouble as with those fellows."[39] Unpaid and living under very harsh conditions, they fought under Brant, who allowed them much more freedom than regular troops. They fought not only like Indians but as Indians. Brant's biographer writes: "his Volunteers dressed and painted themselves as Indians, and during all the border warfare the rebels naturally assumed that their dreaded Mohawk enemy had a large party of grotesquely painted warriors under his command."[40]

Brant, who always had his portraits painted wearing hybrid Indian clothing, was perhaps the "most painted Indian."[41] In 1786 during his second visit to London, Brant sat for several portraits at the request of various friends and patrons, some of whom, like the Duke of Northumberland, wanted to have an image of the famous warrior as a remembrance of their relationship. The duke, who had fought beside Brant during the American Revolution, commissioned Gilbert Stuart to paint Brant's portrait; it hung in the "Duchess' own room" and now hangs in the Print Room of Syon House.[42] Lord Francis Rawdon, Earl of Moira, also a comrade in arms of Brant's, requested that he sit for another portrait by Stuart (Fig. 14). A miniature of it was made for Brant's wife, Christina, and his daughter said that this was the best likeness of her father that she had ever seen.[43] A third portrait was painted by John Francis Rigaud, and this portrait, for which

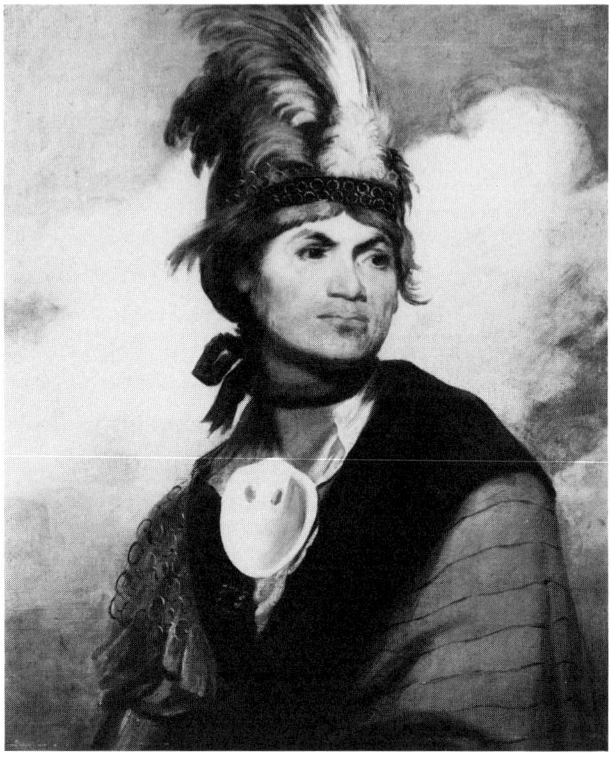

14. Gilbert Stuart, *Joseph Brant*, 1786, oil on canvas.
Courtesy of the New York State Historical Association,
Cooperstown.

Rigaud wanted £50, was, according to Milton Hamilton, Brant's favorite (Fig. 9). He told Rigaud that he would like to purchase it himself
and bring it home. Eventually the painting was sent to him, and it
hung in his home until the mid-nineteenth century, when a fire destroyed it. Fortunately, a nineteenth-century copy was made of it so
that we can see Brant as he wanted to be portrayed, not as the highly
romanticized noble savage that Romney painted or the saddened, defeated warrior, reminiscent of *The Dying Gaul* (a replica of which is
also at Syon House), that Stuart captured in his two portraits.

Stuart's and Romney's portraits are very beautiful, complete with
dramatic play of light and shadow, romantic swirling skies, and feminine pinks, greens, and blues splashed about on the feathers, clothing,

and backgrounds; in contrast, Rigaud's portrait is almost stark in its simplicity. Rigaud's portrait of Brant is, like West's of Guy Johnson, an official portrait. As a captain in the Indian Department, Brant wears an officer's uniform: green coat with epaulets, a black shoulder belt with a silver buckle, and a silver gorget. He is also wearing a feathered headdress decorated with silver rings, which symbolized the Six Nations' covenant chain, and thrown over his shoulder is an Indian blanket.

Brant's wearing of this uniform can be interpreted as an act of what Homi Bhabha calls "colonial mimicry," which is "the affect of hybridity—at once a mode of appropriation and of resistance." In wearing the uniform, Brant looks as if he himself had been appropriated by the Indian Department and the British authorities, as if he were their instrument, and his image seems to become, in Bhabha's words, "the support of an authoritarian voyeurism." But the green coat of the Indian Department signifies resistance also, for, as Bhabha argues, "the insignia of authority becomes a mask, a mockery," and "marks those moments of civil disobedience within the discipline of civility: signs of spectacular resistance."[44] In wearing the green jacket Brant mimics the British, simultaneously recognizing and mocking the authority of the Indian Department.[45] He reproduces on his body an imperfect imitation of a British officer, and in doing so, enacts an ambiguity that calls into question fixed ethnic/national identities and signals the constructedness of British authority.

Performing Sovereignty

Brant's wearing the green military jacket may also be seen as part of his performance designed to make himself recognizable to the British authorities as somehow equivalent to them. Bhabha sees mimicry as an extension of camouflage, but in the case of Brant's uniform, this mimicry is a mimetic act, an attempt to project an image that will somehow be taken for the real thing. Rather than trying to disappear into a British institutional framework, Brant was asserting himself as a member of a people who were not subject to the Crown of England, but, like the British, a sovereign people with sovereign rights. In every interaction with British officialdom, Brant tried to make the British see him as an equal, as a friend and ally, as someone who operated from a parallel position of strength. When Brant was introduced to King George III, he refused to kneel and kiss the king's hand. Not willing to signal his deference to the authority of the king, Brant said he was not the king's subject but rather his ally. In an act of gallantry, however, he did kiss the queen's hand. In his letters to the Duke of Northumberland, Brant would refer to their shared past as comrades in arms in the early years of the American Revolution, signing his letters "Your faithful friend and Brother warrior." [46] In his speech to Lord Sydney, Brant urged the minister to honor the government's promises of friendship, to reward the Indians for their loyalty during the war, and to protect Indian land from American encroachment. Brant said, "We desire to know whether we are to be Considered as his majestys faithfull Allies, and have that Support and Countenance, Such old and true friends Expect." [47]

In asking the British government to honor the terms of their alliance with the Mohawks, Brant was using the "word of the master" against the master himself.[48] He deployed British costume, custom, and law as a strategy to protect Indian lands from British and American depredation. As his biographer writes, "he would dissemble" to the American and British officials, and "he would use their customs against them." [49] Brant's mimicry of British officialdom was, in part, his way of trying to protect his people from disintegration and his lands from dispossession; wearing the green coat was an act of resistance. He performed simultaneously his loyalty as an ally to the king and his resistance to the king's authority by refusing to be the king's subject.

Brant wore his military jacket knowing full well its significance; he was a masterful performer who knew how to employ costume to great effect. In 1780 during the American Revolutionary War, Tories and Mohawks captured a party of rebels and brought them to Fort Niagara as prisoners of war. There the American Captain Snyder was questioned by Guy Johnson and Joseph Brant. In his memoirs Snyder remarked on how magnificently Brant was dressed: "He was a likely fellow, of a fierce aspect—tall and rather spare—well spoken, and apparently about thirty years of age. He wore moccasins, elegantly trimmed with beads—leggings and breech-cloth of superfine blue— short green coat, with two silver epaulets—and a small, lace, round hat. By his side hung an elegant silver-mounted cutlass, and his blanket of blue cloth, purposely dropped in the chair on which he sat, to display his epaulets, was gorgeously decorated with a border of red." [50] A young woman, a prisoner held captive at Niagara, also described Brant as very dramatic in appearance: "The expression of his face was severe and frightful. He was spare and above the medium height of Indians. His dress was very fine; he wore a broadcloth blanket over his shoulders in the usual Indian style, of the finest make, with a deep, rich, red border. When he showed himself about the fort, he was always in full and careful costume, glittering with brooches, etc." [51]

Brant was a careful dresser, always aware that he was posing for an audience, whether in public or in a portrait-painting session. Peggy Phelan, in her discussion of portraiture as performance in her book *Unmarked,* argues that in having one's portrait taken, one can never be oneself because that self is illusionary; one can only act the part of what the viewer expects to see. "Uncertain about what this body looks like or how substantial it is, we perform," Phelan says, "an image of it by imitating what we think we look like. We imagine what people might see when they look at us, and then we try to perform (and conform to) those images. . . . The imitative reproduction of the self-image always involves a detour through the eye of the other." [52] Brant was very aware of these dynamics of representation, especially in portraiture, of creating an image of what the viewer expected to see. In 1806 while visiting the home of his agent, James Caldwell (no relation to Sir John Caldwell), in Albany, Brant was persuaded by the Caldwells to have his portrait painted by Ezra Ames (Fig. 15.) Brant at first protested that he had not brought with him on this trip any Indian clothes and could not be painted without them. Mrs. Caldwell solved the problem by buying some figured calico and quickly sewing an "Indian shirt." His biographer writes: "With the addition of a few beads and an earring, Joseph was able to look as he ought, and he sat for his portrait." [53]

Perhaps the most performative of his attempts at self-representation occurred when he was visiting London in 1786. During his stay and while waiting to discuss with Lord Sydney compensation for the property the Mohawks had lost during the war, Brant was the guest of many fashionable people who entertained him by taking him on tours of the city, to dinner parties, and to the theater. Lord Moira insisted on

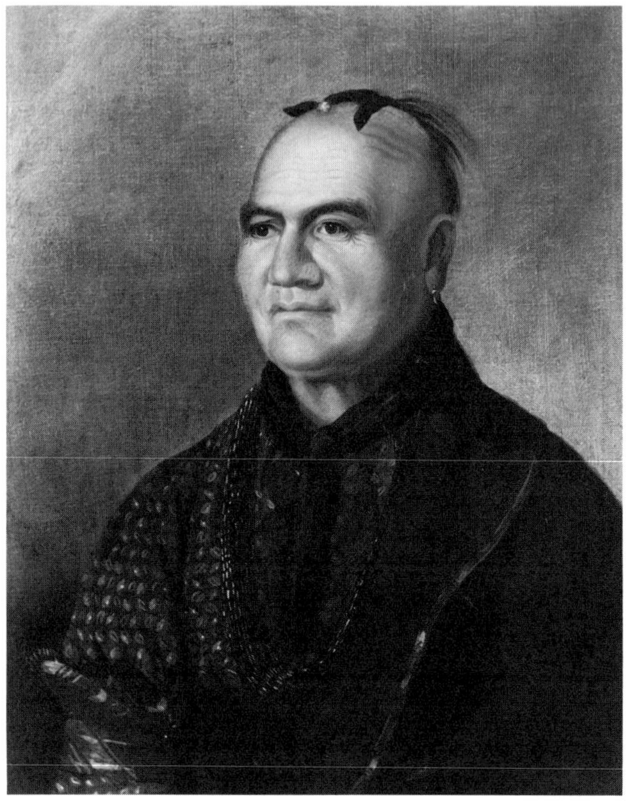

15. Ezra Ames, *Joseph Brant*, 1806, oil on canvas. Courtesy of
the New York State Historical Association, Cooperstown.

taking him to a masquerade where people gathered for entertainment
dressed as "pilgrims and warriors, hermits and shepherds, knights,
damsels, and gipsies." [54] Brant went to the masquerade dressed as an
Indian chief. "Richly dressed in the costume of his nation, wearing no
mask, but painting one half of his face," [55] he wore "a ruffled shirt and
leggings, and a fine blanket which he could carelessly (or carefully) let
fall to disclose his weapons," [56] one of which was a tomahawk. The
crowd contained many fantastically dressed figures, including two
other Indian chiefs, Scottish Highlanders, Turks, and a lady dressed
as a fortress. Brant's costume caught the eye of a man dressed as a
Turkish diplomat, and "mistaking his rouge et noir complexion for
a painted visor, the Turk took the liberty of attempting to handle

his nose. Brant had, of course, watched the workings of his observation, and fell in the humour of the sport." As the Turk reached for Brant's nose, "the Chieftain made the hall resound with the appalling war-whoop, and at the same instant the tomahawk leaped from his girdle, and flashed around the astounded Mussulman's head. . . . The Turk himself trembled with terror, while the female masquers — the gentle shepherdesses, and fortune-telling crones, Turks, Jews and gipsies, bear-leaders and their bears, Sultans, nurses and Columbines, shrieked, screamed and scudded away as though the Mohawks had broken into the festive hall in body. The matter, however, was soon explained, and the incident was accounted as happy in the end as it was adroitly enacted by the good-humoured Mohawk."[57] This incident was reported in the British newspapers, but the papers interpreted Brant's threatening action as a serious response to the masquerader's rude gesture. According to William Stone, one of Brant's early biographers, Brant had acted in jest, and his friends who had taken him to the masquerade knew Brant was playing the part of the proud savage.

Brant's display of his costumed body, carefully constructed to produce a desired effect, was one of the ways that he tried to maintain his position as spokesperson for his people to the British government and as someone to be reckoned with. Hybrid in dress, language, and manners, Brant occupied the middle ground between the British and Indian worlds, traversing the London world of high fashion and the forests of North America with great acumen, courage, and intelligence. Mastering the symbolic orders of two cultures, employing them for his own purposes, Brant fought to maintain the sovereignty of the people he hoped he had represented well. Though he had managed to win from General Haldimand a grant of land consisting of six miles on each side of the Grand River in Canada as a token of British gratitude for Mohawk loyalty, Brant despaired over the loss of their New York lands, wondering if he had failed to protect his people's interests by remaining loyal to the Crown during the American Revolution. On his deathbed he said: "We are an independent people. . . . The English might have lost all America had it not been for the friendship & Assistance of the Indians. . . . Every man thought, that by fighting for the King, we should ensure to ourselves and children a good inheritance. . . . Justice is all I wish for. . . . It seems natural to Whites, to look on lands in the possession of Indians with an aching heart, and never to rest 'till they have planned them out of them. . . . We want nothing more than what we enjoyed before the American War, the land we then lived on was our own and we could do what we pleased with it."[58]

From the Peace of Paris until his death in 1807, Brant fought British and Canadian authorities over Mohawk land rights. He insisted that the Mohawks owned their land in just the same way that any white man owned his land, in freehold tenure and with the right of alienation, that is, the right to sell or to rent their land as they saw fit. Brant delivered the following speech at a council held at Fort Niagara in the presence of several Mohawk chiefs and warriors for the benefit of the government's agent, Colonel William Claus, deputy superintendent general of Indian Affairs (Sir William Johnson's grandson): "We were promised our lands for our services, and these lands we were to hold on the same footing with those we fled from at the commencement of the American war, when we joined, fought, and bled in your cause. Now is published a proclamation forbidding us leasing those very lands that were positively given us in lieu of those of which we were the sovereigns of the soil, of those lands we have forsaken, we sold, we leased, and we gave away, when and often as we saw fit, without the hindrance on the part of your Government, for your Government well knew we were the lawful sovereigns of the soil, and they had no right to interfere with us as independent nations."[59] Canadian authorities argued that the Mohawks had been given the Haldimand grant to use, not to own, and that as wards of the state, they did not have the rights of other landowners. The governor of Canada issued a patent declaring that "no transfer, alienation conveyance sale gift exchange lease property or possession" could be "made or given" by any member of the Six Nations.[60] In addition to not having property rights, the Mohawks of the Grand River were not permitted the legal and political rights that accompanied ownership of land. Francis Gore, lieutenant governor of Upper Canada, wrote to Viscount Castlereagh, foreign secretary, protesting Castlereagh's intention to alter the conditions of the Haldimand grant: "Your Lordship however must be aware, that if they [the Six Nations] are eligible to hold lands by that Tenure, they become subject to His Majesty and entitled to all the privileges of Natural Born Subjects, they will then become Electors, and qualified to be chosen Members of the House of

Assembly. Are we prepared My Lord for such a change? . . . What may not be expected when every Savage in the Country becomes possess'd of the same privilege?"[61] In denying Indians their legal and political rights as owners of land, the Canadian authorities denied them their status as fully realized subjects. They could be objects of charity or reprimand but not masters of their own fates.

When Brant died, the fight did not end. John Norton, Brant's friend and aide, and John Brant, his son, continued to press the government, both traveling to London to argue their case before the Board of Trade and enlisting the help of the Duke of Northumberland, who supported the Mohawk land claims. But when John Brant died suddenly of cholera and John Norton disappeared into Cherokee country in the aftermath of the War of 1812 with the aim of promoting a united Indian nation, also a dream of Brant's, the Grand River Indians lost leaders who, as expert players in the hybrid politics of British America, had skillfully manipulated British laws and customs to promote their struggle for Indian sovereignty.

In wearing the green jacket, Brant had hoped to appropriate the power of the privileged to signal to his viewers his status as a subject and as an agent in the politics of sovereignty. Did he succeed, in the Rigaud portrait, in escaping the position of the romanticized, feminized exotic that he was too often placed in by painters like Romney and Stuart? Brant's construction of himself as hybrid and sovereign creates in the European viewer "mimetic vertigo," which is produced, as Taussig says, when "the "West itself . . . [is] mirrored in the eyes and handiwork of its Others." When these Others reproduce the West on their bodies and in their crafts, the white man is forced to look at himself as an object, "facing himself as Others read him," and when the West is reflected in the "mimetic magic of its Others," then the mastery of the West over its Others is "no longer possible." In displaying his hybridity, the many portraits of Brant destabilize the British/Euro-American viewer's response, disrupting "any possibility of mastering the circulation of mimesis in alterity."[62] Brant's green jacket and his calico "Indian" shirt can send viewers into mimetic vertigo, destabilizing their position as objective observers, causing them to lose their footing in the contest for the subject position. Brant's hybrid dress also signals the impossibility of charting the circuits of desire and capital that permeate and dissolve borders. Destabilizing as this hybridity is to the British and Euro-American viewers' sense of mastery, Brant emerges in his portraits as someone who is at ease in this borderland of fractured and interlocking identities, and as someone who can negotiate this complex world of fragmented allegiances and contending interests.

For Taussig and Bhabha, mimicry and hybridity can be empowering when employed by subalterns like Brant; these displays, they argue, can be destabilizing of imperial hegemonies. However, when British military officers dress in Indian clothing and construct themselves as hybrid, their cultural cross-dressing is not subversive of imperial hegemony. Their mimicry and hybridity worked to maintain the Euro–empire in America. Although Caldwell, Johnson, and Brant are each empowered by their cultural cross-dressing, the political effect of their appropriation of the Other is quite distinct. Caldwell's use of Native American clothing renders Indian cultures incoherent and robs them of their significance. His decontextualizing of Indian artifacts is a classic example of a colonizing strategy that seeks to discredit and devalue native cultures. Also employing an imperialist's trope is Johnson, whose use of Indian clothing, though not as disrespectful as Caldwell's, is an act of appropriation. In wearing Mohawk moccasins, leggings, sash, and blanket, he uses the accoutrements of Mohawk identity to bolster his own and to fuel his personal ambitions. Implicit in Caldwell's and Johnson's cultural cross-dressing is destruction of or depletion of native resources and cultures. They take from native peoples what they want for themselves. When these Britons don Indian garb, the Indian is being displaced by the Briton and his native culture consumed by the foreigner. The implication is that the resources that fuel identity formation are scarce and that competition between Europeans and Indians for these limited resources is intense.

Brant's cultural cross-dressing, unlike Caldwell's and Johnson's, does not partake of the colonizing strategy of decontextualization, nor is it a form of symbolic extraction, as Caldwell's and Johnson's Indian clothing is a mining of Indian culture and power. Brant's cultural cross-dressing does not displace anyone. In wearing the officer's jacket he constructs an identity that is sovereign, and yet it is a sovereignty that does not exist in a state of competition with British subjecthood. Brant's hybrid identity holds out the promise of peaceful coexistence and of exchange, of respect between different but equal parties. Unfortunately, by the mid-nineteenth century, this fragile middle ground of intertwined identities and shared space was obliterated, as Indian cultures, resources, and lands were absorbed into the Euro-American empire. Thus, Caldwell's and Johnson's cultural cross-dressing subtly reveals the cannibalizing dynamics of imperialism.[63]

4

Accommodating India

DOMESTIC ARRANGEMENTS IN ANGLO-

INDIAN FAMILY PORTRAITURE

Cultural cross-dressing for the oppressed and disenfranchised can be empowering, but as we have seen, cultural cross-dressing was also practiced by those in positions of power. The wearing of "native" clothing for Britons often was an index of their ability to master the alien and the exotic. In having their portraits painted wearing native costume, Britons claimed authority over the foreign by displaying alien practices on their bodies. In an act of incorporation, they signaled their pleasure in, and thus their mastery over, the exotic. Sir John Caldwell's portrait of his masquerade as an Indian chief and Lady Mary Wortley Montagu's portrait of herself dressed in Turkish regalia record their sojourns into the unknown, the exotic, and the barbaric and celebrate Britons' successful negotiation of these foreign lands, their survival, and their safe return home. Lady Mary, Caldwell, and Guy Johnson were intensely proud of their experiences among the alien cultures of the Near East and the wilds of North America, respectively, and this pride is visible on their persons in their portraits.

When a European dresses as a native, he or she registers a degree of comfort and familiarity with an alien culture. Cultural cross-dressing, when represented in portraiture, can, therefore, reveal the sitter's attitude toward the exotic culture that he or she has come in contact with. These dynamics of pleasure and mastery are revealed in the portrait of a cultural cross-dresser who resided in India (Fig. 16). In Francesco Renaldi's conversation piece, *A European with his Family* (1794–95), a European man (his identity has been lost), most likely a Briton, is dressed completely as a nawab, a member of the Mughal aristocracy. Renaldi, one of the many British painters who traveled to India to make a small fortune painting portraits of Anglo-Indians and Mughal nawabs, produced this remarkable domestic conversation piece in the 1790s. Like the other cultural cross-dressers we have discussed, this unnamed European's adoption of the clothing of a foreign culture carries with it his attitudes toward that culture. We can read in his clothing, his companions, the surroundings, and his mien his response to the Mughal culture of northern India. In this chapter I examine portraits of Anglo-Indians, the British living in India, for evidence of their pleasures in and anxieties about the people and the land they dominated as agents of British imperialism.

British Gentlemen and Their Bibis

In Renaldi's painting, the European man is surrounded by what seems to be his family: two Indian women and a child. Mildred Archer, expert on British artists in India, suggests that the two women in the painting are the European's two bibis, his two common-law wives, one young and the other older. The child is his offspring, but we do not know which of the two women is the mother. The older woman sits somewhat removed from the others, who form an intimate threesome. The man and younger woman gaze into each other's eyes, he somewhat wistfully and she with intensity. The young bibi leans against him, with one hand resting on his shoulder and the other clutching his arm. He, in turn, has one hand on his son's shoulder and with the other clasps his son's right hand. All these arms and hands link to produce a circle of embraces that excludes the older woman, who gazes in the direction of this happy threesome. The child's eyes break this circle, however, by looking in the direction of the older woman. Is she his mother? Is the child the link to the older bibi? We can only guess, for the man's identity has been lost. But we are not assuming too much when we presume that these two women are this

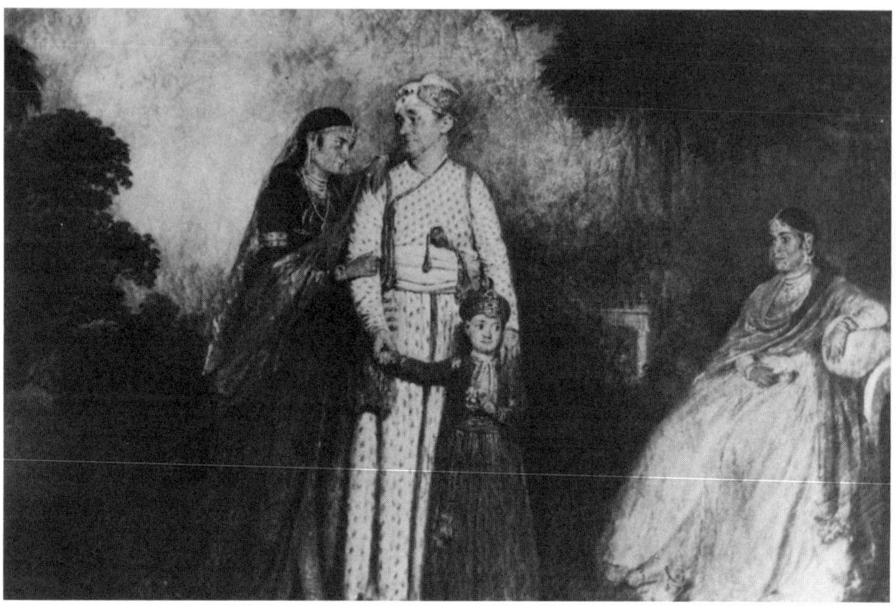

16. Francesco Renaldi, *A European with his Family*, c. 1794–95, oil on canvas. Asiatic Society of Bengal, Calcutta.

European man's bibis, as it was not uncommon for British men living and working in India for long periods of time, decades, even whole lives, to live with Indian women who would assume the position of wife-mistress in the household.[1]

In another Renaldi painting we see a similar domestic relationship, but in this instance the identities of the European and his bibis are known. *The Palmer Family* (c. 1786) depicts a large family with Major William Palmer seated in the center surrounded by his wives, children, and female servants (Fig. 17). Palmer had entered the East India Company's army in 1766 and rose through the ranks to become a general in 1801. In 1776 he became military secretary in Lucknow, and in 1782 Warren Hastings made him his private agent in Oudh. In 1786 he was given command of the 7th Battalion of Sepoys in Calcutta, and in 1798 he was made permanent resident to the Maratha Peswa's court at Poona. According to Palmer's great-granddaughter, Palmer was "a bad old man" who had "two wives."[2] On the left side sits Bibi Faiz Bakhsh, a Muslim lady of aristocratic background with whom Palmer

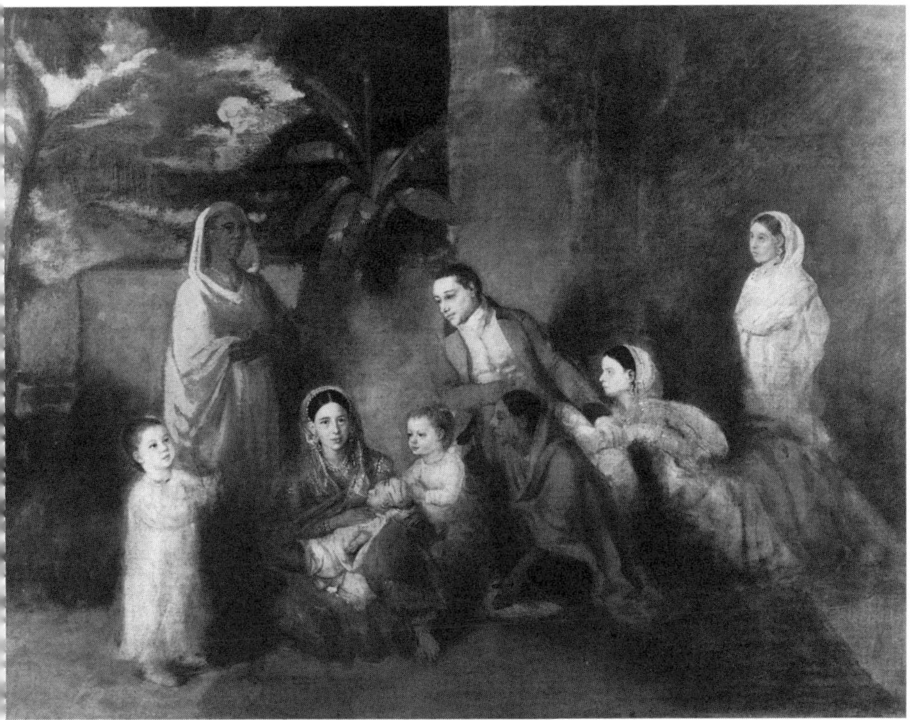

17. Francesco Renaldi, *The Palmer Family*, 1786, oil on canvas.
Oriental and India Office Collections, shelfmark F597. By permission of
The British Library.

lived from 1781 until his death in 1816. In his will he bequeathed to
her his house and described her as "my affectionate friend and companion during a period of more than 35 years." She holds in her lap a
sleeping baby, a boy named Hastings, and on either side of her stands
a toddler, a son William, and a daughter Mary. Of her, Palmer wrote
in 1786 to a friend who had returned to Britain: "Your little Friend
Fyze (sic. ?) sends Bundergee . . . Salaam. She brought me a little Boy
soon after you left Lucknow and another here [Calcutta] last year,
but born dead. I expect another in about four months."[3] On the right
side of the painting sits Palmer's second bibi. Archer believes she is an
aristocratic Muslim lady from Oudh whom Palmer brought into his
household after his removal from Lucknow in 1785. This younger bibi
is childless in the painting, and leans against Palmer's leg. He holds

her hand, but his face is turned away from her and toward Bibi Faiz Bakhsh and her children. Two maidservants stand in opposite corners, echoing the doubling of wives and underscoring the balance between the two sides of the paintings. Renaldi's idyllic rendering of domesticity in the Palmer family portrait conveys the maternal tenderness of Bibi Faiz Bakhsh, the paternal concern of Major Palmer, and the conjugal affection that exists between Palmer and his bibis.[4]

Renaldi's *Palmer Family* and *A European with his Family* represent a serious cultural and moral challenge to English national identity and colonial culture. In having taken Indian wives and producing racially and culturally mixed children, both men appear to have not only succumbed to the "charms" of these beautifully "exotic" women but to have given up themselves to the pleasures of Indian culture. Taking a mistress was generally accepted as a temporary solution to the problem of living abroad without Englishwomen; what was not so acceptable to the thinking of the day was the British men's acculturation to Indian customs and social relations. Perhaps more alarming to British colonial society than the presence of the bibis and their men's apparent affection and lasting attachment was the ease these men felt in the alien culture that was reproduced and maintained by these women. Renaldi's unknown European is *at home* wearing the clothing of a nawab and is at ease living with two wives, something that many Englishmen may have fantasized about but would have felt pressured to reject in keeping with social codes involving notions of respectability. Palmer has retained his British dress but has placed himself in the center of what to the Western colonizing gaze looks like a harem, but which in Indian terms is a household consisting of two wives, three maids, and three children.

Palmer's contented gaze and the unknown European man's sweet face indicate that these men are happy living with women whom British women like Elizabeth Hamilton and Hannah More would have described as morally degenerate and intellectually inferior to British women. As champions of the new cult of domesticity, More and Hamilton, often for rhetorical reasons, would resort to denigrating Muslim cultures for their treatment of women, stressing Turkish and Muslim women's lack of education and repressive social codes that kept them in a helpless state of dependency. In her *Strictures on the Modern System of Female Education* (1799), More writes that under "the laws and the religion of the voluptuous prophet of Arabia," women are excluded from "light, liberty, and knowledge." She continues to say that "in those countries in which fondness for the mere persons of women is carried to the highest excess, *they are slaves; and that their moral and intellectual degradation increases in direct proportion to the adoration which is paid to mere external charms.*" More then turns to a description of Britain, "where our sex enjoys the blessings of liberal instruction, of reasonable laws, of a pure religion, and all the endearing pleasures of an equal, social, virtuous, and delightful [social] intercourse."[5] The new domestic woman that More and Hamilton promoted was a companion to her husband, a nurturing mother, and a disciplined housekeeper. Her concerns were her family's moral and emotional well-being, which she tirelessly promoted. The new domestic woman was pious and disciplined and yet caring and loving, pouring her energies into her family and community.[6]

Palmer's contented gaze acts as an affront to the cult of domestic femininity and to the evolving ideology of British womanhood. His happiness arises out of Indian social customs that are reproduced by Indian women who are represented in Renaldi's paintings as graceful, delicate, shimmering creatures who fawn over their men and whose sexuality is palpable as they seductively lean their bodies against the men's. British women were told by clergymen, moralists, novelists, and conduct book writers to repress their desires in order to be pure and noble; in this way they would earn the respect and love of men. In *Sermons to Young Women* (1766), James Fordyce urges young women to conduct themselves with "humility, contrition, self-denial, solid virtue, and affectionate devotion" so that as wives they will be able to acquire and maintain their husbands' "esteem."[7] But Renaldi's paintings tell another story, in which soft, pliant, and sensual women win the long-lasting love of British men. Renaldi was commissioned to paint several portraits of bibis, a testimonial to British gentlemen's affections for Indian women. As Archer suggests, Renaldi was especially sensitive to "Indian womanhood."[8] These portraits depict bibis as sensuous, graceful, and delicate by carefully reproducing the translucency of their silken robes and glints of light on their profuse jewelry. The face of one bibi in Renaldi's *Muslim Lady Seated with a Hookah* (1787) is, as Archer says, "shy, modest, and reflective and with the same

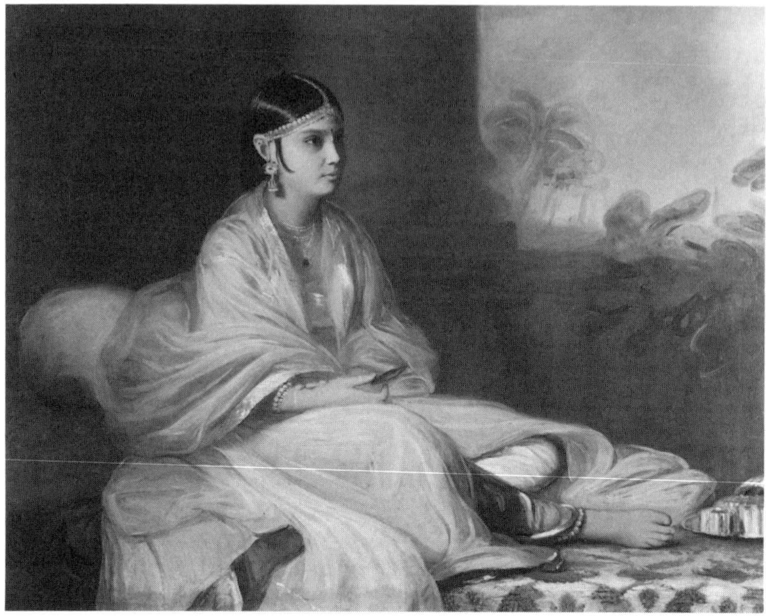

18. Thomas Hickey, *An Indian Girl*, 1787, oil on canvas.
National Gallery of Ireland.

qualities of faithful devotion so clearly present in Palmer's beloved companion."[9] Renaldi's bibis are faithful, devoted, loving, and beautiful, and the British men are attached and affectionate. Thomas Hickey also contributed to this genre when he painted what is thought to be his brother's bibi, Jemdanee, of whom William Hickey wrote: "as gentle and affectionately attached a girl as ever man was blessed with" (Fig. 18).[10]

Francesco Renaldi's *European with his Family, The Palmer Family,* and *Boulone, Bibi of Colonel Claude Martin, Fishing with Martin's Adopted Son* represent a remarkable moment in the history of British and Indian relations when British officers and company employees not only cohabited with Indian women but also adopted the clothing, customs, and familial arrangements of the Indian society in which they lived.[11] Some of the paintings of bibis as the common-law wives of British men belong to the genre of portraits of favorite mistresses; other paintings of bibis, husbands, their children, and extended families are family conversation pieces, much like Zoffany's *The Family of Sir*

William Young (Fig. 4). These paintings by Renaldi present a challenge to British culture, particularly British colonial culture in India, by depicting as appealing a domesticity that is completely alien to British bourgeois notions of domesticity. Renaldi's bibis present a very attractive alternative to British femininity, and Indian customs and social arrangements are portrayed as even more productive of happiness than British culture.[12]

Racial Estrangement

To combat the influence of these bibis, the Indian culture they brought with them, and their racially mixed children, Governor-General Cornwallis in 1793 put into practice race-conscious policies that excluded from government and military office Indians and persons of mixed race. The new colonial administration felt, as C. A. Bayly says, "a deep distrust of miscegenation and the dangers of 'unrestrained colonisation' which was held to increase the likelihood of the mixing of the races."[13] Lord Valentia, a close friend of Wellesley, Cornwallis's predecessor, denounced the people of mixed race: "in every country where this intermediate caste has been permitted to rise, it has ultimately tended to the ruin of that country."[14] Intermarriage between Indian women and British men had resulted in a mingling of cultures reminiscent of the Spanish colonization of South America, where Spanish men married native women, producing a hybrid culture and a creole colonial society. British officials within the company and at home saw a similar kind of colonial practice emerging in India, one that was not like the British methods of settlement in North America or the Caribbean, and one they did not approve of, as it was, for them, too intertwined in Indian social, economic, and political life.

The corruption that ran rampant in the years when Clive and Hastings were in charge of the East India Company was blamed on the company's having assumed Indian social, economic, and political practices. Bayly argues that after 1783 a shift in attitude toward Indians emerged in the "ideologies of state and the mentality of ruling groups both in England and India." "British national character in India," people like Cornwallis and Wellesley thought, "was being undermined by the wiles of the native servants of government and the private Hindu commercial factotums (dubashes and banians) used by Europeans in their private capacity."[15] Cornwallis was sent to reform the company, to purge it of its corruption by instituting policies that removed Indians from all but minor offices, demoted people of mixed race, and prevented the British from mingling in Indian political and commercial structures. Cornwallis objected to the "principles and practices of the native Asiatic governments" and thought that "the corruption spreading from Hindu merchants and Muslim 'tyrants' to the personnel of the Company — exemplified by Hastings' career — was in danger of undermining moral integrity as the basis of good government."[16] Cornwallis practiced a policy of aloofness toward Indian princes and their courts, behaving toward them in a manner "old hands" like Palmer found alarming because insulting to "native dignitaries." Concerned by the studied rudeness of Cornwallis's "mortifying reception" of "Saadit Ally, Mobarem el Dowlah, and N. B. (?) Cawn," Palmer worried that Cornwallis's "most cold and dispiriting style" would offend the "natives" and "estrange them from the person and Government of Lord C. and prevent that cooperation and assistance of which it is but too probable we shall stand in need sooner or later." Palmer mistakenly assumed that Cornwallis's cold manner toward Indian dignitaries was the result of ignorance and bad advice rather than deliberate conduct dictated by a new policy of racial segregation.[17]

Cornwallis's race-conscious policies were part of his effort to separate the British from indigenous communities. According to Bayly, British civil servants were subject to a "new pious standard of behaviour for the once wild Company servants," and they received educations at Haileybury College and Wellesley's Fort William College that sought to isolate them from "the climate and the vices of the people of India" and from the "peculiar depravity" of Indians. In removing the Indian influence from the company's procedures and practices, Cornwallis behaved as though the Indians were responsible for the East India Company's corruption, and as though company employees were in danger of catching moral contagion by proximity with Indians. Bayly suggests that "in a pragmatic, untheoretical way," Cornwallis's reforms were a way of stating "that the social environment and superstitions of Indians made them irredeemably corrupt."[18]

With the introduction of Cornwallis's notion of reform and his anti-Indian policies, British-Indian sexual alliances and domestic arrangements were no longer socially acceptable. Bayly sums up this new morality: "Gone were the days when a senior British resident of Calcutta had himself circumcised to meet the religious requirements of his Muslim womenfolk."[19] Thereafter, as documented in an anonymous cartoon "A Sale of English Beauties in the East Indies" (c. 1800) and in novels of the nineteenth century (e.g., Jane Austen's *Catharine or the Bower* and Charlotte Brontë's *Jane Eyre*), British women were shipped off to India as wives for British military officers, clergy, and company officials. Thus began that peculiar colonial culture of the British Raj, dominated by memsahibs and described in the late nineteenth century by Kipling in such disparaging tones. The cornerstones of this new British society abroad were race and domesticity: racial purity, racial difference, British domesticity, all presided over by a pure British womanhood.[20]

Erasing India

With Cornwallis's reforms and his attempt to remove temptation from company employees by separating the commercial branch from the revenue and administrative branches of the company, a renewed commitment to civic virtue was born in the civil service in India. By the time Wellesley became governor-general in 1798, the effects of Cornwallis's policies could be seen in the conduct of the civilians who were employed under his command. Archer describes these men "of stoical duty" as people who "worked with pious dedication scorning luxury and lackadaisical frolics."[21] Evangelical influence combined with an aristocratic smugness toward commerce produced a new kind of civil servant who would not abuse his position by profiting from it. Philip Lawson describes how Cornwallis tried "to induce Company servants to relinquish their involvement in and need for private trade, along with the unsavoury behavior associated with such transactions," by approving "appointments based on merit with fixed, attractive salary scales."[22] Bayly points out that the professional bureaucrat, this new breed of civil servant, the "virtuous political expert," was supposed to be morally independent from the corrupt-

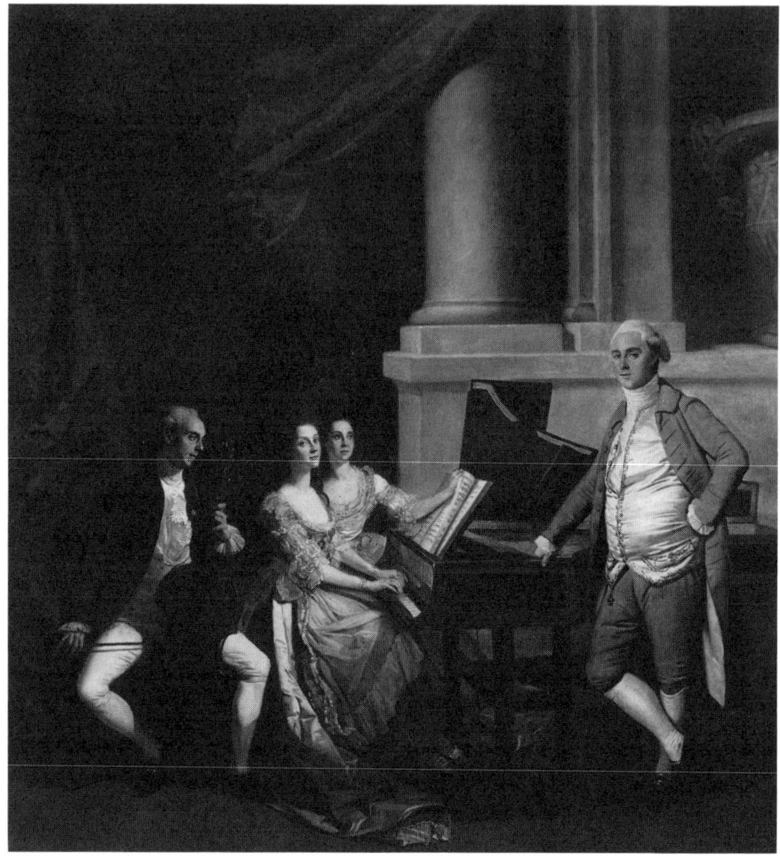

19. Johan Zoffany, *The Morse and Cator Families*, 1784, oil on canvas. City of Aberdeen Art Gallery and Museums Collections, Scotland.

ing influences of "money, sinecure, and hereditary office."[23] His civic virtue was measured not only in terms of his financial independence but also in terms of his independence from Indian customs and practices. "Racial estrangement," as Percival Spear calls the British retreat into its own colonial culture, became a measure of moral conduct.[24]

This new code of conduct that rejected Indian practices and Indian people can be seen in a conversation piece by Johan Zoffany. As Richard Leppert has observed, the painting, *The Morse and Cator Families* (1784) is remarkable for the absence of India in its composition (Fig. 19).[25] The gentleman standing is William Cator, a factor in the

East India Company. He was married to the young woman turning the page of music for the harpsichordist. The women, Sarah and Anne, are sisters, and the cellist is their brother, Robert Morse, who was sheriff of Calcutta and advocate of the Supreme Court.[26] The men represent the administrative and commercial sides of the activities of the East India Company, and yet nowhere in the painting is there a clue to their professions. Compared with Zoffany's almost mannerist rendering of Chief Justice Elijah Impey, whose robes and wig declare his official function (Fig. 12), the Morse-Cator portrait does not contain any of the paraphernalia that would refer to their professions. The obvious explanation for the absence of referents to the police or commerce is that portraits such as Impey's are official portraits, meant to portray the men in their professional function, whereas the Morse-Cator painting is a family conversation piece. True to the demands of the genre, all public duties and functions are eliminated in the representation of the private sphere. Although it is understandable that the India that Morse and Cator dealt with on a professional basis would not be allowed to enter into this painting's iconography, India in its more domestic manifestations is also absent from this painting. The Morse-Cator family scene is strictly British, admitting of no Indian influences at all. No tiger rug is spread beneath the harpsichord; no hookah stands ready for the pleasure of the gentlemen (and ladies); no Indian servant waits in the distance for his master's call; and no banyan tree or plantain peeks in through the window. We see only neoclassical columns, drapes, a Greco-Roman urn, European musical instruments, and the latest London fashions. India exists in this painting, as Richard Leppert remarks in his brilliant essay on colonial culture in India, only as a "semiotic 'present absence.'"[27] India, along with its potential to undermine British justice and commerce, is erased. In removing India from the domestic scene, the Morse-Cator family ensures the purity of the women who preside over the interior space and, even more important for the running of the empire, the absence of India guarantees the incorruptibility of the men who perform their duties in the public world of business and government.

The elegant scene depicted in Zoffany's *Morse and Cator Families* is one in which ladies and gentlemen enjoy an evening of refined amusement gathered around the harpsichord.[28] The private life represented in the Morse-Cator painting is one of adult companionship and rational amusement. Surrounded by the classical architecture, the sitters play music and participate in a culture that, as Leppert argues, values the regularity and harmony of mathematical relations that undergird neoclassical architecture and European music. The harpsichord and the column, as Leppert says, "serve as the standard-bearers of Western self-image: refinement (high culture) in the case of the former, strength and historical patrimony (civilization) for the latter."[29] The neoclassical architecture so beloved by the British in India embodied in stone the mathematical principles of order and symmetry. Harmony, instead of melody, was to dominate eighteenth-century notions of music and was conceived as an extension of mathematics. According to Leppert, music theorists like John Keeble and Jean-Philippe Rameau sought to rationalize the study of music by placing it within the realm of mathematics. Searching for a way to quantify and measure music, Rameau wrote: "all music is founded on harmony, which arises from natural principles derived from the mathematical and physical bases of a vibrating body."[30] An appreciation of European music and architecture implies much more than the simple and immediate feelings of pleasure that are aroused in response to beauty. To appreciate the music the Morse-Cator family is playing requires intellectual faculties such as an aptitude for abstract thinking and the higher-level cognitive skills that are called into play by mathematical relations.

The domestic scene represented in the Morse-Cator portrait partakes of a very different ethos from the domesticity of the Palmer family portrait. The Morse-Cator families derive their pleasures from European Enlightenment values of order, harmony, and reason, and the Palmer family's pleasures seem more sensual and based in the body. Glinting light, luminous colors, and swirling shapes are predominant in the unfinished Palmer painting. Colonel Palmer's fond paternal gaze and the maternal tenderness that shines on Bibi Faiz Bakhsh's face rise above the swirl of saris and the cluster of small children and nursemaids that occupy the foreground of the painting. Children are absent from the Morse-Cator portrait. Although both ladies had had babies the year before they sat for this group portrait, neither child is depicted or referred to. Perhaps the logistics of getting sitters to Calcutta and the brevity of Zoffany's stay in that city dictated who was included in the portrait. (Also missing from the portrait is the harpsichordist's husband, Nathaniel Middleton.) Whatever the reason for the children's not appearing in the painting, their absence emphasizes the rationality of the adults' amusements and the intellectual content of their play. They participate in the refined, cerebral pleasures that only educated Europeans could appreciate. European high culture, represented in this painting by architecture and music, was considered to be culturally superior to anything India could muster. In 1833 Macaulay would summarize what in the late eighteenth century was becoming the British colonial attitude toward India when he said that European arts, philosophy, and morality represented the "triumphs of reason over barbarism," presenting India with an "imperishable empire of our arts and our morals, our literature and our laws."[31] The Morse and Cator families declare their cultural superiority to India by displaying their musical talents; by including women in these rational pleasures, the British men declare themselves morally superior to their Indian counterparts.

A Managed India

The Morse and Cator families' erasure of India and Major Palmer's embracing of India represent the opposite ends of a spectrum of behaviors that the British displayed toward the place and the people of India. The remarkable absence of India in the Morse and Cator family portrait indicates a total rejection of things Indian, as if "everything Indian . . . [was] irrational, superstitious, barbaric, and typical of an inferior civilization."[32] The Morse-Cator family portrait represents an extreme position with regard to India. Most portraits of British families living in India contain references to India by including Indian servants, objects, and landscapes because most wanted to have their stay in India documented. These family portraits reveal a range of attitudes that the British held with respect to the alien culture that India presented to these sojourners.

Unlike the erasure of India in the Morse-Cator family portrait, India's presence is admitted into another domestic conversation piece by Zoffany, *Colonel Blair with his Family and an Ayah* (1786; Fig. 20). Like the Morse and Cator portrait, this painting depicts a family gathered around a musical instrument, not, as Leppert points out,

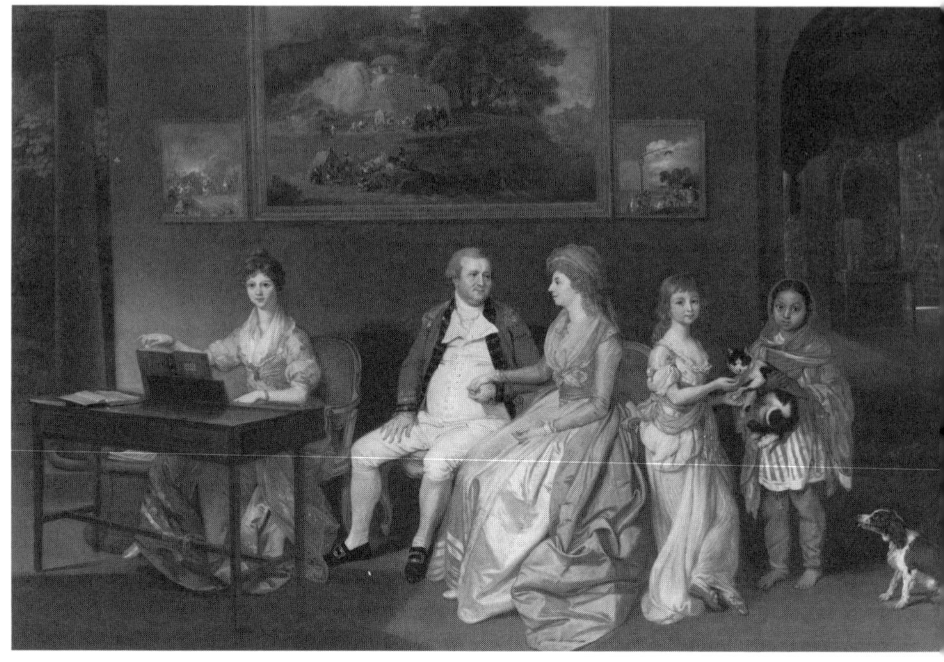

20. Johan Zoffany, *Colonel Blair with his Family and an Ayah,* 1786, oil on canvas. Courtesy of Spink-Leger Pictures, Ltd.

the huge and expensive harpsichord of the Morse-Cator group, but a smaller, square piano, more modest and middle class in its associations. The interior space of the Blair painting is more specific and realistically rendered than the heavily ideological column, curtain, and urn of the Morse-Cator painting. The Blair family is occupying a real sitting room with dim lighting, functional furniture, doorways leading into halls, and paintings on the wall. Less grand in its pretensions to high culture, the Blair family portrait stresses familial harmony and emotional attachment. Colonel Blair is holding his wife's hand and gazing into her eyes, and Mrs. Blair's attention is focused on her musical daughter. The younger daughter caresses a cat in the arms of a maid while a seemingly jealous dog looks up at the cat's enviable position. The younger daughter and the maid are about the same size and look as if they are playmates, judging by their shared interest in the cat.

India is present in this painting most obviously in the form of the maid, who is shown to be an emotionally significant member of the household by her proximity to the littlest Blair. The ayah's youth, gender, and generally sweet air make her incorporation into this British household a fairly modest and easy task. She presents nothing intimidating or frighteningly alien. She does not threaten the British order that dominates this interior space. India is also represented, as Leppert suggests, by the paintings hanging on the wall, paintings that depict typical and exclusively Indian scenes of villages, temples, and elephants carrying people and packages. The India represented in these paintings does not threaten British dominance over the India they rule. As paintings, they are neatly framed packages of interpreted and reproduced India, perhaps paintings that Zoffany himself had painted for the Blairs. The other item that calls India's presence into the portrait is Colonel Blair's uniform. Unlike the absence of referents to the men's official roles in the Morse-Cator portrait, Colonel Blair declares quite boldly his relation to India, one that required him to exercise military power to maintain British dominance over India. Colonel Blair's uniform, his paintings, and the family's ayah convey this family's attitude toward India as being simultaneously intimate with it, incorporating a judicious amount of it into their home, and yet extending over India British control.[33]

The India that is present in this conversation piece is an India contained and firmly located on a hierarchical grid. As Leppert argues, the framed paintings-within-the painting present a British-ordered India despite the absence of things British or European in the paintings; the ayah, as a servant and a child, is at the bottom of the household hierarchy despite her parallel position with the younger daughter alluded to by her proximity and shared interest. Colonel Blair's military jacket announces his own and, by extension, his family's mingling with things Indian, but it is a relation that is dominated by hierarchies that ensure that the British are always on top and in control. India is appreciated by the Blairs, it is even incorporated into this household, but its potential to disrupt and corrupt is contained and not allowed to upset the British order of this domestic space.[34]

Mingling with the Natives

In yet another Zoffany group portrait music is also featured, but instead of European instruments and music, this painting depicts Indian

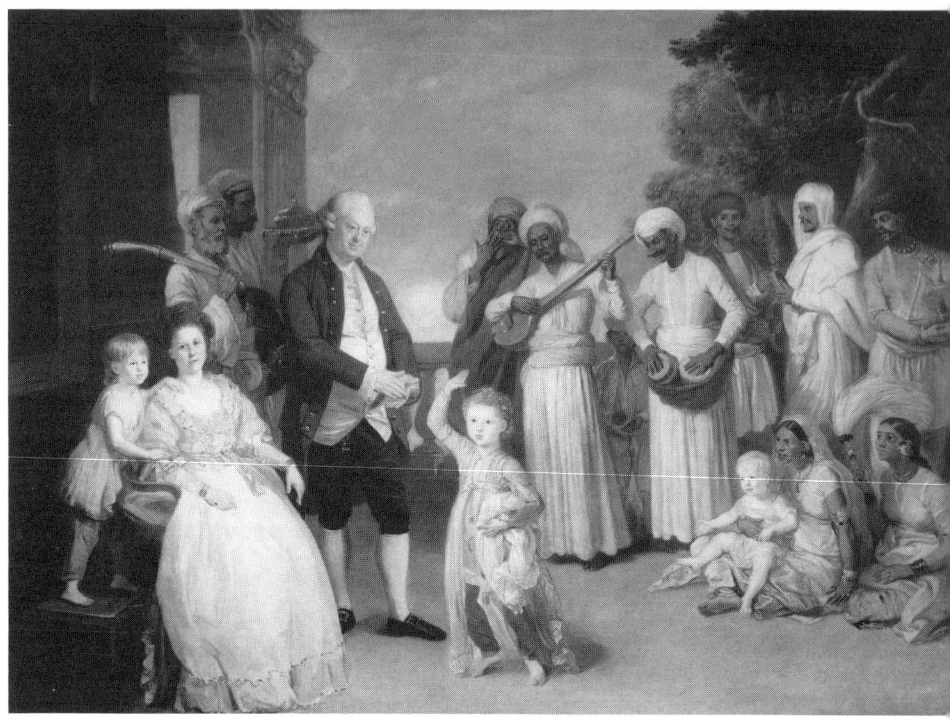

21. Johan Zoffany, *The Impey Family Listening to Strolling Musicians*, c. 1783–84, oil on canvas. Private collection. Sold at Christie's April 18, 1986, lot 132. Photo © Christie's.

musicians entertaining a British family. Far from excluding the presence of India, *The Impey Family Listening to Strolling Musicians* (c. 1783–84) contains the figures of ten Indians, musicians and servants, in addition to the five members of the Impey family (Fig. 21). Sir Elijah Impey, chief justice of the High Court and friend of Warren Hastings, stands near the center of the painting, clapping his hands to the music as if to encourage his small daughter's dancing; his wife sits, looking off into the distance with a somewhat dazed expression on her face, and two smaller children, one on the right and one on the left sides of the painting, look on at the festivities. The children are dressed in Indian clothes, and the dancing daughter moves in the Indian style, her hand crooked over her head. One child rests against Lady Impey while another, a toddler, sits somewhat restively in the lap of an Indian nursemaid. The dancing child is at the center of the composition, with her parents and the musicians forming a half circle around her. The background is divided into two halves, with the columned Impey mansion on the left and a banyan tree on the right.

Unlike the Morse-Cator portrait, India is definitely present in this painting, from the banyan tree to the ayahs to the musicians, and it is an India embraced and enjoyed by British people. Only Lady Impey looks somewhat removed from the happy scene, her gaze traveling out of the painting and into our space, as if asking for our tolerance and understanding. Sir Elijah looks fondly on his daughter who, dressed in Indian-style loose trousers and flowing gown, is intent on her performance. The India that is present in this painting is not the contained, packaged, and boxed India of the Blair family portrait. The India of the Impey painting is powerfully present in the numbers of Indians depicted. Not children, as in the Blair painting, these servants are grown men who carry out their rather meaningless jobs with ceremonial dignity and women who care for the youngest Impeys with tenderness. The Indian figures are depicted as distinct individuals with varying responses to the scene at hand; by individualizing them, Zoffany dignifies the Indian figures. The musicians gain importance not only because the detailed rendering lends them weight but also because they are the organizing principle of the scene depicted. They have the power to entertain and to captivate the Impey family's attention: the chief of the Supreme Court claps his hands in time to their music, and his daughter is caught up in the dance. India is rendered seductive in this Zoffany conversation piece; the Impeys are portrayed as people who can appreciate the arts and culture of India and even know with their bodies India's sensual and aesthetic pleasures. Their appreciation of India is not the remote scholarly, intellectual interest that was adopted by botanists like William Roxburgh and linguists like Sir William Jones. This painting suggests that the Impeys knew India intimately and could dabble in its pleasures without being overwhelmed by powerful stimuli.[35]

Zoffany's arrival in Calcutta coincided with the last two years of Warren Hastings's tenure as governor-general and Impey's tenure as chief justice. Both of these men were Zoffany's patrons, employing him to paint several portraits of themselves and their families. In 1783 and 1784 the administration of the East India Company was under attack in Parliament and in London's popular press. At this time critics of the Company and its servants accused not only Warren Hastings of abusing power but also Sir Elijah Impey of corruption in the administration of British justice in Calcutta. Impey passed the sentence of execution upon Warren Hastings's Hindu adversary, Nanda Kumar, who had been accused of forgery. Macaulay said of Impey's action: "No rational man can doubt that he took this course in order to gratify the Governor-General."[36] If these critics had seen Zoffany's painting of the Impey family, they might have seen in it evidence of Impey's corruptibility, for in their eyes his readiness to embrace and enjoy Indian culture made him suspect. The Impeys' intimacy with Indian culture and their willingness to welcome Indians into their domestic sphere might have made them guilty in the eyes of reformers like Cornwallis of an association that could only lead to corruption of British authority and morality. But although the Impeys enjoy Indian culture, they are not represented by Zoffany as completely acculturated into Mughal manners and mores, as is Renaldi's Colonel Palmer and the unknown European dressed as a nawab. In this Zoffany painting, the interaction between Indians and Britons takes place in a neutral zone, in a space that is in between areas clearly defined as British — the upright columns of the Impey neoclassical mansion — and as Indian — the twisted branches of the banyan tree. Though Sir Elijah claps his hands to the Indian music, he is not necessarily moved by it. He is indulging his daughter by participating in her display. And she, clothed in Indian attire, is not necessarily swept away by the music. She is performing, playing the role of a dancing girl, adopting momentarily the stance and guise of an Indian. Because she is a child, her playful adoption of Indian forms may not have been interpreted as corrupting or damaging, for her mother is there to provide a corrective influence. Lady Impey's eyes, which stare out of the painting at us, assure us that she is emotionally removed enough from this scene of excitement to be a quiet reminder of British domestic manners and morality. Zoffany makes her presence a force of moderation and remediation; her queenly repose may have quieted Hastings's critics with the promise of the continued reign of British feminine domesticity in this foreign place.

Sharing Space

The interaction between the Indian musicians and the Impeys occurs in a no-man's-land, in a liminal space that is neither British-controlled nor Indian-dominated. The representation of space that can accommodate the culture and institutions of both Indians and Britons is found in the work of Arthur William Devis, the nineteenth child of Arthur Devis, an artist who specialized in country house and garden portraits. The younger Devis's portraits of Anglo-Indians depict Indians in British offices, drawing rooms, and gardens and Britons in Indian landscapes. Devis arrived in India in 1784 via the Far East and Polynesia, where he had served as draughtsman for an exploratory expedition. Mildred Archer suggests that his experience in Polynesia of recording exotic peoples and places made Devis sensitive to India's landscape and people. His paintings of Anglo-Indians are, as a result, full of India, its presence felt in his careful depictions of a variety of servants and officials and in his lyrical representation of Indian landscape.[37]

Of several portraits that place Anglo-Indians in outdoor settings, Devis's *Lady Chambers* (1784–85) contains not the usual idealized exotic landscape but the representation of a specific place, the Chamberses' garden house at Bhawanipur. Archer notes that this technique of "placing sitters on their own estates" was something that separated him from his rival painters in India. Devis's sensitivity to landscape and attention to local detail give his portraits the added dimension of specificity of place that is missing from the vague and idealized backgrounds found in most portraits. Archer speculates that the younger Devis may have learned this idiom from his father's many country house portraits.[38] Specificity of place is attended to in the accompanying portrait of her husband, Sir Robert Chambers, who is dressed in his judicial gowns and seated before a window of the New Court House that opens out onto a prospect containing the Hooghly River.[39]

Country houses and their gardens figure in a number of portraits. Robert Grant and his wife are placed against a huge dark and twisted banyan tree which stands on their country house's grounds along the Hooghly River. Charles Russell Crommelin lounges against the gnarled trunk of a massive tree, his neoclassical villa in the back-

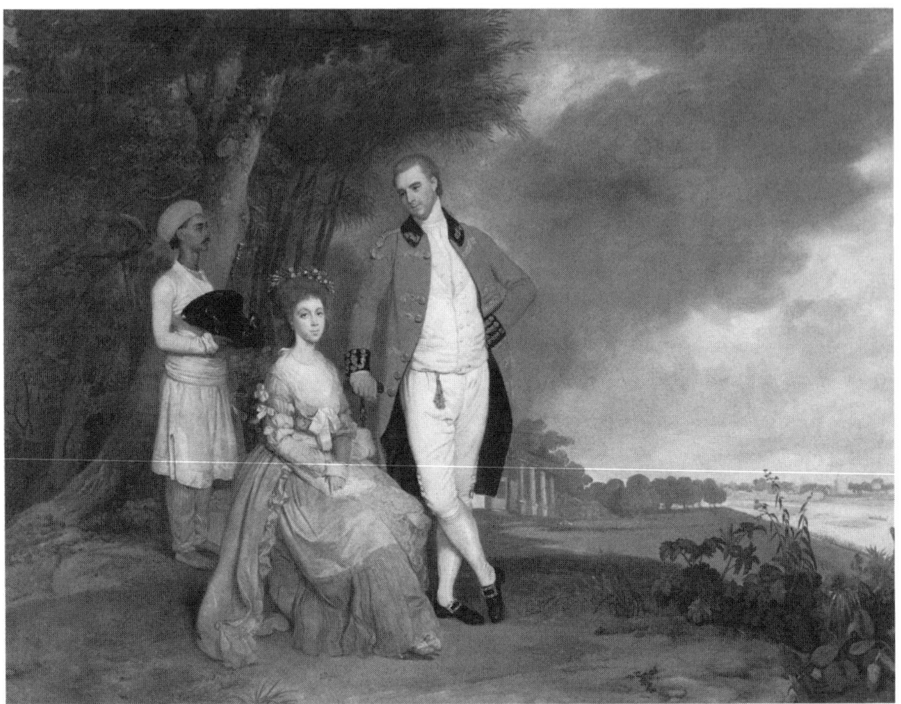

22. Arthur William Devis, *The Honorable William Monson and His Wife, Ann Debonnaire*, c. 1786, oil on canvas. Los Angeles County Museum of Art, William Randolph Hearst Collection.

ground. The Honorable William Monson, his wife, and their servant are placed against a dark clump of trees and the background of a river winding past their columned country villa (Fig. 22). Of the many portraits that Devis painted containing references to real gardens and houses, two paintings, a pair, of a husband and wife on the grounds of their estate, are particularly careful to represent a specific place as well as a specific time.

Devis's portraits *Louisa Dent and her Children* (1790; Fig. 23) and *William Dent with his brother John and an Indian Landlord, Anand Narain* (1790; Fig. 24) commemorate three events: the visit of Dent's brother, who served in the Bengal Infantry; the acquisition of this estate; and the completion of their house. The portrait of Mrs. Dent and her two little children shows her seated in front of the twisting trunk

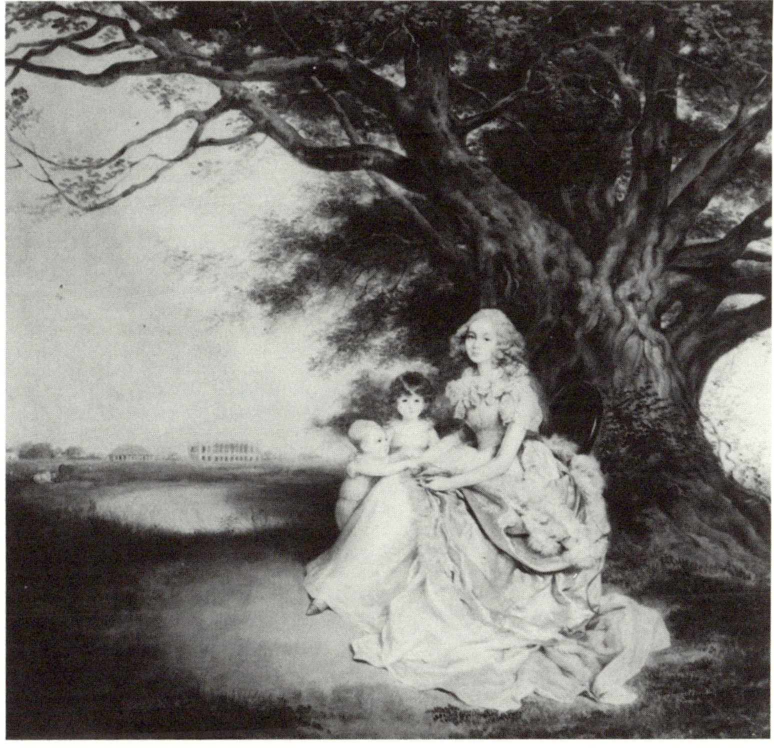

23. Arthur William Devis, *Louisa Dent and her Children*, 1790, oil on canvas. Private Collection. Photograph courtesy of Sotheby's.

and branches of a pipal tree; beyond her in the background is a lake, and beyond the lake is the Dent house, a newly constructed Palladian villa. The painting performs double duty by capturing the likenesses of Mrs. Dent and her children and documenting the Dents' extensive property and grand house. The painting conforms to all the conventions of country house portraiture in which the owners are placed in their beautiful gardens that front their manor houses. The portrait of William Dent contains a bit more than just the lyrical representation of landscape and attractive people. The lake that in Mrs. Dent's portrait glows and shimmers in the distance is seen from a slightly different angle in the Dent brothers' portrait; it is depicted as a work site: a barge floats on it and several laden men walk along its shores. The landscape captured in the Dent brothers' portrait is one that

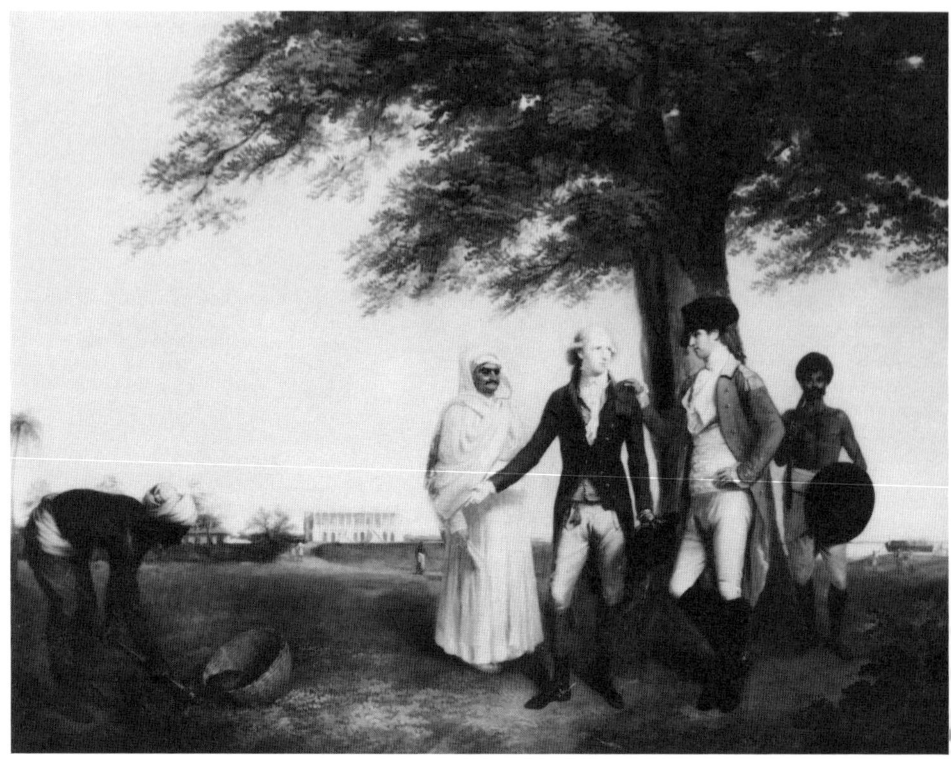

24. Arthur William Devis, *William Dent with his brother John and an Indian Landlord, Anand Narain*, 1790, oil on canvas. Private Collection. Photograph Courtesy of Sotheby's.

is criss-crossed with economic exchanges. The barge is only one instance of the omnipresence of trade in this painting. William Dent resided in Tamluk because, as a member of the Bengal civil service, he was posted there as salt agent of that salt-producing district. The painting commemorates an economic exchange: the receipt of a deed of leasehold title to land by William Dent from the landowner, Anand Narain. Paired, these paintings offer an interesting view on British life in India. Louisa Dent's portrait presents the aesthetically pleasing aspects of their domestic life in Tamluk, and William Dent's portrait alludes to the economic base supported by military force that together maintained the beautiful house, giving us a glimpse into the economic and legal transactions that were a part of British living in India.

India is accorded more weight in this pair of paintings than in most late-eighteenth-century Anglo-Indian portraits. India is not just alluded to, as in the Blair family portrait; here is a tangible India with its land, trees, people and their work represented, and it is an India that is portrayed as an arena for British economic and social action. These paintings portray various exchanges being transacted; some of them are financial and legal, others aesthetic and emotional. On one level of exchange, we see a Briton eager to obtain land on which to build a mansion and thereby to reproduce in India the lifestyle of the landed gentry, imposing on India a British social and economic order. But for William Dent to obtain his seventeen-acre estate (too small to be a real estate in the English sense), he has to pay the Indian owner of this land an annual fee. The presence of the Indian landlord, Anand Narain, is a reminder of who the landowners in India really were, and of pre-British landowning economies that were long-lived, well established, and of ancient origin. The India that the figure of the landlord brings with him into the painting is an India that can absorb British activities into its already time-tested and flexible economic structures. The question arises about the Dent-Narain interaction, Who is dominating whom? The building of the house is one attempt to place a British structure on top of an Indian landscape. The military brother and his Indian orderly holding his shield and sword are reminders of British military might and conquered territories. The Indian laborer who is digging up the piece of sod for the feoffment ceremony is performing an action that has its meaning in British law and custom. He has two masters: British law that instituted such practices and the Indian landlord who is acting in accordance with British law.

In the process of imposing their will on India, these Britons are changed by their contact with the land and the people. They are even absorbed into the Indian landscape and made a part of it. Devis captures this moment of incorporation by making the folds in Mrs. Dent's dress, the curls in her hair, and her feathered shawl mirror the rococo twists and turns of the pipal tree's trunk and branches. The curve of the tree's largest branch is reflected in the curve of the outline made by Mrs. Dent's back and skirt. Even though English order is being imposed on this land with the construction of the Palladian house and, as Archer says, "extensive grounds reminiscent of English parkland,"[40] the mirroring of Mrs. Dent and the Indian tree under-

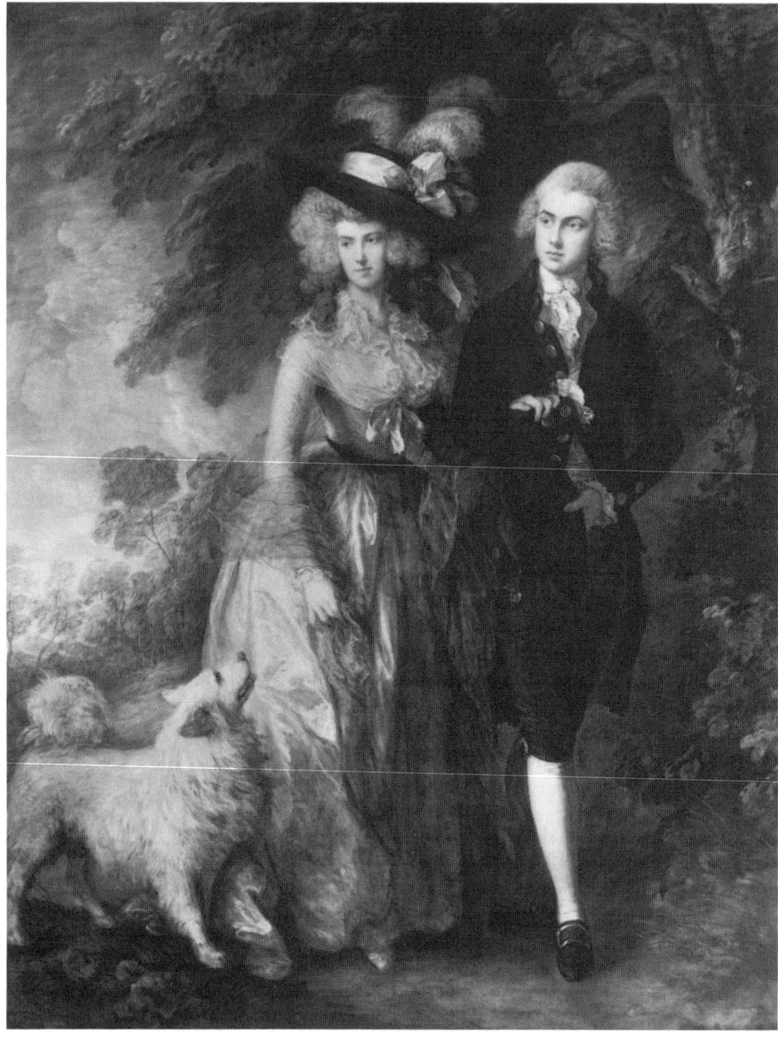

25. Thomas Gainsborough, *The Morning Walk*, 1785, oil on canvas.
Reproduced courtesy of the Trustees, The National Gallery of Art, London.

cuts the power of British structures to transform India, for India is subtly transforming the Britons who occupy it.

By echoing in Mrs. Dent's gown the rococo movement of the tree's trunk, Devis was doing what Gainsborough has been praised for in several of his portraits. In *The Morning Walk*, for instance, Gainsborough gives to the hair and dress of Mrs. Elizabeth Hallett the same wispy, blowing quality that he gives to the coat of their accompanying dog and the tree that stands over the happy couple (Fig. 25). Critics have noted the romantic quality of this painting, the subtle union of nature with human activity.[41] In his Dent portraits Devis may only have been employing Gainsborough's trick of repeating natural patterns in the arrangement and dress of his sitters. But when Gainsborough paints a Briton so that his body imitates the natural world around him and when Devis does the same, the difference in effect is enormous, for in Devis's paintings the natural world is not British but Indian. In Gainsborough's portrait of John Plampin, Plampin's legs are arranged in a way that imitates the positions of branches that loom over him so that together his legs (and his dog's) and the branches of the tree form the bent spokes of a wheel, creating the feeling that this young man is actively engaged in the use and enjoyment of his country estate, that he is "rooted" in the land and is a part of the countryside. When Devis places the two Dent brothers under a neem tree, and their upright stance imitates the tree's straight and sturdy trunk, the iconography of their pose is somewhat confused. Gainsborough, Stubbs, and even the elder Devis often placed British gentlemen against the background of a spreading oak tree to underscore their family's heritage, their moral integrity, and their staunch English independence. But what does it mean when two Englishmen are placed against a neem tree? What associations can such a tree carry for the English viewer or even the Anglo-Indian viewer? Certainly not the same as an oak tree. And in Devis's decision to paint Mrs. Dent's swirling gown in imitation of the swirling patterns on the bark of the pipal tree behind her, did he also send a rather confused message about Mrs. Dent and her susceptibility to the beauty of India? Mrs. Dent does not sit aloof as does Lady Impey, whose abstracted look indicates that she is emotionally removed from the power of India to erode British order. In Devis's desire to record accurately the Indian landscape, combined with his flair for baroque patterning and for putting his sitters in romantic poses, he managed to produce portraits that are almost subversive in that they hint of India's power to absorb British activity and thereby dilute British authority.

British Colonial Culture

The last fifteen years of the eighteenth century were a time of transition, from the wild days of the nabobs, the merchant-kings of the old East India Company, to the newly reformed and government-regulated civil branch of the East India Company. As with all transitions, this one did not happen at a uniform rate. The new ideology of the professional elite was coterminous with customs and habits belonging to the previous generation of company employees. As we have seen, as late as 1795 Renaldi was painting portraits not only of bibis but also of a completely culturally cross-dressed European surrounded by his two bibis and child. Wearing Indian attire had been commonplace for British men in the seventeenth and most of the eighteenth century, especially indoors, as Indian clothing, loose and cool, was much more comfortable than British clothing. However, by the end of the century these "loose coats" were frowned upon, and in the early nineteenth century a government order prohibited Britons from wearing native dress.[42] The nawabi attire of Renaldi's European shows him to be a holdout from another era, a proponent of a hybrid culture that was fast disappearing. Other men in the Company's employ who held onto the residual ideology of the old days were Renaldi's patron, Major General Claude Martin, and Zoffany's patron Colonel Antoine Polier, both of whom carried on their relations with their bibis throughout this period. When Martin died in 1800 he left his adopted son a pension on the condition that he care for all of Martin's female dependents, which included his bibis and their daughters, as well as the children of British gentlemen who had abandoned their mixed-race children when they had returned to Britain.[43]

Attitudes toward India and Indians changed with the advent of bureaucratic reform. According to Bayly, Cornwallis and later Wellesley "fostered a climate of opinion in which drinking, gambling, liaisons with Indian women and gross peculation were no longer admired or tolerated."[44] With this new climate of reform came racial estrangement, so that in 1807 when Lord William Bentinck was governor of Madras, he was able to say, "We do not, we cannot, associate with the natives. We cannot see them in their houses and their families. We are necessarily very much confined to our houses by the heat; all our wants and business which could create a greater intercourse with the native is done for us, and we are in fact strangers in the land." If socializing with Indians was impossible by Bentinck's time, racial mixing was even less acceptable. Bentinck recognized that one of the strengths of the Mughal empire was its policy of intermarriage with their conquered peoples: "In many respects the Mohammendans surpassed our rule; they settled in the countries which they conquered; they intermixed and intermarried with natives; they admitted them to all privileges; the interests and sympathies of the conquerors and conquered became identified. Our policy has been the reverse of this; cold, selfish and unfeeling; the iron hand of power on the one side, monopoly and exclusion on the other."[45] Bentinck's observations get at the heart of the British in India and one of the reasons why they never formed a creole colonial society like those that developed in Spanish South America.[46] The failure to develop a creole colonial society in India was due in part to the failure to develop an interracial elite, one that would have distinguished itself from the metropolitan center and struggled to wrest political power away from Parliament and the Board of Directors of the East India Company.[47]

The British segregated themselves from the surrounding Indian communities, but they also keep themselves apart from each other. By the middle of the nineteenth century the British, according to P. J. Marshall, "did not even constitute a single community on their own." The British in Calcutta, for instance, did not associate much with the British in Madras. Civil servants, army officers, and Britons who were not affiliated with either of these institutions "tended to keep their distance from one another," and class distinctions within British ranks remained even sharper in British India than at home. Marshall contends that "beyond certain mild eccentricities of lifestyle, no clear British-Indian identity ever emerged." Many factors, including the absence of an interracial elite, prevented the development of a creole colonial society, factors such as the huge indigenous population, the complexity of local Indian mercantile economies, and a well-developed peasant agricultural economy as well as the structure of the East India Company itself. Although these difficulties were readily apparent in the eighteenth century, it was not yet clear that the British would not form a colony of settlement like Canada, Jamaica, or Australia, that instead India would become a Crown colony dominated by an official British presence rather than by settlers and the descendants of settlers. Marshall argues that India's fate as a Crown colony, a "colony of exploitation," was not predetermined, and for contemporaries in the late eighteenth century this outcome was not "as inevitable as in retrospect it seems to have been." [48]

Despite the fact that the British never formed a coherent colonial culture, they were, as Marshall suggests, "something more than a collection of British people living temporarily abroad." [49] In their struggle to deal with India and to maintain a sense of their own Britishness, they managed to produce a variety of responses to their sojourn that can be seen in the paintings discussed above. Each painting represents a different way of coping with India, from acculturation to accommodation to estrangement. Not yet hardened into a position of rejecting the influence of Indian culture, some Anglo-Indians in the late eighteenth century could, like the Impeys, appreciate what India had to offer them and enjoy, even relish, their very privileged position in India. Others asserted their superiority over the India they experienced as fascinating but disturbing or as deplorable and corrupting.

The portraits of Anglo-Indians from the late eighteenth century capture the transition from one kind of colonial culture to another, from a time when Company officials would have had themselves circumcised to suit their Muslim bibis to the more evangelically inflected era ushered in by Cornwallis and his race-conscious policies. By Bentinck's tenure in the early nineteenth century, social distance between the British and Indians was considered key by Company officials to maintaining the authority and prestige of the British ruling elite. In 1793 Henry Dundas, president of the Board of Control that oversaw the East India Company, explained to Parliament that India could best be ruled by an aloof elite who would conduct themselves like gentlemen and would awe the Indians with "the superiority of the European character." [50] The degree of aloofness that company officials maintained varied, of course, but in general the British became strangers in the land they had conquered.

5

❧❀❧

Taxonomy and Agency in Brunias's

West Indian Paintings

In my efforts to explore the significance of cultural encounters depicted in late-eighteenth-century colonial art, I have read clothing
semiotically, as a language of signs to be decoded.[1] The orientalized
livery of the black servants and the feminized feathers and jewelry of
Penn's Indians code their wearers as exotic, while the clothing of the
cultural cross-dressers performs mimicry, parody, and hybridity, all
forms of border crossing and the doubling that comes with living in
two cultures simultaneously. Clothing plays a central role in a series of
small (12" × 9") oil paintings by Agostino Brunias, who, in the 1770s,
painted pictures of the people he encountered during his visit to the
Caribbean. However, the function and significance of the clothing in
Brunias's pictures are quite distinct from those depicted in portraits
of cultural cross-dressers. In portraiture, clothing is used to stage
identity or to elicit narratives about a sitter. In Brunias's Caribbean
paintings, clothing serves entirely different ends that have to do with
the genre in which he was working, ethnographic art.[2] The clothing
that Brunias records in his paintings identifies his subjects as types of
Caribbean peoples; the titles of his paintings, *The Barbadoes Mulatto
Girl, Free West Indian Dominicans,* and *A Negroes Dance in the Island of
Dominica,* for instance, indicate that these are taxonomic images of
specimens, not representations of individuals.[3]

Much like the illustrations of plants and animals that accompany natural histories, ethnographic art depicts "exotic" people, their clothing, their habitations, and their activities. Voyages of discovery, such as Captain Cook's three navigations of the Pacific, produced much ethnographic art. Artists on Cook's voyages—Sydney Parkinson and Alexander Buchan on the first voyage, William Hodges on the second, and John Webber on the third—were part of a team of naturalists, botanists and proto-anthropologists whose tasks were to record the new people, plants, animals, and landscapes they encountered. Parkinson was responsible for painting images of plants and Buchan had been hired to draw people; unfortunately, Buchan died in the early stages of the voyage, weakened from the rigors of a disastrous expedition to gather specimens during a surprise snowstorm in Patagonia. In addition to sketching hundreds of plants, some animals, and coastlines, Parkinson had the responsibility of drawing Tahitians, Australian Aborigines, and Maoris (Fig. 26).[4]

At the same time that Cook's artists were drawing images of Polynesians, halfway around the world Brunias was sketching Caribbean peoples. Like Cook's artists, Brunias was employed to record the manners and customs of the inhabitants of a tropical region. His pictures of Caribs, Black Caribs, mulattoes, slaves, freedmen, and planters function as illustrations designed to convey information about exotic peoples and, as such, participate in the conventions of natural history writing. However, Brunias's pictures served a slightly different purpose in that the people he painted—the African Caribbean slaves, the Carib Indians, the free people of color—were familiar to his patrons; these images, I believe, served as momentos and reminders of the Caribbean for planters and colonial officials who had lived in the region but had resettled in England or elsewhere. Several of Brunias's paintings he engraved himself; the plates of these were dedicated to military officers such as Brigadier General Charles O'Hara and to colonial officials such as Sir William Young, who, as mentioned previously, with his love of "music and the fine arts" had made "jovial parties of colonization."[5] Brunias's pictures of West Indians also differ from ethnographic art like Parkinson's in that Brunias's images of African Caribbeans at festivals, in the marketplace, walking, bathing, and buying flowers and fruit from vendors contain elements akin to English "genre" paintings or "fancy" pieces, which depict England's poor, in particular, its agricultural laborers and street vendors, at work. The artistic tradition of depicting the activities of the

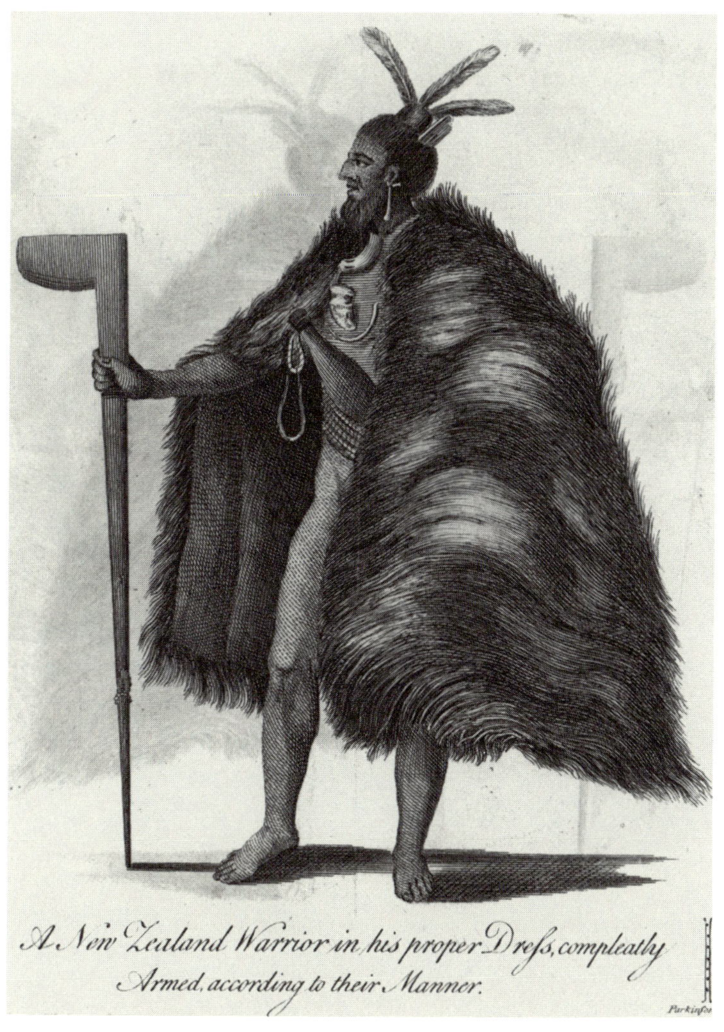

26. T. Chambers after Sydney Parkinson, *A New Zealand Warrior in his Proper Dress, & Compleatly Armed, According to their Manner*, engraving, plate 15 in Sydney Parkinson, *A Journal of a Voyage to the South Seas, In his Majesty's Ship, the Endeavour* (London, 1773). Reproduced by permission of the Bishop Museum, The State Museum of Natural and Cultural History, Honolulu.

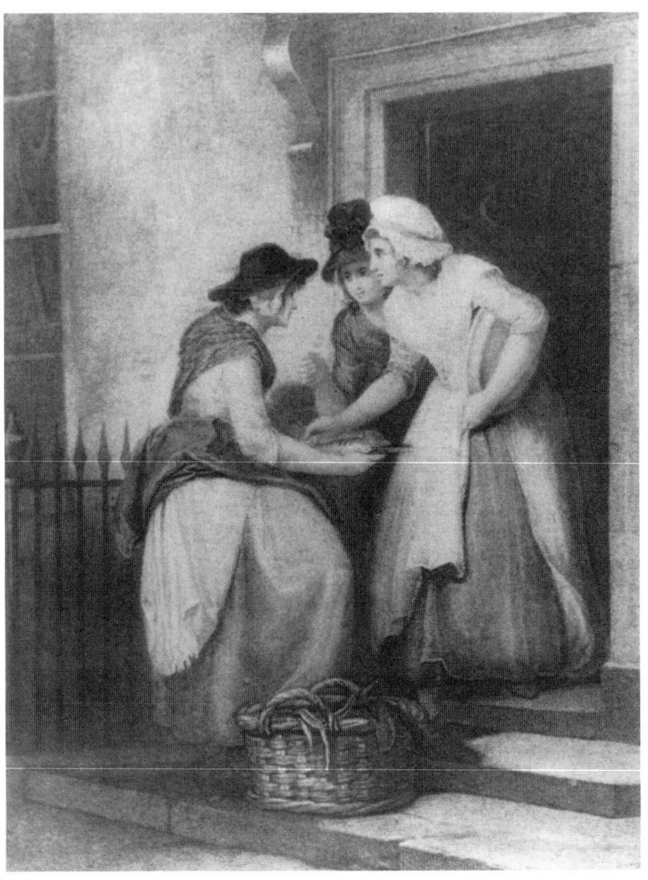

27. Francis Wheatley, *Cries of London: New Mackrel, New
Mackrel*, 1795, engraving by N. Schavemetti. Author's
collection.

urban working class, though European in origin, was developed in
eighteenth-century England by Hogarth with his *Times of Day* and
by Paul Sandby with his *London Cries* (1759–60). The most popular
of these genre paintings are those of Francis Wheatley's series *The
Cries of London* (1792–95), which were widely distributed as prints (e.g.,
Fig. 27).[6] There is an ethnographic quality to these images of England's working classes, in that the people portrayed are not depicted
as individuals but as types, and their activities, depicted with an air of
authenticity, determine their identity—a servant plucking a turkey,

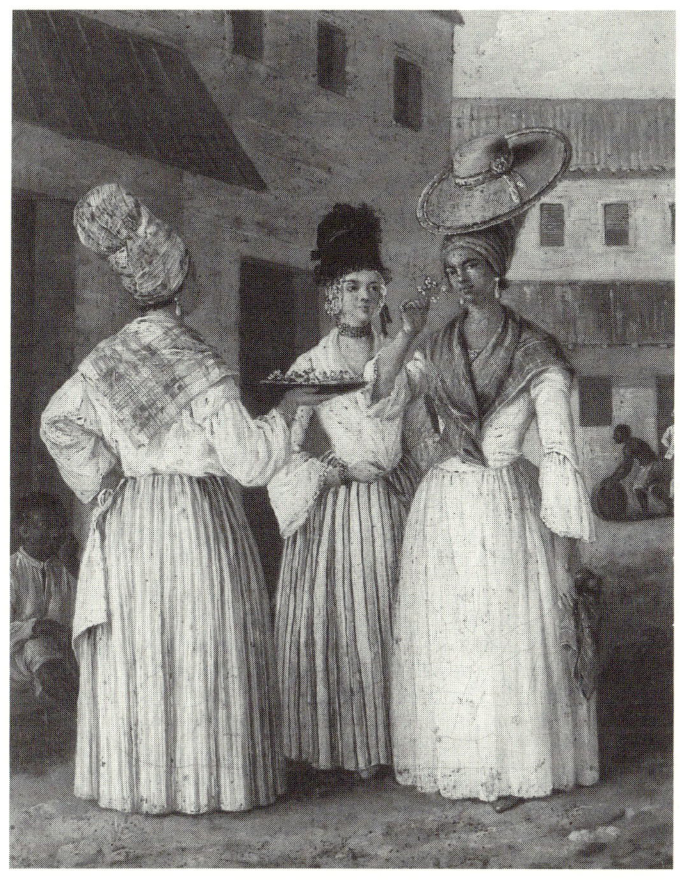

28. Agostino Brunias, *A West Indian Flower Girl*, c. 1769,
oil on canvas. Yale Center for British Art,
Paul Mellon Collection.

a girl selling primroses, a shepherd returning to his cottage, a girl
shucking oysters. Brunias's images of women with baskets of fruits
and flowers soliciting sales from elegantly dressed young women,
such as found in *The Barbadoes Mulatto Girl* and *A West Indian Flower
Girl* (Fig. 28), participate in two genres: the ethnographic art that depicts exotic peoples and the fancy pictures of the laboring poor. Both
genres, in their focus on types of people, work to obscure the individuality of their subjects, Europe's laboring classes and the "exotic"
others from around the globe.

Brunias's ethnographic images of African Caribbean peoples are dominated by meticulous attention to the details of dress, a focus in keeping with the dictates of the genre. However, in depicting the clothing of African Caribbeans as well as their activities of dancing, strolling, selling, and buying, Brunias also captures a quality that moves his African Caribbean figures out of the category of object of natural historical inquiry and into the realm of human subjects capable of agency and possessing history. Brunias's paintings of African Caribbeans, both freed and enslaved, bear traces of the struggle for personhood, and in his representation of clothing we can see both the suppression and presence of narratives of self-actualization for the subjects of his paintings. Brunias's paintings and prints, in recording the quotidian cross-cultural encounters of the "sugar" islands, capture the contradictions inherent in the colonial slave societies of the West Indies, contradictions having to do with the African Caribbean struggle for agency within a slave society that was also a market economy. In representing these contradictory impulses, Brunias's ethnographic art worked explicitly to support but also, however unintentionally, to undermine the plantocracy whose power base was the sugar and slavery economies that dominated the British West Indies of the eighteenth and early nineteenth centuries.[7]

This chapter explores the codes and assumptions of natural history that inform Brunias's representations of the people of the British West Indies, arguing that ethnographic art, as a subset of natural history, depicts people as specimens and seeks to suppress subjectivity and narrative with taxonomy as the organizing principle of the inquiry. Then the focus shifts to an examination of Brunias's depictions of clothing and commerce, images that suggest the liberatory potential of accumulation for slaves, and attempts to assess the power of his paintings to speak beyond taxonomy and ethnology and to narrate personal and public history.

Natural History

Not much is known about Agostino Brunias other than that he had worked with Robert Adams in Italy and had accompanied Adams to England in the late 1750s.[8] Nor is much known about the conditions under which Brunias painted his Caribbean pictures. We can speculate that he was commissioned by planters to produce these images. Sir William Young may have aided him, acting as his patron, as he was the governor of Dominica and one of the three commissioners of St. Vincent, the two sites where Brunias worked in the West Indies. Sir William also owned several of Brunias's paintings of the islands and their people.[9] These paintings are now housed in various collections; many are at the Yale Center for British Art, and others belong to Harvard's Peabody Museum of Archaeology and Ethnology. It is not surprising that paintings by Brunias ended up in an ethnological collection, for many of them in their own era served as illustrations for a work of natural history, Bryan Edwards's *History, Civil and Commercial, of the West Indies* (1796, 1819), providing a visual description of what were presented as specimens of exotic species.

By classifying people into racial categories and recording their dress and manners, Brunias was employing the descriptive codes that belonged to the customs-and-manners section of natural histories, a kind of proto-anthropology that described native peoples in the same terms that natural historians would use to describe botanical or zoological specimens. Natural history, one of the eighteenth century's great preoccupations, was a scientific discourse that encompassed what we now think of as botany, zoology, geology, geography, and anthropology. As part of the Enlightenment project to extend European systems of thought into the unknown regions of the globe, it sought to describe, name, and classify every natural phenomenon that it encountered. As a genre of prose writing, natural history grew out of travel narratives. But the two genres are distinct. Travel writing is organized around a narrative framework as the traveler moves through space and time. Descriptions of what the traveler encounters—plants, animals, people, terrain—are contained within the narrative frame. Natural history, on the other hand, employs the list as its organizing principle. Its method of description is "objective"; the personal and subjective are, by and large, suppressed.[10]

The natural history of the eighteenth century was heavily influenced by Linnaean systems of classification that focused on the observable traits that a specimen displays on its surface. Linnaean nomenclature is based on counting the number of pistils and stamens; consequently, for Linnaean botanists, these were the most important parts of the plant, not its method of reproduction, its anatomy, its biochemical processes, or its relation to its environment, for the number of pistils and stamens would enable them to classify the specimen according to species and to name it as well. The thrust of Linnaean botany was to find a new specimen, to determine in what ways it was typical of a species, to classify and name it.[11]

It is this concern with typicality as well as attention to surface detail that places Brunias's paintings within the discourse of natural history. The customs-and-manners sections of natural histories describe native peoples in terms that stress, as Pamela Regis contends, the "static" and "frozen" and are "concerned with the surfaces of people—their clothing, racial characteristics, dwellings, and diet."[12] Focusing on racial characteristics, dress, and ornament, Brunias's pictures function as a means of identifying types of people. One could use Brunias's pictures to distinguish a planter from a slave by noting surface traits such as skin color, arrangement of hair, clothing, jewelry, and objects that the subjects hold in their hands or surround themselves with. Just as a birdwatcher uses a field guide to identify the bird he has just seen, so one could use Brunias's pictures to identify a French mulatress or a Black Carib, for instance, and to distinguish each of these types from African slaves.

Natural history's focus on types rather than individuals, its concern with surface similarities and differences rather than causality, and its erasure of narrative produced a system of thought that posited a static, timeless universe in which all natural phenomena could be located on a hierarchical grid. According to this way of thinking, the natural world was created all at once, was not subject to change, and existed as part of a divine and ordered universe. In eighteenth-century natural history, species did not evolve nor could they suddenly emerge by way of mutation. Every type of animal, plant, and mineral has existed since the beginning of time and, therefore, has no origin other than the single moment of creation. Each species shares this same history, which is, ultimately, a lack of history. Linnaean botany contributed a scientific cast to this Platonic universe, and, as Arthur Lovejoy argues, had a significant impact on the ancient concept of the Great Chain of Being: "Every discovery of a new form could be regarded, not as the disclosure of an additional unrelated fact in nature, but as a step towards the completion of a systematic structure of which the general plan was known in advance, an additional bit of empirical evidence of the truth of the generally accepted and cherished scheme of things."[13] Once named, a newly discovered plant was classified and its location on the hierarchy of natural phenomena was revealed.

By employing ethnographic conventions, Brunias participated in this discourse of natural history that focused on surfaces, looked for types, and posited a hierarchy of beings. The titles that accompany his paintings reflect the erasure of individuals and their particularities in preference for generalized visual traits: *French Mulatress, Negro Woman, The Barbadoes Mulatto Girl.* Ethnographic art, despite its focus on the human figure, does not share portraiture's goals of reproducing an individual's countenance and conveying a sense of the subject's character. Instead, ethnographic art seeks to represent the typical and to suppress the individual. Brunias also participates in ethnography's classification of people into racial categories. In recording their dress and manners, he contributed to the impression that these groupings of West Indian residents, the hierarchy consisting of planters, mulattoes, and negroes, were fixed and natural categories akin to the categories that divide pine trees from tulips. Not only are these categories fixed, they are timeless. As types, in the natural historical sense, planters, mulattoes, and slaves are portrayed as if they have no history, no origins, and no trajectory into the future. Plantocrats were served by such ethnographic thinking—it erased their participation in the slave trade as well as their culpability as slave owners, and it erased their role in the creation of the so-called mulatto race. The ethnographic tropes imply that slaves and mulattoes, as types of Caribbean peoples, have existed as such since the time of creation. What is erased is the history of slavery, specifically the transformation of Africans into slaves, a process that Europeans had instituted in a particular place at a particular time. Brunias's use of the conventions of natural history implies that slaves are a natural phenomenon, that they occur in nature as do lions and tigers, and that they await collection and classification, as do mulattoes, whose origins are also erased by Brunias's ethnographic conventions. By depicting mulattoes as a subspecies of human being, Brunias elides every mulatto's individual history of miscegenation.

Very few eighteenth-century British observers of the West Indian scene were willing to discuss the origins of mulattoes, for this topic would force them to acknowledge the sexual relationships between slaves and their masters, the white planters and managers of plantations. In a rare moment of candor, Janet Schaw, a Scottish woman visiting friends in 1774 in Antigua, provides an explanation for "the crowds of Mulattoes, which you meet in the streets, houses, and indeed everywhere," saying of the white creole gentlemen, "Alas! my friend, tho' children of the Sun, they [planters] are mortals, and as such must have their share of failings, the most conspicuous of which is, the indulgence they give themselves in their licentious and even unnatural amours . . . a crime that seems to have gained sanction from custom, tho' attended with the greatest inconveniences not only to Individuals, but to the publick in general. The young black wenches lay themselves out for white lovers, in which they are but too successful. This prevents their marrying their natural mates, and hence a spurious and degenerate breed, neither so fit for the field, nor indeed any work, as the true bred Negro."[14] That white men had sexual intercourse with African and African Caribbean women cannot be doubted, but the conditions under which this occurred were most likely quite different from Schaw's explanation, which blames libidinous "black wenches" for seducing these gallant young men, whose "naturally" warm constitutions make them their prey. One can imagine why a slave might seduce the master as a means of survival as well as access to the limited power of a "favorite" servant within the hierarchical social structure of the Big House, but the suggestion that what occurred between white masters and slave women can be described by the word "seduction" is absurd. Given the enormous differential in power between slave women and planters, the sons and nephews of planters, and overseers, the probability of white men, rather than black women, being the aggressors in sexual encounters is quite high.[15] A journal kept by a planter on Jamaica, Thomas Thistlewood, recounts in detail his prodigious number of sexual encounters with his female slaves. In addition to one or two favorites with whom he had sex on a regular basis, he blithely recounts his taking several others by force and providing his gentlemen guests with female slaves as sexual playthings during their stay on his estate. In *Black Ivory: A History of the British Slavery,* James Walvin traces the pattern of predatory and brutal treatment of African women by white men from the slave ships to the plantation's slave quarters. "An unbridled and aggressive white sexuality towards slave women . . . was ubiquitous. . . . There may have been cases where white men fell in love with black women, but for every such case we have scores of examples of sexual exploitation of the basest kind. The slave quarters were the sexual hunting grounds for the predatory local whites. At first trying to persuade a slave with gifts of clothing, money, beads, food or a better post, the white man could, in the last resort, simply use physical force."[16] White men raping African and African Caribbean women was, for the most part, the origin of the mulatto population, and it was this narrative that whites were eager to suppress with stories about seductive "black wenches."

Brunias provides an image that confirms Walvin's statement that "slave women proved a temptation which owners and overseers found difficult to resist; they were the sexual playthings of any white man who took a fancy to them."[17] In his painting *French Mulattresses and Negro Woman Bathing,* Brunias portrays three naked women bathing in a stream; behind them, in a grove of trees, is a white man peeking surreptitiously at them (Fig. 29). His white face appears between the dark green branches of a tree, showing pleasure and surprise as he watches the bathers, who lounge about on the banks of the stream. Though this scene was meant to be amusing, referring perhaps to a bathing scene in Thomson's *Seasons* and the accompanying illustration by William Kent,[18] the racial designations take this image out of the realm of play and harmless innuendo and into the brutal sexual politics of Caribbean slave society, where one cannot ignore the seriousness of the real power possessed by the gazer over these objects of his desire. Clearly, *French Mulattresses and Negro Woman Bathing* appealed to a white male audience. By treating in a playful way white male desire for black women, the painting helps to foster the impression that such desires were harmless and essentially innocent, as signaled by this pastoral setting.

Although the ethnographic conventions that Brunias employed support plantocratic ideas about race and gender, other elements of his paintings, particularly the subject matter, participate in visual conventions and discursive modes that complicate and even contradict the plantocratic ideology at work in these paintings. The paintings that complicate what seem to be simply images circulating as plantocratic propaganda have as their subject matter the representations

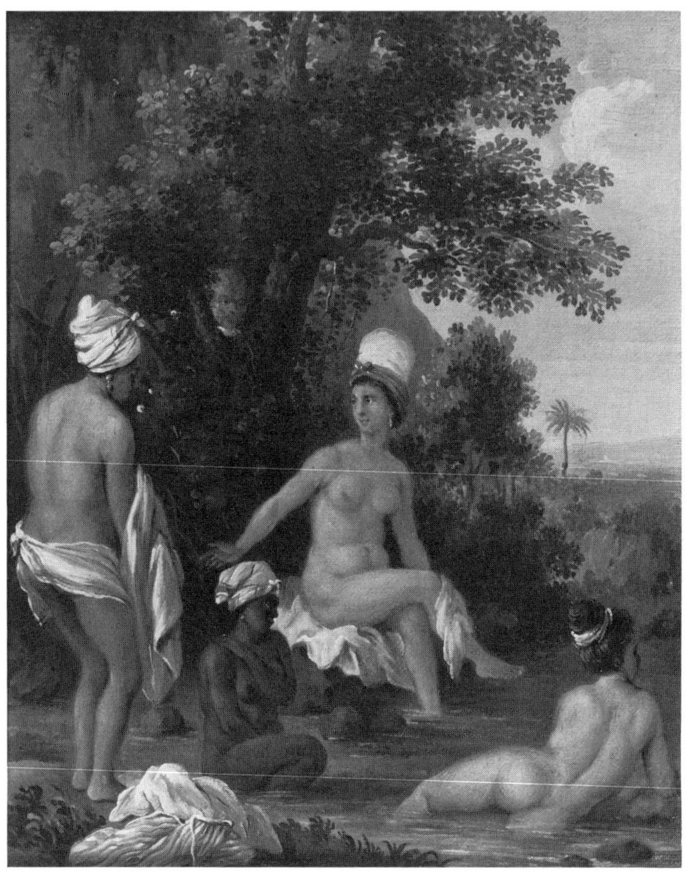

29. Agostino Brunias, *French Mulatresses and Negro Woman Bathing,* c. 1770, oil on canvas. Peabody Museum of Archaeology and Ethnology. © President and Fellows, Harvard College, Harvard University Art Museums.

of slave wealth in the form of expensive clothing and jewelry and the representations of commerce, particularly Africans and African Caribbeans engaged in economic exchange. Despite the strictures of the ethnographic genre, Brunias's images are complex representations of Caribbean peoples. Depicting slave wealth and commerce gives to his subjects, perhaps inadvertently, the possibility of being agents in history and the possibility of undergoing transformation.

Cloth as Fetish

Brunias's careful rendering of the dress and adornment of his Caribbean subjects reflects not only natural history's concern with surfaces but the Caribbean society's obsession with clothing. Brunias's attention to clothing is matched by the descriptions of dress in the journals of Caribbean planters and in the narratives of British visitors to the West Indies. Brunias lavishes attention on clothing, carefully detailing style of dress and quality of cloth. He distinguishes among the elegant dress of "ladies," meaning upper-class whites, the less elegant but quite colorful clothing of "mulatresses," and the simpler clothing of a "Negro Wench." Black Caribs, the descendants of the indigenous Caribs and marooned slaves, are portrayed in various guises, from naked except for armbands, loincloths, and necklaces to fully attired in white linen and straw hats.

Brunias's careful rendering of clothing underscores the importance of cloth in the West Indian economy. Because all cloth was imported, it was expensive and highly valued. Both a commodity as well as the medium of exchange, cloth was fetishized in the West Indies, carrying with it social meanings and displaced energies in addition to its functional role. For instance, cloth was used as a reward or a special gift to slaves. Sir William Young II, pictured as a young man in Zoffany's family conversation piece (Fig. 4), notes that when he returned to the Caribbean to visit his estates, he gave brightly colored cloth as Christmas presents to his favorite slaves. Planter Thomas Thistlewood gave cloth to his slaves in exchange for sexual favors. One entry in his journal gives an account of such an exchange: "For gifts—2 yards of Brown Oznabrig, 4 bitts; 4 yards of striped holland, 8 bitts; and a handkerchief, 3 bitts. Gave them all to Jenny."[19] Matthew Lewis writes in his journal that he used cloth to reward slave mothers who had given birth to healthy babies on his estate, a practice Young mentions in his travel narrative: "such of the women as had reared children, came to the villa, and each received, as a present, five yards of fine cotton, at 2s. 6d. per yard, of the gayest pattern, to make a petticoat."[20] Cloth was redolent with social and economic meanings that went well beyond the commercial or the functional.[21]

In *Domestic Manners and Social Condition of the White, Coloured, and*

Negro Population of the West Indies (1833), A. C. Carmichael, writing about her experiences as the wife of a small plantation owner, describes how her slaves would work in the fields practically naked so as to protect their clothing for special occasions, such as Christmas galas and going to town on Sundays.[22] She writes with derision of "ridiculous dandies," of slaves who had saved hard-earned money so that they could purchase fine material, including silks and lace: "The head boiler-man at Laurel-Hill [her sugar estate], was invariably a dandy; and it was quite a picture to see him . . . watching the sugar, with his air of authority, and his shirt collar stuck up to his ears" (2:170). At Christmas parties or "Negro balls" slave women wear "fine worked muslin gowns, with handsome flounces; satin and sarsenet bodices are very common; their under garments are of the best materials, and they have either good cotton or silk stockings; their kid dancing shoes are often of the gayest colours, while their expensive turbans are adjusted with a grace, that makes the dress really appear elegant" (1:145–46). Her descriptions are filled with a sense of marvel at the elaborate "gala dresses" of slaves, but at the same time her tone is laced with Scottish disapproval of what seemed to her useless expenditure and vain display of finery.

Brunias's depictions of elaborately dressed Africans and African Caribbeans as well as his portrayal of linen market scenes have their verbal equivalents in the accounts of Sunday markets and the finery worn by slaves found in plantocratic texts (Figs. 28–32). Certainly, such market day scenes with their parades of finely dressed folk must have occurred regularly in places like Dominica and St. Vincent, yet plantocratic descriptions of well-dressed slaves and freedmen are so detailed, lengthy, and frequent that their significance seems to be derived from something other than the mere recording of daily life. When Young's descriptions of Christmas day on St. Vincent focus on clothing, his aim is to stress how well off his slaves are, even in comparison with the English peasantry.

The town was like a very gay fair, with booths, furnished with everything good to eat and fine to wear. The negroes (with a very few exceptions) were all dressed in pattern cottons and muslins, and the young girls with petticoat on petticoat; and all had handkerchiefs, put on with fancy and taste about their heads. Returning to the villa . . . the men negroes were dressed in the highest beauism, with muslin frills, high capes, and white hats; and one beau had a large fan. The negro girls were all dressed gay and fine, with handkerchiefs folded tastefully about their heads, and gold ear-rings and necklaces: the girls were nearly all field negroes; there are but four female slaves as domestics in the villa. In England, no idea of "jolly Christmas" can be imagined, in comparison with the three days of Christmas in St. Vincent's. In every place is seen a gaiety of colours and dress, and a corresponding gaiety of mind and spirits; fun and finery are general. (3:258–59)

Young collapses the distinction between appearances and internal states of mind by reading the colorful clothing as indicative of the emotional state of his slaves. They may indeed have been happy at Christmas time but for reasons he might not be able to fathom or to admit to himself and his readers, reasons having to do with time off from work, access to good food, and a chance to participate in recreational and cultural activities denied to them on a regular basis. It is important to Young to stress that these well-dressed young people are mostly field hands, who are the lowest on the plantation hierarchy and who have the least access to personal wealth, for he thinks that if he can prove that field hands possess finery and as such live better than English peasants, slavery is not as bad an institution morally and socially as abolitionists have depicted it. Writing in 1791 as an MP who actively advocated for the West Indian planters in Parliament, Young wanted to portray slavery as a humane institution.

Carmichael reveals her ideological subtext even more directly than does Young when she insists that slavery is a humane institution that serves not only planters but slaves as well. She wrote on the eve of emancipation and in defense of slavery. Of her five-year sojourn in St. Vincent and Trinidad in the 1820s, she speaks with an authority based on personal experience, for as the wife of a planter, she was mistress of many slaves and took an active interest in their moral, physical, and emotional welfare. Whereas Young and Lewis, as absentees, describe their impressions as outsiders, Carmichael establishes her credentials as an insider, someone who can understand what really is happening, things that are not apparent to the casual or uninformed observer. "Being now, as it were, more behind the scenes, I was convinced, that although a casual observer generally will conclude all creoles [whites] to be lazy, luxurious, proud, and even deficient of feeling—

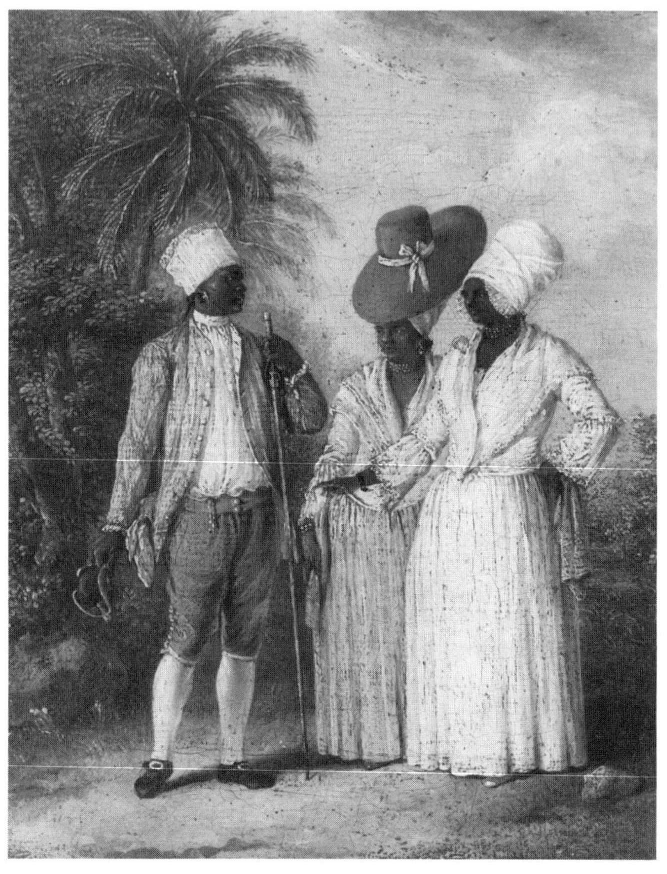

30. Agostino Brunias, *Free West Indian Dominicans*, c. 1770, oil on canvas. Yale Center for British Art, Paul Mellon Collection.

(*Opposite, top*) 31. Agostino Brunias, *Linen Day, Roseau, Dominica — A Market Scene*, c. 1780, oil on canvas. Yale Center for British Art, Paul Mellon Collection.

(*Opposite, bottom*) 32. Agostino Brunias, *The Linen Market, Dominica*, c. 1780, oil on canvas. Yale Center for British Art, Paul Mellon Collection.

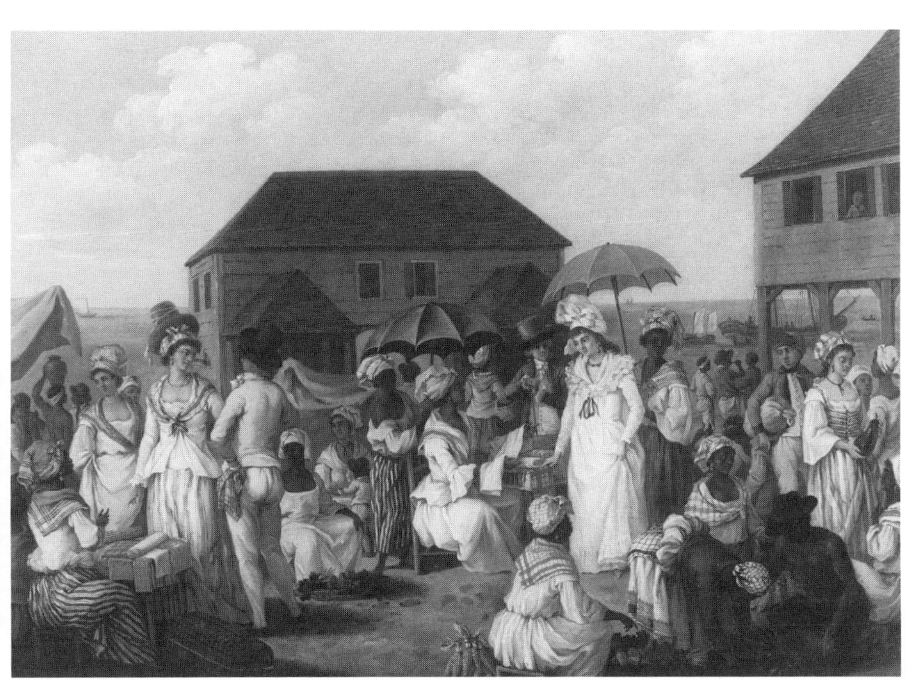

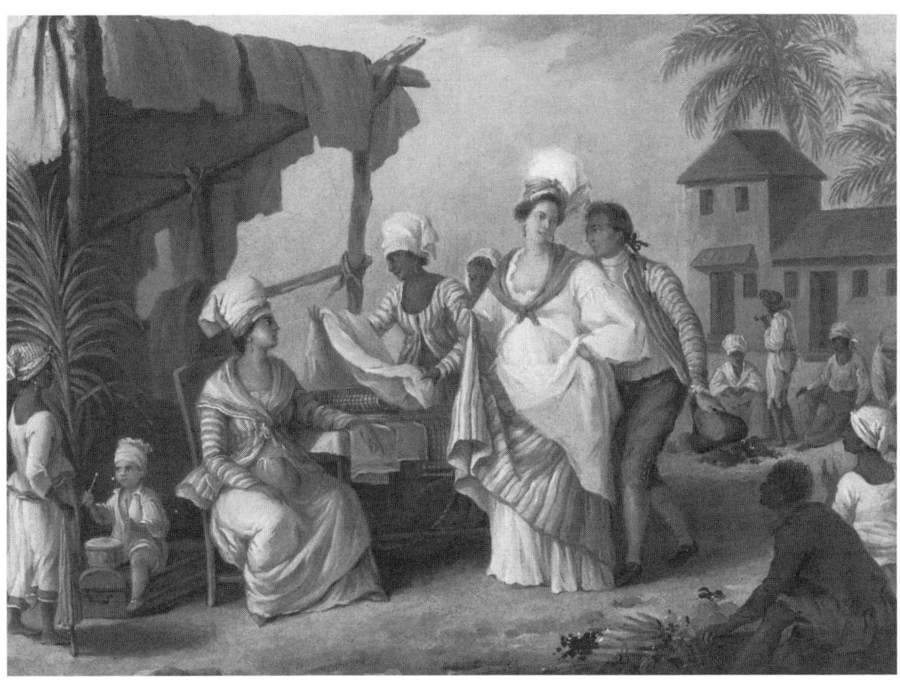

that the cause of his hastily adopting such sentiments proceeds . . .
from seeing only the outside of society" (1:53–54). Discussing British
misconceptions concerning slavery and the white character, she insists
that one has to have lived "long enough in a West India town with
one's own slaves for servants, or in residing at, and taking the active
management of a sugar estate" to arrive at the "truth" (1:55).[23]

Like Lewis and Young, Mrs. Carmichael was a plantocrat, and she
chose to defend slavery by describing how prosperous, well-clothed,
and well-fed slaves were in comparison to the typical British peasant.
Like Brunias's images of well-dressed slaves, Carmichael's descriptions of prosperous slaves support her positive version of slavery and
what was essentially her political project. When describing the clothing of her house slaves, she stresses their taste for expensive items.
"Head negroes," as she calls her upper domestic male servants, "have
all fine broad cloth, either made into jackets, such as gentlemen very
often wear of a morning in the West Indies, or coats . . . their shirt is
always of fine linen, and the collar of a fashionable shape, which, with
the cravat, is as stiff as any reasonable dandy could desire" (1:143–44).
Some of these more expensive items, such as shoes and stockings,
were given as gifts from masters to servants, but most of the clothing
that domestic and field slaves wore they had purchased themselves: "I
have seen an estate negro [plantation slave] in St. Vincent, dressed at
Christmas time as well in every respect as any gentleman could be . . .
he told me every thing he wore was of his own purchasing: he had a
quizzing glass, and as good a hat as any white man in the colony; he
had a watch ribbon and key, but whether or not he wore a watch, I
cannot tell, as I did not put the question to him but I have seen many
with watches and seals" (1:144–45).[24] Carmichael's tone mixes derision with admiration, conveying her disapproval of the expenditure
involved in purchasing this finery and her approval of her slaves' attractive appearance: "All head people upon estates are uniformly well
dressed, neat, and clean; and though it is in their own fashion, they
look nicer and much cleaner than English country people" (1:153).
Even common field slaves, she says, possess greater wealth in fabric
than do English peasants: "I have often been in their [slaves'] houses
at such times, and could not help thinking, how much better off they
were for clothing, bedding, and baby-linen, than the great majority of
the lower ranks in Britain" (1:143). Carmichael suggests that slavery,

with its "security" and material comforts, is preferable to the financial precariousness of free wage labor.

Young's and Lewis's policy of giving cloth as gifts to mothers of healthy children implies a reality other than the one Carmichael describes with her images of well-clothed, prosperous slaves who thrive under slavery. The incredibly high infant mortality rate and very high rate of female infertility among Caribbean slaves bespeak hardships that planters were eager to ignore or deny, hardships having to do with overwork, malnutrition, and venereal disease. Planters believed that the low birth rate and high death rate of babies and small children were the result of maternal indifference, ignorance, or infanticide, and believed that bribing women with a few yards of cloth would cure this presumed maternal negligence. The valence attached to cloth must have been very high indeed if receiving a few yards could be regarded as a reward for keeping one's babies alive or for sleeping with the master. Perhaps when slaves displayed cloth in the form of finery, something more or other was going on than mere vanity and ostentation.

Can the Subaltern Dress?

Carmichael's accounts of slaves and their clothing convey her sense of the absurdity of head servants dressing as "dandies" and of field hands removing their shirts in rainstorms and hiding them under bushes to protect them from being damaged. Perhaps her tone of derision is a defense against recognizing an element of parody in the finery that slaves wore, and her scoffing at the shirtless slave protects her from recognizing the refusal of Africans and African Caribbeans to embrace British systems of signification. In wearing an English gentleman's suit of clothes, was the head servant merely imitating his master, acknowledging his master's superiority by mimicking him, or was he parodying the white man and his privileged position? The dynamics that Bhabha associates with the mimic man come into play here where colonial mimicry is "at once a mode of appropriation and of resistance,"[25] which produces in the European beholder a kind of "mimetic vertigo" that Taussig describes as occurring when the West sees itself "mirrored in the eyes and handiwork of its Others."[26] Plantocratic fascination with slaves' clothing may have stemmed from the discomfort they experienced witnessing their slaves' mimicry of European fashion.

What were slaves performing with their gala dresses and gentlemanly attire? We can begin to interpret slaves' use of clothing if we are alert to the "double inflection" that clothing and other ordinary commodities can carry. As Dick Hebdige has suggested in his *Subculture: The Meaning of Style,* clothing can "be magically appropriated; 'stolen' by subordinate groups and made to carry 'secret' meanings: meanings which express, in code, a form of resistance to the order which guarantees their continued subordination."[27] Slaves could have been displaying their status within their own social hierarchies or, as Orlando Patterson suggests, caricaturing their masters, and in doing so, venting their aggression toward them "in a disguised and permitted form."[28] In performing their contempt for their masters' "natural" superiority, perhaps they were enjoying blurring the boundaries between high and low, masters and slaves, free and bound. Their putting on European dress may have been analogous in effect to the contemporary practice of drag, which in calling attention to the performance of gender, questions the very foundations of gender distinctions. Judith Butler has suggested that parody and, in particular, drag can be quite destabilizing to heteronormativity by denaturalizing the categories of male and female and signaling the constructedness of these gendered categories.[29] Were slaves dressed as upper-class Europeans calling into question the normativity of white access to resources, privilege, and power?

When slaves wore European clothing, women in petticoats and men in breeches, they also performed their cultural and racial difference by inflecting a European style of dress with African idioms. The African Caribbean use of brightly colored cloth (red in particular), the prevalence of gold and semiprecious stones in jewelry, as well as the turbaned headdresses that both men and women wore reflected African styles and tastes in clothing. Such African-inflected dress can be seen in Brunias's paintings, in particular in his depiction of two elegantly attired African Caribbean women conversing with an African Caribbean man (Fig. 30). With his ethnographic attention to details of dress, Brunias reproduces the textures of cloth and the glistening surfaces of jewelry. One woman wears a tall headdress made of white cloth and white lace, and the other woman wears a large,

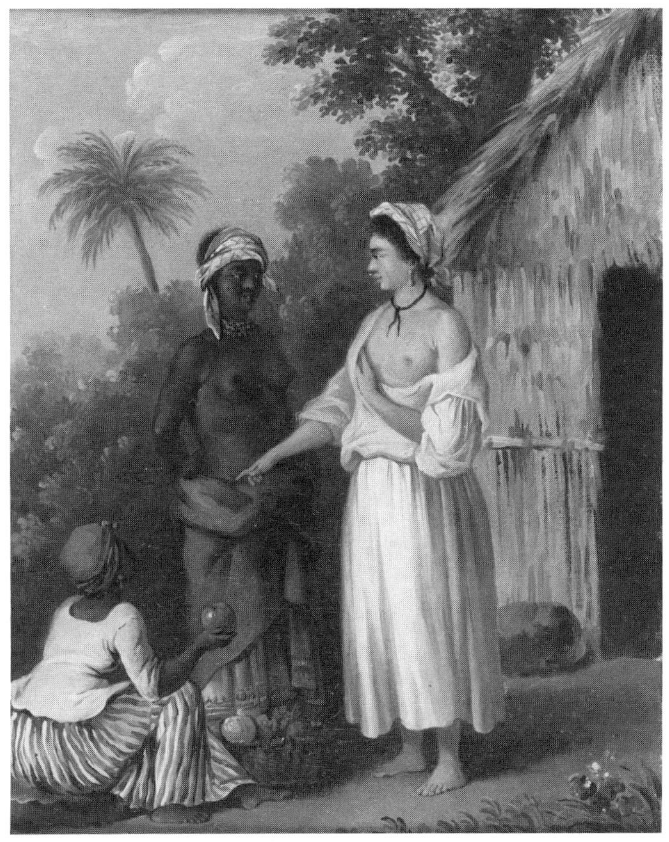

33. Agostino Brunias, *French Mulatress Purchasing Fruit from a Negro Wench*, c. 1770, oil on canvas. Peabody Museum of Archaeology and Ethnology. © President and Fellows, Harvard College, Harvard University Art Museums.

wide-brimmed hat over a white turban. High hair and big flouncy hats as well as turbans were quite popular in England at this time, but the headdresses worn by African Caribbeans reflect an African style rather than the smaller, orientalized headdresses worn by English ladies. In Brunias's other paintings, particularly in his market scenes (Figs. 31–33), he carefully reproduces the headdresses worn by African Caribbean women, detailing the patterns (stripes, checks, plaids) of the cloth and the various ways cloth was tied around the head.

In *Linen Day, Roseau, Dominica—A Market Scene,* Brunias has captured nineteen different ways of wearing head coverings, from simply tied kerchiefs of white cloth to elaborately draped and intricately tied calico and madras turbans (Fig. 31). The cloth used frequently in these turbans was calico and muslin imported by the British from India, though some turbans were made of silk imported from Martinique. Calico, a favorite material among slaves, had been a popular material in West Africa, where cotton cloth, produced locally by cottage industry, carried multiple and complex cultural meanings. The cloth African slaves wore was no doubt invested with significances beyond the apprehension of their white masters.[30] As Hebdige contends, "commodities can be symbolically 'repossessed' in everyday life, and endowed with implicitly oppositional meanings."[31] By carefully altering European styles with African accessories, African Caribbeans assimilated European dress into their African cultural practices and, in doing so, performed tactical maneuvers within the semiotics of European clothing, redefining the significance of what they wore on their bodies.

Whatever the slaves' intentions in wearing elegant European clothing with an African flair, the effect on the British was to destabilize what were to them natural categories having to do with the binaries of civilized-savage and the dressed-undressed, and thereby to unfix the European cultural meanings attached to various kinds of clothing. That slaves sometimes did not wear clothing to protect it from the rain and sun surprised and amused Carmichael. She felt smug in her knowledge that cloth was meant to be worn to protect the body from inclement weather and to cover one's nakedness for modesty's sake. The slaves' use of cloth, however, unhinged the use value attached to clothing and put it into the category of symbolic exchange, where it circulated for reasons other than utility, such as establishing rank within one's community, or as emblematic of favoritism, or for the fun of inverting the hierarchies of race, class, and culture.[32] This sheering off of the use value of clothing destabilized the already complicated and tenuous link between clothing and its "natural" function in British society, where clothing went well beyond use to signify in the most intricate ways class, gender, and regional distinctions. Slaves' wearing gentleman's waistcoats and watch ribbons severed the thread by which the use value of clothing was attached to the exchange value. European style of dress in the hands of and on the bodies of African slaves became fetishized because removed from its European cultural context and systems of signification.[33] Whether parodic in intent or not, slaves' attitudes toward clothing unnerved many British observers of the West Indian scene; perhaps this can account, in part, for the plantocrats' obsession with the topic of slaves' clothing.

Although cloth's importance in the social, moral, and symbolic economy of the Caribbean cannot be doubted, its significance is elusive because overdetermined. Planters claimed that cloth was an index of prosperity and signified that slaves were well taken care of and therefore happy. Slaves, on the other hand, might have read into cloth very different meanings. A red handkerchief, for instance, might have meant a healthy child or a night spent with the master, or it might have functioned to revive a memory of an African past. Brunias's detailed rendering of clothing, though in conformance to the dictates of ethnological conventions, captures the Caribbean fascination with the quality and quantity of cloth a person displays. The fetishizing of surfaces that natural history demands works in Brunias's pictures to reproduce the cloth as fetish, re-creating, albeit for different reasons, the Caribbean obsession with dress.

Sunday Markets and the Accumulation of Wealth

Like his treatment of cloth, Brunias's meticulous depiction of jewelry fulfills the requirements of the ethnographic record but also captures the Caribbean concern with gold jewelry (Figs. 30–33). Travel narratives as well as planter's journals remark repeatedly on the prevalence of slaves wearing gold jewelry, especially earrings. Carmichael notes that "the real value of their jewelry is considerable; it consists of massy gold ear-rings, and rings upon their fingers, coral necklaces, and handsome gold chains, lockets, and other ornaments of this description" (1:146). Young evinces an ambivalence about this show of slave wealth: he is surprised, even taken aback by what he perceives as vanity and display, but he is also pleased to see slaves having access to wealth and private property: "[T]he negroes, with few exceptions, seemed dressed in a style much above even our common artizans, the women especially, and there was such a swagger of importance in the gait of those (and many there were) who had gold ear-rings and necklaces, that I told my friend Mr. O., on his pressing me for my opinion of what struck me on first landing in the West Indies, *That the negro women seemed to me the proudest mortals I had ever seen*" (3:244). The gold earrings in his narrative become emblematic of a defiant and proud stance taken by slaves toward their lot. Far from being servile and cringing, slaves, according to Young, were outspoken, almost rude, while also displaying a sense of humor and employing sarcasm when addressing their masters: "Many pressed their services on our first landing; and some first begged, and then joked with us in the style of a *Davus* of Terence, with great freedom of speech and some humour. I had a higher opinion of their minds, and a better opinion of their masters and government, than before I set my foot on shore" (3:244–45). Slaves having the freedom to express themselves in "a language which characterises a presumption of self-importance" (Young, 3:245) also surprises Carmichael on her arrival in the West Indies.

The marketplace was the site where slaves flirted with freedom by using liberal speech and also where they could enrich themselves, amassing enough money to buy their freedom. To understand the kinds of agency that were available to slaves in the West Indies, I turn to Equiano's autobiography, *The Interesting Narrative of the Life of Olaudah Equiano, or Gustavus Vassa, the African* (1789), as it illustrates the liberatory potential of the marketplace for African Caribbeans. Recounting his Caribbean voyages as a navigator on board his master's sixty-ton sloop, Olaudah Equiano, an African slave, explains how he earned enough money selling fruits and salted meat to buy his freedom. Taking his "whole stock" of "limes and oranges," which he had purchased on Monsterrat with 12 bits, he pooled his produce with another slave's; after having some of their fruit stolen by white men, Equiano and his partner sell the fruit for a profit at a market on Santa Cruz. Equiano is pleased with the success of his foray into merchandizing: "We then proceeded to the markets to sell them; and Providence was more favourable to us than we could have expected, for we sold our fruits uncommonly well; I got for mine about thirty-seven bits" (104). Equiano's narrative at this point, reading a bit like an accountant's ledger, or for that matter like passages in Defoe's *Moll Flanders* or *Roxana,* details his gradual accumulation of wealth, and, like Robinson Crusoe, Equiano is convinced that God's hand has intervened on his behalf and has made him prosperous: "Having made near three hundred per cent by four barrels of pork I brought from Charleston, I laid in as large a cargo as I could, trusting to God's providence to prosper my undertaking" (115). Through buying and selling fruits, vegetables, cured meat, and even live animals, eventually Equiano succeeds in accumulating the £40 he needs to buy his freedom from his master, who is stunned by Equiano's business acumen. "Where did you get the money?" his master asks and comments on how Equiano made "money much faster than he did; and said he would not have made me the promise he did [of freedom] if he had thought I should have got money so soon" (118).

As a skilled navigator and small-time merchant, Equiano finds the language of Calvinist predestination compatible with the workings of mercantile capitalism. Linking the dissenting discourse of election and providence with primitive accumulation was for him, as well as writers like Defoe and George Lillo, crucial to the construction of a liberatory discourse that, in encouraging industriousness and enterprise, set loose self-creating energies. Self-made men like Equiano emerged out of this discursive mingling of providence and business—self-made in the sense not only of accumulation of wealth but in the sense of creating an identity freed from the determining bonds of servitude.

Equiano's marketing abilities were shared by a great many Africans and African Caribbeans, both freed and enslaved, who lived in the British West Indies during the eighteenth century. Sunday markets, run almost exclusively by Africans and African Caribbeans, were crucial sites of exchange in the West Indian domestic economy. The commodities sold in these markets were largely produced by slaves on small plots of land known as provision grounds. Growing produce for market required not only an expenditure of labor above and beyond the arduous tasks and duties assigned to slaves on sugar plantations but also required agricultural expertise, knowledge of animal husbandry, and a talent for merchandizing and bartering. In performing these various activities, West Indian slaves created a space from which to resist some of the consequences of slavery and the machinations of the British legal institutions that enabled slavery.[34]

Narratives of self-actualization and accumulation like Equiano's appear in several of Agostino Brunias's paintings of West Indians who are depicted in the act of selling flowers and fruit (Figs. 28 and 33) as well as participating in the larger economic arenas of the linen and Sunday markets (Figs. 31 and 32). Though the pictures portray the same kind of economic exchange that Equiano describes in his autobiography, Brunias's portrayal of these exchanges differs from Equiano's in that the potential for self-actualization that Equiano emphasizes exists in Brunias's images only in an attenuated and residual form. This disparity can be explained by the differences between Brunias's and Equiano's racial identities and positions within Caribbean society as well as by the differing effects of the genres they employed: the visual versus the verbal and the autobiographical versus the taxonomic approaches to representation. Brunias's art is ethnological, as his purpose is to represent the typical; Equiano's is to describe the individual and his struggle to attain self-definition. Despite these major formal and ideological differences, Brunias's images capture some of Equiano's celebration of agency, for the narrative of self-actualization escapes the bounds of ethnographic conventions. In Brunias's representation of the marketplace as well as in his rendering of the clothing and jewelry of his West Indian subjects, he suggests the liberatory potential of accumulation.

Plantocrats like Young and Carmichael are ambivalent about slaves enjoying prosperity and accumulating wealth. Absentee planters and British visitors were pleased to see well-dressed slaves, yet they were disquieted by the freedom that this prosperity unleashes. Sunday markets were problematic sites for plantocrats: the markets offered pleasing images of industrious and prosperous slaves, but they also presented the possibility of license in the form of freedom of speech and, more important, of liberty.

Sunday was the big market day for slaves because the majority worked on plantations for their masters every day but Sunday. Rural markets as well as established town markets "attracted slaves from far and wide" and were "noisy, boisterous, colourful gatherings," almost carnivalesque in the Bakhtinian sense, a site of licensed liberty.[35] In her description of the "novel spectacle" of a Sunday market, Carmichael reveals her ambivalence about the scene before her: "I saw, for the first time, bands of negroes proceeding from the different estates, some with baskets, and others with wooden trays on their heads, carrying the surplus produce of their provision-grounds to market. Accustomed to a devout observance of the Sabbath day, I could feel little pleasure in gazing on a scene which in other circumstances would have given me unfeigned pleasure—for it was something, to learn that negro slaves were in possession of, and could sell, the loads of surplus produce which I saw, and receive their cash in hand; and it was also something to see that they were, with the exception of very few individuals, dressed in that manner which indicates an approach to real comfort" (1:4–5). Although she is not happy that market day is on Sunday, she is pleased to see slaves with a surplus that is not only the product of their labor but is theirs to sell or exchange. This "freedom" speaks well of the slave economy, for it implies that slaves are industrious and that they can possess property, two conditions that abolitionists argue cannot exist under slavery. Carmichael's defense of slavery consists of arguing that slavery is best for the slaves. In addition to being able to accumulate wealth, they possess all the "benefits" of slavery; they are cared for, given food, shelter, clothing, and medicine, and moral instruction as well as a structured work life. She contrasts the lifestyle of slaves with those of the "free coloured," arguing that "the coloured *slave* domestic is ten to one richer, and more comfortable, than the *free* one; and I never conversed with a free coloured domestic, who did not admit this." She contends that the free African Caribbeans, if unemployed or ill, are "truly wretched, for they have nothing to trust to,—no master, of whom they can demand all the necessaries of life, should they be sick, or unable, from old age, to work any longer." In contrast, the slave lives a life of comfort and security: "No accident, disabling him from work, deprives him of a home, food, clothing, or any necessary comfort, and he looks forward to old age without anxiety, or the chilling dread of poverty, for himself or his family" (1:81–83). Although Carmichael may sincerely believe that her slaves are better off under slavery than free, her position as a planter's wife and her advocacy of slavery undercut the objectivity she claims for her narrative.

Carmichael is eager to stress the slaves' prosperity under slavery, but she is ambivalent about the market scene. She is torn between her pleasure (as a capitalist) in the slaves' access to personal wealth, and her disapproval as a pious Christian of the market activities breaking the Sabbath, which she thinks should be reserved for churchgoing, prayer, and reflection. She is also made uncomfortable by the tone of the Sunday market, which is lively and colorful. Her countrywoman, Janet Schaw, in the narrative of her visit to the West Indies in 1774, registers her ambivalence over the festive atmosphere of the Sunday markets. Aware that she must entertain her audience with pretty pictures and striking vistas, Schaw uses the aesthetic as a way to organize what she sees and to elide the unpleasant power relations that undergird West Indian colonial society.[36] She writes enthusiastically about the beautiful scenes of Sunday markets, with slaves dressed in their finest, men wearing white muslin shirts and trousers and women in white muslin gowns decorated with brightly colored handkerchiefs:

We met the Negroes in joyful troops on the way to town with their Merchandize. It was one of the most beautiful sights I ever saw. They were universally clad in white Muslin: men in loose drawers and waistcoats, the women in jackets and petticoats; the men wore black caps, the women had handkerchiefs of gauze or silk, which they wore in the fashion of turbans. Both men and women carried neat white wicker-baskets on their heads, which they balanced as our Milk maids do their pails. These contained the various articles for Market, in one a little kid raised its head from amongst flowers of every hue, which were thrown over to guard it from the heat; here a lamb, there a Turkey or a pig, all covered up in the same elegant manner, While others had their baskets filled with fruit, pine-apples reared over each other; Grapes dangling over the loaded basket; oranges, Shaddacks, water lemons, pomegranates, granadillas, with twenty others, whose names I forget.

Schaw's account focuses on color and abundance, her description of the overflowing baskets reminiscent of Dutch still life paintings that detail nature's plenty. This market scene, Schaw says, is one of "joy and pleasantry," and suggests that the slaves are happy because on Sundays "the crack of the inhuman whip must not be heard." Schaw's delight in this colorful scene is somewhat mitigated by fear of excess: "It is necessary however to keep a look out during this season of unbounded freedom." She describes how planters arm themselves and accompany the militia on patrols that "go all round the different plantations as well as keep guard in the town." Sunday markets, though colorful and festive, possess the potential for "freedom" in the shape of riot and rebellion, but more important, I would argue, by offering slaves the opportunity to accumulate enough money to buy their freedom.[37] Both kinds of freedom—rebellion and liberation—are nurtured in the marketplace; for this reason, the marketplace is, for planters and the white oligarchy, a site of disruption and danger.

Carmichael is too matter-of-fact, too focused on rendering what she believes is objective truth, to wax lyrical the way Schaw does, but Carmichael registers her surprise at the boisterousness and freedom of movement and attitude that slaves display on market day. "I was again pleased to observe that all were well clothed; their clean white linen trowsers and jacket, with a blue checked shirt, looked tidy and comfortable. I saw nothing of that servile manner which I had antici-pated: all were frank, full of life and spirit, and talked to their master with a freedom which must be seen to be fully comprehended" (1:6). Her comments on slaves' freedom of speech echo Sir William Young's observations and his analogy between the liberal tongue of slaves and "the domestic slaves of the Roman people, [who,] as we deduce from scenes of Plautus and Terence, sometimes talked a language, and took liberties, with their lords and masters which in free servants and citizens would not have been allowed" (3:244–45).

This freedom of manner surprises both Young and Carmichael, but for Carmichael, whose stay in the West Indies outlasts Young's by years, this scene loses its immediate charms. She indicates later in her narrative that the slaves' conduct during market days is disagreeable, calling the Sunday market "a nuisance" and of "no advantage" to the white population (1:49). Another observer of the West Indian scene gives an account of Sunday markets that shares with Carmichael's description a sense of disgust at the noise and confusion: "here an assemblage of many hundred negroes and mulattoes expose for sale poultry, pigs, kids, vegetables, fruit, and other things; they begin to assemble by day-break and the market is generally crowded by ten o'clock. . . . The noise occasioned by the jabber of the negroes and the squalling and cries of the children basking in the sun exceeds anything I ever heard in a London market."[38] Though colorful and lively, the "negro" market is perceived by most white observers as a licentious and disorderly site.

Hinting at the potential for violence if Sunday markets were sup-pressed, Carmichael writes that "although so disgraceful a scene, yet it is one of those customs which were it at once abolished, other worse consequences might follow" (1:49). The markets were held on Sundays, the slaves' only day off. To abolish Sunday markets, in keeping with evangelical measures instituted in Britain, would banish slaves from the marketplace, robbing them of their potential to earn money, to acquire imported items such as salted meat, fish, and cloth, and to prosper. Carmichael realizes that such measures would infuriate the slaves and make life dangerous for the white population. Whites living on their plantations were outnumbered by Africans and African Caribbeans by 100, even 200, slaves to 7 or 8 white family members and overseers. Carmichael laments the "total want of personal security" for the planter and his family: "If any serious apprehension of a rising is entertained, her husband and every white man upon the estate are obliged to join the militia, and she is left with her children in a state of alarm beyond description: surrounded on all sides by negroes, she knows that she has no means of escape, and that she and her family are left entirely in their power" (1:57). These are the "worse consequences" that might follow any abolition of the Sunday markets. For Carmichael to hint at the potential for violence if Sunday markets were suppressed suggests that she must have recognized that the marketplace gave slaves access to resources that made their lives more comfortable and provided them with a measure of freedom and autonomy rare under slavery.

To close the Sunday markets might indeed have been cause for rebellion, for it was primarily through selling or exchanging goods that slaves could accumulate enough money to buy their freedom. Some islands, such as Trinidad, had laws that protected slaves' right to buy their freedom; there, slaves did not need to win their master's approval to gain their manumission, but needed only to present their master with the amount necessary to purchase themselves (Carmichael, 2:105). Planters tell of slaves who became "rich" by selling what they had grown in their gardens. Fruits, vegetables, chickens, and pigs raised by slaves circulated in the West Indian economy through the Sunday markets or through hucksters who came to the plantations to exchange commodities, bringing town items, such as bread and pastries, and leaving with home-grown produce. With an eye for the details of economic exchange, Carmichael describes the role of the African Caribbean hucksters, both enslaved and free, in the circulation of commodities: "[T]hree times a week, hucksters used to come from St. Josephs [Trinidad] to our estate, with great trays on their heads, loaded with bread, cakes, and pastry; and they seldom carried many of their dainties away. The negroes did not give money for these little luxuries; they went on the system of barter and exchange; and these huckster women might be seen, coming across the pasture from the negro houses, equally laden as when they went; but with this difference, that they now carried fruit, vegetables, and eggs, to retail at St. Josephs" (2:166). Arguing that such forms of exchange were an important part of the West Indian economy, Walvin describes how the circulation of commodities was in the hands of slaves: "Produce from the plantations, and from slave plots on the plantations, imported goods and foodstuffs from other West Indian islands, manufactured articles, luxuries and essentials, meat, poultry and fish; all could be had from slave higglers in the towns and cities. Slaves wandered the streets of the towns carrying their wares on their heads (as did London's wandering hawkers), knocking on doors, selling to passers-by and sometimes irritating local propertied society by their intrusiveness."[39]

Planters and townsfolk were dependent on slaves who raised food for sale and on hucksters and Sunday markets to fill their kitchens with fresh fruit, vegetables, eggs, and meat. Carmichael relied on her slaves to grow food for her family, paying them for these commodities, the product of their expertise and labor: "I paid E., a house boy, seven shillings for two chickens. From that date, fruit, vegetables, eggs, fresh fish, game, poultry, and pork, following in succession; and money was fast made" (2:167). One of Brunias's paintings, *French Mulatress Purchasing Fruit from a Negro Wench* (Fig. 33), depicts a young slave woman kneeling before a basket of fruit, her arm outstretched, offering it to the standing, more elegantly attired mulatto woman. This "Negro wench" participates in an economy that could make slaves prosperous, even free through the accumulation of wealth. Walvin suggests that white people felt threatened, their sense of superiority shaken by an autonomous economic system that was built on slaves' diligence, ingenuity, and skill in agriculture, husbandry, and merchandizing: "What whites disliked most was the slaves' independence; that autonomous, self-confident and assertive black presence. . . . It seemed inappropriate in a slave society to have slaves operating successfully at so important a level of economic and social activity."[40] A prosperous slave-run market economy threatened the plantocratic belief that slaves need masters and that Africans need the institution of slavery to manage their lives.[41] Roderick A. McDonald argues that the importance of the internal economy generated by the provision grounds "rests less on the quantities of money accumulated than on its social implications." "Participation in the internal economy fostered slave initiative at odds with the subservience characteristic of much of plantation life. The decision making and choices exercised within the economy contradicted the premises of slavery: in the economy's operation, the slaves made planting, harvesting, and marketing decisions, chose how and when to spend the earnings they accumulated, assessed how to apportion their free time, and weighed the advisability of this or that theft." Working in provision grounds, slaves exercised their skills as agronomists and as managers of their own time and labor, activities requiring an independence that was, as McDonald says, "at odds with the notion of being chattels."[42] Also undermined by this autonomous slave economy was the concept of slavery as a form of benevolence, a belief that Carmichael voices when she says her "negroes" need her to ensure their comfort and happiness.

Another Brunias painting depicts a town scene with three women standing together, examining a tray of flowers that one of them is holding (Fig. 28). They are each beautifully dressed; however, the one most interested in purchasing flowers is the best dressed, without an apron and wearing an elegant, lacy petticoat. She holds a flower to her nose to appreciate its fragrance. All three women are African Caribbean, all three prosperous, graceful, and dignified. *A West Indian Flower Girl* displays none of the desperation or squalor that haunts pictures with similar subject matter in Britain, such as the series of engravings entitled *The Cries of London*. All is grace and elegance in Brunias's market scenes, even in *Linen Day, Roseau* (Fig. 31), which is crowded with a great variety of people: slaves sitting on the ground or seated at booths under umbrellas, selling their cloth to all ranks, including a dramatically dressed mulatto woman and an elegantly attired white woman accompanied by a well-dressed African servant. There is stillness to these market scenes that anticipates the museum display of the late nineteenth century and twentieth century; the subjects are frozen in positions that display them the fullest to our inquiring eyes. Perhaps this woodenness can be attributed to a lack of skill or an inability to capture movement on Brunias's part. Or we can attribute this stillness to other causes: his need to represent these figures as subjects of natural history, and his Italian training as a draughtsman, which included copying classical sculpture. Brunias's hucksters, unlike Carmichael's or Young's, present no menace; they are all grace and elegance, images that reflect the "civilizing" power of commerce.

The power of the market economy to transform people is recognized by Sir William Young in a passage on the civilizing effect on the Black Caribs of growing tobacco and selling sugar. Having fought the British in the 1770s for the right to live unmolested on the windward side of the island of St. Vincent, the Black Caribs, or the Black Charaibes, as the British called them, were a powerful people and were essentially the last large group of native peoples living in the Caribbean islands at the end of the eighteenth century. They lived like Carib Indians, hunting, gathering, owning very few possessions, and defending their borders against the depredations of British planters and the military. Young's father had waged war against them, hoping to acquire their vast tracts of fertile land on St. Vincent for British use, but had failed to extirpate the Black Caribs from their portion of the island. Twenty years later Sir William Young II is pleased to see the Black Caribs' adoption of tobacco and sugar agronomy. Ironically, what his father could not do with soldiers, money could effect: the conversion of "vacant" land into "productive" land and the conversion of a "primitive" people into a "civilized" society. "The Charaibes thus begin to taste of money, and are already become very industrious at this work. Moreover, they plant tobacco, and want nothing but a market to encourage them to plant more. Chatoyer's brother (Du Vallee) [Chatoyer is the chief] has nine negroes [slaves], and plants cotton. Money civilizes in the first instance, as it corrupts in the last; the savage labouring for himself, soon ceases to be a savage . . . the slave to money becomes a subject to government, and he becomes a useful subject" (3:282). This statement disconcerts Young's editor, Bryan Edwards, who supplies a long footnote qualifying what Young has proposed rather flippantly as a solution to the problem posed by the Black Caribs. Buried in Young's enthusiasm for commerce is the implication that money and commerce can civilize not only Indians but Africans as well. Edwards has to explain away what looks like Young's advocacy of wage labor, a position that was unacceptable to slave owners in the Caribbean, as free wage labor was the rallying cry of abolitionists and those who were against the West Indian sugar monopoly.[43] Edwards writes: "[T]he doctrine of my amiable friend, without some qualification, seems to sanctify an assertion which has been maintained by speculative writers, with some plausibility; namely, 'that if the negro slaves were allowed wages for their labour, coercion would become unnecessary.' What effect a system of gradual encouragement, by means of wages, operating slowly and progressively, might produce in a long course of time, I will not presume to say; but I am persuaded that an attempt to introduce such a system among the labouring negroes in general, without great caution and due preparation, would be productive of the greatest of evils" (3:283). Edwards believes that having money itself will not change the slave into a responsible member of society, rather, that it is "the new desires springing up in his mind, from the prospects and examples before him, that have awakened his powers, and called the energies of his mind into action" (3:283). Edwards and Young seem to have underestimated the extent to which slaves were already participating in a market economy and were already working hard to satisfy their desires, producing commodities so that they could enter into economic exchange. These economic transactions possessed the promise of transformations, not only from poor to prosperous, and barbaric to civilized (Young's language), but from slavery to freedom.

In West Indian society, clothing, and to a lesser extent jewelry, were sites of multiple and competing narratives about slavery, property, and identity. Slaves' access to fine clothing was a source of pride and discomfort for plantocrats. Planters would boast of their slaves' fine apparel as a sign of their slaves' financial and emotional well-being under the institution of slavery. But slaves' access to wealth in the form of clothing and gold jewelry unsettled plantocrats, by presenting them with the conundrum of property owning property, disturbing the neat binary that equates personhood with property ownership and slavery with the absence of property.

Brunias's depictions of slaves engaged in economic exchange and slaves possessing material wealth in the form of clothing and jewelry generate narratives about change, and these narratives challenge the power of the ethnographic to erase human agency and history. However, as suggestive as these narratives are of potential change, they are still presented within the limitations of the ethnographic conceptual framework. Two contradictory discourses are at work in Brunias's Caribbean paintings: one that assumes the universe is static, timeless, unchanging, and hierarchical, and the other that posits the possibility of change, even transformation through individual agency. The clothing and jewelry in these pictures participate in both discursive realms: they can be interpreted as surface traits, used to identify a type and to place that type in the great chain of being, and they can also signal narratives of slaves who have accumulated wealth through hard work and commercial craft. The significance of these little paintings lies in their ability to embrace both the stasis of natural history's systems of classification and the narrative progression associated with primitive forms of accumulation. As a result of the presence of elements that refer to these contending discourses, Brunias's images come closer than one might expect on first glance to capturing the complexity and contradictions of West Indian slave society.

6

Imperial Designs

BOTANICAL ILLUSTRATION AND

THE BRITISH BOTANIC EMPIRE

Previous chapters have focused on British enslavement of Africans and the appropriation of Native American land; this chapter examines another form of imperial power, one that Mary Louise Pratt has termed the "anti-conquest" narrative of natural history. Unlike the brute power exercised by slavers and planters or the physical violence of backwoods Indian haters and squatters, the kind of power exercised by naturalists was epistemological and discursive, for the goals of natural history were to describe and to organize natural phenomena, and as such, natural history was portrayed by its proponents as benign and innocent. Poet laureate James Henry Pye wrote a poem celebrating the plant-collecting activities of Sir Joseph Banks as a benevolent extension of George III's imperial powers:

> George's parental sway and Albion's laws
> Spreading where Ammon's empire never spread . . .
> Sudden, a buoyant Vessel meets his eyes,
> Not launch'd by thirst of wealth, or hope of fame,
> Science alone directs the bold emprise . . .[1]

Despite claims that natural history was a disinterested enterprise, the botanizing practices of natural historians, explorers, and gentleman scholars performed the important work of locating and documenting natural resources ripe for imperial appropriation. Dependent on as well as an extension of imperial power, natural history, as Pratt argues, takes "possession without subjugation and violence."[2]

This chapter focuses primarily on botanical illustrations commissioned by or published under the direction of Sir Joseph Banks, who, as president of the Royal Society and unofficial director of the Royal Botanic Gardens at Kew, was one of the most powerful men in the late-eighteenth-century British scientific community. My aim is to explore the ways in which botanical illustration was employed by the British botanical establishment in their discovery of plants new to Europe, in their management of information about these global resources, and in their manipulation of the world's plant life. Before examining specific illustrations produced by English and Indian artists, I survey the activities and mentalities of the late-eighteenth-century British botanical establishment so that we may understand the context in which these illustrations were produced. I then examine the way botanical art's complex formal codes simultaneously lent themselves to the imperial aims of British botany and undermined some of the basic tenets of this Linnaean-inflected botany.

Sir Joseph Banks

In 1768 Sir Joseph Banks, gentleman and amateur botanist, sailed with Captain Cook on his first voyage around the world. Banks brought with him Dr. Daniel Solander, a botanist and pupil of Carl von Linné, the naturalist Herman Sporing, two artists, Sydney Parkinson and Alexander Buchan, and four servants to assist in an ambitious undertaking: the cataloguing of all the new plants they encountered on their voyage. The *Endeavour* stopped at Madeira, Rio de Janeiro, and Tierra del Fuego on the way to Tahiti, where they were to stay for several months before embarking on an exploration of the mysterious south continent. While the *Endeavour* lay anchored off Rio de Janeiro, Banks had been ordered by the viceroy of Brazil to remain on board because the colonial governor believed that Banks and his team of botanists and artists were spies. Banks's desire to collect new plant life was so strong that he ignored the Brazilian governor's directive,

and under the cover of darkness he and Solander slipped off the ship
and rowed ashore so that they might gather a few botanical specimens. Solander described and named the three hundred or so items,
using the latest scientific classification system developed by Carl von
Linné, and Sydney Parkinson painted pictures of the plant specimens.[3]
In addition to these specimens, Banks also collected Brazilian fruits:
melons, pineapples, oranges, limes, lemons, mangoes, and bananas.
Banks tasted each, recording in his journal his judgments as to their
quality, and saved the seeds, which several months later he planted
in Tahiti. Proud of his cultivation skills, he wrote: "I have very little
Doubt of the former [seeds] especialy coming to perfection as I have
given away large quantities among the natives and planted also in the
woods; they now continualy ask me for seeds and have already shewd
me melon plants of their raising which look perfectly well."[4]

In transferring seeds from one ecosystem into another—planting
Brazilian seeds in Tahiti—Banks anticipates his career as director of
the Royal Gardens at Kew, a position that not only entailed the supervision of the collection and cataloguing of plant life new to Europeans but included the management of what Daniel Headrick calls
the "British Botanical Empire."[5] According to Frans Stafleu, Kew Gardens played "a role in the development of the empire through the
introduction of useful as well as ornamental plants from all parts of
the globe, for the benefit of the home country as well as of the colonial settlements."[6] During Banks's supervision of Kew (1772–1820),
approximately seven thousand new plants arrived in England from
around the world.[7] Under Banks's leadership, Kew became, in the
words of his biographer, the "great exchange house of the Empire"
and served "as an advisory centre for all practical activities in botany
while at the same time it controlled the development of botanical
exploration and experiment."[8] In her history of the Royal Botanic
Gardens, Lucille Brockway describes Kew as sharing in the "spirit of
crusading imperialism" with its "scientific development of the plants
transferred." She concludes that "Kew converted knowledge to profit
and power, for the Empire and for the industrial world system of
which Britain was then the leader."[9]

Under the direction of Banks, Kew Gardens became the center of
the British Empire's management of tropical and subtropical agriculture. Banks monitored the activities of botanical gardens that were

established by the British in their West Indian and East Indian colonies. From the Botanic Garden in St. Vincent, he received regular inventories of plants collected and cultivated for ornamental and commercial use. He was in constant correspondence with the various directors of the Calcutta Botanic Garden, offering them advice on which plants to cultivate, arguing that India, with its "advantages of soil, climate & population so eminently above its mother country, seems by nature, intended for the purpose of supplying her fabrics with raw materials."[10] Banks encouraged the East India Company to invest in the cultivation of plants, such as cotton, indigo, pepper, cinnamon, and hemp, insisting that these would be not only profitable ventures but patriotic as well, by reducing Britain's dependence on foreign powers' access to these commodities. As Ray Desmond observes, "Banks never once wavered in his conviction that the prosperity of Britain and its colonies could be enhanced by the bold and imaginative utilization of the world's natural resources."[11]

Banks did not think only in terms of the benefits that Britain would accrue from the consumption of its colonies' plant material; he also thought that the colonial territories would benefit from this worldwide traffic in plants. He encouraged the various colonial botanical gardens to exchange seeds and cultivate plants from other tropical and subtropical zones. For instance, the Calcutta Botanic Garden cultivated West Indian mahogany, one of the sixty West Indian plants adapted to the Bengal climate. Banks masterminded, unbeknownst to the East India Company, a secret mission that had as its goal the smuggling of cotton seeds out of India for experimental cultivation in the Caribbean. Banks wrote to his agent, a Kew gardener he recruited, "the real object of your mission is to procure for the West Indies seeds of the finer sorts of cotton with which the Ahmood Country where you are ordered to reside abounds."[12] Most famous, or infamous, of Banks's early attempts to manage plant transfers for the benefit of the empire is the transportation of Tahitian breadfruit to the West Indies as a cheap source of food for the slaves who worked on British sugar plantations. This transfer of plant material ended with the mutiny on Captain Bligh's *Bounty* and with the death of one of the Kew gardeners sent by Banks on the voyage to keep the plants alive en route to Jamaica. This early fiasco did not dissuade Banks from espousing the cause of the international circulation of plants and the benefits such trade would bestow on Britain and its colonies.

Botanical Illustration

Botanists like Banks, eager to collect and catalogue "new" plants, employed botanical draughtsmen to aid in their efforts to identify and classify plants. Botanical art in late-eighteenth-century Britain was heavily influenced by its role in the classification of plant life and, in effect, became an extension of botany. What was represented and what was not represented in botanical illustrations of the late eighteenth and early nineteenth century reflect the concerns of a botany shaped simultaneously by Linné's system of classification and by the colonial imperative of the era.

Europe's most famous botanical draughtsman, Georg Dionysius Ehret (1708–70), worked with Carl Linné to produce the illustrations for *Hortus Cliffortianus* (1737), which depicted the rare plants in the private botanical garden of George Clifford, an Anglo-Dutch financier. At Clifford's residence in Haarlem, Ehret and Linné shared ideas and information. Ehret wrote in his autobiography that he and Linné "were the best of friends: he showed me his new method of examining the stamens, which I easily understood, and privately resolved to bring out a Tabella of it." With this Tabella, Ehret made "some money," but it was included without acknowledgment in the second edition of Linné's *Genera Plantarum* (1742).[13] Ehret transformed botanical art subtly by focusing on those details of the plant that Linné declared the most significant to his taxonomic project. Ehret focused on the flower, depicting clearly the number of pistils and stamens so that botanists who were employing Linné's binomial system could use the illustrations to study and identify plants.

Conventions of botanical illustration that are accepted today as normal developed over the course of the eighteenth century and were influenced by the Linnaean system of classification. Typically the late-eighteenth-century botanical illustration is diagrammatic, depicting the stem, leaves, and flowers of a plant against a white background. Sometimes fruit is shown hanging from the plant; sometimes fruit is drawn as separate items and set off from the plant, either beneath or beside it. Sometimes the flower, placed near the bottom border, is drawn in its various stages of blooming, even dissected to show its parts of fructification. Not represented is the whole plant—its size and shape — nor is there any attempt to record how the plant's vital properties function. Root systems are represented infrequently. Dissected, cross-sectioned stems, limbs, and leaves rarely appear in late-eighteenth-century drawings of plants. Also eliminated from the Linnaean-influenced botanical illustration is the plant's environment, which includes the kind of soil it grows in and the kind of climatic conditions that it needs to survive. Not represented also is the plant's relationship with other plants and with animals.[14]

The cultural as well as environmental context of each plant is missing in these illustrations. The local name of the plant is not recorded; instead, the European "discoverer's" name is often assigned to the plant along with a Latinate name that places it in a classification system that has been deemed "universal." Nor are local uses of the plant recorded, nor is there any attempt to understand and record the significance of the plant to a particular human culture, such as the myths and cultural uses of the ironwood to the Tahitians or the banana plant to the Hawaiians.[15] The late-eighteenth-century botanical illustration was heavily influenced by Linnaean botany, which sought to erase the environmental and cultural contexts of plants. What Mary Louise Pratt has said of Enlightenment natural history can be applied to Linnaean botany: "Natural history extracted specimens not only from their organic or ecological relations with each other, but also from their places in other peoples' economies, histories, social and symbolic systems."[16] The white border and snipped twig of late-eighteenth-century botanical illustration reinforced the idea that a plant could be plucked from one cultural and ecological context and inserted into another with ease and with little regard for negative consequences. To understand the way some of the conventions of late-eighteenth-century botanical illustration worked to decontextualize plant life, it may be helpful to examine briefly pre-Linnaean botanical illustration, which often represented plants in either their natural or cultural contexts.

Pre-Linnaean Botanical Illustration

Before Linnaean botany dominated European and, in particular, English botanical art, illustrations of plants were included in herbals (books that detailed the medicinal uses of plants) and in landscape gardening books and horticultural treatises. According to Blanche Henrey, between 1500 and 1600, nineteen botanical illustrated books were published in England; eleven were herbals and eight were concerned with horticulture.[17] An example of a horticultural book is William Lawson's *A New Orchard and Garden* (1618, 1623), a dissertation on how to grow various kinds of trees. The title-page of Lawson's book contains a scene in which gardeners are in the process of transplanting young trees; large holes have been dug and trees complete with roots await their new home. The illustrations in John Evelyn's *The French Gardiner* (1658) are framed with words that instruct the reader in the latest horticultural techniques and contain images of women cooking the fruits of such horticultural endeavors. In seventeenth- and early-eighteenth-century books on garden design, illustrations of layouts of elaborate French and Dutch gardens were popular, along with nurserymen's seed catalogues, which contained pictures of flowers and fruits according to their season. Robert Furber, a florist and seedsman, commissioned Pieter Casteels to paint flowers and fruits in the Dutch manner for his seed catalogues, *The Twelve Months of Flowers* (1730) and *The Twelve Months of Fruit* (1732). For each of the twelve months, there is a print containing an abundance of fruit or flowers, gorgeously colored, beautifully sensuous, spilling out of bowls and baskets; beneath the luscious image is a chart with all the names of the fruits and flowers and with numbers so that a customer can easily identify the plants he or she wants to order.

In addition to seed catalogues, herbals, and treatises on horticulture, also popular were books with "serious botanical content: plant surveys . . . [and] floras of European, Asian, and American regions," according to John Brindle and James White.[18] An example of a book containing illustrations of plants from an exotic locale is Maria Sibylla Merian's *Dissertation sur la Génération et les Transformations des Insectes de Surinam* (1726). Although her focus is the insects of Surinam, Merian's emphasis on the insects' life cycle led her to incorporate plant life into her pictures. The brilliantly colored picture of the pepper plant *Capsicum annuum*, for instance, contains a caterpillar creeping on a stem of the plant; it has fed on a yellowish pepper, exposing its seeds to our view (Fig. 34). The pupa form is attached to an immature green pepper, and a butterfly rests on a curling stem. Merian's

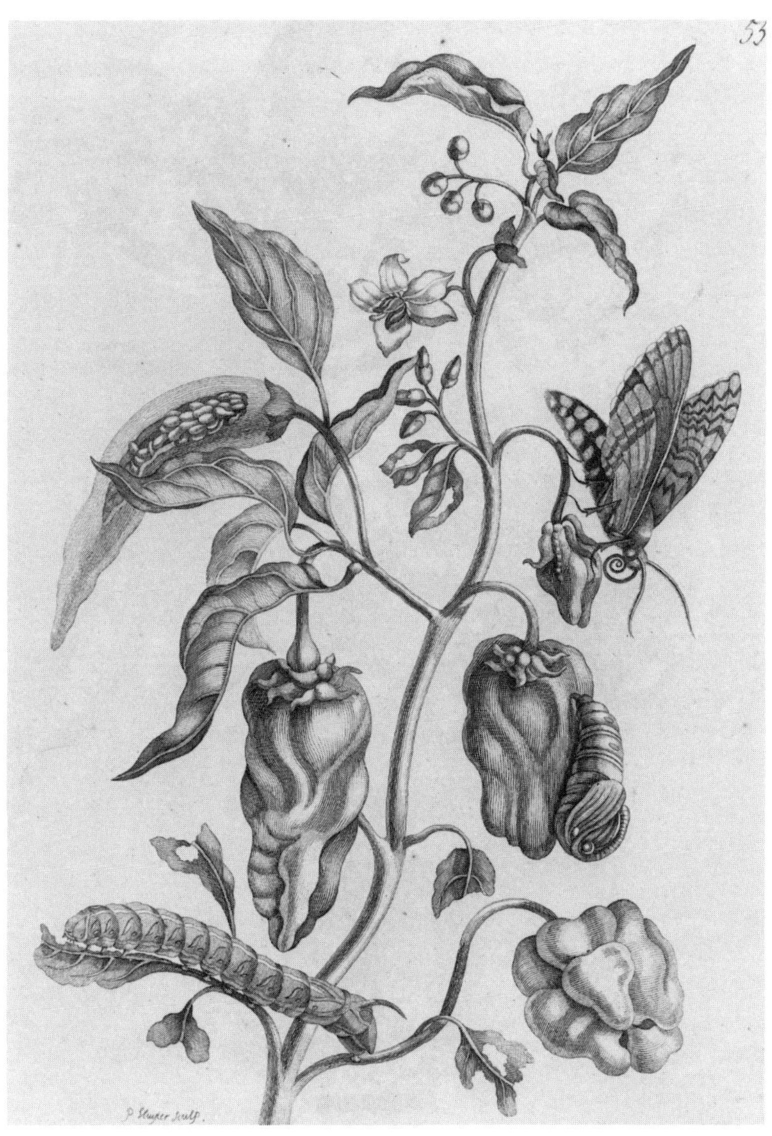

34. Maria Sibylla Merian, *Dissertation sur la Génération et Les Transformation des Insectes de Surinam*, 1726, engraved by Jan Pieter Sluyter, *Capsicum annuum*. By permission of The British Library.

drawing of the life cycle of this butterfly that lives in and around the pepper plant demonstrates a sensitivity to what we now call the ecosystem, the various and specific relationships that exist between plants and animal life. Mark Catesby in his *Natural History of Carolina, Florida and the Bahama Islands* (1730–47) also includes animals in his pictures of plants. His *Sweet Flowering Bay Tree* contains a bird, "The blew Grosbeak," which is precariously perched on a twig, stretching its neck up and twisting around to reach a suspended reddish nutlike fruit from the tree.

Early-eighteenth-century botanical illustrations usually conveyed more than a description of the leaf and flower of a particular plant. Merian's and Catesby's illustrations attempt to capture a plant's ecological relations, but other artists focused on plants in their human context. Herbals, like Elizabeth Blackwell's *A Curious Herbal, Containing 500 Cuts of the most useful plants which are now used in the Practice of Physick* (1737–39), contained information on medicinal uses of plants. The illustration of the tobacco plant, which Blackwell drew, engraved, and hand painted, contains the English common name as well as a Latinate name and a breakdown of the plant's parts—flower, calix, seed vessel, and seed. The accompanying text relates the tobacco leaf's efficacy in curing ulcers, piles, and the king's evil (scrofula). This book was meant to be used by the housewife, the apothecary, and the herbalist. Michael Bernard Valenti's *Historia Simplicium Reformata* (1716) describes non-European plants and explains the various uses of these new, exotic items. He depicts a coffee tree full of coffee berries growing in a mountainous region. In the white space surrounding the dark engraving of the tree there is Arabic writing and in Roman characters the word "Coffi." The Arabic conveys the ethnic origin of the exotic plant and drink, and the accompanying text tells the reader how to prepare this Turkish treat. Valenti's sensitivity to the cultural significance of plants and their uses can be seen also in the text accompanying his illustration of nutmeg and mace, for he includes the Indian and Javan as well as European names for these spices.[19] Valenti's as well as Blackwell's representations of plant life, like those of sixteenth- and seventeenth-century herbals, are closely allied to the study of medicine and stress the usefulness of plants. The knowledge of plants that is found in herbals, according to Londa Schiebinger, is "local and particular, derived from direct experience with plants in agriculture, gardening, or medicine, or from knowledge handed down based upon that experience." By the mid-eighteenth century, however, botanists turned from "medical application to more general and theoretical issues of pure taxonomy, as botanists sought simple principles that would hold universally."[20]

Linnaean Botany

By the mid-eighteenth century Linné's taxonomic system began to exert a powerful influence on British botany and its handmaiden, botanical illustration. In his history of the reception of Carl von Linné's *Species Plantarum* (1753) in England, W. T. Stearn suggests that the "publication of the finest illustrated works ever produced" was made possible by botany's popularity with wealthy and influential amateurs.[21] Stearn argues that Linnaean classification dominated British botany from the 1760s to the early nineteenth century because it was embraced by professional and amateur botanists alike. A contemporary observer, Robert Pulteney, wrote in 1790 that the Linnaean system "had given the author of it a literary dominion over the vegetable kingdom; which in the rapidity of its extension, and the strength of its influence, had not perhaps been paralleled in the annals of Science." Pulteney explains how Linné's doctrines "insinuated themselves" into the minds of British botanists: "The simplicity of the classical characters as the basis, the uniformity of the generical notes, confined wholly to the parts of fructification, and that precision which marked the specific distinctions, advantages of which all foregoing systems were destitute, soon commanded the assent of the unprejudiced; and after an interval of a few years, gave Linnaeus's method a decided superiority with English botanists."[22]

In his efforts to construct a systematic botany, Linné searched for a system that would, as John Lesch observes, "bring uniformity, consistency, and coherence to the representation of a clearly defined domain of natural objects."[23] Linné's taxonomic system was centered on the parts of the flower or, as he called it, "the sexual system of classification."[24] Stearn characterizes Linné's system as "a basically simple but ingenious arithematical system, whereby the genera are grouped into twenty-four classes according to the number of the stamens (together with their relative lengths, their distinctness or fusion, their occurrence in the same flower as the pistil or their separation in unisexual flowers, or their apparent absence), the Monandria having one stamen, the Diandria two stamens, the Triandria three stamens, and so on; it ends with the Cryptogamia whose reproductive habits were not then understood. Within each class the genera are arranged into smaller groups or orders according to the number of pistils."[25] By focusing on the number and connections of the parts of fructification, Linné rationalized the study of plants; as Lesch argues, he "impose[d] unity, consistency, and logical order on the whole field of botany."[26] In his drive to construct a coherent and universal system of classification, Linné excluded from consideration any part or function of the plant other than pistils and stamens. According to Stafleu, he had an "extremely narrow view of nature";[27] he ignored plant anatomy, physiology, and ecology, focusing only on the number and connection of the parts of fructification, criteria that, according to Stearn, are ironically "exactly those characters of the androecium and gynoecium which are least important as regards their sexual function."[28] As Gunnar Eriksson observes, botany before Linné had been dominated by "questions about the general nature of the plant, its growth and survival, its observance of chemical and physical laws, and its dependence on external environment, climate, and soil." Although Linné did not dismiss such matters, Eriksson notes that "he regarded them as being of secondary importance to his efforts to master the names of all forms of plants and to obtain a comprehensive view of their place in the whole."[29] Lesch argues that Linné "embraced an artificial system placing clarity of concept over empirical intuition."[30]

The simplicity of Linné's system of classification can account for its popularity with amateur botanists, and its ascendancy with amateur botanists like Banks can be explained by the fact that the Linnaean system limited botanical study to the identification and naming of plants and ignored more complicated (and more scientific) analyses of anatomy and physiology. As Lesch notes, Linné characterized "his science as one of 'describing and picturing,' and defines a naturalist as one who distinguishes and names the parts of natural bodies by sight."[31] Previous systems, according to Stearn, "demanded a more detailed knowledge of plants and a more expert user than did the Linnaean system which replaced them." With the help of Linné, British botany was transformed from "being the preserve of the pharmacist and the medical man" into a field of study in which the amateur could play a significant role.[32] No amateur played a more significant role in the scientific community of late-eighteenth-century London than Sir Joseph Banks.

The Exotica of the Empire

Linnaean classification's domination of British botany can also be explained by the influx of plants into England from the Americas. Stafleu argues that the "rapidity with which Linnaean thought gained ground in England in the 1760s must be seen in the light of . . . a need for a practical system and nomenclature in . . . a period of rapidly increasing plant introductions from many parts of an expanding empire."[33] British botany developed side by side with the discovery and conquest of foreign lands.

Having accompanied Cook on his navigation around the globe, Banks was celebrated by poets and fellow botanists as a conquering hero. Using language reserved for heroic feats, James Henry Pye, poet laureate, sings the praises of Banks and his plant-hunting expeditions:

> Advent'rous BANKS! . . .
> Now 'mid the rigour of antarctic frost,
> Where the chill stream of life scarce keeps its way;
> Now where the day-stream on the sultry coast
> At noon-tide sheds th' insufferable ray . . .
> His pride, on every land, in every clime,
> From the low shrub that clothes the arid plane,
> To where the cedar waves her boughs sublime,
> Careful to trace the vegetable reign.

Robert Thorton, who included this poem in his *Temple of Flora* (1799–1807), provides the reader with a lengthy footnote on Banks that makes explicit the connection between botany and empire. He associates Banks's botanical collecting with the spoils of empire when he cites Pliny on the origin of cherry trees, which were brought to Italy by Lucullus after his defeat of Mithridates. Thorton describes the botanical spoils of other conquering heroes: Pompey and Vespasian bore "in their triumphs the trees of the conquered countries, producing a remembrance of their victories more useful and durable than columns of brass or marble." The "science of Botany," writes Thorton, has enlisted "the fine Arts into her service,"[34] and that service was the British colonial project.

By representing only the flowering stem of a plant from Australia or Tahiti, for instance, on a white background, botanical illustrators exoticized their subject. As we have seen in the discussion on Caldwell's Indian souvenirs, exoticism, according to Harriet Guest, "inscribes its object with an acultural illegibility, isolated from any coherence of origin." Guest suggests that the process by which an object is exoticized is through the "colonizing displacement or dislocation of its object from any signs of the personal estate or cultural context that might produce legible or potent significance." In Guest's discussion of Banks's wish to bring an islander back with him "as a souvenir of his trip to the South Pacific," she quotes from his journal, calling attention to his own perception of himself as a collector of curios: " 'Thank heaven I have a sufficiency and I do not know why I may not keep him as a curiosity, as well as some of my neighbours do lions and tygers at a larger expense than he will probably ever put me to.' " Guest argues that the curiosity that this Polynesian figure aroused in Banks "thrives on the isolation of its exotic object" and is replicated in the zoos to which Banks refers. Guest's analysis of "the colonialist curiosity . . . which demands that its objects be presented stripped of context, and feeds on the wondrous exoticism" can be applied to Banks's work as a collector of botanical specimens.[35] Banks's expedition to the South Pacific, in fact his whole career as a botany enthusiast, was fueled by this curiosity about the exotic. He was not a scientist; he did not even practice taxonomy, but employed others to perform this task. He was a collector of curios and even had himself represented this way.[36] Banks commissioned a portrait of himself surrounded by the curios he had collected on the South Pacific voyage (Fig. 11). In Benjamin West's portrait, Banks stands erect, proud, and confident, dominating the exotic collection that surrounds him.

Banks enjoyed his role as collector par excellence; he enjoyed having the largest collection of botanical curios in England. The fact that Banks never published *The Florilegium*, Parkinson's illustrations and Solander's taxonomic descriptions of the plants collected on the South

Pacific voyage, can be explained, in part, by his being a collector who lacked the scientist's commitment to publishing and thus to sharing new ideas and information. He liked to maintain control over his botanical domain, and to publish would be to lose this control. His role at Kew was an outgrowth of his role as a private collector. Under his direction Kew Gardens became the site of the largest collection of botanical specimens in the world. At Kew Gardens, the botanical version of the zoo, the exoticism of plants from tropical zones is heightened by the dislocation of these plants from their ecological and cultural contexts. The famed Palm House, the nineteenth-century realization of a Banksian dream, works to decontextualize plant life. Even though it recreates the hot and humid air of the tropics, it is an idealized tropics, not a re-creation of an ecosystem specific to Jamaica or Tahiti, for instance. In this undifferentiated tropical setting, bananas from Tahiti grow side by side with bananas from the Caribbean, and ginger from Jamaica grows next to ginger from Brazil. No attempt has been made to replicate a specific place's tropical ecosystem (as opposed to, for instance, the San Diego Zoo's sun bear exhibit that re-creates a Malaysian rainforest.) The Palm House represents the triumph of Britain's power to collect, analyze, and manage the world's resources for Britain's benefit.[37]

The Local and the Universal

Banks's voyage with Cook is emblematic of the dual thrust of voyages of discovery: to claim for the Crown lands and peoples and to control information about these places. But although both Banks's and Cook's collecting of information was an exercise in imperial power, their ways of knowing were quite distinct.[38] In an insightful assessment of Banks's activity as a botanizer on the voyage of the *Endeavour*, Paul Carter compares Banks's and Cook's approaches to their tasks of naming their discoveries. Carter argues that Cook's exploration of coastlines and seas and his mapmaking were very different epistemological processes from Banks's discovery of new plants and his use of taxonomy and botanical illustration to represent his discoveries. "Cook's geo-graphy, his writing of lands, was inseparable from the conditions of the inquiry itself," argues Carter, and the maps he made of the Australian coastline recorded his own experience with that particular place. His maps "did not mirror the appearance of natural objects, but preserved the trace of encountering them." While Cook's knowledge of new lands "was indistinguishable from the conditions of knowing," Banks's use of Linnaean botany to name and classify new plants concealed "the discovering process." Plants were inserted into a system that assumed they already existed before discovery, that they had occupied a place in the grand taxonomic scheme and were only waiting to have their existence confirmed by being sighted and named. Banks's way of knowing the new was to move from "a superficial acquaintance to grand generalization." In contrast to Cook's mapping, which was an interactive process that had come to terms with a place's specificity, Banks's use of Linnaean nomenclature and botanical illustration attests to adherence to a universal system of ideal types, a system that ignores the specificity and individuality of an object. Carter contends that the "botanizing mind" is indifferent to the "claims of locality," and in detaching an object "from historical and geographical surroundings," botany steals from its object of study the "power to signify beyond itself, to suggest lines of development or the subtler influences of climate, ground, and aspect." [39]

Banks's botanizing mind was a product of the Enlightenment; he was, as a civic humanist, bent on erasing the particular and on relegating the specific and the local to the realm of fashion and custom. British civic humanists rewrote the particular and the local as trivial in their search for a transhistorical and transcultural universality. Banks had the same agenda as did Dr. Samuel Johnson and Sir Joshua Reynolds: to deny to the local the power to constitute the significance of an object. Johnson insists that "the business of a poet . . . is to examine, not the individual, but the species; to remark general properties and large appearances." To explicate this process whereby the individual and the specific are suppressed in the search for general properties, Johnson describes how a poet (or, for our purposes, an artist) should depict plants: "he does not number the streaks of the tulip, or describe the different shades in the verdure of the forest. He is to exhibit in his portraits of nature such prominent and striking features, as recal the original to every mind; and must neglect the minuter discriminations." To ignore the appeal of the particular and to focus on discovering general principles, the poet, Johnson says, "must divest himself of the prejudices of his age and country; he must consider right and wrong in their abstracted and invariable state; he must disregard present laws and opinions, and rise to general and transcendental truths, which will always be the same."[40] Reynolds asserts in his third *Discourse* that "the whole beauty and grandeur of the art consists, in my opinion, in being able to get above all singular forms, local customs, particularities, and details of every kind."[41] The universalizing impulse insists that there is a universally applicable truth that exists outside time, place, and culture, and yet, as Foucault points out in *The Order of Things*, this Enlightenment obsession with the universal is a product of a particular time and place: eighteenth-century Europe.[42] To invoke the universal was to impose a European order on the world, usurping the power to make meaning from cultures peripheral to the European core.

Late-eighteenth-century British botany worked to establish British dominance over the world's botanical resources by employing ideal types of a universalizing system to diminish a plant's relation to its ecological and cultural contexts. This particular kind of botany was a colonial discourse; its goal was to erase the power of the local to determine meaning and to insist that there was only one legitimate order, and that this order was best understood by Europeans who were adept in managing this world system.

Botany's Handmaiden

Botanical artists satisfied the taxonomic needs of Linnaean botany by arranging the specimen so that the pistils and stamens were visible and by carefully delineating the parts of the sexual system. By placing the image of a snipped twig on a field of white, botanical artists reinforced the decontextualizing thrust of Linnaean botany, which sought to place plant life into static, preexistent, Platonic categories. In these ways botanical illustration of the late eighteenth century conformed to the demands of a botany heavily influenced by Linné's system of classification and by the need to manage information about the huge influx of plants new to Britain.

However obliging botanical illustration may have seemed to be in fulfilling the aims of Linnaean botany, it draws upon artistic traditions and conventions that ultimately contradict the aims of this "cult of botany."[43] Botanical illustration is internally inconsistent because it is informed, as Bernard Smith argues, by the "central paradox of naturalism." Smith explains this paradox: "The object of the natural-history draughtsman was to draw the *type* rather than the individual specimen with all its imperfections. Yet how was the artist to decide upon those characteristics that were typical of a particular animal and those that were accidental? To achieve this the draughtsman . . . required a conceptual framework to give order to his observations."[44] This absence of this conceptual framework is apparent in the illustrations that Hans Weiditz made for the woodcuts in Brunfels's *Herbarum vivae eicones* (1531). Weiditz's drawing of a specimen of *Arctium Lappa* shows wilted leaves and insect-damaged stems; his attention to these details indicates that he was copying what he saw and failed to omit those individual characteristics that were not general to this species. In *Herbals: Their Origin and Evolution* Agnes Arber argues that Weiditz's representation of "the actual example he had before him, whether it was normal or not," arose out of a conceptual problem: "The notion had not then been grasped, that the drawing which is ideal from the standpoint of systematic botany, avoids the accidental peculiarities of any individual specimen, seeking rather to portray the characters fully typical for the species."[45]

In its efforts to produce an image of a plant that is not meant to be a reproduction of an individual specimen but a representative of that plant's whole species, botanical illustration elides the distinction between the particular and the typical. In reality, ideal types do not exist; ideal types are a construct that belongs to a Platonic vision of the universe that is static, unchanging, and timeless. Linné's system of classification pivoted on the concept of the ideal type; the true vegetable kingdom existed, for him, on an ideal plane divorced from the particular, the local, and the agency of time.[46]

All botanical illustrations to some extent struggle to construct ideal types; in those illustrations produced under the auspices of Linnaean botany, this struggle to eliminate the particularities of individual specimens as well as the influence of time and place is even more intense. Despite the efforts of botanical artists to create ideal types untouched by historical processes, time is not that easily banished from botanical illustration for the reason that one of botanical illustration's antecedents is, as Bernard Smith observes, still life. The "aesthetic strength" of still life "lay not in a rendering of the ideal but in depicting the palpable presence of the object in all its particularity."[47] Dutch still life of the seventeenth century celebrates the objects that belong to everyday life with its detailed rendering of the colors, shapes, and textures of material surfaces.

Seventeenth-century Netherlandish still life not only rendered the particular in all its glorious detail, but it also alluded to the passage of time in its representation of natural and built objects. In her discussion of Dutch pictorial art, Svetlana Alpers notes that "an insistent feature" of David Bailly's *Still Life* is "the traditional reference made by almost every object (candle, bubbles, hourglass, skull, jewels, coins, books) and the inscription at the lower right to vanity and hence to the transience of all human endeavor and particularly of life itself."[48] Ingvar Bergstrom argues that seventeenth-century Dutch still life was "designed to make the observer contemplate the brevity of life, the frailty of man and the vanity of all worldly things." Seventeenth-century Dutch flower painting, as a type of still life, concerns itself with the ephemeral nature of life. Flowers were often seen as "symbols for . . . fleeting life," and, as Bergstrom points out, biblical references to the brevity of life couched in flower metaphors permeated Dutch Calvinist culture with phrases such as "Man that is born of a woman is of few days. . . . He cometh forth like a flower, and is cut down," and "All flesh is grass, and all the goodliness thereof is as the flower of the field: The grass withereth, the flower fadeth: because the spirit of the LORD bloweth upon it; surely the people is grass."[49] Seventeenth-century Dutch flower paintings, in particular, and still life in general are, as Norman Bryson says, laced with "emblems of . . . ephemerality."[50]

Because botanical illustration as an art form draws upon techniques developed within the conventions of still life painting, time as well as the particular often make themselves present. The drawings that Parkinson made during the *Endeavour* voyage provide an excellent example of the complex interplay of contending conventions at work in the representation of plant life. Time creeps into many of Parkinson's illustrations even though they were produced literally right under Sir Joseph Banks's superintending gaze. In his journal Banks describes how he and Solander supervised Parkinson: onboard the *Endeavour,* Banks and Solander catalogued their specimens while sitting at a "great table with our draughtsman opposite and showed him in what way to make his drawings." [51] The Netherlandish influence surfaces in Parkinson's drawings despite his being surrounded on shipboard by models from Banks's extensive botanical library, including, of course, Linné's *Species Plantarum* and *Genera Plantarum*.

In drawing upon the older Netherlandish idioms, several of Parkinson's illustrations allude to the passage of time and thus subtly resist the totalizing project of Linnaean botany. Plate 275 of Banks's *Florilegium*, based on Parkinson's 1770 drawing and engraved by John Sebastian Miller in 1773, contains the image of the snipped twig of an Australian plant from Botany Bay (Fig. 35). *Xylomelum pyriforme (Gaertner)*, as Solander classified the plant, is depicted as a beautiful swirling bunch of graceful leaves and suggestively pendulant seedpods. The composition of Parkinson's drawing stresses the plant's vitality. The branch, placed upright on the left side of the picture, splits into two smaller branches that gracefully arch out, one moving down and right and the other moving up and left. Each of these branches contains a cluster of long, tapered, green leaves, forming two circular shapes, one above the other. The leaves, radiating out from the clusters' centers, twist and curl, and reveal in their midst two oval-shaped, dark gray seedpods, one for each cluster of leaves. The upper pod is smaller and less developed than the lower, which hangs down, slightly split and exposing the light brown nut inside. This larger pod looks heavy, as if it is about to drop its seed. Parkinson, though drawing from a snipped specimen that was in the process of dying (hence the curling leaves?), manages to invest this twig with energy and movement, giving it a life of its own. By depicting the two pods, one ripe, the other immature, he implies a developmental life cycle for this plant. He constructs a time continuum, one that implies a past—the plant's growth from a seed and into a mature seed-bearing plant—and projects a future, the propagation of this plant through its seed, a future that has been arrested by its involvement in Banks's botanizing project. This image of the pendulant pod also suggests the plant's relation to the earth and its interaction with its habitat: we visualize the seed falling into the earth, implanting itself, growing and reproducing. The seedpod also carries with it the idea of kinship, that plants have genealogies and that they can inherit characteristics from their "parents," an idea that was to assume major significance in

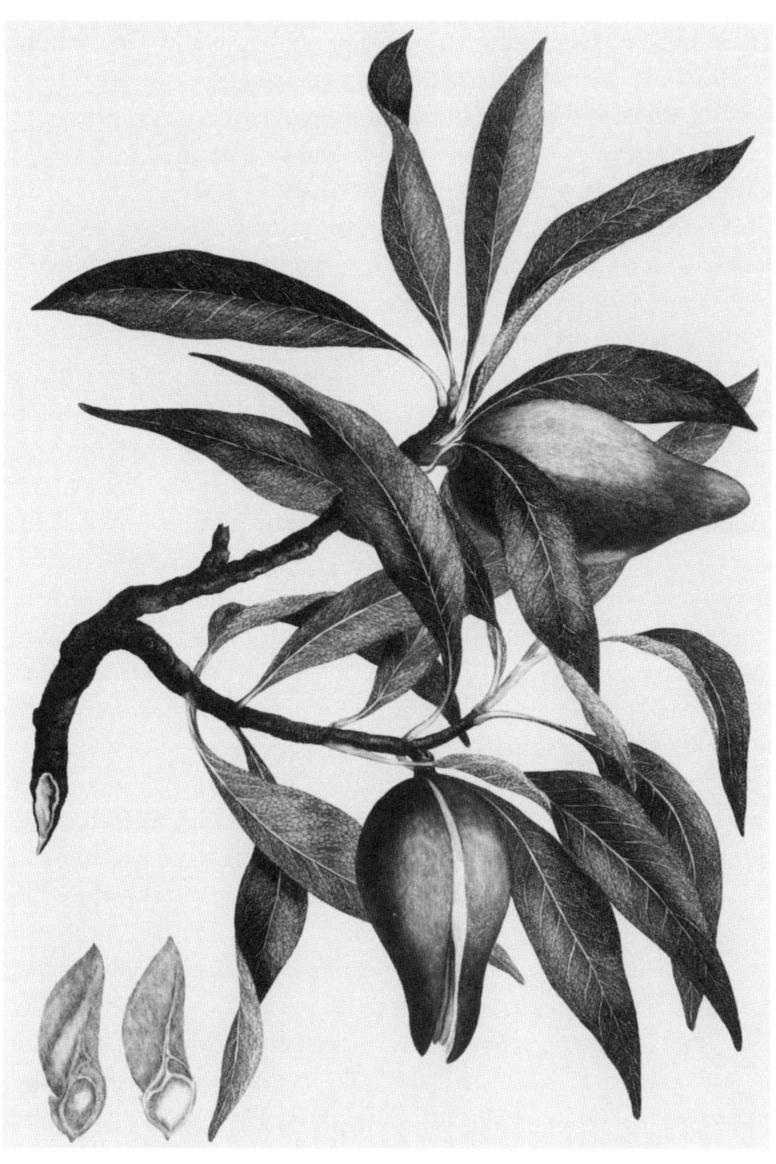

35. Sydney Parkinson, *Xylomelum pyriforme,* 1770, plate 275 from *Banks' Florilegium* (1980–), engraved by J. F. Miller (1773). © British Museum (Natural History) and Alecto Editions. Reproduced by the kind permission of the publishers.

nineteenth- and twentieth-century genetic biology. With this drawing Parkinson has managed to complicate the taxonomic process that inserts the plant into a static and timeless hierarchy of ideal types, not only by portraying the plant's vitality but by placing the plant in a constantly changing realm of time and space.

Not only does Parkinson render plants' temporality in some of his illustrations, in a few he also conveys a sense of place. His drawing of an unusual plant collected by Banks and Solander on the Endeavour River represents this particular plant's relation to its environment. The plant, named by Solander *Epidendroides tetranda* and known today as *Rubiaceae* or the anti-house plant, is represented as having eight elongated, dark olive green leaves, attached to a short, stubby stem that is growing out of a large, round, bulbous trunk. Thin, white, spindly roots emerge from the bulblike lower portion of the plant, suggesting the plant's physiology. The plant's large and bumpy bulbous lower portion has been sliced through, revealing a catacomb of holes, the home of a particular species of ants, *Irdomyrmex cordatus,* and the larvae of a butterfly, the Apollo Jewel. Parkinson's rendition of the many dark holes suggests an "intimate association" with these ants; without representing the insects, he manages to evoke their presence and portray their symbiotic relation to the plant.[52] In another drawing of a symbiotic relation, Parkinson depicts a specimen of the orchid family, the *Taneniophylum fasciola,* which, according to F. R. Fosberg and Marie-Hélène Sachet, is "a curious genus of leafless . . . autotrophic orchids." The green, spiderlike "aerial roots" are shown "firmly adhering to the bark of the host tree." The plant's tiny flowers are barely visible, and its tenacious grasp on what looks like a rotting branch of a tree conveys a sense of this plant's delicate relation with its environment.[53] Parkinson's sketches, in drawing upon older traditions such as Netherlandish still life, created images of plants that, while satisfying the need to identify plants according to Linné's sexual system, also subtly undermined the Linnaean erasure of the workings of time and place on plant life.

Company Art

Like Parkinson, other botanical artists called upon older artistic traditions to produce images that undercut the aims of their botanizing patrons.[54] Striking examples of the (con)fusion of artistic practice and scientific method can be found in the botanical art produced by Indian artists for their British patrons during their tenure in India. One of the earliest British patrons of Indian botanical art was Lady Impey, wife of Sir Elijah Impey, whose subdued but regal countenance was captured by Zoffany in *The Impey Family Listening to Strolling Musicians* (Fig. 21). Stuart Cary Welch describes the natural history paintings she commissioned as representing "a transitional stage between purely Mughal and Company idioms." He notes that while the paintings use English paper, the "pigments have been applied in the very time-consuming, traditional Mughal burnished layers, a method given up for purposes of economy in the later Company studies." A painting of a double Rose of Sharon (*Hybiscus syriacus*) signed by the artist, Shaykh Zayn-al-Din, blends the idioms of European art—"the flowers as specimens, with cut stems"—with Muslim traditions. Welch sees in Zayn-al-Din's "twittering, lively composition, which 'reads' like Urdu and Persian, from right to left," the artist's "Muslim education." The painting is very busy and full of life. A centipede undulates across the lower stretches of the paper while a caterpillar creeps toward its delicious meal, the foliage of the *Gloriosa superba,* or Malabar glory lily; birds perch on the stems of the flowers and two butterflies stretch their wings, one resting on the blooming hibiscus and the other having alighted on the seedpod of the *Gloriosa superba.* The plants are intricately depicted: the details of the life cycle from blossom to seed are included in the representation of the lily, and the hibiscus bloom contains a careful rendering of the details of the flower's reproductive organs that were so important to British botanists. Welch makes the point that these paintings were not natural history illustrations or studies and did not meet the standards required by "scientific accuracy," and yet their beauty, the product of the blending of two cultural traditions, were "seldom surpassed" in company botanical painting.[55]

In the 1790s under the direction of men like William Roxburgh and Nathaniel Wallich, the East India Company employed native artists to record the natural history of India. Roxburgh, as director of the Calcutta Botanic Garden, employed native artists to draw specimens of plants in the garden unknown to Europeans. As Phyllis Edwards surmises, Roxburgh must have trained his Indian draughtsmen in the "proper method of presentation," perhaps giving them plates from

Curtis's *Flora Londinensis* as examples.[56] Altogether, these artists produced drawings for 2,542 of the species in the Sibpur Botanic Garden in Calcutta.[57] Roxburgh often had difficulty persuading the East India Company that paying these artists a salary was a worthwhile expenditure. He enlisted the aid of Sir Joseph Banks, who, as England's best-known collector of exotic plants, managed to oversee, sometimes at great distances, the publication of many illustrated botanical books, including Roxburgh's *The Plants of the Coast of Coromandel*. Banks thought that botanical illustrations were crucial in the process of identifying and cataloguing new species and encouraged the British East India Company to support Roxburgh's efforts to record Indian plant life. Banks intervened between Roxburgh and the Court of Directors of the Company, and explained to them that Roxburgh's project would not only aid scientific discovery but would provide useful information on the cultivation and uses of these plants. He wrote to the Court of Directors insisting that Roxburgh's drawings and descriptions of plants on the coast of Coromandel would enable "company servants . . . to know readily the vegetable production" of this area as well as "the uses of each, both commercial or medicinal," and that this knowledge would eventually profit the company.[58] Successful in persuading the company to finance Roxburgh's project, Banks also insisted that the drawings be sent to him to see if they met his high standards for scientific accuracy and artistic merit. Banks informed the company that the drawings had been executed with skill: "the accuracy with which the parts illustrative of the sexual system are delineated, the intelligence with which interesting views of these parts are selected, and the patience and detail with which the descriptions are drawn up, do great honor to the abilities of Dr. Roxburgh."[59] Only when he had approved of Roxburgh's descriptions of the plants and the accompanying drawings were they published. Banks oversaw the reproduction of the drawings in London and *The Plants of the Coast of Coromandel* was published "under the direction of Sir Joseph Banks" in twelve parts over twenty-five years (1795–1820).[60]

The Indian artists, most anonymous with the exception of the famed Vishnupersaud and Gorachaud, produced illustrations of plants that, while conforming to the demands of Linnaean botany, do not completely erase their ecological and cultural contexts. *Cylista scariosa* and *Caesalpinia sappan,* or sappan-wood tree, plate 16 of Roxburgh's *Plants of the Coast of Coromandel,* volume 1 (1795), are full of

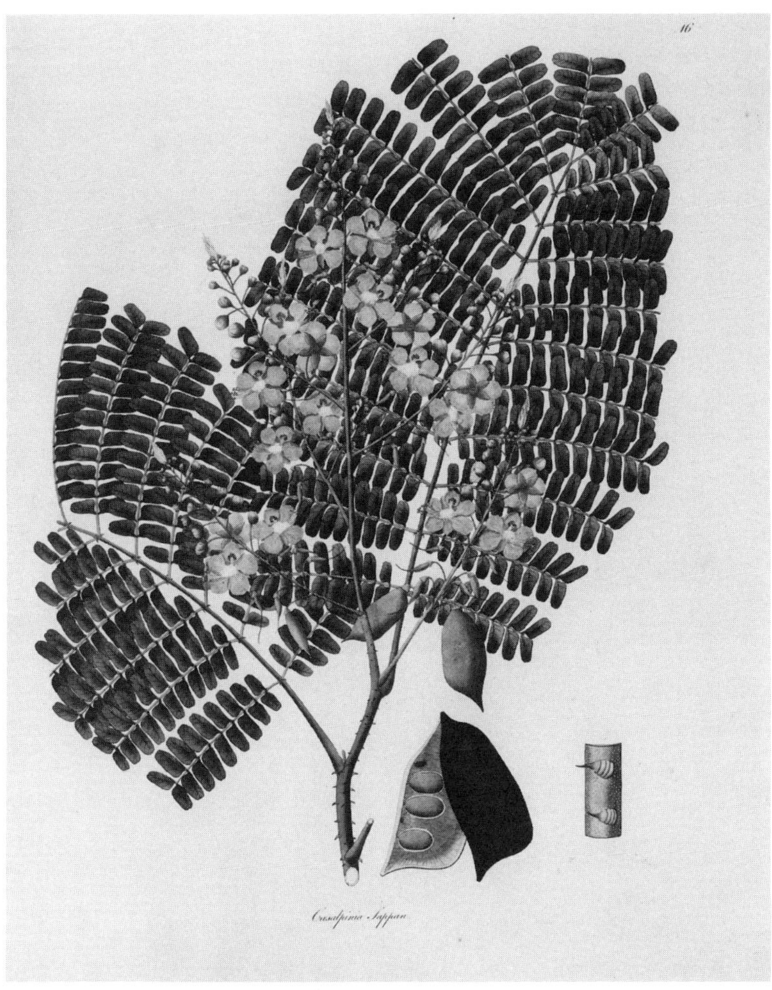

36. After an anonymous artist employed by the Calcutta Botanic Gardens, *Caesalpinia sappan,* plate 16 from William Roxburgh, *Plants of the Coast of Coromandel,* vol. 1 (London, 1795). Hamilton Library, University of Hawai'i at Mānoa.

intricate details that swirl and move in rhythmic patterns. Each of the sappan-wood tree's tiny leaves are detailed, filling the paper with an intricate pattern, their fanlike shape and position suggesting movement. Placed against this intensely detailed background of little leaves that spill over the edges of the paper are the delicate clusters of flowers,

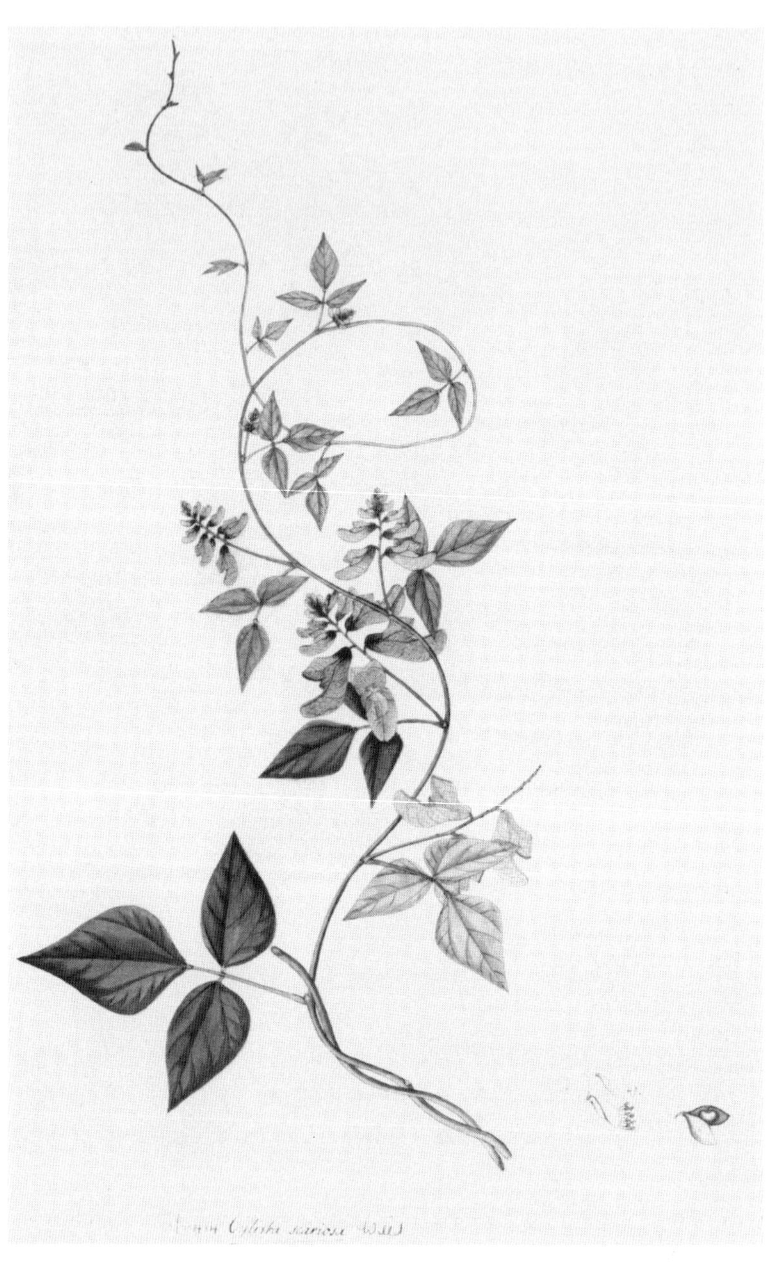

37. Anonymous, Royal Botanic Gardens, Kew, William Roxburgh
Collection, no. 414, watercolor, *Cylista scariosa,* n.d. © RBG, Kew.
Reproduced with kind permission.

which have to compete with the leaves for our attention (Fig. 36). The tendrils of the *Cylista scariosa,* a vine-like plant, twist and turn around each other, practically dancing off the page. The plant's largish, dark, diamond-shaped leaves capture our attention, but quickly our eyes move up the vine as its leaves and clusters of little yellow and red-dotted flowers decrease in size, and all that remains at the top of the picture is a single waving tendril, eager to be off wandering beyond the page's boundaries (Fig. 37).

The intricacy of pattern in these illustrations reflect the artists' training in the Mughal traditions of natural history painting. The seventeenth- and eighteenth-century Mughal courts were patrons of vast numbers of artists whose detailed depictions of flora and fauna stress pattern and color. Traditionally, Mughal artists would painstakingly lay down layers of gouache to create luminous colors, but this technique was too time consuming and expensive for the purposes of the East India Company. Roxburgh's Indian artists abandoned this technique to work faster and at less expense. They also struggled to satisfy the European tastes of their patrons and tried to produce sketches of plants that were more in keeping with the traditions of naturalism, but frequently their images of plants are rather flat and lacking in perspective, and as a result, the illusion of three dimensions is somewhat diminished in a number of their illustrations. This flatness should not necessarily be interpreted as the failure of these artists to master the illusion of depth, but rather as a return to their own cultural traditions.

The Indian artists employed by Roxburgh, however, excelled in their representation of *Leguminosae,* many of which are vines, for their sensitivity to pattern and to intricate detail creates images so full of rhythm that the plants seem to move. Although some critics have suggested that the Calcutta artists' attention to pattern makes for flat and static images, I think that their patterns create rhythm and thus the illusion of movement. For instance, the composition of three pictures made for the Botanic Gardens in Calcutta, duplicates of which were sent off to the Company in London, highlights movement. A dramatic diagonal stroke dominates the composition of the painting of *Casalpinea simora, Buch.* and organizes the abundantly detailed rendering of paired leaflets and clusters of blossoms (Fig. 38). The arch of yellow blossoms mirrors the bold line of the dark green leafy branch that

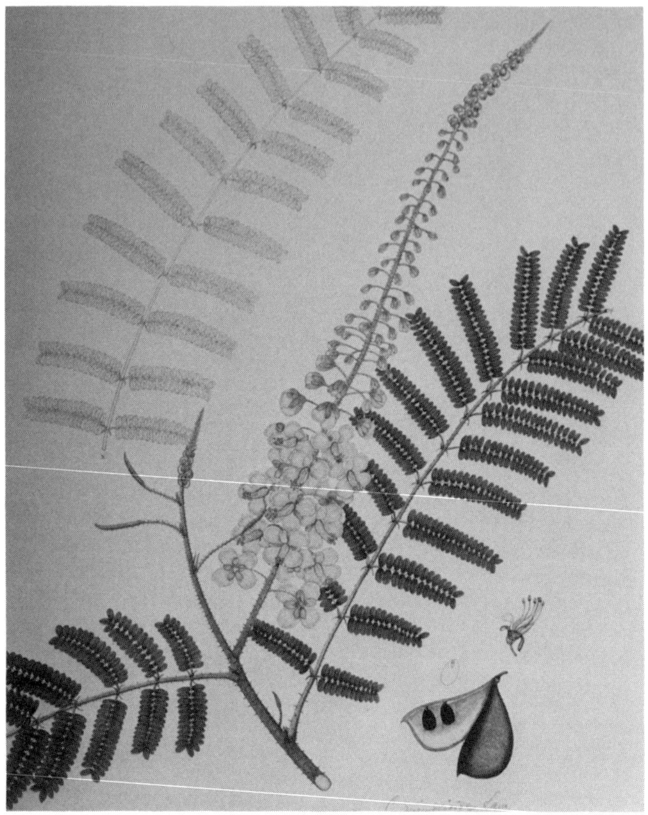

38. Anonymous, Royal Botanic Gardens, Kew. William
Roxburgh Collection, No. 1841, watercolor, *Casalpinea simora
Buch,* n.d. © RBG, Kew. Reproduced with kind permission.

lies beneath the blossoms, which climb from the center of the composition out and up to the right-hand corner in increasingly smaller,
rhythmically spaced buds. The painting of *Momordica dioica* presents
a profusion of heart-shaped leaves, large-petaled flowers, and curly-
cue tendrils arching from the bottom left up through the full center
and to the top left, moving in and out of the picture. The image of
Luffa graveolens, which is also a vine, seems to move and swirl as the
graceful stem of the vine extends right off the top of the paper. On the
left side of this vine heart-shaped leaves move up the vine's stem in
increasingly smaller shapes. These leaves are balanced on the right by

whimsically spiraling tendrils, to which the leaves are counterparts. Where the tendrils join the leaves on the vine's stem is where flowers and their seedpods grow. The vine moves through the picture in a slow and open backward S, and the whole picture—leaves, tendrils, flowers, and seedpods—undulates, dancing together with harmony and grace. These images of plants convey an energy that cannot be contained by the blank white borders of the botanical illustration. The natural history illustrations produced by the Calcutta artists are suffused with a Muslim delight in design and intricacy, which, I would argue, worked to complicate and even undermine the static Platonic hierarchies of Linnaean botany with its drive to turn living structures into ideal types, converting them into manageable units ripe for incorporation into a world system.

Botanical art was employed by a British botanical establishment eager to assert European systems of control over the natural resources of the world. Some aspects of botanical illustration, such as the snipped stem placed on a field of white, were well suited for the Linnaean project of cataloguing the world's plants according to a static, universal system. Such aspects of botanical illustration worked to decontextualize plant life and reinforced the idea of the efficacy of plant transfers, which undergirded the worldwide traffic in plants orchestrated by Kew Gardens.[61] Resistant, however, to this Linnaean-inflected botanizing were other aspects of botanical illustration that were informed by the conventions of Dutch still life, as in the case of Parkinson's illustrations, and by the traditions of natural history painting in the Mughal courts of the seventeenth and eighteenth centuries, as in the case of the drawings by the Calcutta artists. Centipedes creeping right to left, tendrils spiraling out of the frame, and seeds about to burst from their pods imply that not only do plants have cultural and ecological contexts, but that they have a vitality of their own that cannot be completely contained by the colonizing discourse of late-eighteenth-century botany. Parkinson's *Xylomelum pyriforme* and the unknown Indian artist's sappan-wood tree refuse to be subsumed by a universalizing discourse that sees them only as ideal types in an abstract and static hierarchical system. These images suggest that plants have an existence that lies outside European systems of control and management, an existence and a significance that escape British domination.

7

The Imperial Politics of

the Local and the Universal

In this concluding chapter, I explore the larger implications of what I have traced out in my readings of individual paintings and their specific social, economic, and political contexts and offer an analysis of the role of representation in the operations of colonialism. I have suggested in my chapters on representations of the black servant and Native American land that colonialism is a process of extraction; in the case of African Caribbeans, labor was extracted to produce commodities consumed in Britain, and in the case of the Delawares, land was expropriated and transformed into a commodity that enriched colonial elites within North America and Britain. In this chapter I focus on another kind of colonial technology, one that is the discursive equivalent of extraction—abstraction—a process whereby traces of a distant place, people, or resource are gathered up and consolidated at the metropolitan center. I begin with a description of a painting by John Singleton Copley, one that depicts an agent of empire in a manner that might seem to us today brutal and unsubtle in its portrayal of colonial power. I will use this painting's deployment of colonial imagery to think through the similarities between the eighteenth-century aesthetic categories of the universal and particular and the creation of core-periphery relations within the global imperial regime of eighteenth- and nineteenth-century Britain, and in doing so, illustrate how re-representation, a form of abstraction, operates in the context of colonialism.[1]

I first encountered John Singleton Copley's portrait of Major Hugh Montgomerie, 12th Earl of Eglinton (1780), as I was strolling through the Los Angeles County Museum of Art on one of those recreational visits one makes to museums as a tourist and, in this case, as a member of a large, disjointed family expedition involving grandparents, uncles, aunts, and restless cousins. Copley's painting, housed upstairs above an incredible Mayan art collection, in the European painting section, was hung in such a way that one could easily miss it: not flat against a wall of the room but on the back of a partition that divides one room from another. Only as I left the room of eighteenth-century paintings and turned to look for straggling members of our party did I see Copley's portrait (Fig. 39). It caught my breath, jolting me out of my preoccupation with the whereabouts of my family, and surprised me with its blatant and, in this pleasant setting, ludicrous display of colonial power. In what is clearly a battle scene, Montgomerie is positioned so that he seems, at first glance, to be standing triumphantly on top of a heap of dead Indians. He looms quite large in this painting, which is hung so that one has to look up at him, while at eye level are the bodies of dead and dying Indians. My response to this painting was a mixture of surprise, pity, moral outrage, and amusement. Despite his commanding pose, Montgomerie failed to intimidate me. That I could muster a smile of derision at this image had a lot to do with the fact that his portrait was hanging in late-twentieth-century Los Angeles, severed so completely from its origins and discursive community, a feeble remnant of "glories" long past, a reminder of those truisms about the abuse of power and the rise and fall of empires (Mayan, Roman, British, and now the American).

Looking more carefully at Copley's painting reveals that Montgomerie is not really standing on the bodies of dying Indians. He stands on a ledge in the foreground; behind him, in the lower third of the painting, we see a battle being waged between his advancing troops and defending Native Americans. His Highlander troops, dressed in kilts (as is he), are engaged in hand-to-hand combat with Native Americans, their heads cleanly shaven except for a "Mohawk" stripe of spiky hair. Montgomerie stands calmly in a modified *Apollo Belvedere* pose, his left arm stretched across himself pointing to the battle raging behind and under him.[2] Beneath Montgomerie, a fallen Indian lies splayed on his back, one arm thrown back, his eyes wide with astonishment that he has been defeated and is dying; another

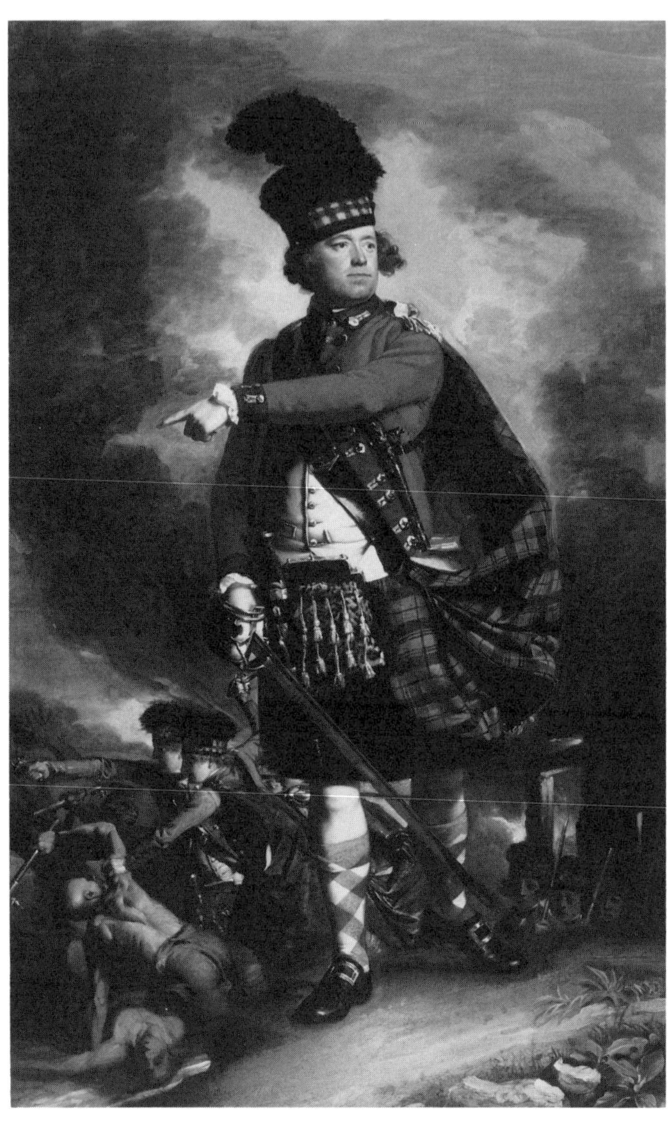

39. John Singleton Copley, *Hugh Montgomerie, Twelfth Earl of Eglinton,* 1780, oil on canvas. Los Angeles County Museum of Art, Gift of Andrew Norman Foundation and Museum Acquisitions Fund.

Indian, on his knees, raises his tomahawk to strike at two of Montgomerie's advancing troops. The Indians, doomed to defeat, are idealized and generalized; they are brave, handsome, and athletic, their muscular physiques reminiscent of the *Dying Gaul,* all of which suggesting they are worthy opponents for a noble leader. Surrounded by alien and exotic beings from the wilds of North America, the Briton retains his composure and resolve amid the screams of tomahawked soldiers and bayoneted Indians. His remove from the fray—standing slightly above on a rise overlooking the scene—gives him an air of command. His classical pose takes him out of a specific time and aligns him with the mythical heroes of antiquity, bestowing on him a timelessness and a universality that belie the heat of the moment. The dramatic elements in the painting heighten the heroic aspect of Montgomerie's character—his bravery, boldness, decisiveness. By alluding to events in Montgomerie's military career, Copley creates not only a heroic portrait but an unusual mix of portraiture, reportage, and history painting. Like Sir Joshua Reynolds, Copley has used a classical pose to elevate the sitter and to heighten the grandeur of the scene; like Benjamin West, he has paid careful attention to the details of British military uniforms and Native American dress to stress the contemporaneity of the heroic deed being performed before our eyes (Fig. 40).[3]

A generic hybrid, this painting mingles classical idioms with contemporary details as well as combining two very different ways of treating the human figure: portraiture, the depiction of a specific, named individual (Montgomerie, in this case), with genre painting, the depiction of figures who represent types of people, usually the laboring poor and sometimes colonial subjects, as in Brunias's paintings. This mixing of portraiture with the representation of generalized figures produces tensions between Montgomerie and the other figures in the painting, for Montgomerie, whose "likeness" is captured, possesses subjectivity and individuality, whereas the Highland troops and Native Americans, functioning as types, are reduced to the category of objects. In this painting two different orders of human subjects occupy the same space, and through various devices, such as Montgomerie's *Apollo Belvedere* pose (which will be discussed at length later in this chapter), hierarchies are established to deal with ideological tensions produced by the painting's participation in maintaining

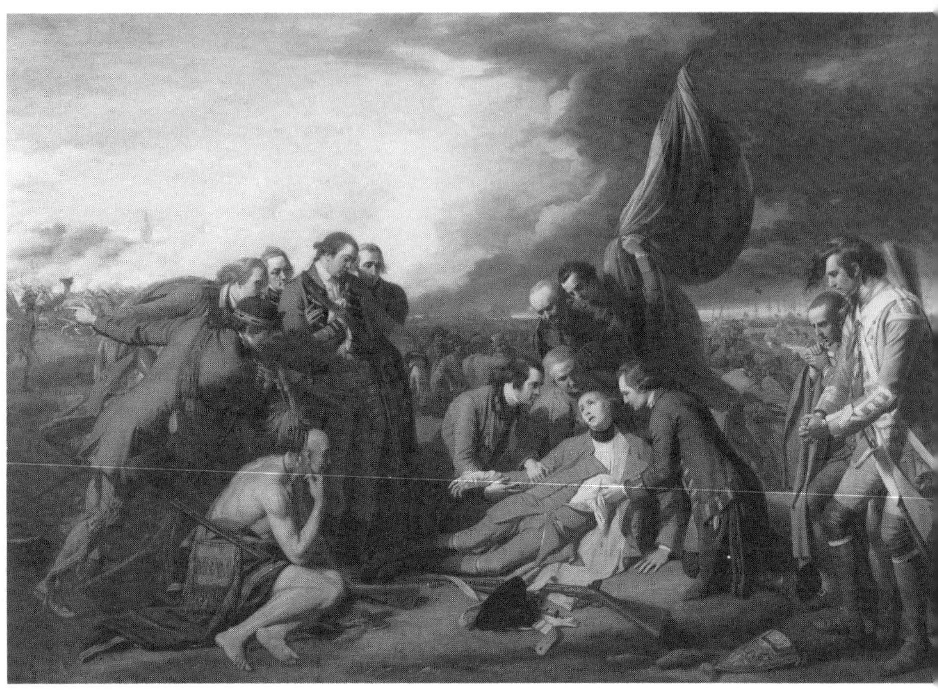

40. Benjamin West, *The Death of General Wolfe*, 1770, oil on canvas. National
Gallery of Canada, Ottawa. Transfer from the Canadian War Memorials,
1921. Gift of the 2nd Duke of Westminster, Eaton Hall, Chesire, 1918.

distinctions between classes and races. In this painting only the upper-
class Briton achieves personhood, while foot soldiers and Indians are
reduced to props to help tell the great man's story.[4]

Painted in the midst of the American Revolution by an American
loyalist living in Britain, this portrait alludes to Montgomerie's activities in North America during the Seven Years' War (1756–63). Why
would Montgomerie want to have himself represented as a slayer of
Native Americans, especially during a time when most Native Americans were allied to the British cause?[5] I can only raise and not answer
this question, but the image of Montgomerie directing his troops
to kill Indians might be easier to explain if this were a portrait of
Archibald Montgomerie, the eleventh Earl of Eglinton and Hugh's
distant relation, because Archibald Montgomerie's military career as
lieutenant-colonel commandant of the 77th Highlanders includes en-

counters with the Cherokee in the battle of Etchocy in 1760 and War-Woman's Creek in 1761. Archibald Montgomerie's 77th was raised in 1757, fought in New York and in the Ohio River Valley, and in 1762 was sent to the Caribbean to fight with General Monkton in Martinique and the Earl of Albermarle in Havana. The 77th returned in 1763 to the Ohio River Valley to accompany Colonel Bouquet's troops as he marched to Fort Duquesne (now Pittsburgh) and fought at the battle of Bushy Run, where, incidentally, Sir William Young's son Brook died.[6] Although Archibald Montgomerie participated in some of the few famous battles that Britons fought against Indians, why would Hugh Montgomerie, who was a captain in the 78th foot, which primarily saw action in what is now Canada, want to memorialize his military career in such a way? One can only speculate that he wished to be associated with British victories in American colonial wars and that the Native American figures were painted into the scene not only to mark the locale as North America but to function as emblems of a conquered America, and not necessarily to refer to a specific battle he fought against Indians.[7]

What interests me about this painting is not so much the obvious exercise of colonial power that is conveyed by hierarchical and racialized relations among the figures in the painting, as the subtle and complicated ideological work it performs by manipulating the temporal and spacial dimensions that mirror the colonial structures of the core and its peripheries. The juxtaposition of the timelessness of Montgomerie's classical pose and the details of contemporary dress as well as the particulars of an exotic setting inject this painting with a tension derived from a powerful dialectic between the universal and the particular, a dialectic that structured the late-eighteenth-century imperial project. By interrogating how the core-periphery relation is structured through the idea of the universal, we can perhaps gain a greater understanding of the epistemic violence that is inherent in the figuring of the global and the local.[8]

The Universal

Before explaining how aesthetic issues in eighteenth-century portraiture mirror essential patterns within the structures of colonialism, I will sketch here the argument that Sir Joshua Reynolds made concerning the use of classical poses and antique dress in portraiture, an argument that he couched in a discussion of the artist's search for universal forms. In his *Discourses* Reynolds worked hard to reconstruct the figure of the artist, transforming him from the craftsman, the "mechanic" and draughtsman, into the gentleman who, when provided with a liberal education, possessed the ability to see beyond the limits of the material present. Not wanting to be thought of as what Shaftesbury had termed a "mere face-painter" who "copies what he sees, and minutely traces every feature and odd mark," Reynolds redefined portraiture as a search for universal forms.[9] He urges the artist to shun "the humbler walks of painting"—the kind of botanical illustration that Parkinson did, for instance—to aspire to create paintings that "consider nature in the abstract."[10] Thus, painting as an art form will have "true dignity," entitling it "to the name of a Liberal Art, and . . . a sister of poetry" (50). The artist who has long contemplated general nature and universal forms will be able to "distinguish the accidental deficiencies, excrescences, and deformities of things, from their general figures" and to make out "an abstract idea of their forms more perfect than any one original" (44). Reynolds echoes what his good friend Dr. Johnson wrote in *Rasselas* about the role of the poet, whose business "is to examine, not the individual, but the species; to remark general properties and large appearances." Dr. Johnson's Imlac describes how a poet must remove himself from the local and the specific so that he can see transhistorical and transcultural "truths": "He must divest himself of the prejudices of his age or country; he must consider right and wrong in their abstracted and invariable state; he must disregard present laws and opinions, and rise to general and transcendental truths which will always be the same. . . . He must write as the interpreter of nature, and the legislator of mankind, and consider himself as presiding over the thoughts and manners of future generations; as a being superiour to time and place."[11] Sharing Johnson's notions of the universal nature of man, Reynolds in his "Discourse III" argues that great art is created when it is "able to get above all singular forms, local customs, particularities, and details of every kind" (44). Reynolds's linking of the particular and the local with the defective and deformed reveals his anxiety about the fragility of the concept of disinterested contemplation, which, as

Elizabeth Bohls argues, is founded on a series of exclusions, aimed primarily at women, the laboring classes, and the non-European peoples of the world, as a means of consolidating the political and cultural authority of England's governing elite.[12] Reynolds's *Discourses* participated in the maintenance of this gentlemanly authority through his articulation of aesthetic theories that privileged the universal over the particular.[13]

The problem for Reynolds was that portraiture was considered a lesser genre compared to history painting, because portraiture was concerned with capturing the specific and the singular in likenesses and history painting was allegorical and general in its treatment of the human figure: "An History-painter paints man in general; a Portrait-painter, a particular man, and consequently a defective model" (70). To elevate the status of portraiture, to remove it somewhat from the debased realm of the local and particular and invest it with some of the grandeur associated with history painting, Reynolds suggested that artists paint sitters in poses that refer to classical sculpture and in clothing that alludes to the flowing togas and robes of Greek and Roman statuary: "He therefore who in his practice of portrait-painting wishes to dignify his subject, which we will suppose to be a lady, will not paint her in the modern dress, the familiarity of which alone is sufficient to destroy all dignity. He takes care that his work shall correspond to those ideas and that imagination which he knows will regulate the judgment of others; and therefore dresses his figure something with the general air of the antique for the sake of dignity, and preserves something of the modern for the sake of likeness" (140). Familiarity, for Reynolds, destroys dignity. By referring to the antique in dress and pose, he could remove the sitter's image from the familiarity of the here and now and evoke a distant time and place. A contemporary defended Reynolds from accusations that he was plagiarizing the old masters by identifying Reynolds's use of classical dress and pose as a form of citation. In his defense of Reynolds, Horace Walpole wrote: "When a single posture is imitated from a historic picture and applied to a portrait in a different dress and with new attributes, this is not plagiarism, but quotation: and a quotation from a great author, with a novel application of the sense, has always been allowed to be an instance of parts and taste; and may have more merit than the original."[14] Reynolds's borrowing of "attitudes from

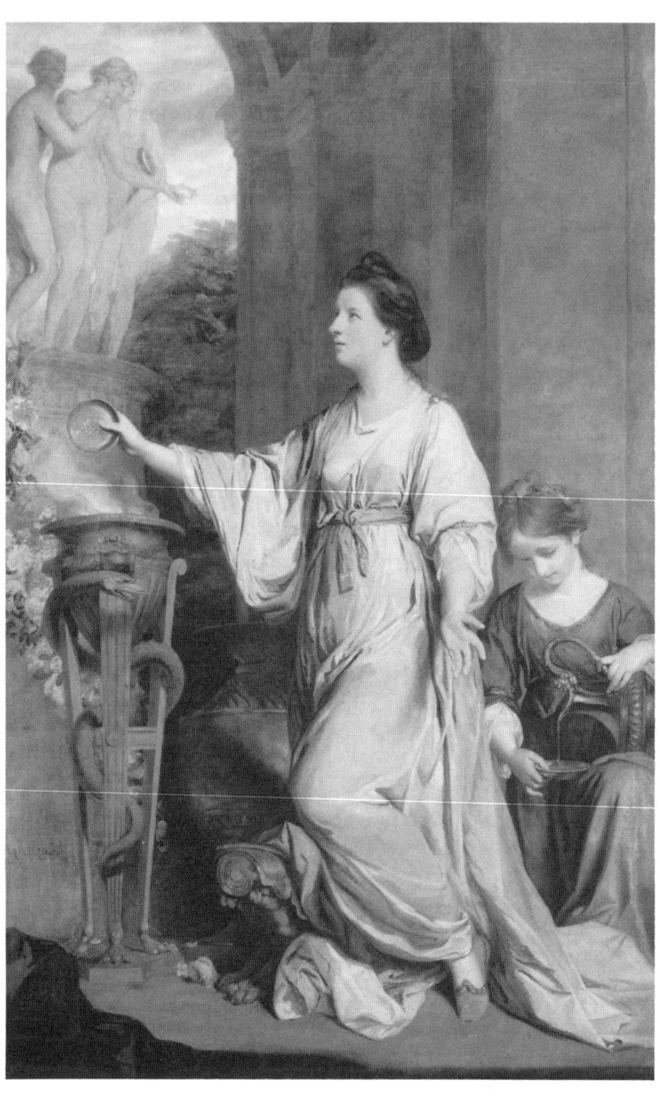

41. Sir Joshua Reynolds, *Lady Sarah Bunbury Sacrificing to the Graces,* 1765, oil on canvas. Chicago, The Art Institute of Chicago, Mr. and Mrs. W. W. Kimball Collection. Photograph © 1996, The Art Institute of Chicago. All rights reserved.

ancient masters" was an important strategy in his attempt to lend the dignity of the past to his contemporary sitters and to link them to a larger frame shaped by the cultures of classical Rome and Greece and the Italian Renaissance. He frequently painted women as muses, graces, virtues, or goddesses (Fig. 41), and he arranged men in poses that recalled Roman statesmen, heroes, or gods.

Reynolds's borrowing of poses from the ancients and his citation of the masters were his way of depicting what he called the "central forms" that reveal general human nature. This search for the "central form" was a process of abstraction, whereby an artist would "disregard all local and temporary ornaments, and look only on those general habits which are every where and always the same" (49). "Perfect form," argues Reynolds, "is produced by leaving out particularities, and retaining only general ideas" (57); as John Barrell explains, for Reynolds "common form" is achieved through "a process of averaging the various different forms exhibited by the objects of any species, be they swans, doves, or men." Summarizing Reynolds's position, Barrell writes: "The central form is thus what is 'analogous' to the original frame of the minds of all of us, and it is a representation of the highest common factor of our nature—for if our true nature is grounded on universal principles, and our actual natures are only various as they are variously deformed by accident, the central form is the means by which, in recognising what our minds have in common, we recognise our nature in its highest, its universal form."[15] Reynolds suggests that this ability to abstract is a kind of thinking limited to those men who have read widely and traveled extensively, who have leisure and taste, and whose economic and political interests are not narrow and selfish. In possessing a breadth of understanding and a range of experience, such men, usually educated (and usually landed) gentlemen, can hold, supposedly, extensive views on the nature of mankind and can generalize from the particular to the universal.[16]

Abstraction

Reynolds's embrace of the general and his rejection of the particular are typical of Enlightenment thinking, the kind of thinking that Bruno Latour, sociologist and historian of science, traces in the work of eighteenth-century geographers, natural historians, and astronomers who participated in voyages of discovery. As noted in chapter 6, tensions between the individual and the typical within the field of botanical illustration mirrored the larger issues within botany having to do with Linnaean systems of classification and Linné's notion of ideal types and their place in the Great Chain of Being. Looking for ideal types in botany shares with Reynolds's search for central forms a way of thinking that Latour identifies as "abstracting," which is a process that involves taking the local and translating it into what we have come to call the universal.

Latour argues that there are only various local understandings of the world, and the universal is created when one local dominates another local.[17] As for the technological, economic, and military infrastructure that ensures the epistemological domination of one local "truth regime" over another, Dipesh Chakrabarty, a postcolonial historian, has suggested, it is "physical, institutional, and symbolic violence, often dispensed with dreamy-eyed idealism . . . that plays a decisive role in the establishment of meaning, in the creation of truth regimes, in deciding, as it were, whose and which 'universal' wins."[18] Latour's example of how this happens is taken from an eighteenth-century French voyage of discovery, Jean François La Pérouse's exploration of the Pacific. La Pérouse had orders from the king to make an accurate map of the Pacific and to clear up various unknowns such as whether Sakhalin in the western Pacific was an island or a peninsula. When La Pérouse arrived at Sakhalin, he tried sailing around the land form to see if it were an island, but fog and bad weather did not permit circumnavigation. He sent a team to inquire of the local Chinese who lived there whether this land mass was an island. The local fishermen knew, of course, that it was indeed an island and sketched a map of it for La Pérouse in the sand. Latour makes a point here in his argument that at this stage in the geographic expedition, the Europeans' knowledge of Sakhalin is inferior to its inhabitants; La Pérouse's knowledge is "weaker" compared to the local Chinese fishermen's, and as a result, the Europeans are weaker in that they are vulnerable, easily lost, and dependent on their guides. In fact, La Pérouse and his ship disappeared somewhere in the southern Pacific several months after trying to chart Sakhalin. However, before he sailed south, La Pérouse dispatched an officer to carry the data he had collected thus far back to France overland through Russia. The balance of power between the Europeans and Chinese would change dramatically when the measurements and maps that La Pérouse had been collecting on his voyage reached Europe, where they were organized and arranged so that when other European ships would return to this land mass, they would know in advance that it was an island and would not have to ask anyone living there about it. The kind of knowledge that the Europeans would bring with them on subsequent voyages would enable them to "know" a place without having seen it. This kind of knowledge is empowering, Latour argues, because of its relation to "cycles of accumulation," which he describes as "how to bring things back to a place for someone to see it for the first time so that others might be sent again to bring other things back. How to be familiar with things, people, and events, which are *distant*" (220). An important part of gaining global dominance is the ability to visualize without actually seeing a place, its people, its plants, and other resources, and this kind of visualization relies on accumulating traces—sketches, descriptive notes, specimens, measurements—from those places.

Latour argues that the difference between the knowledge that the Sakhalin islanders have of their own land and the scientific cartography of the Europeans is not that the islanders' knowledge is "local, implicit, uncertain, and weak" (228–29), but that the European knowledge, which is also a local knowledge, contains devices that enable extraction and mobilization that act to marginalize and include others' knowledge as a subset of their own. The way a local explanation becomes stronger than another is not through the discovery of universal laws but, as Latour argues, through a process involving inscription, networks, and centers of calculation. Although this process of inscription and circulation requires a material base—ships to sail across oceans, navigational instruments to guide those journeys, and military power to protect those ships from people on shore and in other ships—just as important to the creation of a cycle of accumulation is inscription: drawings of plants, people, coastlines; measurements of longitude, latitude, distances, depths, heights; charts of the stars' movements, of tides, weather patterns.[19] Inscription is perhaps what distinguishes the voyages funded by the courts of Spain and Portugal from the earlier Norse voyages that have left barely a trace of their impact on the New World. Through the process of inscription and mobilization, La Pérouse's drawings, maps, and measurements, once they arrived in Paris, had already undergone the change from local knowledge into "universal" knowledge.

Art played an important part in this inscription process: botanical, ethnographic, and landscape illustrations were employed as carriers of traces of distant places in the cycle of accumulation by which Europeans were made familiar with things they had never seen. The process of inscription involves extraction and translation, the lifting of particulars out of one context and placing them into another. Think of Parkinson's sketches of the New Zealand coastline; his ink strokes on paper are a part of a process of abstraction that involves selection and translation from one visual register into another.[20] As inscriptions, they fulfill Latour's criteria in that they are stable, mobile, and combinable. Parkinson's drawings were stable in that they did not deteriorate significantly over time or in harsh climactic conditions (although flies sometimes tried to eat the paint). They were mobile, far more transportable than actual specimens, and they were combinable with other kinds of information and inscriptions to produce maps. Parkinson's sketches of coastlines could, in combination with Cook's soundings and tracings of the New Zealand shoreline, produce what Latour calls a second-degree "paper form" from which elements can be extracted to produce yet another paper form, a map of the south Pacific, which, for instance, could be used on a second voyage to New Zealand to aid the crew in knowing this place before having seen it. This is a process of "abstraction" by which "each stage extracts elements out of the stage below so as to gather in one place as many resources as possible" (241). With each successive extraction and translation of elements, "*nth* order" inscriptions create networks that "mobilise, cumulate and recombine the world" (228), and "they all help to reverse the balance of forces between those who master and those who are mastered" (227).

Latour's work on technoscience is tremendously suggestive for the study of colonialism. His question—"how to act at a distance on unfamiliar events, places and people"—provides a model with which to examine the operations of colonialism. The goal of the Board of Trade and Plantations, for instance, in the 1760s and 1770s was to act at a distance on unfamiliar events, places, and people. They wanted to control the westward movement in North America of white settlers into Indian territory so that they could protect the lucrative fur trade with Native Americans and keep settlers within a few days' march from the coast. How did the Board of Trade act at a distance on the events taking place in North America? Latour's model provides the answer: "by *somehow* bringing home these events, places and people." This can be achieved, he says, "By inventing means that (a) render them *mobile* so that they can be brought back; (b) keep them *stable* so that they can be moved back and forth without additional distortion, corruption or decay, and (c) are *combinable* so that whatever stuff they are made of, they can be cumulated, aggregated, or shuffled like a pack of cards. If those conditions are met, then a small provincial town, or an obscure laboratory, or a puny little company in a garage, that were at first as weak as any other place will become centres dominating at a distance many other places" (223). The means by which the world is rendered mobile, stable, and combinable is a process of inscription combined with a material base that can support and extend the ideological work of inscription. The Board of Trade made itself powerful, in part, through its accumulation of maps, drawings, reports, and lists — all mobile, stable, and combinable — which brought the distant world of North America closer and enabled the Board to act on people and places it never physically encountered. One has only to read a small portion of the hundreds of volumes of letters from colonial officials to the Board of Trade or to a governor such as General Haldimand to see how colonial networks extract traces from distant events, people, and places and send them to the center where they are extracted even further, made even more abstract, more mobile, more combinable, and ultimately more powerful. Economic, political, and technological factors contributed to the construction and maintenance of these networks that brought these traces back to Europe and conspired together to allow "a point to become a *centre* by acting at a distance on many other points." The technosciences that Latour describes grew up inside of imperialism, so that they are structurally indistinguishable from each other: "Expeditions, collections, probes, observatories and enquiries are only some of the many ways that allow a centre to act at a distance" (227–28).

To avoid centers being flooded with traces from around the world, centers developed ways of "devising inscriptions that retain simultaneously as little and as much as possible by increasing either their mobility, stability or combinability. This compromise between presence and absence is often called information" (Latour, 243). An example taken from the archives of Sir William Johnson illustrates this process. After having attended a gathering of Mingoes, Shawnees, and Senecas, Daniel Claus, an agent for the Department of Indian Affairs, wrote a letter to his superior, the superintendent of Indian Affairs for the Northern Department, Sir William Johnson, to report on the various concerns and complaints that had been aired by Indians who had been chosen to act as the representatives of various villages in the Ohio River Valley. After receiving Claus's letter, which was in itself already a second-, third-, or fourth-order stage of extraction from the Indian villages in the Ohio River Valley, Johnson sent his report to the Board of Trade; there it was read and analyzed by officials who then extracted from Johnson's letters details about Indian complaints concerning white encroachment, and combined some of Johnson's concerns with similar problems related by John Stuart, the superintendent of Indian Affairs for the Southern Department. Using this information, the Board of Trade was able to discuss the problem of white encroachment on Indian territory and to devise solutions to the problem of permeable boundaries along the North American frontier.

This network of inscriptions—Claus's, Johnson's and Stuart's letters, for instance—is a "cascade of re-representation" that enables those at the center to represent the world "in its absence" (Latour, 246–47). This means that when all these pieces of paper, these abstractions, or "*nth* order forms" of inscription came to London, and the staff of the Board of Trade performed even more extractions in the forms of lists, tables, summaries, and agendas, the Board could then meet, for instance, to discuss Penn's acquisition of land in the Ohio River Valley without ever having seen Penn's agents, the Susquehanna River, or any Delaware or Iroquois, and they could at the same time discuss the Spanish garrisons in Florida and French traders along the Mississippi as well as turning their attention to the consequences of tariffs on East Indian sugar as opposed to duty-free West Indian sugar. When in one afternoon men in a room in London can conjure up through inscription the presence of Pennsylvania, Florida, the Mississippi, Jamaica, and Calcutta, time and space are collapsed into the here and now of London. Centers of calculation, like the Board of

Trade, used inscriptions that could represent the world in its absence to localize distant places such as Pennsylvania and Calcutta and to figure themselves as working in a universal register. The activities that took place in that room in London, a particular place with specific qualities, had shed for the men in that room their local qualities to assume the authority of general principles. With the construction of centers of accumulation there is a rearrangement of temporal and spacial relations so that the center assumes a universality while the peripheries become a collection of disparate sites, contained and limited in their effect, part of the process whereby they become localized.

Double Time

The key terms in Latour's analysis of technoscience—abstraction, local, and universal—are central concepts in Reynolds's and Johnson's discussions of the liberal arts. Technoscience, particularly cartography, geography, astronomy, and botany, all of which developed within imperialist voyages of discovery, shares similar discursive strategies with Reynolds's search for central forms and "general and invariable ideas of nature" (16) and with Johnson's desire to uncover "general and transcendental truths" that appear in their "abstracted and invariable state." Latour's critique of the category of the universal when applied to Reynolds's efforts to discover central forms reveals the absurdity of Reynolds's claim that classical sculpture reflects the universal, the "invariable ideas of nature." Classical poses reflect, in reality, only another specific time and place, first-century Rome, for instance. However, in insisting that eighteenth-century England and first-century Rome share similarities in aesthetics, values, and notions of power, Reynolds, along with countless other British artists, poets, essayists, and philosophers of the eighteenth century, sought to create in their audiences the sensation of a doubling of time and space and a simultaneous erasure of temporal and spacial differences so that Cicero's speeches, Virgil's poetry, and Caesar Augustus's imperial policies could speak beyond temporal confines and across the centuries to the "Augustan" period in England. By borrowing antique styles and imitating classical genres, neoclassical artists and writers were claiming the politics and art of Caesar Augustus's empire as Britain's inherited past, a legacy from which they could forge models for Britain's imperial ambitions.[21]

In arranging his sitters in classical poses and arraying them in antique dress, then, Reynolds was not merely raising the stature of portraiture by investing his subject matter with a grandeur that belonged to a heroic age, he was clothing his subjects in imperial trappings. Those classical sculptures that he admired so much carried with them connotations associated with the empire building and military conquests of Greece and Rome. His portrait of Commodore Augustus Keppel makes use of the *Apollo Belvedere* pose to suggest that Keppel, who is dressed as an English gentlemen, possesses the qualities of a god and an imperial hero.[22] In solving what seems to be a genre problem—how to lend grandeur to portraiture, or in short, how to paint heroic portraits—Reynolds's use of classical poses for his male models invests them with a heroic quality that is implicated in nationalist narratives of superiority and imperial conquest.

Although it is important to recognize the implicit imperial agenda of Reynolds's heroic portraits, what has greater significance for our study of colonialism and art is his manipulation of time and space in his heroic portraits, a trick that Copley borrows in his portrait of Montgomerie. Reynolds's use of the antique partakes of the same dynamics as Latour's centers of calculation, in that Reynolds extracts from classical statuary traces of the original—the turn of a wrist, the placement of a foot, the definition of the calves, the tilt of the head—and then incorporates those traces somewhat eclectically into his own work.[23] Combining these classical traces with elements that convey a "likeness" produces a doubling of time and space whereby a sitter is taken out of the local, limited, and finite and placed into a realm that hovers outside of these parameters as if he were, in Johnson's terms, "a being superiour to time and place." In this temporal and spacial doubling, there is a heightening of specific patterns that are assumed to be universal and an erasure of details that call attention to the particulars of time and space. A sculpture like the *Apollo Belvedere,* an idealized version of the human body, is already an abstraction; in the work of someone like Reynolds or West, the *Apollo Belvedere* is further abstracted by focusing on a pattern of gestures (Fig. 42). In bringing together a contemporary likeness and an ancient pose, Reynolds collapses historical periods into one timeless continuum, and Rome, as a

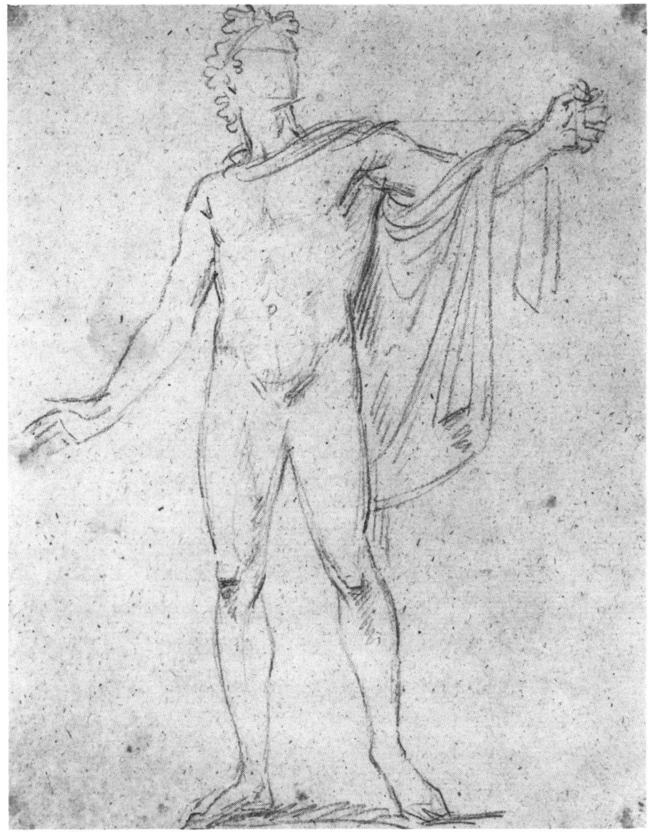

42. Benjamin West, drawing of the *Apollo Belvedere*, c. 1760–62, conte crayon on paper. Swarthmore College Art Collection, Swarthmore, Pennsylvania.

specific place existing in particular time, is absorbed into the painting, reduced to an echo in Reynolds's image of a contemporary Briton.[24]

Of course, all portraiture tries to move beyond mere representation by adding iconographic elements that provide a homologic framework to remind viewers of narratives about status and power ("the king is like Alexander the Great"), mortality and morality ("the queen is like the Virgin Mary"), or by stressing the visual structure of the image, the underlying interrelations of light, line, mass, and color. There is always some kind of doubling going on in portraiture — some visual or verbal reference beyond mere representation — but I would argue that this doubling of time and space is crucial to colonial art's conceptual and aesthetic foundations.[25]

Localized Space

Centers are constructed so that they contain various forms of the local, albeit as inscripted abstractions, so that at centers of accumulation there is a knowing and an imagining going on that absorbs, even consumes the distant regions of the world. Those at the centers of accumulation localize others who are distant and subordinate them to what they believe are general principles and truths. This localizing of distant places and people combined with a universalizing of a British "hero" occurs frequently in colonial art. In his *Hugh Montgomerie* (Fig. 39), Copley combines an evocation of the universal with a detailing of dress and exotic locale. With this combination of classical pose with the specifics of military costume and historical incident, Copley brings into play what might seem contradictory elements, and yet, in his management of the tensions between the universal and the particular, he constructs a very complex image that mirrors key colonial issues having to do with the core and its peripheries.

While the modified *Belvedere* pose imparts those universal qualities Reynolds thought so important, Copley's use of costume flies in the face of Reynolds's and other academicians' beliefs about a sitter's dress. Ignoring Reynolds's dictum "to get above all singular forms, local customs, peculiarities, and details of every kind," Copley chose to follow in the footsteps of his fellow countryman and mentor, Benjamin West, and portray a military hero in his contemporary uniform. Although West did not originate this practice, he became famous for it with his *Death of General Wolfe*, which depicts fourteen military men in a variety of uniforms, ranging from those of ordinary foot soldiers to provincial rangers and militia to regimental officers (Fig. 40).[26] Despite his use of contemporary military garb, West managed to avoid what Reynolds thought would be the outcome of portraying the details of contemporary clothing: loss of dignity for the sitter. Reynolds feared that familiarity would breed contempt and that ordinary clothing would make his sitters seem less than dignified. West countered these tendencies in his painting by evoking the pietà with Wolfe's languishing body. In addition to alluding to idioms of martyrdom and sacrifice associated with Christ's body, West also dignified the scene by exoticizing it. As Edgar Wind so brilliantly suggests in his discussion of modern history painting, distance lends dignity. Wind argues that the figure of the American Indian in West's painting of Wolfe's death, in leading "the imagination into a distant land effectively offsets the shock of seeing the hero die in a modern uniform." Quoting Racine, Wind continues: " 'Distance of country compensates in some sort for nearness of time: for people do not distinguish between that which is . . . a thousand years, and that which is a thousand miles away from them.' " [27] Reynolds achieved this distance by referring to the past, and West achieved it by referring to a remote place with the exoticized and idealized body of the noble savage, a Native American who watches with interest Wolfe's last moments. The Indian's quiet contemplation of this hero's death subtly implies that even this Indian warrior, accustomed to bravery and stoicism in the face of torture and death, has something to learn from this great man and his manner of dying. West's detailing of the tattooed and near-naked body of the Indian creates "that sense of the extraordinary and marvelous," a necessary ingredient in arousing spectators' feelings of "reverence and astonishment" for the dying hero.[28]

Copley borrows West's use of the exotic locale and the exotic body of the Native American to create the distancing effect requisite for the heroic. He also follows West's example of dressing his hero in contemporary clothing. However, Copley's use of modern dress is complicated by the fact that Montgomerie's military uniform is that of one of the Highland regiments, Fraser's 78th, sent to North America during the Seven Years' War. The kilts, tartan plaid, and broadswords unique to the Highland regiments were potent emblems that spoke beyond the Highland regiments' participation in colonial wars by referring to a particular place, the Scottish Highlands, and to a particular political past involving insurgency and resistance to English colonial rule.[29] While some Highland regiments, like the Black Watch, had a counterinsurgency role in the rebellion of 1745, others were raised after the defeat of the Jacobites and were mostly made up of Highlanders, some of whom sought "absolution for having taken part in the rebellion." Highland regiments were known for their battle readiness and the quickness with which they could be mustered. Montgomerie's

78th was raised in 1757 and disbanded in 1763, when "they were given the option of taking their discharge (and a substantial land-grant) in North America."[30] The prime minister, William Pitt the Elder, suggested that raising Highland regiments was an efficient way to maintain control over different parts of the empire. The appropriateness of sending half-naked, kilted Scotsmen to North America to fight other half-naked "barbarians" appealed to the popular imagination of the English, who regarded Highlanders as near savages in comparison to themselves. By dispatching potentially unruly Scottish subjects to America, the government quelled unrest in Scotland, defeated the French in North America and the Caribbean during the Seven Years' War, fought the American rebels during the American Revolution, and secured India for Britain in the 1780s and 1790s.[31]

Copley's portrait of Montgomerie is rich in emblems that convey complex narratives involving nationalist wars, colonial uprisings, and the assertion of imperial authority. However, Montgomerie's classical pose dominates the painting so that the elements that allude to barbarians and rebels, disruption and insurgency are localized, limited, and contained. The bodies of the Indian warriors and the kilts of the Highlander troops are rooted in specific locales—North America and Scotland—but Montgomerie manages to rise above these specific markings even though he himself is standing in North America clad in Highland dress. Not limited to a specific time and place, Montgomerie is figured as a superior being, for he exists on several temporal and spacial planes simultaneously: in colonial North America, in the rebellious Scottish Highlands, and in ancient Rome. With his classical pose, Montgomerie has been given an unfair advantage over his enemies. This is not a battle between two well-matched opponents; Montgomerie's resources are enormous, while his foes' are limited. The Indians are at a disadvantage because they are fixed in time and space, tied to very narrow coordinates, whereas Montgomerie, as military leader, floats above time and place, his powers reaching into a mythical and heroic past, his actions contiguous with all heroes, Greek, Roman, and British.

Copley's use of the exotic locale, the specificity of incident and costume, and the *Belvedere* pose create an image that triples time and space for Montgomerie. The Highland troops exist on two temporal planes—the Jacobite Rebellion and contemporary colonial wars—

while the Native Americans, who as "primitives" are regarded as
a people without history, are limited to one dimension, a timeless
present.[32] In keeping with West's example, Copley depicts Native
Americans as noble savages who, as the popular conceit portrayed
them, lived simple lives devoid of the corrupting influences of luxury and the excesses of commercialized and urbanized "civilization."
Their bodies, athletic and anatomically perfect, reflect the purity of
simple relations with their environment. In figuring Indians as noble
savages complete with idealized bodies, Copley produced an image
of Native Americans that was reminiscent of the idealized bodies of
classical sculpture, particularly *The Dying Gaul,* Emperor Commodus
as Hercules, and even the *Apollo Belvedere.* This link between bodies
of Native Americans and statues of classical heroes was consciously
articulated when West went to Rome as a young man fresh from
the "wilds" of Pennsylvania, for upon seeing the Vatican's *Apollo Belvedere,* he said, "My God, how like it is to a young Mohawk Warrior."[33] (See West's drawing of the *Apollo Belvedere,* Fig. 42.) West's
clever statement was a strategic act of self-exoticization; he reinvented
America simultaneously as exotic and as having a direct tie to antiquity.[34] Through the naked bodies of muscular men, he lay claim
to the art of the classical period as his legacy, thereby circumventing
Britain's appropriation of Roman culture and establishing himself as
having a vital and authentic appreciation of classical sculpture that
was denied Europe's more academic appreciation of the art of the
classical period. Perhaps West was trying to bolster his inferior sense
of cultural capital as a colonial American by laying a direct claim to
the antiquities of the past through the body of the noble savage, which
he also claimed as a part of his heritage.[35] West's and Copley's idealized and generalized images of Indians allude to classical sculpture;
as a result, these images create that doubling effect, albeit somewhat
attenuated, that we see in portraits with the *Apollo Belvedere* pose, portraits such as Reynolds's *Commodore Keppel* and, of course, Copley's
Hugh Montgomerie. However, in spite of what might seem to be a
subversive reference to classical sculpture in his portrayal of Native
Americans, Copley manages to give greater weight to Montgomerie
with the explicit allusion to the *Apollo Belvedere* and with the Highlander costume, allowing Montgomerie the exalted position not only
in terms of his size and placement within the composition but also

in terms of possessing a greater number of temporal and spacial levels than do either his troops or his enemies. The *Belvedere* pose dominates this portrait, creating a hierarchical relation so that Native Americans are dominated by Scots who are dominated by a Briton, who is himself Scottish but has risen out of his provincial ties through his rank in the British army and his identification with classical culture and enlightened civic humanism.

Copley's allusions to classical sculpture and his use of exotic locale and contemporary dress create a multilocality and polytemporality that play out the dynamics of the dialectic between the universal and the particular that structure this painting. Copley's reference to three different places—North America, the Highlands of Scotland, and ancient Rome—and his allusion to the classical era, to Jacobite rebellions, and to colonial wars in the New World are organized and harmonized by the figure of Montgomerie, who, as someone who stands outside time and place, can absorb temporal and spacial difference. "A being superior to time and place," Montgomerie operates in the realm of the universal while his troops and enemies operate in the more limited realm of specific times and places; consequently, by virtue of his universality, he can encompass their experiences. Like Latour's centers of calculation, the figure of Montgomerie can extract traces from various times and places and recombine and mobilize them in such a way that empowers him, enabling him to perform his task as an agent of empire. In spite of, or rather because of his alignment with universality, Montgomerie achieves individuality while the other figures in the painting remain generalized, nonindividuated entities, reduced to "soldiers" and "Indians."

The complex interplay of time and space that Copley sets into motion with his portrait of Hugh Montgomerie constructs a multilocality and a polytemporality that figure global relations in such a way as to participate in the construction and maintenance of the core-periphery relations key to the imperialist project. Simultaneously abstracting and localizing, the colonial dynamic structures time and space, universalizing the center and localizing the peripheries of the global network, making peripheral sites interchangeable, combinable, cumulative. Complex negotiations of time and place are therefore typical of eighteenth-century paintings that deal with colonial subject matter. Sometimes this multilocality is evoked by a subject's clothing, such as the Africanized European attire of Caribbean slaves, or Sir John Caldwell's Indian masquerade. At other times this multilocality is created by hybrid genres, such as the Calcutta artists' botanical illustrations, Brunias's genre-like ethnographic paintings; or modern history paintings such as West's *William Penn's Treaty with the Indians*. In paintings such as Zoffany's *Family of Sir William Young* or the Elihu Yale conversation piece, colonial sites are evoked by the bodies of colonial subjects so that a simultaneity of place is present within these pictures, and yet it is an extracted and attenuated form of the colonial site (the West Indies), which is, in turn, ultimately subordinated to British aesthetic, social, or spacial structures.

Central to the rendering of cultural encounters is the figuring of multiple sites. However, the evocation of colonial space is not always so tidily contained within British structures. In Brunias's paintings, for instance, tensions between British and colonial spaces are not so decidedly resolved as in the Elihu Yale conversation piece. The slaves' gala costumes, in mimicking European styles and evoking their masters' presence, appropriate the masters' symbolic power and assert a subjectivity that resists containment. This doubling of presences—British and Other—that occurs in mimicry is disruptive of hierarchies, destabilizing of the abstracting-localizing dynamic of the colonial relation. In other paintings that display cultural cross-dressing, such as Guy Johnson's portrait or Renaldi's Anglo-Indian family, another kind of doubling occurs, one that emerges in images of hybridity where both British and colonial worlds exist simultaneously as if in a borderland where dominance has yet to be attained. The hybridity of these images is suggestive of alternative pasts and acts as a reminder that British dominance was not foreordained, natural, or necessarily inevitable.

Imperial art's figuring of multiple spacial dimensions performs some of the same ideological work that abstracted inscriptions such as maps, charts, and reports perform: making the distant familiar by extracting, condensing, and localizing colonial sites. And yet, as I argued in my chapters on cultural cross-dressing and natural history illustration, the representation of otherness holds out the possibility of resisting incorporation and containment within British structures. By stressing hybridity as well as the possibility of resistance to colonial domination in addition to pointing to the ambivalence within colonial authority, my aim has been to suggest that colonialism was not simply a matter of domination—exertion on the part of British conquerors and capitulation on the part of native and enslaved peoples. Within the formal structures of colonialism, cultural encounters were complicated and diverse, and cultural, national, and ethnic identities were fluid as colonial subjects negotiated the multicultural terrain of British America and British India. My readings of colonial art illuminate the complexity of cultural interactions between colonizers and colonized with the goal of denaturalizing colonialism's discursive and material technologies of power.

Notes

Introduction: *Toward a Cultural History of Colonialism*

1 *The British Army in North America, 1775–1783,* text by Robin May and plates by G. A. Embleton (1974; London: Osprey, 1989), 18.

2 Linda Nochlin, *The Politics of Vision: Essays on Nineteenth-Century Art and Society* (New York: Harper & Row, 1989), 56–57.

3 Ibid., 57.

4 By using the term "colonial art," I am stretching the boundaries of what is usually meant by the term: art produced during a colonial period by indigenous/settler artists, as in American colonial art, which refers to the work of artists such as John Singleton Copley during his Boston career. Under the rubric of colonial art, I am including art produced by British artists in the colonies; art produced for British patrons by native and foreign artists, which in India would include Hindu and Muslim artists as well as someone like Zoffany or Devis; and art produced by Americans in Britain.

5 Ann Laura Stoler, "Rethinking Colonial Categories: European Communities and the Boundaries of Rule," in *Colonialism and Culture,* ed. Nicholas B. Dirks (Ann Arbor: University of Michigan Press, 1992), 321.

6 Laura Chrisman, "The Imperial Unconscious? Representations of Imperial Discourse," *Critical Quarterly,* 32 (1990): 38–58, suggests that "one colony, India, inadvertently begins to occupy a privileged site of representativeness, of conceptual supremacy for imperial 'worlding,' at the expense of other colonies such as those in Africa and the Caribbean" (39).

7 Vincent T. Harlow, *The Founding of the Second British Empire, 1763–1793,* 2 vols. (London: Longmans and Green, 1964). See also Lawrence Henry Gipson, *The British Empire before the American Revolution,* 13 vols. (1942; New York: Knopf, 1961).

8 See Immanuel Wallerstein, *The Modern World System*, 3 vols. (New York: Academic Press, 1989). For a site-specific analysis of the way colonies served the "mother" country, see Eric Williams, *Capitalism and Slavery* (1944; Chapel Hill: University of North Carolina Press, 1994), and Sidney W. Mintz, *Sweetness and Power: The Place of Sugar in Modern History* (New York: Penguin, 1986).

9 George Marcus, "Ethnography in/of the World System: The Emergence of Multi-Sited Ethnography," *Annual Review of Anthropology* 24 (1995): 102. For an example of this method, see Laura Lyons and Pernima Bose, *boundary 2*, forthcoming.

10 For an attack from within postcolonial studies, see Aijaz Ahmad, *In Theory: Classes, Nations, Literatures* (London: Verso, 1992), and from outside of the field, see John MacKenzie, *Orientalism: History, Theory and the Arts* (Manchester, UK: Manchester University Press, 1995).

11 See Edward Said, *Orientalism* (New York: Vintage, 1979); Homi Bhabha, *The Location of Culture* (New York: Routledge, 1994); and Gayatri Chakravorty Spivak, "Can the Subaltern Speak?," in *Marxism and the Interpretation of Culture*, ed. Cary Nelson and Lawrence Grossberg (Urbana: University of Illinois Press, 1988), 271–313.

12 Benita Parry, "Problems in Current Theories of Colonial Discourse," *Oxford Literary Review* 9 (1987): 34; Ranajit Guha, "The Prose of Counter-Insurgency," in *Selected Subaltern Studies*, ed. Ranajit Guha and Gayatri Chakravorty Spivak (New York: Oxford University Press, 1988), 84; Nicholas Thomas, *Colonialism's Culture: Anthropology, Travel and Government* (Princeton, NJ: Princeton University Press, 1994), 3.

13 Bart Moore-Gilbert, *Postcolonial Theory: Contexts, Practices, Politics* (London: Verso, 1997), 147.

14 Bhabha, *The Location of Culture* 239; Moore-Gilbert, 151.

15 Edward Said, *Culture and Imperialism* (New York: Knopf, 1993), xx. For discussions that complicate the binary oppositions of global-local, core-periphery, and colonizer-colonized, see also Anne McClintock, "The Angel of Progress: Pitfalls of the Term 'Post-Colonialism'" *Social Text* 31/32 (1992): 84–98; Ella Shohat, "Notes on the 'Post-Colonial,'" *Social Text* 31/32 (1992): 99–113; and Inderpal Grewal, "Autobiographical Subjects and Diasporic Locations: *Meatless Days* and *Borderlands*," 231–254, and Inderpal Grewal and Caren Kaplan, "Introduction: Transnational Feminist Practices and Questions of Postmodernity," 1–33, both in *Scattered Hegemonies: Postmodernity and Transnational Feminist Practices*, ed. Inderpal Grewal and Caren Kaplan (Minneapolis: University of Minnesota Press, 1994).

16 In *Colonialism's Culture*, Nicholas Thomas argues persuasively that the study of colonialism needs to focus on specific locales: "only localized theo-

ries and historically specific accounts can provide much insight into the varied articulations of colonizing and counter-colonial representations and practices" (ix). Thomas's book on the colonial encounter in the Pacific critiques current colonial discourse theory and offers examples of readings of specific colonial encounters. Nicholas Dirks, an anthropologist and historian, insists that "colonialism was neither monolithic nor unchanging through history. Any attempt to make a systematic statement about the colonial project runs the risk of denying the fundamental historicity of colonialism, as well as conflating cause with effect" (7). He argues that "linked together, colonialism and culture can . . . provide a new world in which to deploy a critical cartography of the history and effects of power" (5). See Dirks, "Introduction: Colonialism and Culture," in *Colonialism and Culture,* ed. Nicholas B. Dirks (Ann Arbor: University of Michigan Press, 1992). Also exemplary in attention paid to the local operations of colonialism are Anne McClintock, *Imperial Leather: Race, Gender and Sexuality in the Colonial Contest* (New York: Routledge, 1995); David Spurr, *The Rhetoric of Empire: Colonial Discourse in Journalism, Travel Writing, and Imperial Administration* (Durham, NC: Duke University Press, 1993); and Ann Laura Stoler, *Race and the Education of Desire: Foucault's History of Sexuality and the Colonial Order of Things* (Durham, NC: Duke University Press, 1995), which combine theoretical sophistication with analysis of particular nineteenth- and twentieth-century colonial practices.

17 Frantz Fanon quoted in Orlando Patterson, *The Sociology of Slavery: An Analysis of the Origins, Development and Structure of the Negro Slave Society in Jamaica* (London: MacGibbon and Kee, 1967), 10–11.

18 Stuart Hall, "The Local and the Global: Globalizations and Ethnicity," in *Culture, Globalization and the World-System: Contemporary Conditions for the Representation of Identity,* ed. Anthony King (Binghamton: Department of Art and Art History, State University of New York, 1991), 34–35. See also Hall's essay "Old and New Identities, Old and New Ethnicities," 41–68, in the same volume, in which he argues: "I have a little local politics to tell you about. It may be that all we have, in bringing the politics of the local to bear against the global, is a lot of little local politics" (52).

19 Hilary M. Beckles, *Natural Rebels: A Social History of Enslaved Black Women in Barbados* (New Brunswick, NJ: Rutgers University Press, 1989), 176.

20 In my effort to recover slaves' experience, I have modeled my approach on that of the Subaltern Studies collective and their use of colonialist texts to represent "the phenomenality of subaltern consciousness," as Gayatri Chakravorty Spivak describes this endeavor in her introduction, "Subaltern Studies: Deconstructing Historiography," in *Selected Subaltern Studies,* ed. Ranajit Guha and Gayatri Chakravorty Spivak (New York: Oxford University

Press, 1988), 32. See Ranajit Guha's discussion of his methodology, which utilizes the writings of colonialists to make the subaltern the subject of history, "On Some Aspects of the Historiography of Colonial India" (37–44) and "The Prose of Counter-Insurgency" (45–84) in *Selected Subaltern Studies*.

21 For a discussion of the difficulties of using elite, imperialist texts to recover subaltern subjectivity, see Edward Said's foreword to *Selected Subaltern Studies* and his treatment of the Subaltern Studies collective's attempt "to wrest control of the Indian past from its scribes and curators in the present. . . . And if there can be no actual taking of power in the writing of history, there can at least be a demystifying exposure of what material interests are at stake, what ideology and method are employed, what parties advanced, which deferred, displaced, defeated" (vii).

22 See Guha's essay "The Prose of Counter-Insurgency," and Dipesh Chakrabarty, "Conditions for Knowledge of the Working-Class Conditions," in *Selected Subaltern Studies,* ed. Ranajit Guha and Gayatri Chakravorty Spivak (New York: Oxford University Press, 1988), 179–230; Said, *Culture and Imperialism,* 66–67. For a similar reading strategy, see Chrisman, "The Imperial Unconscious?" For a discussion of reading history psychoanalytically and psychoanalysis historically, see Anne McClintock's introduction to *Imperial Leather,* 8–9.

23 Richard Leppert, "Music, Domestic Life and Cultural Chauvinism: Images of British Subjects at Home in India," in *Music and Society: The Politics of Composition, Performance and Reception,* ed. Richard Leppert and Susan McClary (Cambridge: Cambridge University Press, 1990), 80.

24 Said, *Culture and Imperialism,* 66–67.

25 For a discussion of varying sorts of resistances to dominant ideologies, see Stuart Hall and Tony Jefferson, eds., *Resistance through Rituals: Youth Subcultures in Post-War Britain* (New York: Holmes and Meier, 1976): "Negotiation, resistance, struggle: the relations between a subordinate and a dominant culture, wherever they fall within this spectrum, are always intensely active, always oppositional, in a structural sense. . . . The subordinate class brings to this 'theatre of struggle' a repertoire of strategies and responses — ways of coping as well as of resisting. Each strategy in the repertoire mobilises certain real material and social elements: it constructs these into supports for the different ways the class lives and resists its continued subordination. Not all strategies are of equal weight: not all are potentially counter-hegemonic" (44–45).

26 W. J. T. Mitchell, *Picture Theory* (Chicago: University of Chicago Press, 1994), 8.

27 Norman Bryson, Michael Ann Holly, and Keith Moxey, eds., *Visual Culture: Images and Interpretations* (Hanover, NH: Wesleyan University Press, 1994), xviii.

28 I do not mean to imply that memorabilia and collectibles are trivial forms of cultural production; they are as powerful as "high" art in the production of cultural practice and ideologies.

29 Susan Wolff, *The Social Production of Art* (London: Macmillan, 1981), 66.

30 Paul Gilroy, *The Black Atlantic: Modernity and Double Consciousness* (Cambridge, MA: Harvard University Press, 1993), chap. 1. David H. Solkin's discussion of consumption of luxury items and the new commercial nature of polite society does not analyze to what extent these commodities are imbricated in imperialist practices; he does, however, discuss briefly images of imperial conquest in *Painting for Money: The Visual Arts and the Public Sphere in Eighteenth-Century England* (London: Yale University Press, 1993), chap. 5, "Exhibitions of Sympathy," 190–99. Marcia Pointon's discussion of conversation pieces incorporates the idea of "military dominance and cultural conquest" into her discussion of Zoffany's painting of Queen Charlotte and her sons; see *Hanging the Head: Portraiture and Social Formation in Eighteenth-Century England* (New Haven: Yale University Press, 1993), 164.

31 Gauri Viswanathan, "Raymond Williams and British Colonialism," *The Yale Journal of Criticism* 4 (1991): 49.

32 Pointon, *Hanging the Head,* 141–57 (a version of which was also published in Barrell's volume as "Killing Pictures," 39–72); Harriet Guest, "Curiously Marked: Tattooing, Masculinity, and Nationality in Eighteenth-Century British Perceptions of the South Pacific," in *Painting and the Politics of Culture: New Essays on British Art, 1700–1850,* ed. John Barrell (Oxford: Oxford University Press, 1992), 101–34.

33 Harriet Guest, "The Great Distinction: The Figures of the Exotic in the Work of William Hodges," *Oxford Art Journal* 12 (1989): 36–58.

34 Leppert, "Music, Domestic Life and Cultural Chauvinism," 63–104. Another important text that explores the relationship between art and colonialism is David Dabydeen's *Hogarth's Blacks: Images of Blacks in Eighteenth-Century English Art* (Athens: University of Georgia Press, 1982). Dabydeen recovers the ways in which black figures were used in seventeenth- and eighteenth-century portraiture and in popular prints and contrasts this tradition with Hogarth's treatment of Afro-Caribbeans, which, according to Dabydeen, is unusually sympathetic toward them.

35 William L. Stone, *The Life of Joseph Brant — Thayendanegea,* 2 vols. (1838; New York: Kraus Reprint Co., 1969), 2:259–60.

36 Peggy Phelan, *Unmarked: The Politics of Performance* (New York: Routledge, 1993), 36.

37 Artists often felt that they must deliver what their patron paid for, out of a sense either of gratitude, of obligation, or of prudence. Some artists, like some novelists, poets, architects, surveyors, stewards, and landscape designers, were identified with the interests of the landed classes and par-

ticipated in promulgating ideas and images of the upper classes that were not necessarily in concert with their own more middle-class interests. For a discussion of "artists' ideological affinity — real or faked — with those whom they painted" (111), see Richard Leppert, *Music and Image: Domesticity, Ideology and Socio-Cultural Formation in Eighteenth-Century England* (Cambridge: Cambridge University Press, 1988).

38   As Mark Girouard points out, country houses were "power houses — the houses of a ruling class" (2); see *Life in the English Country House* (New Haven: Yale University Press, 1978). See also John Harris, *The Artist and the Country House: A History of Country House and Garden View Painting in Britain, 1540–1870* (1979; London: Sotheby's, 1985).

39   Bruno Latour, *Science in Action: How to Follow Scientists and Engineers through Society* (Milton Keynes: Open University Press, 1987), 243, 220. For a discussion of absence and presence, see his "Opening One Eye While Closing the Other . . . a Note on Some Religious Paintings," in *Picturing Power: Visual Depiction and Social Relations,* ed. Gordon Fyfe and John Law, *Sociological Review Monograph* 35 (London: Routledge, 1988): 15–38.

40   Raymond Williams, *Marxism and Literature* (Oxford: Oxford University Press, 1977), 112.

1. Bringing the Empire Home:
The Black Servant in Domestic Portraiture

Versions of this chapter were read before the Northeast American Society for Eighteenth-Century Studies in 1996 and at the conference "Icon/Texts/ Icono-texts" held in Eichstadt, Germany, in 1993.

1   Hall, "Old and New Identities," 48.

2   For seventeenth- and eighteenth-century representations of black figures, see Hugh Honour, *The Image of the Black in Western Art* (Cambridge, MA: Harvard University Press, 1989), Ellwood Perry, *The Image of the Indian and the Black Man in American Art, 1590–1900* (New York: George Braziller, 1974), and Dabydeen, *Hogarth's Blacks.* For the use of the black figure in advertisements, see Dabydeen, 86–100.

3   For a discussion of the exotic as an aesthetic category other than the beautiful or the ugly, see Bernard Smith, *Imagining the Pacific: In the Wake of the Cook Voyages* (London: Yale University Press, 1992), chap. 1: "The exotic was what the European was not and so helped Europe to define itself. In the visual arts exotic representations acquired a tenuous and shifting quasi-aesthetic character, opposed to the beautiful, in a spatial sense, as the ugly and the grotesque were opposed to the beautiful in more direct, qualita-

tive senses. The exotic is a fringe dweller among the aesthetic categories"
(9). See also Nochlin, *The Politics of Vision,* chap. 3, "The Imaginary Orient";
G. S. Rousseau and Roy Porter, *Exoticism in the Enlightenment* (New York: St.
Martin's Press, 1990); and Hugh Honour, "Science and Exoticism: The European Artist and the Non-European World Before Johan Maurits," in *Johan
Maurits van Nassau-Siegen, 1604–1679: A Humanist Prince in Europe and Brazil,*
ed. E. van den Boogaart (The Hague: Government Publishing Office, 1979),
268–96.

4 Fanny Burney, *A Busy Day,* ed. Tara Ghoshal Wallace (New Brunswick,
NJ: Rutgers University Press, 1984), 32. Subsequent references to this text are
in parentheses.

5 Richard Leppert uses this phrase in his illuminating study of portraits of
British families in an Indian setting, "Music, Domestic Life and Cultural
Chauvinism," 80.

6 The maidservant, who has served her mistress in India, also describes
Calcutta as one of "those Negro places" (36). This confusion over African
and Indian identities was commonplace in the eighteenth century, as Moira
Ferguson points out in her treatment of the many versions of the Inkle and
Yarico story. Inkle, an Englishman, betrays his lover, Yarico, who as a native
of a Caribbean island is represented as an Indian, a Carib. As the century
progressed and several writers took up this pathetic tale, Yarico takes on an
African aspect. See Ferguson's *Subject to Others: British Women Writers and
Colonial Slavery, 1670–1834* (New York: Routledge, 1992), chap. 4.

7 Oliver Goldsmith, "The Deserted Village," in *Collected Works of Oliver
Goldsmith,* ed. Arthur Friedman (London: Oxford University Press, 1966),
4:287–304, lines 385–88.

8 See John Sekora's excellent study of luxury as an important moral and
political concept, *The Concept of Luxury in Western Thought, Eden to Smollett*
(Baltimore: Johns Hopkins University Press, 1977).

9 For the debate over the importation of foreign luxury goods, see Louis
Landa, "Of Silkworms and Farthingales and the Will of God," in *Studies in
the Eighteenth-Century,* ed. R. F. Brissenden (Toronto: University of Toronto
Press, 1973), 259–77, and "Pope's Belinda, the General Empories of the
World, and the Wondrous Worm," *South Atlantic Quarterly* 70 (spring 1971):
215–35; and J. G. A. Pocock, *The Machiavellian Moment: Florentine Political
Thought and the Atlantic Republican Tradition* (Princeton, NJ: Princeton University Press, 1975), especially chaps. 13 and 14. For an enlightening discussion
of how this discourse on luxury and intemperance was negotiated visually
in the conversation piece, see chap. 2, "Conversation at the Crossroads," and
chap. 3, "Hogarth's Refinement," in Solkin's *Painting for Money.* For gender's
intersection with the discourse on commerce, see Laura Brown, "Reading

Race and Gender: Jonathan Swift," *Eighteenth-Century Studies* 23 (summer 1990): 424–43, and *Ends of Empire: Women and Ideology in Early Eighteenth-Century English Literature* (Ithaca, NY: Cornell University Press, 1993); and Suvir Kaul, "Why Selima Drowns: Thomas Gray and the Domestication of the Imperial Ideal," *PMLA* 105 (March 1990): 223–32. For the debate surrounding the consumption of exotic commodities by women, see Beth Kowaleski-Wallace, "Tea, Gender, and Domesticity in Eighteenth-Century England," *Studies in Eighteenth-Century Culture* 23 (1993): 131–45, "Women, China, and Consumer Culture in Eighteenth-Century England," *Eighteenth-Century Studies* 29 (1995–96): 153–67, and *Consuming Subjects: Women, Shopping, and Business in the Eighteenth Century* (New York: Columbia University Press, 1997).

10 Alexander Pope, "The Rape of the Lock," in *The Poems of Alexander Pope,* ed. John Butt (London: Methuen, 1963), book 3, lines 133–36.

11 Joseph Addison, *The Spectator* no. 69 (Saturday, May 19, 1711), in *Addison and Steele: Selections from* The Tatler *and* The Spectator, ed. Robert J. Allen (New York: Holt, Rinehart and Winston, 1970), 213, 210.

12 Ibid., 213.

13 Richard Steele, *The Conscious Lovers* (1722), in *British Dramatists from Dryden to Sheridan,* ed. George H. Nettleton et al. (1939; New York: Houghton Mifflin, 1969), IV.ii.59–62.

14 Addison, *The Spectator* no. 69, 213.

15 George Lillo, *The London Merchant; or, The History of George Barnwell* (1731), in *British Dramatists from Dryden to Sheridan,* ed. George H. Nettleton et al. (Boston: Houghton Mifflin, 1969), I.i.19–21, I.i.601, III.i.14–23.

16 Jonathan Swift, "Answer to Several Letters," cited in *Gulliver's Travels,* ed. Paul Turner (New York: Oxford University Press, 1990), 368.

17 Jonathan Swift, "A Voyage to the Country of the Houyhnhnms," in *Gulliver's Travels,* ed. Paul Turner (1726; New York: Oxford University Press, 1990), 256.

18 Bernard Mandeville, *The Fable of the Bees* (New York: Penguin, 1970), 68.

19 Ibid., 239, 74, 238.

20 John Woodward, *The State of Physick, and of Diseases* (London, 1718), 194–95.

21 See Solkin's *Painting for Money,* chap. 3, "Hogarth's Refinement," for a brilliant treatment of Hogarth's participation in this discourse on luxury, trade, and virtue.

22 This reading of the print might be a bit extreme, especially because the printed image is the reverse of the oil painting. However, as Ronald Paulson pointed out to me in a conversation, Hogarth painted the *Progresses* in oil, not as a final product, but as a stage in the printing process. In effect, Hogarth painted his oil paintings of the *Progresses* backward.

In "Black Bodies, White Bodies: Toward an Iconography of Female Sexuality in Late Nineteenth-Century Art, Medicine, and Literature," in *"Race," Writing, and Difference,* ed. by Henry Louis Gates Jr. (Chicago: University of Chicago Press, 1986), Sander Gilman states that "the figures of the black servants" in European art of the eighteenth and nineteenth centuries "mark the presence of illicit sexual activity." He argues that due to the European "association of the black with concupiscence," the black figure "becomes an icon for deviant sexuality in general." Gilman cites as an example Hogarth's *A Harlot's Progress,* noting that Moll Hackabout's "decline as a sexualized female" is signaled by the presence of a black servant (228). But, as David Dabydeen has shown, the figure of a black servant does not always signal the presence of illicit sexuality, and I agree that the figure of the black servant can best be understood in the context of mercantile and imperialist activities.

23 See Gerald Newman's discussion of Hogarth's dislike of France, the English aristocracy's aping of French fashion, and his "Gate of Calais, O the Roast Beef of Old England" (1749), in *The Rise of English Nationalism, a Cultural History, 1740–1830* (New York: St. Martin's Press, 1987), 63–84. For Hogarth's participation in the construction of an English national identity that resisted foreign influences while absorbing foreign luxury goods (95), see chap. 3 of Solkin's *Painting for Money.* See also Ronald Paulson's discussion of Hogarth's distrust of "the Italianate, operatic, allegorical mode" in his chapter "The Bad Taste of the Town," in *Hogarth* (New Brunswick, NJ: Rutgers University Press, 1991–93), 1:65–94. For a detailed analysis of *A Harlot's Progress,* see Paulson's *Hogarth,* vol. 1, chaps. 8, 9, and 10.

24 For a discussion of masquerades, see Paulson, *Hogarth* 1:74–82.

25 Dabydeen argues that Hogarth was critical of the opulence and immorality of the upper classes and sympathized with the " 'nobodies,' that is, the lower classes" and with "black people who belong to the same category" (*Hogarth's Blacks,* 131).

26 See Dabydeen on this genre of painting of ladies and their pets, which include lambs, dogs, and black pages (ibid., 22–36).

27 According to Leppert, one way that British power over black colonial subjects was explained and legitimated was in the representation of English domesticity in a colonial context. Conversation pieces that depicted Englishmen with their wives and children in the presence of their colonial subjects worked to support various ideologies that justified British colonial power. The colonial figure or setting, according to Leppert, functions as a reminder of colonial domination; at the same time, the way the colonial subject or locale is presented works to erase from that relation the brute force that was necessary to create and maintain British colonial power. I am indebted to Leppert's discussion of British domesticity in a colonial context in his essay "Music, Domestic Life and Cultural Chauvinism." For a sensitive reading of

Zoffany's conversation pieces, see Ronald Paulson, *Emblem and Expression: Meaning in English Art of the Eighteenth Century* (Cambridge, MA: Harvard University Press, 1975), chap. 9. For conversation pieces as a genre, see Solkin, *Painting for Money,* chaps. 2 and 3; Pointon, *Hanging the Head,* chap. 6, "The Conversation Piece: Generation, Gender, and Genealogy"; E. D. H. Johnson, *Paintings of the British Social Scene from Hogarth to Sickert* (New York: Rizzoli, 1986), chap. 2, "Domestic Portraiture"; and Ellen D'Oench, *The Conversation Piece: Arthur Devis and His Contemporaries* (New Haven: Yale Center for British Art, 1980).

28 The Walker Art Gallery assigns 1770 as the date Zoffany painted this family portrait, but I believe that Sir William Young was still in the West Indies then. He petitioned the government in 1773 to return to England, according to his son's account, *Observations respecting the Conduct, the Accounts, and the Claims of the late Sir William Young, Bart.* (London, 1793), 28. Also, Brook Young, according to a letter his father wrote to the Earl of Liverpool, died at the battle of Bushy Run (Pennsylvania) in 1763. Was he painted into the family piece after his death, or was the picture painted much earlier? See Young to Lord Liverpool, 1764, British Library, Add. MSS. 38,200:215 and 38,202:5.

29 For names of figures, see G. C. Williamson, *English Conversation Pictures of the Eighteenth and Early Nineteenth Centuries* (1931; New York: Hacker Art Books, 1975), 19, and Robin Simon, *The Portrait in Britain and America* (Boston: G. K. Hall, 1987), 246.

30 The groupings on the left and right sides of the painting were reproduced by Zoffany as separate paintings.

31 The Youngs were friends of the Garricks and often gave family theatricals and masquerades. The Van Dyck costume was a favorite at masquerades. See Anne Buck, *Dress in Eighteenth-Century England* (London: Batsford, 1979), 39. For a detailed history of masquerades in England, see Terry Castle, *Masquerade and Civilization: The Carnivalesque in Eighteenth-Century English Culture and Fiction* (Stanford, CA: Stanford University Press, 1986), chaps. 1 and 2; and Aileen Ribeiro, *The Dress Worn at Masquerades in England, 1730 to 1790, and Its Relation to Fancy Dress in Portraiture* (New York: Garland Publishing, 1984).

32 Sacheverell Sitwell, *Conversation Pieces: A Survey of English Domestic Portraits and Their Painters* (London: Batsford, 1936), 38.

33 Sir William Young II, "Tour through the several Islands of Barbadoes, St. Vincent, Antigua, Tobago, and Grenada in the years 1791 and 1792," in *The History, Civil and Commercial, of the British West Indies,* 5 vols., ed. Bryan Edwards (1796, 1819; New York: AMS Press, 1966), 3:241–84, 264.

34 This figure is derived from the information Sir William's son provides in his defense of his father's financial dealings as a colonial official. Unfortu-

nately for the Young family, Sir William was accused of owing the Crown £156,764, a debt he incurred in the performance of his duties as governor of Tobago and commissioner of St. Vincent. As a result, most of his West Indian property was signed over to trustees to sell if necessary to pay off the debt to the Crown or to hold until the debt was liquidated (*Observations*, 54).

35 Simon, 64. Brook Taylor, mathematician and scientist, was Sir William Young's father-in-law. Brook Taylor's mother, Olivia, was the daughter of Sir Nicholas Tempest. See Sir William Young II's edition of and introduction to Brook Taylor, *Contemplatio Philosophica* (London, 1793).

36 Sitwell, 38.

37 See Charles Shephard, *An Historical Account of the Island of St. Vincent* (1813; London: Cass, 1971), 30. For an account of these events, see Virginia Heyer Young, *Becoming West Indian: Culture, Self, and Nation in St. Vincent* (Washington, DC: Smithsonian Institution Press, 1993), chap. 1; Peter Hulme and Neil L. Whitehead, eds., *Wild Majesty: Encounters with Caribs from Columbus to the Present Day* (Oxford: Clarendon Press, 1992), 189–229; Peter Hulme, *Colonial Encounters: Europe and the Native Caribbean, 1492–1797* (London: Methuen, 1986), chap. 6. Virginia Young suggests that Sir William Young's estate, Calliaqua, was located on what had been Black Carib land and that the Caribs continued to use this land to camp on as they made their way from the interior to Kingstown: "Clearly the Caribs treated the Calliaqua estate as Carib territory" (27).

38 See, for instance, Eric Williams, *Capitalism and Slavery* (1944; Chapel Hill: University of North Carolina Press, 1994); Michael Craton, *Sinews of Empire: A Short History of British Slavery* (New York: Doubleday, 1974); and Barbara Solow and Stanley L. Engerman, eds., *British Capitalism and Caribbean Slavery: The Legacy of Eric Williams* (New York: Cambridge University Press, 1987).

39 The British planters desired the windward side of the island because it was, as Sir William Young's son wrote in his "Tour through the Several Islands," "a beautiful and rich country, mostly in possession of the Charaibes" (270). The British had won the windward and leeward islands of St. Vincent, Dominica, Grenada, and Tobago from the French in 1763 with the Treaty of Paris (the conclusion of the French and Indian War) and wanted to begin cultivating sugar on these islands. St. Vincent's Black Caribs resisted British attempts to dominate them militarily during the First Black Carib War of 1772–73, but during the Second Black Carib War of 1795–96, the Black Caribs surrendered to the British, fearing extermination, and acquiesced to their transportation from St. Vincent to Roatan, an island off the coast of Central America.

40 David Richardson, "The Slave Trade, Sugar, and British Economic

Growth, 1748–1776," in *British Capitalism and Caribbean Slavery: The Legacy of Eric Williams,* ed. Barbara Solow and Stanley L. Engerman (New York: Cambridge University Press, 1987), 112.

41 Eric Williams, 29. As Richardson argues, there is a "direct, but lagged relationship between changes in Jamaican planters' gross receipts from sugar shipments to Britain between 1748 and 1775 and the number of imported slaves retained in the island" (109). Planters bought more slaves when their revenues from sugar increased. According to James Walvin, the total number of Africans to be imported to the New World (Spanish and Portuguese as well as British) has been estimated to be somewhere between 8 and 10 million; see *The Black Presence: A Documentary History of the Negro in England, 1555–1860* (London: Orbach and Chambers, 1971), 7.

42 Eric Williams, 52.

43 Craton, 145.

44 Eric Williams, 52.

45 M. Postlewayt, "The National and Private Advantages of the African Trade Considered" (1746), excerpted in Walvin, *Black Presence,* 52.

46 R. Norris, "Memoirs of the Reign of Bossa Ahadee . . . and a Short Account of the African Slave Trade" (1789), excerpted in Walvin, *Black Presence,* 55.

47 See Craton, 140–56. According to Solow and Engerman, "These colonies may be responsible for more than half of the growth of English domestically produced exports in the third quarter of the century, and about 8.5 percent of the growth in English industrial output during that time" (8).

48 Craton, 140–41.

49 Ibid., 141–42.

50 Young had inherited a "considerable" fortune derived from the possession of landed property in the West Indies (10). Living the life of a "fine gentleman" (19), he left enormous debts when he died. His son defended his father, arguing that these debts were incurred in his capacity as a colonial official and should be liquidated by the Crown; see his *Observations.*

51 See Richard S. Dunn, " 'Dreadful Idlers' in the Cane Fields: The Slave Labor Pattern on a Jamaican Sugar Estate, 1762–1831," in *British Capitalism and Caribbean Slavery: The Legacy of Eric Williams,* ed. Barbara Solow and Stanley L. Engerman (New York: Cambridge University Press, 1987), 163–90, for a discussion of the health and physical welfare of the West Indian slave. Dunn's essay focuses on the "brutal and exploitive labor regimen" in his exploration of the question "Why did the slaves imported to the West Indian sugar islands die faster than they propagated, while the slaves imported to North America experienced marked natural increase?" (163). Drawing on West Indian sugar plantation estate records, Dunn states, "Almost all of

the field workers were described in the inventories as 'able' when they first entered into adult gang labor, but their health broke down rapidly, which surely suggests the deleterious effect of cane planting, weeding, and harvesting upon the strength and health of these slave laborers" (179). Noting that most of the slaves died childless and in their early forties, he concludes that the labor system "sentenced the slave workers to broken health and early death" (190).

52 The representation of their appreciation of and participation in European cultural heritage works to justify British domination of non-European peoples. As Richard Leppert argues in "Music, Domestic Life, and Cultural Chauvinism," Western culture, declared to be superior to all other cultures, was used to justify the repression of native cultures and exploitation of native peoples. Leppert notes that Thomas Babington Macaulay makes explicit this "connection between Western cultural superiority (defined as art and morality) and the suppression of India by British political power (defined as law)," Macaulay celebrating the " 'imperishable empire of our arts and our morals, our literature and our laws' " (103).

53 William Young, *Observations*, 19–20.

54 Thomas Babington Macaulay, *The Works of Lord Macaulay*, 12 vols. (London, 1898), 11:567.

55 During the debates in Parliament, Sir William Young, 2nd Baronet, defended the slave trade and slavery against the attacks of the abolitionists by portraying his slaves, as does Zoffany, as happy, healthy, industrious, and devoted to their master. Describing his return to his Antigua estates, he writes, "A mulatto boy getting before, gave notice of *Massa* being on the way. Every hoe was now thrown down, and a general huzza followed; and my good creoles, man, woman, and child, ran to meet me with such ecstacy of welcome, embracing my knees, catching my hands, clothes, &c. &c. that I thought I should never have reached the house. At length, in joyous procession, with handkerchiefs for flags, I was conveyed to the old mansion of my ancestors, and gave my good people a treat of rum, and all was dance and song" (*A Tour*, 264). The slaves' affection for the master in Young's narrative and in Zoffany's painting works to erase the brutality of slavery, suggesting that slaves can find satisfaction and pleasure in being slaves.

56 Though not referring specifically to Bigg's *A Lady and Her Children*, E. D. H. Johnson, in *Paintings of the British Social Scene* (83), is describing the qualities of late-eighteenth-century genre painting. Johnson goes on to state, "No theme provided a wider field of subject-matter to genre painting in the later eighteenth century than that of charity" (93). See also Solkin, *Painting for Money*, chap. 5, "Exhibitions of Sympathy," for history paintings featuring a charitable theme.

57 The sex of this child is ambiguous, especially for twentieth-century viewers, who see the child in what looks like a dress and assume it is a girl. By the 1760s children of both sexes under the age of four wore frocks to allow for freedom of movement and (I suspect) made toilet training easier. There are several portraits of male children wearing frocks; for instance, in Nathaniel Dance's painting of Lady Palk with her two children, a boy and a girl, both are wearing frocks with sashes, and in Sir Henry Raeburn's painting of John Tait and his grandson, the child is dressed in a frock. Starting in the late 1780s boys between four and eight began to wear trousers. The child in Bigg's painting may be older than four, and this might lead one to assume it is a girl. But I think that all the Christian imagery surrounding the child—its hat a halo, its white dress reminiscent of Jesus' robes—works to equate the child with Christ. Not knowing whether the child is a girl or a boy does not interfere with our recognizing the kind of ideological work this painting performs in portraying an upper-class mother teaching her children their Christian duty to be charitable. For children's clothing, see Buck, *Dress in Eighteenth-Century England*, 204–7.

58 On the eighteenth-century construction of motherhood, see Ruth Bloch, "American Feminine Ideals in Transition: The Rise of the Moral Mother, 1785–1815," *Feminist Studies* 4 (1978): 101–26; Elizabeth Fox-Genovese, "The Ideological Bases of Domestic Economy: The Representation of Women and the Family in the Age of Expansion," in *The Fruits of Merchant Capital: Slavery and Bourgeois Property in the Rise and Expansion of Capitalism*, ed. Elizabeth Fox-Genovese and Eugene D. Genovese (New York: Oxford University Press, 1983), 299–336; Marlene LeGates, "The Cult of Womanhood in Eighteenth-Century Thought," *Eighteenth-Century Studies* 10 (1976): 21–39; Beth Kowaleski-Wallace, "Home Economics: Domestic Ideology in Maria Edgeworth's *Belinda*," *The Eighteenth-Century: Theory and Interpretation* 29 (1988): 242–62; Mitzi Myers, "Impeccable Governesses, Rational Dames, and Moral Mothers: Mary Wollstonecraft and the Female Tradition in Georgian Children's Books," *Children's Literature* 14 (1986): 31–59; Ruth Perry, "Colonizing the Breast: Sexuality and Maternity in Eighteenth-Century England," *Eighteenth-Century Life* 16 (1992): 185–213; and Beth Fowkes Tobin, " 'The Tender Mother': The Social Construction of Motherhood in the *Lady's Magazine*, 1770–1837," *Women's Studies* 18 (1990): 205–21.

59 See Mitzi Myers, "Reform or Ruin: 'A Revolution in Female Manners',," *Studies in Eighteenth-Century Culture* 11 (1982): 199–216.

60 In one *Lady's Magazine* story, a mother of a seven-year-old boy is distressed by her husband's decision to send him away to private school. He is jealous of her nurturance of this child and wants her attentions for himself. The boy dies while at school and the mother goes mad and dies of grief.

Such examples of a mother's intense feelings for her children are frequent in women's periodicals of the late eighteenth century. See *Lady's Magazine* 20 (1789): 545–47.

61 William Duff, *Letters on the Intellectual and Moral Character of Women* (Aberdeen, 1807), 294–95.

62 Ann Taylor, *Practical Hints to Young Females on the Duties of a Wife, a Mother, and a Mistress of a Family* (London, 1816), 2; *The Ladies' Cabinet* (1847), quoted in Cynthia White, *Women's Magazines, 1693–1968* (London: Michael Joseph, 1970), 42.

63 In *Vindication of the Rights of Woman* (1792; New York: Norton, 1988), Mary Wollstonecraft argues that without a proper education, a woman becomes "the toy of man, his rattle" that "must jingle in his ears whenever, dismissing reason, he chooses to be amused" (118). "This barren blooming" (79) she attributes to "a false system of education" which has rendered women "insignificant objects of desire — mere propagators of fools" (83). For Hannah More's rewriting of femininity as morality, see Nancy Cott, "Passionlessness: An Interpretation of Victorian Sexual Ideology, 1790–1850," in *A Heritage of Her Own: Toward a New Social History of American Women*, ed. Nancy F. Cott and Elizabeth H. Pleck (New York: Simon and Schuster, 1979), 162–81. See also chap. 3, " 'The Nursery of Virtue': Domestic Ideology and the Middle Class," in Leonore Davidoff and Catherine Hall, *Family Fortunes: Men and Women of the English Middle Class, 1780–1850* (Chicago: University of Chicago Press, 1987), 149–92.

64 See Solkin, *Painting for Money*, 157–213.

65 For novels of sensibility, see R. F. Brissenden, *Virtue in Distress: Studies in the Novel of Sentiment from Richardson to Sade* (New York: Barnes and Noble, 1974); John Mullan, *Sentiment and Sociability: The Language of Feeling in the Eighteenth Century* (Oxford: Clarendon Press, 1988); Janet Todd, *Sensibility, an Introduction* (London: Methuen, 1986); and Jane Tompkins, *The Popular Novel in England 1770–1800* (1932; Lincoln: University of Nebraska Press, 1961).

66 William Clarkson, "Inquiry on Pauperism and Poor Rates," *Pamphleteer* 8 (1816): 390.

67 For the displacement and pauperization of the small farmer, see, for instance, J. L. Hammond and Barbara Hammond, *The Village Labourer* (London: Longmans, Green, and Co., 1927); Howard Newby, *A Social History of Rural England* (London: Weidenfeld and Nicholson, 1987); E. P. Thompson, *The Making of the English Working Class* (New York: Random House, 1964); and Raymond Williams, *The Country and the City* (New York: Oxford University Press, 1973). For a celebration of the technologies of the agricultural revolution, see J. D. Chambers and G. E. Mingay, *The Agricultural Revolution 1750–1880* (New York: Schocken Books, 1966). For an interesting assessment

of this debate, see John Barrell, *The Idea of Landscape and a Sense of Place, 1730–1840* (Cambridge: Cambridge University Press, 1972), 189–215. On infant mortality rates, see Lawrence Stone, *The Family, Sex and Marriage* (New York: Harper & Row, 1977).

68 See, for instance, Joseph Townsend, *A Dissertation on the Poor Laws* (1786; Berkeley: University of California Press, 1971), who argues that the poor laws encourage "idleness and vice" by misapplying funds for "industry in distress." People who wish to be charitable are "harassed by the clamours and distracted by the incessant demands of the most improvident and lazy of the surrounding poor" (17–19); and William Cowper on "clam'rous importunity in rags" in "Winter Evening," *The Task* (4:413–19), in *Cowper's Poems,* ed. Hugh I'Anson Fausset (London: Dent, 1966), 374. On the homeless, see Patrick Colquhoun, *A Treatise on Indigence* (London, 1806).

69 Townsend, *Dissertation,* 17.

70 Ibid., 19.

71 Craton, 249.

72 See chaps. 4, 7, 8, and 9 of Roger Anstey, *Atlantic Slave Trade and British Abolition, 1760–1834* (Atlantic Highlands, NJ: Humanities Press, 1975). In "'Paradigms Tossed': Capitalism and the Political Sources of Abolition," in *British Capitalism and Caribbean Slavery: The Legacy of Eric Williams,* ed. Barbara Solow and Stanley L. Engerman (New York: Cambridge University Press, 1987), Seymour Drescher argues that the opposition to the slave trade was not confined to a few religious zealots. In 1787 Manchester manufacturers organized an abolition petition campaign that mobilized over 20 percent of the city's population in gaining the signatures of 11,000 of its male inhabitants. Thus Manchester petitioners placed "abolition on the political map" (Drescher, 207) so that "by 1787 it had become impossible for Parliament to continue ignoring the slave trade and the conditions under which slaves labored on the plantations" (Craton, 260).

73 Little is known about Bigg's life, or for that matter his religious feelings or his political sentiments. According to William Gaunt in *The Great Century of British Painting: Hogarth to Turner* (London: Phaidon, 1971), William Sandby said that Bigg's work portrayed "benevolence or the tender feelings either of parental affection or rustic society" (217).

74 See Thomas Clarkson, *History of the Abolition of the Slave Trade,* 2 vols. (1808; London: Cass, 1968), 1:228–29. Granville Sharp's actions as an abolitionist were motivated by Christian doctrine: "The same benevolent principles—viz. *universal love and charity*—founded on the great commandment, 'Thou shalt love thy neighbour as thyself' which obliges the true Christian most disinterestedly to forgive all personal injuries, and pass over every affront offered to his own person, will necessarily engage him, on the other hand, as disinterestedly to oppose every degree of oppression and injustice

which affects his brethren and neighbours, when he has a fair opportunity of asserting them" (quoted in Anstey, *Atlantic Slave Trade*, 243).

75 Craton, 249.

76 Moira Ferguson's *Subject to Others: British Women Writers and Colonial Slavery, 1670–1834* (New York: Routledge, 1992) is a welcome addition to the literature on abolition, which has been dominated by tracing the political activity of men like Sharp, Clarkson, and Wilberforce. Ferguson demonstrates women's political engagement with abolition, focusing on the surprisingly large number of British women writers who, with their poems, novels, and short stories, sought to persuade readers to support abolition. Unlike Anstey and Davis, Ferguson is careful to qualify the work of these "do-gooders" by situating the abolition movement within colonial discourse: "The classic colonial topos—that Europeans have an unquestioned right to colonize—invisibly informs every [abolition] text; so does the notion that right-minded people are divorced from corrupt colonial practice" (141). Ferguson makes the case that these women writers, in positing slaves as subjects and as inferiors in need of their help, "ultimately denied the full humanity of the colonized other" (9); thus these British women, themselves subjected to another form of patriarchal tyranny, found empowerment in subjecting others.

77 For Hannah More's relationship to the poor, see Mitzi Myers, "Hannah More's Tracts for the Times: Social Fiction and Female Ideology," in *Fetter'd or Free? British Women Novelists, 1670–1815*, ed. Mary Anne Schofield and Cecilia Macheski (Athens: Ohio University Press, 1986); Beth Kowaleski-Wallace, *Their Fathers' Daughters: Hannah More, Maria Edgeworth, and Patriarchal Complicity* (New York: Oxford University Press, 1991); and Beth Fowkes Tobin, *Superintending the Poor: Charitable Ladies and Paternal Landlords, 1770–1860* (New Haven: Yale University Press, 1993).

78 Ferguson, *Subject to Others*, 8, 119; see chaps. 8 and 10 for Hannah More and abolition. For a similar attitude toward using Christianity to keep freed Africans in their place in the social and racial hierarchy, see William Cowper's poem "Charity":

> Farewell my former joys! I sigh no more
> For Africa's once loved, benighted shore;
> Serving a benefactor I am free;
> At my best home, if not exiled from thee.
> (*Cowper's Poems*, lines 240–44)

79 John Barrell, *The Dark Side of the Landscape: The Rural Poor in English Painting, 1730–1840* (Cambridge: Cambridge University Press, 1980), 118.

80 Linda Colley, *Britons: Forging the Nation 1707–1837* (New Haven: Yale University Press, 1992), 359.

81 John Singleton Copley's paintings *The Death of Major Pierson* (1783) and

Brook Watson and the Shark (1778) contain black servants who are depicted in the midst of performing dramatic actions. Unlike the small, childlike pages in earlier British art, these servants are clearly men of physical vigor and mental courage, and they are placed at the center of the action in both scenes. Perhaps Copley's American origins can explain to some extent his portrayal of black servants as men of action.

2. Native Land and Foreign Desires:
William Penn's Treaty with the Indians

I have stolen (an act in keeping with my forbears) this chapter title from Lili-kala Kame'eleihiwa's powerful book about the dispossession of the Hawaiians at the hands of American missionaries and sugar planters, *Native Land and Foreign Desires: Pehea La E Pono Ai?* (Honolulu: Bishop Museum Press, 1992).

1 These words, according to his biographer, were uttered on Brant's deathbed; see Isabel Thompson Kelsay, *Joseph Brant, 1743–1807: A Man of Two Worlds* (Syracuse, NY: Syracuse University Press, 1984), 652.

2 "Justice and benevolence" are West's words. See Helmut von Erffa and Allen Staley, *The Paintings of Benjamin West* (New Haven: Yale University Press, 1986), 207. Ann Urhy Abrams, "Benjamin West's Documentation of Colonial History: *William Penn's Treaty with the Indians*," *Art Bulletin* 64 (1982): 59–75, suggests that "This painting has been reproduced and reinterpreted perhaps more than any other American work, appearing often in textbooks as an actual portrayal of the historic event" (59–60). I am much indebted to Abrams's work, especially her insistence that "one must look beyond the William Penn legend" to understand the work's significance, for "it spoke on many levels" (75). See also Solkin, *Painting for Money,* for a discussion of painting by Hayman that performs similar ideological work: "This is a marvelous piece of eighteenth-century imperialist propaganda: a brutal seizure of power . . . is described in terms that transmute a violent conquest into a demonstration of the victor's sensitivities" (195).

Although it is customary to claim William Penn as belonging to American history and Benjamin West as an American painter, I think of both of these men as belonging to the British Empire. (Besides, to call Penn an American is anachronistic; he would not have labeled himself so.) West used his Pennsylvania birth and colonial upbringing to exoticize and market himself, but he was loyal to Britain and active in the loyalist and expatriate American community in London. In his portrait of John Eardley-Wilmot (1812) West included images of himself and his wife among representations of various loyalists, all of whom are shown seeking shelter under the spreading cloak of a benevolent Britannia.

3 I use the terms "Native American" and "Indian" interchangeably, recognizing that both are inaccurate and problematic.

4 For a history of the various ways Euro-Americans have projected their needs and anxieties onto Native Americans in their construction of the figure of the Indian, see Robert F. Berkhofer Jr., *The White Man's Indian: Images of the American Indian from Columbus to the Present* (New York: Random House, 1979), part 3. See also Hugh Honour, *The New Golden Land: European Images of America from the Discoveries to the Present* (New York: Pantheon, 1975), and Ellwood Parry, *The Image of the Indian and the Black Man in American Art, 1590–1900* (New York: George Braziller, 1974).

5 John Gregory, *A Father's Legacy to His Daughters* (1774), ed. Gina Lurie (Facsimile ed., New York: Garland Publishing Co., 1974), 55; Jonathan Swift, "A Letter to a Young Lady on Her Marriage" (1727), in *Satires and Personal Writings by Jonathan Swift*, ed. William A. Eddy (London: Oxford University Press, 1973), 67.

6 Wollstonecraft, 186–87. An advocate of education for women, Wollstonecraft argues here that European women because they lack formal education, are emotionally, intellectually, and morally inferior to European men.

7 Von Erffa and Staley's commentary on this painting suggests that the Indian costumes are authentic, though not necessarily Lenape in origin. West seems to have combined dress from Iroquois, Lenape, and other Algonquian peoples to create an artistic effect. See von Erffa and Staley's commentary in *The Paintings of Benjamin West*, 207, and J. C. H. King, "Woodland Artifacts from the Studio of Benjamin West 1738–1820," *American Indian Art Magazine* 17 (1991): 34–42.

8 Menno Boldt, *Surviving as Indians: The Challenge of Self-Government* (Toronto: University of Toronto Press, 1993), 3.

9 See Urs Bitterli, *Cultures in Conflict: Encounters between Europeans and Non-European Cultures, 1492–1800*, trans. Ritchie Robertson (1986; Cambridge: Polity Press, 1989), chap. 5, especially 122–32. See also Francis Jennings, "Brother Minquon: Good Lord!," in *The World of William Penn*, ed. Richard S. Dunn and Mary Maples Dunn (Philadelphia: University of Pennsylvania Press, 1986), 196–97. Acquiring Indian quitclaims also bolstered Penn's claims against Maryland's for land along the Susquehanna River. See Francis Jennings, *The Ambiguous Iroquois Empire: The Covenant Chain Confederation of Indian Tribes with English Colonies from Its Beginnings to the Lancaster Treaty of 1744* (New York: Norton, 1984), 225.

10 For Penn's construction of himself as a man of peace in his dealings with the Delawares, see his letter "To the Kings of Indians," dated October 18,

1681, in *William Penn and the Founding of Pennsylvania, 1680–1684, a Documentary History,* ed. Jean R. Soderlund (Philadelphia: University of Pennsylvania Press, 1983), 88: "I am very sensible of the unkindness and injustice that has been too much exercised towards you by the people of these parts of the world, who have sought themselves, and to make great advantages by you, rather than be examples of justice and goodness unto you; which I hear has been matter of trouble to you and caused great grudgings and animosities, sometimes to the shedding of blood, which has made the great God angry. But I am not such a man, as is well known in my own country. I have great love and friendship toward you, and I desire to win and gain your love and friendship by a kind, just, and peaceable life."

11 Vivien Green Fryd's term; see her *Art and Empire: The Politics of Ethnicity in the United States Capitol, 1815–1860* (New Haven: Yale University Press, 1992), 28.

12 See Francis Jennings, *The Invasion of America: Indians, Colonialism, and the Cant of Conquest* (Chapel Hill: University of North Carolina Press, 1975), chap. 8, "The Deed Game," and chap. 17, "Outrage Bloody and Barbarous." For the deed of Penn's first purchase from the Lenni Lenape, see Soderlund, 156–62.

13 In von Erffa and Staley, 207.

14 A popular theme in eighteenth-century British mercantile thought was the civilizing influence of trade on the primitive peoples of the world. See chapter 1's discussion of the celebration of mercantile capitalism.

15 The language describing the "gifts" is ambiguous and multivalent. In the first deed from the Lenni Lenape, the gifts are described as "goods, merchandize, and utensils," as "presents," and as indicating that the sachems "have granted, bargained, sold, and delivered . . . unto William Penn, his heirs and assigns, forever, all that or those tract or tracts of land" ("Deed from the Delaware Indians," in Soderlund, 156–57). Penn refers to these exchanges as purchases. For another version of the meaning of these kinds of exchanges of commodities, see Richard White, *The Middle Ground: Indians, Empires, and Republics in the Great Lakes Region, 1650–1815* (New York: Cambridge University Press, 1991), and his discussion of the French-Algonquian alliance, which was cemented by such gift-giving ceremonies.

16 Abrams, "Benjamin West's Documentation," 75. See also Anne Cannon Palumbo, "Averting 'Present Commotions': History as Politics in 'Penn's Treaty,'" *American Art* 9 (1995): 29–55 for the ideological implications of the representation of trade and the threat of conflict implicit in *Penn's Treaty.*

17 See Francis Jennings's account of the Walking Purchase in *Ambiguous Iroquois Empire,* chaps. 16 and 17, especially 330–42 and appendix B.

18 Nutimus to Jeremiah Langhorne, November 21, 1740, mss., Penn Mss.,

Indian Affairs 4:30, Historical Society of Pennsylvania; quoted in Jennings, *Ambiguous Empire*, 320–21, 341. Jennings, *Ambiguous Empire*, 346.

19 Council Minutes, July 1, 1742, Philadelphia; reprinted in Cadwallader Colden, ed., *The History of the Five Indian Nations of Canada*, 2 vols. (1727–47; New York: Allerton Book Co., 1922), 2: 104–11.

20 Michael N. McConnell, *A Country Between: The Upper Ohio Valley and Its Peoples, 1724–1774* (Lincoln: University of Nebraska Press, 1992), sees the Penn–Six Nations alliance as "an instrument of coercion and dispossession" (59–60); for a discussion of the Six Nations' impact on the westward movement of the Delawares, see chap. 3 of McConnell. David K. Richter, *The Ordeal of the Longhouse: The Peoples of the Iroquois League in the Era of European Colonization* (Chapel Hill: University of North Carolina Press, 1992), agrees that "Iroquois behavior in selling lands out from under the Delaware and Shawnee 'Props of the Longhouse' was certainly one of the less admirable moments in the Six Nations' history" (275). But he suggests that this Pennsylvania-Iroquois connection was "the work of a particular faction of headmen" who claimed "to speak for the Confederacy Council" (274). See chap. 11 of Richter.

21 See Jennings, *Ambiguous Empire*, 341–46.

22 Richter, 22–23, 42–43.

23 Jennings, *Ambiguous Empire*, 362. Elsewhere, Jennings puts it even more dramatically: "The fateful alliance between Pennsylvania and the Iroquois changed history on the large scale. When James Logan [Penn's agent] seduced the Iroquois into serving his purposes against their tributaries instead of protecting the tributaries against him, he opened the gate to colonial settlement beyond the Appalachians, insured that the French would respond in arms, and guaranteed the deaths of hundreds of Pennsylvania's back settlers at the hands of Delawares seeking righteous, though misdirected, vengeance" (345).

24 The Board of Trade to the King's Privy Council, June 1, 1759, 2:780; Board of Trade to the King, December 11, 1755, 2:704; Board of Trade to the King's Privy Council, June 1, 1759, 2:778, all in Edmund O'Callaghan, ed., *The Documentary History of the State of New-York* (Albany: Weed, Parsons, 1849), hereafter *DHNY*.

25 Johnson to the Board of Trade, September 10, 1756, *DHNY* 2:736. I have not regularized the spelling and shorthand of Sir William Johnson, George Croghan, or Benjamin Franklin, each of whom has his own spelling of Pennsylvania.

26 Johnson to the Board of Trade, May 28, 1756, *DHNY* 2:719; Johnson to the Board of Trade, September 10, 1756, *DHNY* 2:736–37; Johnson to the Board of Trade, September 10, 1756, *DHNY* 2:737.

27 Proceedings of Commissioners From 6 Provinces met at Albany Anno 1754 on Indian Affairs, July 9, 1954, *DHNY* 2:610–11.

In his history *The British Empire before the American Revolution*, Lawrence Henry Gipson stresses the inability of London and the Crown to control the colonial scene in North America: "It is exceedingly important to grasp the fact—something that many students of British colonial history have not fully appreciated and that the failure of the British ministry to comprehend before 1775 cost the British people dearly—that none of the mechanisms evolved by the British government to keep the Empire in due subordination were really adequate to the task with the growing maturity of the American colonies" (5:viii). Georgiana C. Nammack, *Fraud, Politics, and the Dispossession of the Indians: The Iroquois Land Frontier in the Colonial Period* (Norman: University of Oklahoma Press, 1969), argues that colonial governors were not able (and frequently did not want to) enforce the Board of Trade's policies that regulated the sale of Indian land. "In America, colonial officials were not only reluctant to satisfy Indian complaints [about fraudulent land purchases], but also were apparently unwilling to enforce Crown regulations pertaining to land grants." Such regulations stipulated that "lands were to be properly surveyed in the presence of the Indians, and surveys and deeds were to be recorded within a specified period of time" (91). Colonial governors and officials, most visibly in New York, Pennsylvania, and Virginia, participated in land speculation deals that ignored the Crown's policies. Nammack describes the various ways colonists perpetrated fraud, one of which was by using the phrase "more or less" in describing the portion of land so that the possessor of a deed could claim as much as one hundred times more land than the Indians had intended to sell (99–100).

28 Francis Jennings, " 'Pennsylvania Indians' and the Iroquois," in *Beyond the Covenant Chain: The Iroquois and Their Neighbors in Indian North America, 1600–1800*, ed. Daniel K. Richter and James H. Merrell (Syracuse, NY: Syracuse University Press, 1987), argues that the idea that the Iroquois had ascendancy over the Delawares was a "myth, originated with English colonial officials," and insists that the Iroquois did not have a "position of importance" among Pennsylvania's many bands of Delawares (75). Michael N. McConnell, "Peoples 'In Between': The Iroquois and the Ohio Indians, 1720–1768," in *Beyond the Covenant Chain*, explores the relationship of the Six Nations Confederacy with the Ohio Indians, among them the Delawares, Shawnees, and Mingos. He argues that the Ohio region was not simply a part of the Iroquois empire: "Instead of a land subdued and controlled by the Six Nations, there was an Ohio Indian world created by a variety of people—Shawnees, Delawares, and Iroquois. Into this world the councils of the Six Nations rarely intruded; and when they did, it was with little influence and less au-

thority" (93). The Penn sale and the Fort Stanwix Treaty of 1768 are instances of what McConnell sees as the Iroquois abandoning "reciprocal obligations to their own people in the west and to others whom the Iroquois periodically found it useful to call 'dependent' " (112). Richard White, *Middle Ground* chap. 8, argues that both the Iroquois and the British exploited this myth for their own advantages, both knowing that it was not as true as they wished.

29 Croghan is quoted in a letter from the Proprietors of Pennsylvania to the Board of Trade, September 1757, *DHNY* 2:754.

30 See Nammack for the ways colonial officials benefited from the sale of Indian lands, especially the appendix on fees officials charged every time land changed hands (107–8). Attorney General for New York John Tabor Kempe explained to Sir William Johnson why he wanted to speculate in Indian lands: "It is the only way I can have of making my office of any advantage to me . . . because I . . . am but illy supported in my office" (Kempe to Johnson, May 23, 1766, cited in Nammack, 101). Menno Boldt summarizes the effect of the Royal Proclamation in 1763: "the Crown was establishing itself as the exclusive real-estate agent for vast tracks of Indian land that were destined to be surrendered under treaties. Then, on the basis of purchase and grants, the Crown transferred proprietary title to land surrendered by Indians, from itself to the provinces, to settlers, and to corporations (e.g., the Hudson's Bay Company) [in Johnson's case, the Indiana Company]. But it consistently denied Indians proprietary title to any of their ancestral lands, even to their reserves" (4–5).

31 For Delaware land tenure, see Jennings, *Ambiguous Empire*, 325–28.

32 Treaty minutes, July 3, 1755, in Edmund B. O'Callaghan and Berthold Fernow, eds., *Documents Relative to the Colonial History of the State of New York*, 15 vols. (Albany: Weed, Parsons, 1856–87), 6:984; quoted in Jennings, *Empire of Fortune: Crown, Colonies, and Tribes in the Seven Years War in America* (New York: Norton, 1988), 107.

33 Nammack details colonial land fraud practices, focusing on provincial New York and Iroquois lands. She cites an Onondaga speaker who complains about the use of deeds and patents to defraud Indians of their lands: "we were always ready to give, but the English don't deal fairly with us, they are more cunning than we are; they get our names upon paper very fast, we often don't know what it is for" (104).

34 Proprietors of Pennsylvania to the Board of Trade, September 10, 1757, *DHNY* 2:751.

35 Board of Trade to Privy Council, June 1, 1759, *DHNY* 2:773.

36 Proprietors of Pennsylvania to the Board of Trade, December 11, 1756, *DHNY* 2:738; Thomas and Richard Penn to Mr. Richard Peters (their agent), March 12, 1757, *DHNY* 2:743.

37   For Franklin's position on Indian affairs, see Jennings, *Empire of Fortune,* 87–95, 280–81.

38   Franklin's Petition to the Board of Trade, *DHNY* 2:771–72.

39   Treaty Minutes, November 13, 1756, in Samuel Hazard, ed., *Minutes of the Provincial Council of Pennsylvania,* 16 vols. (Harrisburg, PA: Theo. Fenn, and Co., 1851), 7:324–26.

40   Franklin's petition stated "that all the Purchase Deeds and Writings by which . . . Thomas and Richard Penn . . . now hold any Lands within the back Parts of the Province of Pennsylvania, should be examined and Copies laid before Your Majesty for Your Royal Decision, of the Bounds and Limits between the Lands heretofore bought of the Indians, and those yet unpurchased." For Franklin's petition, see *DHNY* 2:771–72. For Johnson's re-action to the petition, see Johnson to the Board of Trade, June 5, 1760, *DHNY* 2:792. For the Board of Trade's analysis of the affair, see Report on the Pre-ceding Petition, June 1, 1759, *DHNY* 2:774–75.

41   When the Delawares complained about the Penn purchase, Thomas Penn wrote to the Board of Trade insisting that the land had been sold with-out fraud and legally belonged to the proprietaries of Pennsylvania, Thomas and Richard Penn. But to prevent further violence and possible defection from the British alliance, the Penns decided to return the land west of the Allegheny Mountains. In their letter to the Board of Trade, the proprietaries let the Board know that this reparation was not done lightly. They end their letter reminding the British government of its duty to protect private prop-erty: "they hope [that] private Property will ever be as much regarded, and as unwillingly given up by the Crown as Land in Provinces under His Maj-esty's immediate Government, and where the Lands are granted by virtue of his Commission" (*DHNY* 2:741). The implication here is that the Penns felt they were forced to return land to the Indians, something that any other province would never have allowed to have happened.

42   For an interesting discussion of the repercussions of the royal proclama-tion, see Boldt, who argues that under the proclamation of 1763, "the British Crown unilaterally asserted its sovereignty over self-governing indigenous nations in North America, and claimed proprietary title to lands on which Indians had lived and survived from time immemorial. . . . The Royal Proc-lamation was uniquely framed to dispossess Indians of their sovereignty and lands" (3). In claiming sovereignty over Indian land, the Crown was simulta-neously protecting Indian land from unauthorized white encroachment and depriving Indians of property rights over their land.

43   Nammack, 95.

44   For a discussion of Indian discontent leading up to "Pontiac's Rebellion," see Richard White, *Middle Ground,* chap. 7, and McConnell, *Country Between,* chap. 8.

45   See Johnson to Hillsborough, November 18, 1768, *DHNY* 2:917–19. Giving away lands belonging to the Cherokees, Johnson extended the border westward, far beyond the Board of Trade's suggested boundary, which was where the Ohio and Kanawha Rivers met to the Tennessee River, only thirty miles from the Mississippi. He negotiated this boundary not with the Cherokees or other southern nations, but with the Six Nations Confederacy, which claimed to be the Cherokees' overlords by ancient right of conquest. Johnson's decision to ignore Cherokee rights was expedient as well as convenient. He could pretend that the Iroquois' suzerainty extended over their neighbors in the Ohio and their enemies in Kentucky, and in this way gain legal control over vast interior tracts of land. Johnson's actions can be explained as "enlightened" British policy. By alienating and insulting the Cherokees, he kept jealousies alive between the Indians of the North and the South and helped to prevent the formation of what could have been a very powerful pan-American Indian alliance, one that could have threatened British control of not only the western frontier but provinces such as New York, Pennsylvania, and Georgia.

46   Johnson's motives for ignoring the Board of Trade's directives and redrawing the boundary have been criticized by historians who point out that he benefited materially from this redrawn boundary, receiving large tracts of land along the Ohio River. The Iroquois benefited by the treaty because the boundary line left most of their lands on the Indian side. "In effect," Michael McConnell writes, "the Six Nations maintained their own territorial integrity by selling land occupied by people on the fringes of the Iroquois world" ("Peoples 'In Between,'" 111). Richard White characterizes the Treaty of Fort Stanwix as "a cynical compact born of the mutual weakness of its two major parties: the Iroquois and the British empire" (*Middle Ground,* 351). The British "effectively abdicated their role" as protectors of Indian lands and mediators between tribes, and "the Iroquois betrayed those people who were nominally under their protection." For a defense of Johnson's redrawing of the boundary, see James Thomas Flexner, *Mohawk Baronet: Sir William Johnson of New York* (New York: Harper, 1959), chap. 23. For a discussion of Johnson's motives and conduct during the negotiations of the Treaty of Fort Stanwix, see Jack M. Sosin, *Whitehall and the Wilderness: The Middle West in British Colonial Policy, 1760–1775* (Lincoln: University of Nebraska Press, 1961), 175–78. For a discussion of the Treaty of Fort Stanwix, including Johnson's and the Iroquois' motives, see McConnell, *Country Between,* 244–58.

47   Flexner, 326.

48   Abrams, "Benjamin West's Documentation," 69.

49   In 1780 after running out of funds to pay its soldiers, the State of New York promised men who joined the militia that they would be paid in Indian land. After the war the federal government tried to stop New York from dis-

tributing land to militia men, arguing that the state had no right to cede Indian land; that right rested with the federal government. The federal government had this fight with other states in the decades after the Revolutionary War. For a discussion of the way Iroquois land was distributed after the war, see Richard H. Schein, "Framing the Frontier: The New Military Tract Survey in Central New York," *New York History* 74 (1993): 5–28.

3. Cultural Cross-Dressing in British America:
Portraits of British Officers and Mohawk Warriors

I am grateful to Daniel A. Baugh and Kristina Straub for their insightful comments on earlier drafts of this chapter as well as the thoughtful comments and questions by audiences who heard versions of it at the North American Conference on British Studies (1994), Northeast American Society for Eighteenth-Century Studies (1996), and at Cheltenham-Gloucester College in Cheltenham, England (1997).

1 My discussion of eighteenth-century British appropriations of Indian culture and Indian resistance to imperialism is indebted to Marta Savigliano's thinking on appropriating the power of the exotic. See her book *Tango and the Political Economy of Passion* (Boulder, CO: Westview Press, 1994).

2 Vern L. Bullough and Bonnie Bullough, *Cross-Dressing, Sex, and Gender* (Philadelphia: University of Pennsylvania Press, 1993), define cross-dressing as a complex phenomenon: "It ranges from simply wearing one or two items of clothing to a full-scale burlesque, from a comic impersonation to a serious attempt to pass as the opposite gender, from an occasional desire to experiment with gender identity to attempting to live most of one's life as a member of the opposite sex" (vii).

3 See Stevens's thorough treatment of Lieutenant Colonel Caldwell's career at Fort Niagara in Paul L. Stevens, *A King's Colonel at Niagara, 1774–1776: Lt. Col. John Caldwell and the Beginnings of the American Revolution on the New York Frontier* (Youngstown, NY: Old Fort Niagara Association, 1987). I am grateful to Daniel A. Baugh for informing me of this source.

4 An inscription on one of three copies of this portrait states: "Sir John Caldwell, 5th Bart., An officer of the 8th Regiment of Foot, elected chief of the Ojibboway Indians, N. America, and given the name A petto or 'The Runner' as he appeared at a grand War Council held by him at the Wakeetomike village January 17, 1780." See David Boston, "The Three Caldwells," *White Horse and Fleur de Lys* 3 (1964): 316–17. I doubt the accuracy of the inscription because Lt. Colonel Caldwell died in 1776, and his nephew, only an ensign, would hardly have the stature to hold a war council. However,

Boston suggests that the younger Caldwell's stay in North America included acting as an Indian negotiator. Though it may be possible that the younger Caldwell was stationed in North America during the American Revolution, no correspondence from him is to be found in the Haldimand Papers or in *Official Appointments in North America and West Indies, 1780*, BL, Add. MSS 22,129. A family history, a bound manuscript handwritten in the late eighteenth century, confirms Lieutenant Colonel John Caldwell's ill health and death: he "embarked to join his Regiment at Quebec nor was his ardour for his majesty's service in the less damped by his Delicate State of Health, or the Physician's opinion that the American climate would not agree with his constitution." "Lt Col. John Caldwell died on the 31 day of October 1776 at Niagara where he commanded the 8th Regiment," Caldwell Family Papers, (Royal King's 427, British Library, 87).

5 The correspondence between Caldwell and Guy Carleton reveals Caldwell's concern over the "starving Indian women and children" and his desire to relieve them with commissary stores, an action that Carleton approved of: "you could not see them perish for want of food when it was possible to relieve them." Carleton praises Caldwell's efforts at "keeping the Indians in the King's interests" (f. 191); "I hope that result of the deliberation of the Indian Chiefs, may prove, as you are led to expect, favourable to us, and that they are dispos'd to live on a friendly footing with us." See Carleton to Caldwell, October 5, 1774, in Correspondence and Papers of Governor General Sir Frederick Haldimand, 1758–91, British Library, Add. MSS. 21,678: f. 188b; f. 191; f. 189a.

6 I owe this observation to Dian Kriz. For classical sculptural models, see David H. Solkin, "Great Pictures or Great Men? Reynolds, Male Portraiture, and the Power of Art," *Oxford Art Journal* 9 (1986): 42–49.

7 Colin G. Calloway, *Crown and Calumet: British-Indian Relations, 1783–1815* (Norman: University of Oklahoma Press, 1987), 57.

8 Guest, "Curiously Marked," 104. For the relationship between exoticism and "a process of dismemberment and fragmentation" (42), see Deborah Root, *Cannibal Culture: Art, Appropriation, and the Commodification of Difference* (Boulder, CO: Westview Press, 1996). See also Bernard Smith's discussion of the exotic in *Imagining the Pacific*, chap. 1.

9 Ward Churchill, "Fantasies of the Master Race: Categories of Stereotyping of American Indians in Film," in *Fantasies of the Master Race: Literature, Cinema and the Colonization of American Indians*, ed. M. Annette Jaimes (Monroe, ME: Common Courage Press, 1992), 236.

10 Susan Stewart, *On Longing: Narratives of the Miniature, the Gigantic, the Souvenir, the Collection* (Durham, NC: Duke University Press, 1993), 147, 148.

11 Lady Mary Wortley Montagu was painted several times in her famous

Turkish dress, complete with pantaloons, pointed-toe slippers, and low-cut bodice. However, Lady Mary did not wear her Turkish outfit frivolously; it meant a great deal to her, for she carried it with her back to England and then into self-imposed exile in Italy. For an analysis of the way Lady Mary's sojourn in the Ottoman Empire transformed her life, see Jill Campbell, "Lady Mary Wortley Montagu and the Historical Machinery of Female Identity," in *History, Gender, and Eighteenth-Century Literature,* ed. Beth Fowkes Tobin (Athens: University of Georgia Press, 1994), and Joseph Lew, "Lady Mary's Portable Seraglio," *Eighteenth-Century Studies* 24 (1991): 432–50. For a discussion of the way Lady Mary positioned herself as powerful while presenting herself as an object of male desire, see Pointon, "Killing Pictures."

12 Cultural cross-dressing was a regular occurrence at eighteenth-century British masquerades. Dressing in costumes of nuns and priests, shepherdesses and shepherds, Turkish dancing girls and Oriental potentates, pleasure seekers could slide over what were rigidly fixed boundaries of propriety that governed the upper class's daily lives. For a detailed history of masquerades in England, see Castle, chaps. 1 and 2, and Ribeiro.

13 I owe this observation to the generosity and collegiality of the audience who attended the session of the North American Conference on British Studies during which I presented a portion of this chapter in October 1994. I do not know who said that Caldwell looked like a tourist, but I am grateful and want to acknowledge this brilliant insight.

14 This phrase alludes to Stephen Greenblatt's *Marvelous Possessions: The Wonder of the New World* (Chicago: University of Chicago Press, 1991). See Marcia Pointon's discussion of exotic objects in Zoffany's conversation piece of Queen Charlotte and her sons: "The English royal lineage is constructed . . . from a mass of imported and gifted goods—forms of cultural annexation" ("Killing Pictures," 162). See also Pointon's discussion of Lady Mary's construction of herself through her contact with the alien in chap. 5, "Going Turkish in London: Lady Mary Wortley Montagu and Her Portraits," in *Hanging the Head.*

15 Diana Fuss, "Freud's Fallen Women: Identification, Desire, and 'A Case of Homosexuality in a Woman,'" in *Fear of a Queer Planet: Queer Politics and Social Theory,* ed. Michael Warner (Minneapolis: University of Minnesota Press, 1993), 66.

16 Judith Butler, *Gender Trouble: Feminism and the Subversion of Identity* (London: Routledge, 1990), 137–38.

17 Ibid., and Mikhail Bakhtin, *Rabelais and His World,* trans. Helen Iswolsky (Bloomington: Indiana University Press, 1984), chap. 1.

18 Marjorie Garber, *Vested Interests: Cross-Dressing and Cultural Authority* (New York: Routledge, 1992), 103; and McClintock, *Imperial Leather,* 67. On

the importance of positionality when it comes to performing gendered identities on stage and in autobiography, see Kristina Straub, *Sexual Suspects: Eighteenth-Century Players and Sexual Ideology* (Princeton, NJ: Princeton University Press, 1992).

19 Fuss, 66.

20 Sorting out the differences among terms such as mimicry, parody, and masquerade is difficult, especially because there is little agreement among theorists as to the differences between masquerade and mimicry. Luce Irigaray, *This Sex Which Is Not One* (Ithaca, NY: Cornell University Press, 1985), 220, defines mimicry as the self-conscious adoption of a gendered identity, in this case, femininity, as a way to deal with and disrupt the masculinist discourse that denies subjectivity to women. Mimicry is "an interim strategy . . . in which the woman deliberately assumes the feminine style and posture assigned to her within this discourse in order to uncover the mechanisms by which it exploits her." Masquerade, on the other hand, Irigaray defines as "an alienated or false version of femininity" that posits the woman as the object of man's desire and denies to her the subject position and the experience of desire. Diana Fuss, commenting on and building from Irigaray's "slippery distinction between 'masquerade' (the unconscious assumption of femininity) and 'mimicry' (the deliberate and playful performance of femininity)," sees the difference between mimicry and masquerade as located in "telltale signs of excess." The difference between the " 'straight' imitation of a role and a parodic hyperbolization of that role—depends on the degree and readability of its excess." Mimicry overdoes masquerade, "intentionally ironizing it" (66–67). See Mary Ann Doane, "Film and Masquerade: Theorizing the Female Spectator," *Screen* 23 (1982): 74–88.

21 James Axtell, *The Invasion Within: The Contest of Cultures in Colonial North America* (New York: Oxford University Press, 1985), 302.

22 For a discussion of the evolution of state portraiture in England, see Richard Wendorf, *Elements of Life: Biography and Portrait-Painting in Stuart and Georgian England* (Oxford: Clarendon, 1990), chap. 3.

23 I do not mean to suggest that American Indians were primitive (less cultured or civilized than Europeans), but rather that this was how Europeans and Euro-Americans thought of Indians. The notion that the primitive possesses power is discussed by Michael Taussig in *Mimesis and Alterity: A Particular History of the Senses* (New York: Routledge, 1993).

24 Some art historians have expressed doubt as to the identity of these sitters. Von Erffa and Staley entertain the possibility that the Briton is not Guy Johnson but instead either John Johnson, son of Sir William Johnson, or Sir William himself. The only problem with this suggestion is that Sir William never returned to England after leaving it in the 1730s, and John Johnson was

in England in 1765–67 and did not return until the 1780s. They argue that the dry brushwork of the painting belongs to West's earlier work, and suggest that the National Gallery's dating is off by six to nine years. See von Erffa and Staley, 523–25. Likewise, Brant's biographer Isabel Kelsay doubts that the Mohawk is meant to be Brant, as his face looks only vaguely like Brant's. The National Gallery identifies the Indian as Karonghyontye (David Hill), who did indeed accompany the Johnson-Brant delegation. For a discussion of Hill, see Leslie Reinhardt, "British and Indian Identities in a Picture by Benjamin West," *Eighteenth-Century Studies* 31 (1998): 283–305.

25 In a similar reading of a painting of another cultural cross-dresser (Van Dyck's portrait of the Earl of Denbigh), Wendorf writes: "By placing his main figure in the extreme foreground, Van Dyck has in effect opened up the pictorial space in this painting so that Denbigh seemingly inhabits a middle ground: what lies in front of him is just as important as what Van Dyck has depicted in the background" (102).

26 Thomas Gage to Commanding Officer at Niagara, July 25, 1774, Haldimand Papers 21,678, f. 185.

27 For Guy Johnson's career, which ended with charges of corruption and accusations of exorbitant expenditures in the name of maintaining good relations with Iroquois chiefs, see Colin Calloway, "Fort Niagara: The Politics of Hunger in a Refuge Community," in *The American Revolution in Indian Country: Crisis and Diversity in Native American Communities* (Cambridge: Cambridge University Press, 1995), 129–57.

28 "If Molly was firmly ensconced in the favor of the whites, she was even more thoroughly entrenched in the favor of the Indians. Molly dispensed largess with a lavish hand, and this was the most direct way to the hearts of any people so poverty-stricken as the Mohawks. . . . In just a few years she had made herself the most powerful woman among the Mohawks" (Kelsay, 120). For more information on Molly Brant, see Kelsay's biography and Lois M. Feister and Bonnie Pulis, "Molly Brant: Her Domestic and Political Roles in Eighteenth-Century New York," in *Northeastern Indian Lives, 1632–1816*, ed. Robert S. Grumet (Amherst: University of Massachusetts Press, 1996), 295–320.

29 Donald Grinde demonstrates that both British and American diplomats actively and eloquently courted the Six Nations as allies; see *The Iroquois and the Founding of the American Nation* (San Francisco: Indian Historian Press, 1977).

30 In Kelsay, 165.

31 Quoted in Grinde, 69.

32 Taussig describes this appropriation of the primitive by the colonizer: "this mimicry by the colonizer of the savagery imputed to the savage is what I call the colonial mirror of production" (66).

33 Calloway, *Crown and Calumet*, 56.

34 Richard White, *Middle Ground*, ix–x. It is important to recognize that British America was a site where race, culture, and ethnicity intermingled, for, as Frank Shuffelton argues in his introduction to *A Mixed Race: Ethnicity in Early America*, ed. Frank Shuffelton (New York: Oxford University Press, 1993): "to fail to understand this is to risk always the misconception that later immigration is a dilution or contamination of some supposed founding ethnic purity (7).

35 Of the British wool trade with the Indians, Francis Jennings, *Invasion of America*, writes: "One region, in particular, had reason to be pleased with the Indian trade. The scarlet and blue cloth made in the Stroud and Stroud-water valley of Gloucestershire became an Indian favorite and remained so during the eighteenth century. The valley was distant from the great highways leading to London, and its clothiers turned naturally to nearby Bristol for outlet. . . . The clothiers of the Bristol region enjoyed their greatest prosperity between 1690 and 1760, the span of greatest activity in the English-Indian trade" (99).

36 Richard White argues that trade goods never really became an economic necessity for Indians but rather achieved "symbolic value" (99). "Algonquians fitted European goods into existing social niches, for Algonquians increasingly relied on Europeans for culturally required items. Acquiring sufficient European goods became a requirement of Algonquian ceremonials and diplomacy. In one sense, such goods became as 'Indian' as moccasins, but in another complementary sense they remained exotic, for this is what gave them their value" (104). For typical trade goods, see "An Account of Goods in His Majesty's Indian Stores at Niagara March 31, 1779," which included: 100 lbs. glass wampum, 19 dozen shirts, 12 yards of Stroud blue, 25 yards of scarlet cloth, 75 yards of linen, 10 pieces of muslin for "ruffling shirts," and 24 hat feathers (in *Haldimand Papers*, 21,769: 16–17).

37 Taussig, 246.

38 Kelsay, 229.

39 Ibid., 192.

40 Ibid.

41 See Milton Hamilton's discussion of the many portraits of Joseph Brant in two articles: "Joseph Brant—'The Most Painted Indian,'" *New York History* 39 (1958): 119–32, and "Joseph Brant Painted by Rigaud," *New York History* 40 (1959): 247–54.

42 William Stone, 2: 337.

43 Kelsay, 389.

44 Homi K. Bhabha, "Signs Taken for Wonders: Questions of Ambivalence and Authority under a Tree outside Delhi, May 1817," in *"Race," Writing, and Difference*, ed. by Henry Louis Gates Jr. (Chicago: University of Chi-

cago Press, 1986), 181. The potential for mimicry to disrupt the dominant culture's discourse is pursued by Bhabha in his discussion of the "mimic men" who occupy subaltern status in colonial societies like the British Raj. These mimic men, in their adoption of the affect of their colonial oppressors, turn the colonial gaze back onto itself and present to the colonizer his image reflected. Bhabha, like Fuss, sees this mirroring as disruptive of oppressive systems of representation. He argues that "the *menace* of mimicry is its *double* vision which in disclosing the ambivalence of colonial discourse also disrupts its authority." Bhabha explains that "the look of surveillance returns as the displacing gaze of the disciplined, where the observer becomes the observed and 'partial' representation rearticulates the whole notion of *identity* and alienates it from essence" ("Of Mimicry and Man: The Ambivalence of Colonial Discourse," *October* 29 [1984]: 129). For Bhabha, as for Fuss and Butler, mimicry's power lies in its destabilizing discursive strategies by calling attention to the constructedness of systems of representation and to the absence of essence, whether it be sexual, racial, or cultural.

45   Several critics have commented on how parody incorporates the object of the parody. See Bakhtin on the parodying of high culture in chap. 1 of *Rabelais*. See also Fredric Jameson, "The Cultural Logic of Late Capitalism," in *Postmodernism, or the Cultural Logic of Late Capitalism* (Durham, NC: Duke University Press, 1992).

46   For Brant's audience with the king, see William Stone, 2:251. Captain Brant to the Duke of Northumberland, January 24, 1806, in ibid., 2:425.

47   Quoted in Kelsay, 382.

48   Bhabha writes: "To the extent to which discourse is a form of defensive warfare, mimicry marks those moments of civil disobedience within the discipline of civility: signs of spectacular resistance. When the words of the master become the site of hybridity—the warlike sign of the native— then we may not only read between the lines but even seek to change the often coercive reality that they so lucidly contain" ("Signs," 181). Bhabha here has appropriated Bakhtin's term "hybridity," which applies to double-voiced speech; see M. M. Bakhtin, "Discourse in the Novel," in *The Dialogic Imagination: Four Essays*, ed. Michael Holquist, trans. Caryl Emerson and Michael Holquist (Austin: University of Texas Press, 1981), 362.

49   Kelsay, 394.

50   Quoted in William Stone, 2:67.

51   Jane Whitaker, narrative, extract from *Daily National Democrat*, July 26, 1853, quoted in Kelsay, 279.

52   Phelan, 36.

53   Kelsay, 645.

54   William Stone, 2: 259.

55 Ibid.

56 Kelsay, 384.

57 William Stone, 2:259–60.

58 In Kelsay, 651–52.

59 Council, August 17, 1803, State Papers, Upper Canada, Q301:87–99. Brant's speech is quoted in *The History of the County of Brant, Ontario* (Warner, Beers, and Co., 1883).

60 The patent was issued by Lieutenant Governor John Simcoe on January 14, 1793. It is cited in James J. Talman, Historical introduction to *The Journal of Major John Norton*, ed. Carl F. Klinck and James J. Talman (Toronto: The Champlain Society, 1970), c.

61 Gore to Castlereagh, September 4, 1809, quoted in ibid., civ.

62 Taussig, 236–37, 238, 69, 237, 246.

63 Dean MacCannell, *Empty Meeting Grounds: The Tourist Papers* (New York: Routledge, 1993), equates incorporation with cannibalism, arguing that U.S. contemporary corporate culture is a cannibalizing capitalism that consumes global resources and cultures. See also Root, *Cannibal Culture*, chap. 3. Ward Churchill discusses white theft of native lands and Native American traditions as a form of genocide; see "Fantasies of the Master Race," and *Struggle for the Land: Indigenous Resistance to Genocide, Ecocide and Expropriation* (Monroe, ME: Common Courage Press, 1993). Churchill delineates the ways whites have colonized Indians and have expropriated their culture, land, and resources, focusing his attention on the various contemporary colonizing strategies of whites, who range from professors of religion to New Age ecologists to so-called friends of Indians. As M. Annette Jaimes writes in her introduction to *Fantasies of the Master Race: Literature, Cinema and the Colonization of American Indians* (Monroe, ME: Common Courage Press, 1992), "Each part of the book focuses on a particular device—from the outright invention of spiritual rituals to the rewriting of history—designed to obliterate Native American culture and people, or to absorb them into a system of Euroamerican values" (2).

4. Accommodating India:
Domestic Arrangements in Anglo-Indian Family Portraiture

1 See Mildred Archer, *India and British Portraiture, 1770–1825* (London: Sotheby Parke Bernet, 1979), for details concerning British artists' sojourns in India and for details about their patrons. I am indebted to Archer's work on British painting in India.

2 Apparently, Palmer had an English wife living in England during his

decades-long sojourn in India. Palmer to D. Anderson, March 4, 1792, Correspondence and Papers of David Anderson, British Library (hereafter BL), Add. MSS 45,427:200–203.

3 Palmer to Anderson, November 12, 1786, BL, Add. MSS 45,427:198.

4 For details about the Palmer household, see Archer, *India*, 282–83.

5 Hannah More, *Strictures on the Modern System of Female Education* (1799), in *The Works of Hannah More*, 2 vols. (New York: Harper, 1851), 1:313.

6 See Davidoff and Hall, chaps. 1, 2, and 3 for a treatment of gender and evangelicalism.

7 John Fordyce, *Sermons to Young Women* (1766; Philadelphia: Thomas Dodson, 1787), 274, 332. For a discussion of feminine propriety, see Kathryn Kirkpatrick, "Sermons and Strictures: Conduct-Book Propriety and Property Relations in Late Eighteenth-Century England," in *History, Gender, and Eighteenth-Century Literature,* ed. Beth Fowkes Tobin (Athens: University of Georgia Press, 1994), 198–226.

8 Archer, *India*, 291.

9 Ibid., 286.

10 Quoted in ibid., 208.

11 It should come as no surprise that Martin and Palmer were friends, for they seem to have shared a similar attitude toward living in India.

12 For the rivalry between British and native women and its connection to racial superiority, see Ann Laura Stoler's discussion of early twentieth-century Sumatra in "Rethinking Colonial Categories": "[White] women championed a moral order that both restricted their husbands' sexual activities and reconstituted the domestic domain as a site demanding their vigilance and control" (333). See also Kenneth Ballhatchet, *Race, Sex and Class under the Raj: Imperial Attitudes and Policies and Their Critics, 1793–1905* (New York: St. Martin's Press, 1980), chap. 6.

13 C. A. Bayly, *Imperial Meridian: The British Empire and the World, 1780–1830* (London: Longman, 1989), 143. For discrimination against Eurasians, see Ballhatchet, chap. 4.

14 Valentia, Viscount George, *Voyages and Travels in India* (1809), quoted in Bayly, *Imperial Meridian*, 143.

15 Bayly, *Imperial Meridian*, 148.

16 C. A. Bayly, *The New Cambridge History of India: Indian Society and the Making of the British Empire* (Cambridge: Cambridge University Press, 1988), 2:78.

17 Palmer to Anderson, November 12, 1786, BL, Add. MSS 45,427:196–97.

18 Bayly, *Imperial Meridian*, 143, 150, 149.

19 Ibid., 115.

20 For a discussion of "English ladies, those guardians of racial purity"

(148), see Ballhatchet, chap. 6. For a discussion of colonialist fears of moral and racial contamination of the bourgeois self due to the proximity of natives, particularly native women, see Stoler, *Race and the Education of Desire*, chap. 4, "Cultivating Bourgeois Bodies and Racial Selves," and chap. 5, "Domestic Subversions and Children's Sexuality."

21 Archer, *India*, 357.

22 Philip Lawson, *The East India Company: A History* (London: Longman, 1993), 129.

23 Bayly, *Imperial Meridian*, 150–51.

24 Percival Spear, *The Nabobs: A Study of the Social Life of the English in Eighteenth-Century India* (1932; London: Oxford University Press, 1963), 141.

25 See Richard Leppert's essay, "Music," and his discussion of the Morse-Cator and Blair portraits. My readings of these paintings recapitulate his argument and extend to other works his brilliant insight into the presence or absence of India in these paintings.

26 Anne, seated at the harpsichord, was married to Nathaniel Middleton, a company employee, who had criticized Palmer for having too much influence in Lucknow.

27 Leppert, "Music," 80.

28 See ibid., 70–76, on the significance of the harpsichord as an emblem of the harmony and reason of high European culture.

29 Ibid., 70.

30 In ibid., 76.

31 In ibid., 103.

32 Spear, 129.

33 Pointon makes a similar point about the exotic detail in Zoffany's conversation piece of Queen Charlotte and her eldest sons, how it is used to display the monarchy's global reach, "cultural conquest," and "forms of cultural annexation" (*Hanging the Head,* 162–66).

34 Leppert concludes his discussion of the ayah and the paintings-within-the-painting: "All in all this is a striking painting which in a small way mediates the visual norm in cultural relations between the Anglo-Indian and Indian peoples. The painting still confirms the order of colonialism and reiterates the hierarchy. But it does not acknowledge as legitimate the racial estrangement evident in the other images I have discussed" ("Music," 101–2).

35 Lady Impey is famous today for her patronage of Indian artists who painted some of the most beautiful watercolors of Indian flora and fauna. See chap. 6 below.

36 Quoted in Ramkrishna Mukherjee, *The Rise and Fall of the East Indian Company: A Sociological Appraisal* (New York: Monthly Review Press, 1974), 319. For a discussion of Warren Hastings's administration, see ibid.

37 Devis's representations of Indian servants and officials are as detailed as Zoffany's Impey family portrait. In several portraits by Devis, Indians, even servants, are portrayed as dignified, fully realized, and individualized adults. The tall, somewhat stooped servant in the portrait of *Claud and Boyd Alexander* has his head turned away from the interaction that engrosses the brothers (and their dog); facing out, he stares at us as if linking us with him in not fully understanding the brothers' conversation over a letter that has just arrived. His somewhat bored look deflates the excitement that the two brothers display over the letter. Devis's interest in accurately depicting Indians led to a scheme that never materialized, in which he proposed to draw pictures of the customs and occupations of Indian villagers that then would be engraved for publication.

38 For Devis's career, see D'Oench, *Conversation Piece,* and for country house portraiture, see Mary Spivy, Joy Breslauer, and Ellen D'Oench, *Country Houses in Great Britain* (New Haven: Yale Center for British Art, 1980).

39 Archer, *India,* 239.

40 Ibid., 254.

41 See, for instance, Ellis Waterhouse, *Painting in Britain from 1530–1790* (1953; Harmondsworth: Penguin Books, 1988), 257.

42 Pratapaditya Pal and Vidya Dehejia, *From Merchants to Emperors: British Artists and India, 1757–1930* (Ithaca, NY: Cornell University Press, 1986), comment on the British rejection of Indian clothing for the wearing of "totally inappropriate, uncomfortable, and even unhealthy clothing that had been designed to be worn in the climate of the British isles. . . . It was not uncommon for a British gentleman even in remote outposts to eat dinner alone at home in full dress solely for the benefit of his servants" (61). Not only were Indian clothes rejected by the British but by the 1820s Indian cloth was socially taboo. "It was the extremity of bad taste to appear in anything of Indian manufacture—neither muslin, silk, flowers nor even ornaments however beautiful" (quoted in Spear, 142). This attitude seems to me to be particularly ridiculous, given that acquiring Indian cloth was one of the original goals of the East India Company. For a discussion of the significance of clothing in nineteenth-century India, see Bernard S. Cohn, *Colonialism and Its Forms of Knowledge: The British in India* (Princeton, NJ: Princeton University Press, 1996), 106–62.

43 Archer, *India,* 292.

44 Bayly, *Indian Society,* 78.

45 Lord William Bentinck, quoted in Pal and Dehejia, 45.

46 For creole colonial societies, see Benedict Anderson, *Imagined Communities: Reflections on the Origin and Spread of Nationalism* (London: Verso, 1983).

47 P. J. Marshall, "The Whites of British India, 1780–1830: A Failed Colonial

Society?," in *Trade and Conquest: Studies on the Rise of British Dominance in India* (Aldershot, UK: Variorum, 1993), 39.

48 Ibid., 43, 27, 28.

49 Ibid., 44.

50 Quoted in Ballhatchet, 96.

5. Taxonomy and Agency in Brunias's West Indian Paintings

1 For clothing as a signifying practice, see Dick Hebdige, *Subculture: The Meaning of Style* (London: Methuen, 1979), chaps. 1 and 8 in particular.

2 For the fullest discussion of this genre in the context of voyages of discovery, see Smith, especially chap. 4, "Portraying Pacific People," where he states that Joseph Banks wanted his artists to portray Pacific people "in a manner similar to that of natural history, as type specimens, accompanied by detailed verbal descriptions" (81). "Ethnographic convention . . . defines by means of costume and adornment" (80). See also Rudiger Joppien and Bernard Smith, *The Art of Captain Cook's Voyages*, vol. 2: *The Voyage of the Resolution and Adventure, 1772–1775* (New Haven: Yale University Press, 1985), for a discussion of William Hodges's ethnographic art and how Hodges's paintings of Maori warriors avoid the conventions of ethnographic art to create images that are "humanized and individualized" (45). Joppien and Smith argue that Hodges's images of Maoris are "significant exceptions during a period when generalizing, allegorical, ethnographic or philosophic conventions largely determined the portrayal of native peoples, casting them into well-established visual types" (46).

3 The word "negro" was used by planters to refer to slaves. Perhaps uncomfortable with the bare politics of domination that the word slave carries, planters preferred to call their slaves negroes and sometimes creoles (if born in the Caribbean). See, for instance, Matthew Gregory Lewis, *Journal of a West India Proprietor; Kept during a Residence in the Island of Jamaica* (1834; New York: Negro Universities Press, 1969).

4 For discussions of Parkinson's role as draughtsman on this voyage, see Rudiger Joppien and Bernard Smith, *The Art of Captain Cook's Voyages*, vol. 1: *The Voyage of the Endeavour* (New Haven: Yale University Press, 1985). For a treatment of scientific aspects of Parkinson's art, see D. J. Carr, ed., *Sydney Parkinson: Artist of Cook's Endeavour Voyage* (Canberra: Australian National University Press, 1983).

5 Young, *Observations*, 19–20.

6 Like Wheatly's *Cries of London*, Brunias's Caribbean pictures were painted with the intention of having them engraved for the lucrative print trade.

Like Hogarth, Brunias engraved many of his paintings himself. For the impact of the print trade on fancy pieces and a history of genre painting in Britain, see E. D. H. Johnson, chap. 4, "The Triumph of Genre."

7   See chapter 1 for a discussion of the sugar-slavery nexus in the West Indies. For seventeenth-century images of sugar and slavery in the New World, see Rudiger Joppien, "The Dutch Vision of Johan Maurits and His Artists," in *Johan Maurits van Nassau-Siegen, 1604–1679: A Humanist Prince in Europe and Brazil*, ed. E. van den Boogaart (The Hague: Government Publishing Office, 1979).

8   For information on Brunias's career, see Hans Huth, "Agostino Brunias, Romano," *Connoisseur* 151, no. 610 (1962): 265–69, Neville Connell, "Colonial Life in the West Indies as Depicted in Prints," *Antiques* 99 (1971): 732–37, and Hugh Honour, *The Image of the Black in Western Art*, 4:32–37.

9   See a brief discussion of Brunias's relationship with Sir William Young in Hulme and Whitehead, 201.

10   My discussion of natural history is indebted to Pamela Regis, *Describing Early America: Bartram, Jefferson, Crevecoeur, and the Rhetoric of Natural History* (Dekalb: Northern Illinois University Press, 1992), chaps. 1 and 5. Anthropology has been criticized for ignoring change within a culture as well as the history of particular societies. See Johannes Fabian, *Time and the Other: How Anthropology Makes Its Object* (New York: Columbia University Press, 1983), chap. 3. Fabian interrogates the use of the ethnographic present: "the statement 'the X are matrilineal' is taken to imply a static view of society, one that is inattentive to the fact that all cultures are constantly changing" (81). See also John Comaroff and Jean Comaroff's elegant discussion of the strengths and weaknesses of anthropology in the first chapter of *Ethnography and the Historical Imagination* (Boulder, CO: Westview Press, 1992): "Anthropology will continue to cast 'other cultures' in the timeless shadows of its own dominant narratives," denying to "primitive peoples" their own histories (24–25). For an exception to this dehistoricizing tendency in an eighteenth-century proto-anthropological travel narrative, see Nicholas Thomas's discussion of Forster's work in "Johann Reinhold Forster and His *Observations*," in *Observations Made during a Voyage round the World*, by Johann Reinhold Forster, ed. Nicholas Thomas, Harriet Guest, and Michael Dettelbach (Honolulu: University of Hawaii Press, 1996), xv–xxii.

11   For an extended discussion of Linnaean botany, see chapter 6 below.

12   Regis, 148.

13   Arthur Lovejoy, *The Great Chain of Being* (Cambridge, MA: Harvard University Press, 1973), 232.

14   Janet Schaw, *Journal of a Lady of Quality; Being the Narrative of a Journey from Scotland to the West Indies, North Carolina, and Portugal, in the years 1774*

to 1776, ed. Evangeline Walker Andrews (New Haven: Yale University Press, 1921), 112.

15 John Luffman, a traveler to Antigua in the 1780s, writes in *A Brief Account of the Island of Antigua* (London, 1789): "Many of these gentlemen-managers, as well as the overseers under them, contribute, in a great degree, to stock the plantation with mulatto and metee slaves. It is impossible to say in what number they have such children, but the following fact is too often verified, 'that, as soon as born, they are despised, not only by the very authors, under God, of their being, but by every white, destitute of humane and liberal principles,' such is the regard paid to the hue of complexion in preference to the more permanent beauties of the mind" (45–56).

16 James Walvin, *Black Ivory: A History of the British Slave Trade* (London: Fontana Press, 1993), 218–20. See also Edward Brathwaite, *The Development of Creole Society in Jamaica, 1770–1820* (Oxford: Clarendon Press, 1971), especially chap. 19, for a description of the various interactions between slaves and their masters in creole society. For a description of a particular plantation, see Michael Craton and James Walvin, *A Jamaican Plantation: The History of Worthy Park, 1670–1970* (Toronto: University of Toronto Press, 1970).

17 Walvin, *Black Ivory*, 219.

18 See "Summer," lines 1269–370, for the story of Damon and Musidora, in which Damon watches the woman he loves but who scorns him swim naked in a stream. In an earlier version of the poem, Damon spies upon "three naked bathers, who are likened to Juno, Minerva, and Venus" (224). See James Thomson, *The Seasons and the Castle of Indolence*, ed. James Sambrook (1972; Oxford: Oxford University Press, 1987). See John Berger, *Ways of Seeing* (London: Penguin and BBC, 1977) for the politics of the male gaze and the nude female body. Feminist scholarship on the representation of the female body is too vast and complex to recapitulate here. See the following useful collections of essays, *Women as Sex Objects: Studies in Erotic Art, 1730–1970*, edited by Thomas B. Hess and Linda Nochlin (New York: Newsweek, 1972); *Feminism and Art History: Questioning the Litany*, edited by Norma Broude and Mary D. Garrard (New York: Harper & Row, 1982); *Looking On: Images of Femininity in the Visual Arts and Media*, edited by Rosemary Betterton (New York: Routledge, 1987). See also Linda Nochlin, *Women, Art, and Power: and Other Essays* (New York: Harper and Row, 1988), and Griselda Pollock, *Vision and Difference: Femininity, Feminism, and Histories of Art* (New York: Routledge, 1988).

19 *In Miserable Slavery, Thomas Thistlewood in Jamaica, 1750–1786*, ed. D. Hall (London, 1989), quoted in Walvin, *Black Ivory*, 215.

20 Lewis, 123; William Young, "Tour through the several Islands," 3:241–84, 253. Hereafter, citations to this text will appear in parentheses.

21 For a similar discussion of the importance of cloth and clothing in Indian society, see Cohn, chap. 5, "Cloth, Clothes, and Colonialism: India in the Nineteenth Century."

22 A. C. Carmichael, *Domestic Manners and Social Condition of the White, Coloured, and Negro Population of the West Indies*, 2 vols. (1833; New York: Negro Universities Press, 1969), 1:142–60. Hereafter, citations to this text will appear in parentheses.

23 Carmichael's account has been regarded by most historians and anthropologists as reliable. More skeptical of Carmichael's narrative, anthropologist Virginia Heyer Young contrasts Ashton Warner's narrative with Carmichael's, both of which record life on St. Vincent in the 1820s, and urges scholars to be cautious in using Carmichael as an authority and "to pick out neutral and unprejudiced data from Carmichael's account" (48).

24 Watches were quite expensive, and as Davidoff and Hall argue, were emblematic of a self-regulation associated with evangelicalism and the work ethic (85–91). See Hannah More, "On Time," in *Practical Piety* (London, 1813). A slave with a watch would be a contradiction in terms because a slave is denied self-regulation, his or her time being superintended by the master. Perhaps this accounts for what Carmichael feels is ludicrous about a slave owning a watch.

25 Bhabha, "Signs," 181.

26 Taussig, 236–37.

27 Hebdige, 18.

28 Patterson, 248.

29 Butler, 137–38.

30 See Carmichael on turbans and handkerchiefs (1:145–46). Equiano describes how his Ibo people grew "vast quantities of cotton" (39) and how the women's "usual occupation is spinning and weaving cotton, which they afterwards dye, and make into garments" (36). See Olaudah Equiano, *The Interesting Narrative of the Life of Olaudah Equiano, or Gustavus Vassa, The African, Written by Himself,* ed. Robert Allison (Boston: Bedford Books, 1995). Subsequent references to this text appear in parentheses. In West Africa, woven cotton cloth was used in rituals marking the stages in the life cycle (birth, puberty, marriage, death) and in ceremonies celebrating status and prestige as well as functioning as a medium of exchange similar to money. See B. W. Hodder, "Indigenous Cloth Trade and Marketing in Africa" and Lisa Aronson, "History of Cloth Trade in the Niger Delta: A Study of Diffusion" in *Textiles in Africa,* ed. Dale Idiens and K. G. Ponting (Bath, England: The Pasold Research Fund, 1980).

32 I am thinking here, of course, of Marx's discussion of commodity fetishism, which occurs when commodities are severed from their use value and

from human production. See *Capital,* trans. Ben Fowkes (New York: Random House, 1977), 1:164–65.

33 Summarizing Susan Pearce's ideas on collecting as a form of fetishism, John Windsor, "Identity Parades," in *The Cultures of Collecting,* ed. John Elsner and Roger Cardinal (Cambridge, MA: Harvard University Press, 1994), writes that "fetishism is the removal of the object from its historical and cultural context and its redefinition in terms of the collector" (50).

34 For a discussion of the significance of peasant economies as a form of resistance to slave and wage labor economies in the Caribbean, see Sidney W. Mintz, "From Plantations to Peasantries in the Caribbean," in *Caribbean Contours,* ed. Sidney W. Mintz and Sally Price (Baltimore: Johns Hopkins University Press, 1985), 127–54.

35 Walvin, *Black Ivory,* 114. Caribbean market days bear a strong resemblance to Bakhtin's description of the medieval marketplace as a site of licensed freedom of speech as well as his description of the carnivalesque. Bakhtin, *Rabelais and His World,* trans. Helen Iswolsky (Bloomington: Indiana University Press, 1984), explores the subversive quality of the carnival but concludes that the carnival and the marketplace allow for highly ritualized and self-contained acts of rebellion that vent dangerous energies and work ultimately to maintain the hegemonic order.

36 See Elizabeth Bohls's brilliant discussion of Schaw's use of the aesthetic to organize her portrayal of West Indian society and scenery: "The Aesthetics of Colonialism: Jane Schaw in the West Indies, 1774–1775," *Eighteenth-Century Studies* 27 (1994): 363–90.

37 Schaw, 107, 108–9.

38 Luffman, 139–41.

39 Walvin, *Black Ivory,* 114.

40 Ibid.

41 See Roderick McDonald, *The Economy and Material Culture of Slaves: Goods and Chattels on the Sugar Plantations of Jamaica and Louisiana* (Baton Rouge: Louisiana State University Press, 1993), 18.

42 Ibid. According to Hilary Beckles, slaves regarded taking things from the master as a matter of survival and an exercise in ingenuity rather than theft. Apparently, stolen goods were a significant portion of the internal economy of slaves in Barbados because slaves did not have provision grounds on that island. See Beckles, chap. 4, "Marketeers: The Right to Trade."

43 See Eric Williams, chaps. 9 and 10.

6. Imperial Designs: Botanical Illustration and
the British Botanic Empire

I am grateful to the staff of the Herbarium and Library of the Royal Botanic Gardens, Kew, the staff of the Hawaiian and Pacific Collection of Hamilton Library, University of Hawai'i, and the staff of the Botany Library of the Natural History Museum for their help in finding and reproducing the Indian artists' illustrations and locating Banks's correspondence concerning the Roxburgh collection. A portion of this essay was presented at a 1993 Northeast American Society for Eighteenth-Century Studies session on "Illustrating Science in the Eighteenth Century," and at the International Congress on the Enlightenment, Munster, Germany, 1995.

1 In Robert John Thorton, *The Temple of Flora: A New Illustration of the Sexual System of Linnaeus* (London, 1799, 1807), n.p.

2 Mary Louise Pratt, *Imperial Eyes: Travel Writing and Transculturation* (New York: Routledge, 1992), 57; for an incisive analysis of the imperialism implicit in natural history and travel writing, see chaps. 2, 3, and 4. For the relationship between exploration, imperial ambitions, and science, see Derek Howse, ed., *Background to Discovery: Pacific Exploration from Dampier to Cook* (Berkeley: University of California Press, 1990); David Mackay, *In the Wake of Captain Cook: Exploration, Science, and Empire, 1780–1801* (Wellington: Victoria University Press, 1986); John Mackenzie, ed., *Imperialism and the Natural World* (New York: St. Martin's Press, 1990); Roy MacLeod and Philip F. Rehbock, eds., *Nature in Its Greatest Extent: Western Science in the Pacific* (Honolulu: University of Hawaii Press, 1988); and Patrick Petitjean et al., *Science and Empires: Historical Studies about Scientific Development and European Expansion* (Dordrecht: Kluwer, 1992).

3 Wilfrid Blunt, "The Voyage of the *Endeavour*" in *Sidney Parkinson: Artist of Cook's Endeavour Voyage*, ed. D. J. Carr (Honolulu: University of Hawaii Press, 1983), 1–13.

4 Joseph Banks, *The Endeavour Journal of Joseph Banks*, ed. J. C. Beaglehole, 2 vols. (Sydney: Angus and Robertson, 1962), 1:308–9. For Banks's description of Brazilian fruit, see J. C. Beaglehole, "Introduction: The Young Banks," in *The Endeavour Journal of Joseph Banks*, 1:192–93, 200–201.

5 Daniel R. Headrick, *The Tentacles of Progress: Technology Transfer in the Age of Imperialism, 1850–1940* (New York: Oxford University Press, 1988), 211.

6 Frans A. Stafleu, *Linnaeus and the Linnaeans: The Spreading of Their Ideas in Systematic Botany, 1735–1789* (Utrecht: Oosthoek's Uitgeversmaatschappij N.V., 1971), 231.

7 W. B. Turrill, *The Royal Botanic Gardens, Kew, Past and Present* (London, 1959), 23, quoted in ibid., 232.

8 Hector Charles Cameron, *Sir Joseph Banks: The Autocrat of the Philosophers* (London: Batchworth Press, 1952), 63.

9 Lucille H. Brockway, *Science and Colonialism: The Role of the British Royal Botanic Gardens* (New York: Academic Press, 1979), 192. See also the collection of essays in David Philip Miller and Peter Hanns Reill, eds., *Visions of Empire: Voyages, Botany, and Representations of Nature* (Cambridge: Cambridge University Press, 1996), in particular David Philip Miller, "Joseph Banks, Empire, and 'Centers of Calculation' in Late Hanoverian London," 21–37; David Mackay, "Agents of Empire: the Banksian Collectors and Evaluation of New Lands," 38–57; and Alan Frost, "The Antipodean Exchange: European Horticulture and Imperial Designs," 58–79.

10 Sir Joseph Banks to East India Company, December 27, 1788, *The Correspondence of Joseph Banks,* Natural History Museum, 6:109; hereafter cited as Correspondence of Joseph Banks.

11 Ray Desmond, *The European Discovery of the Indian Flora* (Oxford: Oxford University Press, 1992), 205.

12 Banks to Hove, January 7, 1787, *Correspondence of Joseph Banks,* 5:124–27.

13 William Thomas Stearn, introduction to *Species Plantarum and Cognate Botanical Works of Carl Linnaeus: A Facsimile of the First Edition, 1753,* by Carl Linnaeus (London: The Ray Society, 1957), 1:44–45.

14 An exception might be Thorton's *Temple of Flora,* which does depict flowers in a landscape. However, the landscape is highly romantic, governed by the picturesque, and quite fanciful, for on occasion the illustrations contain Roman goddesses and cupids. See Janet Browne, "Botany in the Boudoir and Garden: The Banksian Context," in *Visions of Empire: Voyages, Botany, and Representations of Nature,* ed. David Philip Miller and Peter Hanns Reill (Cambridge: Cambridge University Press, 1996), 153–72.

15 Tahitians used the ironwood tree's very hard wood to make hooks and weapons. Spears and clubs made of ironwood were thought to possess *mana* (supernatural powers): "Ironwood became so intimately associated with war that when ever trees were felled one automatically assumed that war was imminent. The association with war is also reflected in language; throughout Polynesia the word for ironwood, *tea,* is synonymous with that for warrior and bravery" (Angela Kay Kepler, *Hawaiian Heritage Plants* [Honolulu: Oriental Publishing Company, 1983], 67–68). The banana was the embodiment of the great god Kanaloa, who had brought the first plants to Hawaii from his ancestral homeland (22). Lilikalā Kame'eleihiwa explains in her book that the banana was forbidden to women because it was not only a phallic symbol but it was "*kinolau* (one of the many physical forms) of the major male *Akua*" (33). Kame'eleihiwa writes, "For women to eat these foods would not only allow their *mana* to defile the sacrifice to the male *Akua* [god], but would also encourage them to devour male sexual prowess. . . . Given that

the word *'ai* means 'to eat, to devour' and also 'to rule and to control,' if women ate the *kinolau* of the *Akua,* they would gain the *mana* to rule the domains represented by these *Akua;* women would then rule male sexual prowess, including war, agriculture, ocean travel, and deep-sea fishing. What would be left for men to do?" (34).

16 Pratt, 31. See also Nicholas Thomas's discussion of the decontextualizing white background of illustrations of exotic artifacts, which he suggests is derived from the conventions of natural history illustration, in "Licensed Curiosity: Cook's Pacific Voyages," in *The Culture of Collecting,* ed. John Elsner and Roger Cardinal (Cambridge, MA: Harvard University Press, 1994), 116–36.

17 Blanche Henrey, *British Botanical and Horticultural Literature before 1800,* 3 vols. (London: Oxford University Press, 1975). For a history of botanical illustration, see Wilfrid Blunt and William T. Stearn, *The Art of Botanical Illustration* (1950; Woodbridge, Suffolk: Antique Collectors' Club, in association with The Royal Botanic Gardens, Kew, 1994).

18 John V. Brindle and James J. White, *Flora Portrayed: Classics of Botanical Art from the Hunt Institute Collection* (Pittsburgh: Hunt Institute, 1985), 11.

19 Bernard McTigue, *Nature Illustrated: Flowers, Plants, and Trees 1550–1900: From the Collections of the New York Public Library* (New York: Harry Abrams, 1989), 95.

20 Londa Schiebinger, *Nature's Body: Gender in the Making of Modern Science* (Boston: Beacon Press, 1993), 14.

21 Stearn, 1:3.

22 Robert Pulteney, *Historical and Biographical Sketches of the Progress of Botany in England from Its Origin to the Introduction of the Linnaean System,* 2 vols. (London, 1790), quoted in Stearn, 80, 75.

23 John E. Lesch, "Systematics and the Geometrical Spirit," in *The Quantifying Spirit of the 18th Century,* ed. Tore Frangsmyr, J. L. Heilbron, and Robin E. Rider (Berkeley: University of California Press, 1990), 75.

24 See Schiebinger's study of the way science employs gender in constructing so-called natural categories; see chap. 1, "The Private Lives of Plants," for an examination of the ways Linnaean taxonomy "came to recapitulate the sexual hierarchy of Western Europe" (4).

25 Stearn, 24.

26 Lesch, 76.

27 Stafleu, 58.

28 Stearn, 24.

29 Gunnar Eriksson, "Linnaeus the Botanist," in *Linnaeus: The Man and His Work,* ed. Tore Frangsmyr (Berkeley: University of California Press, 1983), 78, 79. Michel Foucault, *The Order of Things: An Archaeology of the Human Sciences* (1966; New York: Vintage, 1973), makes a similar point when he says

that natural history writing in the Renaissance included "the virtues it was thought to possess, the legends and stories with which it had been involved, its place in heraldry" (129).

30 Lesch, 78.

31 Ibid., 77.

32 Stearn, 3.

33 Stafleu, 211.

34 Thorton, n.p.

35 Guest, "Curiously Marked," 102–4.

36 For a discussion of Banks's relation to collecting and the virtuoso tradition, see John Gascoigne, *Joseph Banks and the English Enlightenment: Useful Knowledge and Polite Culture* (Cambridge: Cambridge University Press, 1994), chap. 3. Gascoigne traces what he describes as Banks's growth from a "macaroni," a mere amateur and leisured gentleman who regarded science as "a source of gentlemanly amusement" (62), into a "major naturalist and scientific patron in his own right" (95).

37 Brockway sees the Palm House at Kew as "a symbol, like the Crystal Palace in the industrial sphere, of the importance of Kew Gardens to Britain in its relations with the non-European world, the tropical world, the world of the colonies, a necessary complement to the home island as a source of wealth and raw materials" (187).

38 Bernard Smith points out that Cook's voyages and the collection and recording of botanical and other scientific information that were a part of these voyages were dependent on imperial might. While art was "in the service of science and travel . . . both science and travel were subordinated to the demands of commerce, power and ideology" (10).

39 Paul Carter, *The Road to Botany Bay: An Exploration of Landscape and History* (Chicago: University of Chicago Press, 1987), 22–24. For a critique of Carter, see Bernard Smith, who argues that Cook (just as much as Banks) operated within preconceived systems of conceptualization when he employed the principles of trigonometry to aid in his cartography (242).

40 Samuel Johnson, *The History of Rasselas* (Oxford: Oxford University Press, 1990), 26–27.

41 Sir Joshua Reynolds, *Discourses on Art,* ed. Robert R. Wark (New Haven: Yale University Press, 1975), 44.

42 See Foucault, particularly chap. 5 on "Classifying."

43 Stearn, 75.

44 Smith, 37.

45 Agnes Arber, *Herbals, Their Origin and Evolution: A Chapter in the History of Botany, 1470–1670* (1912; Cambridge: Cambridge University Press, 1988), 206.

46 A. G. Morton, in *History of Botanical Science: An Account of the Devel-*

opment of Botany from Ancient Times to the Present Day (London: Academic Press, 1981), argues that Linné's Platonic system of ideal types is a result of his having "never escaped from the restricting circle of idealist-essentialist thought in which his early high-school training had confined him. This was the background . . . to his narrow view of botany, his blindness to the advances of plant physiology and anatomy, his unquestioning acceptance of special creation" (276). See also Lisbet Koerner, "Purposes of Linnaean Travel: A Preliminary Research Report," in *Visions of Empire: Voyages, Botany, and Representations of Nature,* ed. David Philip Miller and Peter Hanns Reill (Cambridge: Cambridge University Press, 1996), 117–52.

47 Smith, 33.

48 Svetlana Alpers, *The Art of Describing: Dutch Art in the Seventeenth-Century* (Chicago: University of Chicago Press, 1983), 106–7.

49 Ingvar Bergstrom, *Dutch Still-Life Painting in the Seventeenth Century,* trans. Christina Hedstrom and Gerald Taylor (New York: Thomas Yoseloff, 1956), 155, 214. The biblical passages are Job 14:1–2 and Isaiah 40:6–7, quoted in Bergstrom, 155.

50 In his discussion of still life, Norman Bryson, *Looking at the Overlooked: Four Essays on Still Life Painting* (London: Reaktion Books, 1990), notes that while Dutch still life contains "emblems of human ephemerality" (107), it also takes place within a culture that celebrates consumption and revels in the material. Bryson traces out the "vast colonial network" that is implicit in the Dutch paintings of exotic flowers, such as the Turkish import, the tulip. He sees in these Dutch paintings of flowers a kind of denial of exotic origins, a "complete dislocation, the abolition of space" (105–6), and "a symbolic association between horticulture and political power" (108). See also Blunt and Stearn, chap. 10, "Holland: The Flower-piece and the Dutch Influence."

51 Beaglehole, 1:33–34.

52 R. J. Henderson, "Plants of Australia," in *Sydney Parkinson: Artist of Cook's Endeavour Voyage,* ed. D. J. Carr (Canberra: Australian National University Press, 1983), 155.

53 F. R. Fosberg and Marie-Helene Sachet, "The Plants of the Society Islands," in *Sydney Parkinson: Artist of Cook's Endeavour Voyage,* ed. D. J. Carr (Canberra: Australian National University Press, 1983), 106–7.

54 In 1831 Goethe lamented that "a great flower-painter is not now to be expected: we have attained too high a degree of scientific truth; and the botanist counts the stamens after the painter and has no eye for picturesque grouping and lighting" (cited in Wilfrid Blunt, "Sydney Parkinson and His Fellow Artists," in *Sydney Parkinson: Artist of Cook's Endeavour Voyage,* ed. D. J. Carr [Canberra: Australian National University Press, 1983], 15).

55 Stuart Cary Welch, "A Confluence of East and West, of Art and Science,"

in *A Selection of Late 18th and Early 19th Century Indian Botanical Paintings* (Pittsburgh: Hunt Institute for Botanical Documentation, 1980), 17–18.

56 Phyllis I. Edwards, "Company Sponsorship and the Beginnings of Indian Botany," in *A Selection of Late 18th and Early 19th Century Indian Botanical Paintings* (Pittsburgh: Hunt Institute for Botanical Documentation, 1980), 25.

57 Mildred Archer, *Natural History Drawings in the India Office Library* (London: Her Majesty's Stationary Office, 1962), 21.

58 Banks to the East India Company, July 4, 1794, Correspondence of Joseph Banks, 9:55.

59 Banks to the East India Company, July 4, 1796, The Correspondence of Joseph Banks, 9:52.

60 Desmond, chaps. 6 and 11.

61 Some of the more famous examples of Britain's control over the agricultural production of its empire are its introduction and wide-scale cultivation of plants and their produce for sale in the world market, products like sugar grown in the West Indies for English consumption, opium grown in India for sale in China, and tea grown in India and Sri Lanka and coffee in Africa for European consumption.

7. The Imperial Politics of the Local and the Universal

1 "Re-representation" is Bruno Latour's term. *Science in Action: How to Follow Scientists and Engineers through Society* (Milton Keyes: Open University Press, 1987), 241. To clarify my terms, colonialism is not merely a power differential but a formal state apparatus complete with ideological and repressive state apparatuses—a state formation with police, military, laws, educational, religious and cultural institutions that are controlled more or less completely by a combination of bureaucratic elites in the "home" country and in the colony. Too often the term colonialism has been borrowed to describe power differentials (usually class based) that have nothing to do with a formal colonial state apparatus. For instance, in multicultural studies the phrase "internal colonialism" is often used to describe relations between dominant and minority communities within one state and its legal borders (an exception to this would be Native Americans in Canada and the United States who are indeed colonized). Colonialism in this context is being used as a metaphor rather than as a descriptor, deployed for effect rather than for analysis. Imperialism differs from colonialism in that imperialism, a relationship between two or more countries, can exist without the formal state structures of colonialism through the exercise of political influence, infiltration of economic structures (banking, labor unions, multinational com-

panies, etc.), and the threat of military violence (U.S. relations with South America and Britain's with Argentina, for instance). The terms core and periphery are derived, in part, from Immanuel Wallerstein's world-system theory, in which he carefully traces out Europe's construction of itself as a core in a global economic and political network, a process that began in the fifteenth century, was consolidated in the eighteenth and nineteenth centuries, and only in the early twentieth century began to dissolve into less visible, because more fragmented and mobile, cores of power (the board rooms of multinational corporations, for instance, instead of the "home office").

2 Robin Simon argues that Copley had the *Apollo Belvedere* in mind when he painted Montgomerie in this pose because Copley's preliminary sketches reveal various attitudes that are clearly derivative of that work (81–83). For an argument that the *Apollo Belvedere* is not necessarily the referent but instead a "particular type of ancient Roman statue, one commonly used for the official portrayal of magistrates" (44), see David H. Solkin, "Great Pictures or Great Men? Reynolds, Male Portraiture, and the Power of Art," *Oxford Art Journal* 9 (1986): 42–49. Although Solkin's convincing argument focuses on Allan Ramsay's *Norman, Twenty-second Chief of Macleod* (1748) and Reynolds's portrayal of *Commodore Augustus Keppel* (1752–53), many critics have taken up Solkin's position and applied it to figures previously identified as standing in the *Apollo Belvedere* pose. For the purposes of my argument, it does not really matter if Montgomerie's pose is that of the *Apollo Belvedere* or a Roman statesman; what is important is that the pose refers to classical antiquity. For an argument, which Solkin also makes, that Reynolds was not interested in citation per se or allegorical reference, but rather used allusions for the sake of heightening the grandeur of a portrait, see Andrew Wilton, *The Swagger Portrait: Grand Manner Portraiture in Britain from Van Dyck to Augustus John* (London: Tate Gallery, 1992), 46–47, and Edgar Wind, "Hume and the Heroic Portrait" and " 'Borrowed Attitudes' in Reynolds and Hogarth," in Wind, *Hume and the Heroic Portrait: Studies in Eighteenth-Century Imagery,* ed. Jaynie Anderson (Oxford: Clarendon Press, 1986), in particular 16–20, 69–73.

3 For an extremely suggestive treatment of Copley's contribution to history painting and the role of exotic locale, see Wind, chap. 9, "The Revolution of History Painting," and for a discussion of contemporary versus antique clothing, see chap. 10, "Penny, West, and 'The Death of General Wolfe.' "

4 Copley's mingling of individuals and types has precedent in paintings that portray military leaders' benevolence to their conquered subjects and/or their troops. In *The Death of General Wolfe* West combined portraiture with the figuring of types: the Native Americans and foot soldiers are types, and the officers standing around the dying Wolfe are identifiable individuals.

Francis Hayman, with his *Surrender of Montreal to General Amherst* (1760–61), and Edward Penny, with his *Marquess of Grandby Relieving a Sick Soldier* (1765), combined types with individuals: soldiers and their families are generalized figures much like those in Gainsborough's fancy pictures. See chap. 5, "Exhibitions of Sympathy," in Solkin, *Painting for Money.*

5 For the Revolution's impact on Indian people, see Calloway, *American Revolution.*

6 For the 77th Highlander troop's movements, see "British Losses at Havanna" (1762), in *Papers of Sir William Johnson* ed. James Sullivan (Albany: University of the State of New York, 1921), 3:990–91. See also David Stewart, *Sketches of the Highlanders of Scotland* (Edinburgh, 1822). For Brook Young's death, see Sir William Young to Earl of Liverpool, Correspondence and Papers of the Earl of Liverpool, British Library, Add. MSS. 38,200:215 and 38,202:5. For the Cherokee during the American Revolution, see Calloway, *American Revolution,* chap. 7, "Chota: Cherokee Beloved Town in a World at War."

7 In her discussion of the Indian in *The Death of General Wolfe,* Ann Uhry Abrams, *The Valiant Hero: Benjamin West and Grand-Style History Painting* (Washington, DC: Smithsonian, 1985), 177, suggests that the figure of a Native America personifies the continent of America. This might help make sense of Montgomerie's portrait.

8 Another point I would like to clarify: Too often in recent discussions of the local/global, there is a somewhat thoughtless celebration of the local as a site of resistance to the global forces of postindustrial capitalism with its concomitant cultural imperialism. Although I applaud the kind of work that Stuart Hall suggests with his phrase "All we have is a little local politics," I question whether the embrace of the local solves the problems that originate in the structural relation between the global and the local. Critiquing and resisting the global is not sufficient, nor is cultivating the local; what must accompany any real change is a refusal of the structural dynamics that create the global and the local. Rather than embrace the local as a form of resistance, it seems to me that one should refuse to be "localized" by the global, and instead to step outside of this dynamic, establish (through recovery of precolonial relations?) an epistemology that is not universal and not "local" in the sense of marginalized and of limited import. For an interesting discussion of place as a form of resistance to core-periphery dynamics, see Nochlin, "Courbet, Oller, and a Sense of Place: The Regional, the Provincial, and the Picturesque in 19th-Century Art," in *Politics of Vision,* 19–32. For discussions that complicate the binary oppositions of global-local, core-periphery, and colonizer-colonized with categories such as transnational and diasporic, see Grewal, 231–54, and Grewal and Kaplan, 1–33.

9 Anthony Ashley Cooper, 3rd Earl of Shaftesbury, *Characteristics of Men, Manners, Opinions, Times,* quoted by Solkin, 10. See Solkin's discussion of Shaftesbury's disdain for portraiture in *Painting for Money,* 1–26. See also Wind's "Penny, West, and 'The Death of General Wolfe,' " in *Hume and the Heroic Portrait,* 100–104.

10 Reynolds, 50. Subsequent references to this text are in parentheses.

11 Samuel Johnson, 26–27.

12 For a discussion of Reynolds's distrust of and distaste for material particularity, see Elizabeth A. Bohls, "Disinterestedness and Denial of the Particular: Locke, Adam Smith, and the Subject of Aesthetics," in *Eighteenth-Century Aesthetics and the Reconstruction of Art,* ed. Paul Mattick Jr. (Cambridge: Cambridge University Press, 1993), 16–51; and Wendorf, 261–72.

13 Another way to interpret Reynolds's construction of the impartial observer of universal forms is in terms of his rearticulation of a Cartesian notion of subjectivity as positing "an historical, disinterested, disembodied subject outside of the world it claims to know only from afar" (Jay, 10). See Martin Jay's illuminating discussion "Scopic Regimes of Modernity," in *Vision and Visuality,* ed. Hal Foster, Dia Art Foundation Discussions in Contemporary Culture, no. 2 (Seattle: Bay Press, 1988), 3–23. For Cartesian perspectivalism, see William M. Ivins Jr., *On the Rationalization of Sight* (New York: Metropolitan Museum of Art, 1938); Samuel Y. Edgerton Jr., *The Renaissance Rediscovery of Linear Perspective* (New York: Basic Books, 1975); and John White, *The Birth and Rebirth of Pictorial Space* (London: Faber and Faber, 1987).

14 Horace Walpole, "Advertisement," in *Anecdotes of Painting in England,* ed. R. N. Wornum (1862), quoted in Wind, 19.

15 John Barrell, *The Political Theory of Painting from Reynolds to Hazlitt* (New Haven: Yale University Press, 1986), 93.

16 See ibid., 76–82. See also Barrell's important discussion of class, gender, and the idea of civic virtue in *English Literature in History 1730–1780: An Equal, Wide Survey* (London: Hutchinson, 1983), as well as Solkin's discussion of civic humanism under attack by commercial culture in *Painting for Money.* For an analysis of civic humanism, see J. G. A. Pocock's seminal *Machiavellian Moment.*

17 Latour, *Science in Action,* 229. Subsequent references to this text are in parentheses. David Philip Miller brings Latour's ideas about centers of calculation to bear on Banks's botanical activities; Miller's work has encouraged me to extend Latour's ideas to other Enlightenment projects, including art and colonialism. See Miller, "Joseph Banks, Empire, and 'Centers of Calculation' in Late Hanoverian England," in *Visions of Empire: Voyages, Botany, and Representations of Nature* (Cambridge: Cambridge University Press, 1996).

18 Dipesh Chakrabarty, "Postcoloniality and the Artifice of History: Who Speaks for 'Indian' Pasts?" *Representations* 37 (1992): 20. On the subject of the historicity of the universal, Marx wrote: "Even the most abstract categories, despite their validity—precisely because of the abstractness—for all epochs, are nevertheless . . . themselves . . . a product of historical relations" (*Grundrisse,* trans. Martin Nicholas [New York; Random House, 1973], 105). Chakrabarty argues that with this gesture Marx engages in a kind of critique of modernity and history that Chakrabarty calls "the project of provincializing 'Europe,' the 'Europe' that modern imperialism and (third-world) nationalism have, by their collaborative venture and violence, made universal" (20).

19 Science could not exist without art and the scopic regime of modernity, as Martin Jay suggests: "the Western scientific tradition may have only been made possible by Cartesian perspectivalism or its complement, the Baconian art of describing" (19). See Alpers for descriptive as opposed to narrative art, and Norman Bryson, *Word and Image: French Painting of the Ancien Regime* (Cambridge: Cambridge University Press, 1981). For a brilliant treatment of the interrelations of art, science, and voyaging, see Barbara M. Stafford, *Voyage into Substance: Art, Science, Nature, and the Illustrated Travel Account, 1760–1840* (Cambridge, MA: MIT Press, 1984).

20 Perhaps I should qualify this statement by limiting what I am saying about inscription to art and other forms of inscription that have some explicit representational function, or, in other words, that occupy the position of the signifier in relation to the signified. Religious art would fall outside this category; for example, a statue of the Virgin Mary might combine and blur the signifier and signified so that it is unclear whether the statue represents or is the Virgin Mary. See Bruno Latour's brilliant discussion of the different "regimes of re-presentation" that are presented by religious art and art informed by scientific principles (perspective, for instance): "There is a huge difference between a visual display that solves the problem of renewing in the heart the ever present God, and a visual display that solves the problem of the absence of distant things" ("Opening One Eye," 24).

21 See, for instance, Howard D. Weinbrot, *Augustus Caesar and "Augustan" England* (Princeton, NJ: Princeton University Press, 1978), for eighteenth-century Britain's identification with classical art, literature, and politics of the Roman Empire. Searching for an English idiom, artists and architects, for instance, rejected Baroque and religious art as models as too Catholic for their tastes. For a brief discussion of the sympathies and antipathies for a style associated with Catholicism and the continent, see Wilton's introduction to *Swagger Portrait,* especially his treatment of Van Dyck, 26–38.

22 Although Solkin's argument is quite persuasive, I still think that the

Apollo Belvedere is Reynolds's referent for the Keppel portrait, and not the Roman statuary of magistrates and statesmen, because Apollo was associated with war and in particular with naval victories. Claiming Apollo as his personal guardian, Caesar Augustus credited the god with his naval victory at Actium in 31 B.C.

23 "Eclectic" is Wind's term; see 19–20.

24 As Christopher Flint, " 'The Family Piece': Oliver Goldsmith and the Politics of the Everyday in Eighteenth-Century Domestic Portraiture," *Eighteenth-Century Studies* 29 (1995–96), puts it: "In Reynolds's harmonic display of past and present, history either becomes attenuated, insofar as the artist prolongs the continuity between classical Greece and eighteenth-century Britain; or it disappears altogether, as the two periods generalize each other out of existence" (134).

25 See Latour on how the two art regimes (the religious and the scientific) define "space-time" differently; he argues that the scopic regime of the modern creates a "new specific type of space" ("Opening One Eye," 25–28).

26 See Wind's "Penny, West, and 'The Death of General Wolfe,' " in *Hume and the Heroic Portrait,* 100–104.

27 Wind, 89.

28 Ibid. For the role of the Native American in West's painting of Wolfe, see Abrams, *Valiant Hero,* 176–80.

29 Tartan plaids, which were worn as filibegs (something like kilts), were outlawed in Scotland after the 1745 rebellion was put down but were resurrected as part of the uniform for Highland regiments. See Hugh Trevor-Roper, "The Invention of Tradition: Highland Tradition of Scotland," in *The Invention of Tradition,* ed. Eric Hobsbawm and Terence Ranger (Cambridge: University of Cambridge Press, 1993), 15–41.

30 Stuart Reid and Mike Chappell, *18th Century Highlanders,* Men-At-Arms Series (London: Osprey, 1993), 6–8.

31 See Trevor-Roper, 25–27.

32 See Fabian.

33 John Galt, *The Life, Studies, and Works of Benjamin West, Esquire* (1820; Gainesville, FL: Scholars' Facsimiles, 1960), 105–6.

34 On West's self-exoticization, see Wind, 97–98. On his linking of classical poses with Native Americans to create the "noble savage," see Jules David Prown, "Benjamin West and the Use of Antiquity," *American Art* 10 (1996): 28–49.

35 See Hugh Honour, "Benjamin West's 'Indian Family,' " *Burlington Magazine* 125 (1983): 726–33.

Selected Bibliography

Unpublished Manuscripts

Caldwell Family Papers. British Library, King's 427.

Correspondence and Papers of David Anderson. Add. MSS. 45,427, ff. 76–213b.

Correspondence of Joseph Banks, Dawson Turner copies, Natural History Museum.

Correspondence and Papers of Governor General Sir Frederick Haldimand, 1758–91. British Library. Add. MSS. 21,661–21,892.

Correspondence and Papers of the Earl of Liverpool. British Library, Add. MSS. 38,200:215 and 38,202:5.

Printed Documents

Documents Relative to the Colonial History of the State of New York. Ed. Edmund O'Callaghan and Berthold Fernow. 15 vols. Albany: Weed, Parsons, and Co., 1856–87.

Documentary History of the State of New-York. Ed. Edmund O'Callaghan. 4 vols. Albany: Weed, Parsons and Co., 1849.

Minutes of the Provincial Council of Pennsylvania. Ed. Samuel Hazard. 16 vols. Harrisburg: Theo. Fenn, and Co., 1838–53.

Papers of Sir William Johnson. Ed. James Sullivan. Albany: University of the State of New York, 1921.

Books and Articles

Abrams, Ann Urhy. "Benjamin West's Documentation of Colonial History: *William Penn's Treaty with the Indians*." *Art Bulletin* 64 (1982): 59–75.

———. *The Valiant Hero: Benjamin West and Grand-Style History Painting.* Washington, DC: Smithsonian, 1985.

Addison, Joseph. *The Spectator* no. 69 (Saturday, May 19, 1711). In *Addison and Steele: Selections from* The Tatler *and* The Spectator. Ed. Robert J. Allen. New York: Holt, Rinehart and Winston, 1970.

Ahmad, Aijaz. *In Theory: Classes, Nations, Literatures.* London: Verso, 1992.

Alpers, Svetlana. *The Art of Describing: Dutch Art in the Seventeenth Century.* Chicago: University of Chicago Press, 1983.

Anderson, Benedict. *Imagined Communities: Reflections on the Origin and Spread of Nationalism.* London: Verso, 1983.

Anstey, Roger. *Atlantic Slave Trade and British Abolition, 1760–1834.* Atlantic Highlands, NJ: Humanities Press, 1975.

Arber, Agnes. *Herbals, Their Origin and Evolution: A Chapter in the History of Botany, 1470–1670.* 1912; Cambridge: Cambridge University Press, 1988.

Archer, Mildred. *India and British Portraiture, 1770–1825.* London: Sotheby Parke Bernet, 1979.

———. *Natural History Drawings in the India Office Library.* London: Her Majesty's Stationary Office, 1962.

Aronson, Lisa. "History of Cloth Trade in the Niger Delta: A Study of Diffusion." In *Textiles of Africa.* Ed. Dale Indiens and K. G. Ponting. Bath, England: The Pasold Research Fund, 1980. 89–107.

Axtel, James. *The Invasion Within: The Contest of Cultures in Colonial North America.* New York: Oxford University Press, 1985.

Bakhtin, Mikhail. "Discourse in the Novel." In *The Dialogic Imagination: Four Essays.* Ed. Michael Holquist, trans. Caryl Emerson and Michael Holquist. Austin: University of Texas Press, 1981.

———. *Rabelais and His World.* Trans. Helen Iswolsky. Bloomington: Indiana University Press, 1984.

Ballhatchet, Kenneth. *Race, Sex and Class under the Raj: Imperial Attitudes and Policies and Their Critics, 1793–1905.* New York: St. Martin's Press, 1980.

Banks, Joseph. *The Endeavour Journal of Joseph Banks.* Ed. J. C. Beaglehole. 2 vols. Sydney: Angus and Robertson, 1962.

Barrell, John. *The Dark Side of the Landscape: The Rural Poor in English Painting, 1730–1840.* Cambridge: Cambridge University Press, 1980.

———. *English Literature in History 1730–1780: An Equal, Wide Survey.* London: Hutchinson, 1983.

————. *The Idea of Landscape and a Sense of Place, 1730–1840.* Cambridge: Cambridge University Press, 1972.

————. *The Political Theory of Painting from Reynolds to Hazlitt.* New Haven: Yale University Press, 1986.

————, ed. *Painting and the Politics of Culture: New Essays on British Art, 1700–1850.* Oxford: Oxford University Press, 1992.

Bayly, C. A. *Imperial Meridian: The British Empire and the World, 1780–1830.* London: Longman, 1989.

————. *The New Cambridge History of India: Indian Society and the Making of the British Empire.* Cambridge: Cambridge University Press, 1988.

Beaglehole, J. C. "Introduction: The Young Banks." In *The Endeavour Journal of Joseph Banks.* 2 vols. Ed. J. C. Beaglehole. Sydney: Angus and Robertson, 1962.

Beckles, Hilary M. *Natural Rebels: A Social History of Enslaved Black Women in Barbados.* New Brunswick, NJ: Rutgers University Press, 1989.

Berger, John. *Ways of Seeing.* London: BBC and Penguin, 1972.

Bergstrom, Ingvar. *Dutch Still-Life Painting in the Seventeenth Century.* Trans. Christina Hedstrom and Gerald Taylor. New York: Thomas Yoseloff, 1956.

Berkhofer, Robert F., Jr. *The White Man's Indian: Images of the American Indian from Columbus to the Present.* New York: Random House, 1979.

Betterton, Rosemary, ed. *Looking On: Images of Femininity in the Visual Arts and Media.* New York: Routledge, 1987.

Bhabha, Homi. *The Location of Culture.* New York: Routledge, 1994.

————. "Of Mimicry and Man: The Ambivalence of Colonial Discourse." *October* 29 (1984): 125–33.

————. "Signs Taken for Wonders: Questions of Ambivalence and Authority under a Tree outside Delhi, May 1817." In *"Race," Writing, and Difference.* Ed. Henry Louis Gates Jr. Chicago: University of Chicago Press, 1986. 163–84.

Bitterli, Urs. *Cultures in Conflict: Encounters between Europeans and Non-European Cultures, 1492–1800.* Trans. Ritchie Robertson. 1986; Cambridge: Polity Press, 1989.

Bloch, Ruth. "American Feminine Ideals in Transition: The Rise of the Moral Mother, 1785–1815." *Feminist Studies* 4 (1978): 101–26.

Blunt, Wilfrid. "The Voyage of the *Endeavour.*" In *Sidney Parkinson: Artist of Cook's Endeavour Voyage.* Ed. D. J. Carr. Honolulu: University of Hawaii Press, 1983. 1–13.

————. "Sydney Parkinson and His Fellow Artists." In *Sydney Parkinson: Artist of Cook's Endeavour Voyage.* Ed. D. J. Carr. Honolulu: University of Hawaii Press, 1983. 14–45.

Blunt, Wilfrid, and William T. Stearn. *The Art of Botanical Illustration.* 1950;

Woodbridge, Suffolk: Antique Collectors' Club, The Royal Botanic Gardens, Kew, 1994.

Bohls, Elizabeth A. "The Aesthetics of Colonialism: Jane Schaw in the West Indies, 1774–1775." *Eighteenth-Century Studies* 27 (1994): 363–90.

———. "Disinterestedness and Denial of the Particular: Locke, Adam Smith, and the Subject of Aesthetics." In *Eighteenth-Century Aesthetics and the Reconstruction of Art.* Ed. Paul Mattick Jr. Cambridge: Cambridge University Press, 1993. 16–51.

Boldt, Menno. *Surviving as Indians: The Challenge of Self-Government.* Toronto: University of Toronto Press, 1993.

Boston, David. "The Three Caldwells." *White Horse and Fleur de Lys* 3 (1964): 316–17.

Brathwaite, Edward. *The Development of Creole Society in Jamaica, 1770–1820.* Oxford: Clarendon Press, 1971.

Brindle, John V., and James J. White. *Flora Portrayed: Classics of Botanical Art from the Hunt Institute Collection.* Pittsburgh: Hunt Institute, 1985.

Brissenden, R. F. *Virtue in Distress: Studies in the Novel of Sentiment from Richardson to Sade.* New York: Barnes and Noble, 1974.

Brockway, Lucille H. *Science and Colonialism: The Role of the British Royal Botanic Gardens.* New York: Academic Press, 1979.

Broude, Norma, and Mary D. Garrard, eds. *Feminism and Art History: Questioning the Litany.* New York: Harper & Row, 1982.

Brown, Laura. *Ends of Empire: Women and Ideology in Early Eighteenth-Century English Literature.* Ithaca, NY: Cornell University Press, 1993.

———. "Reading Race and Gender: Jonathan Swift." *Eighteenth-Century Studies* 23 (summer 1990): 424–43.

Browne, Janet. "Botany in the Boudoir and Garden: The Banksian Context." In *Visions of Empire: Voyages, Botany, and Representations of Nature.* Ed. David Philip Miller and Peter Hanns Reill. Cambridge: Cambridge University Press, 1996. 153–72.

Bryson, Norman. *Looking at the Overlooked: Four Essays on Still Life Painting.* London: Reaktion Books, 1990.

———. *Word and Image: French Painting of the Ancien Regime.* Cambridge: Cambridge University Press, 1981.

Bryson, Norman, Michael Ann Holly, and Keith Moxey, eds. *Visual Culture: Images and Interpretations.* Hanover, NH: Wesleyan University Press, 1994.

Buck, Anne. *Dress in Eighteenth-Century England.* London: Batsford, 1979.

Bullough, Vern L., and Bonnie Bullough. *Cross-Dressing, Sex, and Gender.* Philadelphia: University of Pennsylvania Press, 1993.

Burney, Fanny. *A Busy Day.* Ed. Tara Ghoshal Wallace. New Brunswick, NJ: Rutgers University Press, 1984.

Butler, Judith. *Gender Trouble: Feminism and the Subversion of Identity.* London: Routledge, 1990.

Calloway, Colin G. *Crown and Calumet: British-Indian Relations, 1783–1815.* Norman: University of Oklahoma Press, 1987.

———. "Fort Niagara: The Politics of Hunger in a Refuge Community." In *The American Revolution in Indian Country: Crisis and Diversity in Native American Communities.* Cambridge: Cambridge University Press, 1995. 129–57.

Cameron, Hector Charles. *Sir Joseph Banks: The Autocrat of the Philosophers.* London: Batchworth Press, 1952.

Campbell, Jill. "Lady Mary Wortley Montagu and the Historical Machinery of Female Identity." In *History, Gender, and Eighteenth-Century Literature.* Ed. Beth Fowkes Tobin. Athens: University of Georgia Press, 1994. 64–85.

Carmichael, A. C. *Domestic Manners and Social Condition of the White, Coloured, and Negro Population of the West Indies.* 2 vols. 1833; New York: Negro Universities Press, 1969.

Carr, D. J., ed. *Sydney Parkinson: Artist of Cook's Endeavour Voyage.* Canberra: Australian National University Press, 1983.

Carter, Paul. *The Road to Botany Bay: An Exploration of Landscape and History.* Chicago: University of Chicago Press, 1987.

Castle, Terry. *Masquerade and Civilization: The Carnivalesque in Eighteenth-Century English Culture and Fiction.* Stanford, CA: Stanford University Press, 1986.

Chakrabarty, Dipesh. "Conditions for Knowledge of the Working-Class Conditions." In *Selected Subaltern Studies.* Ed. Ranajit Guha and Gayatri Chakravorty Spivak. New York: Oxford University Press, 1988. 179–230.

———. "Postcoloniality and the Artifice of History: Who Speaks for 'Indian' Pasts?" *Representations* 37 (1992): 1–26.

Chambers, J. D., and G. E. Mingay. *The Agricultural Revolution 1750–1880.* New York: Schocken Books, 1966.

Chrisman, Laura. "The Imperial Unconscious? Representations of Imperial Discourse." *Critical Quarterly* 32 (1990): 38–58.

Churchill, Ward. "Fantasies of the Master Race: Categories of Stereotyping of American Indians in Film." In *Fantasies of the Master Race: Literature, Cinema and the Colonization of American Indians.* Ed. M. Annette Jaimes. Monroe, ME: Common Courage Press, 1992. 231–41.

———. *Struggle for the Land: Indigenous Resistance to Genocide, Ecocide and Expropriation.* Monroe, ME: Common Courage Press, 1993.

Clarkson, Thomas. *History of the Abolition of the Slave Trade.* 2 vols. 1808; London: Cass, 1968.

Clarkson, William. "Inquiry on Pauperism and Poor Rates." *Pamphleteer* 8 (1816): 385–420.

Cohn, Bernard S. *Colonialism and Its Forms of Knowledge: The British in India.* Princeton, NJ: Princeton University Press, 1996.

Colden, Cadwallader, ed. *The History of the Five Indian Nations of Canada.* 2 vols. 1727–47; New York: Allerton Book Co., 1922.

Colley, Linda. *Britons: Forging the Nation 1707–1837.* New Haven: Yale University Press, 1992.

Colquhoun, Patrick. *A Treatise on Indigence.* London, 1806.

Comaroff, John, and Jean Comaroff. *Ethnography and the Historical Imagination.* Boulder, CO: Westview Press, 1992.

Connell, Neville. "Colonial Life in the West Indies as Depicted in Prints." *Antiques* (1971): 732–37.

Cott, Nancy. "Passionlessness: An Interpretation of Victorian Sexual Ideology, 1790–1850." In *A Heritage of Her Own: Toward a New Social History of American Women.* Ed. Nancy F. Cott and Elizabeth H. Pleck. New York: Simon and Schuster, 1979. 162–81.

Cowper, William. *Cowper's Poems.* Ed. Hugh I'Anson Fausset. London: Dent, 1966.

Craton, Michael. *Sinews of Empire: A Short History of British Slavery.* New York: Doubleday, 1974.

Craton, Michael, and James Walvin. *A Jamaican Plantation: The History of Worthy Park, 1670–1970.* Toronto: University of Toronto Press, 1970.

Cumberland, Richard. *The West Indian* (1771). In *British Dramatists from Dryden to Sheridan.* Ed. George H. Nettleton et al. Boston: Houghton Mifflin, 1969. 711–49.

Dabydeen, David. *Hogarth's Blacks: Images of Blacks in Eighteenth Century English Art.* Athens: University of Georgia Press, 1982.

Davidoff, Leonore, and Catherine Hall. *Family Fortunes: Men and Women of the English Middle Class, 1780–1850.* Chicago: University of Chicago Press, 1987.

Desmond, Ray. *The European Discovery of the Indian Flora.* Oxford: Oxford University Press, 1992.

Dirks, Nicholas B. "Introduction: Colonialism and Culture." In *Colonialism and Culture.* Ed. Nicholas B. Dirks. Ann Arbor: University of Michigan Press, 1992. 1–25.

Doane, Mary Ann. "Film and Masquerade: Theorizing the Female Spectator." *Screen* 23 (1982): 74–88.

D'Oench, Ellen. *The Conversation Piece: Arthur Devis and His Contemporaries.* New Haven: Yale Center for British Art, 1980.

Drescher, Seymour. " 'Paradigms Tossed': Capitalism and the Political Sources of Abolition." In *British Capitalism and Caribbean Slavery: The Legacy of Eric Williams.* Ed. Barbara Solow and Stanley L. Engerman. New York: Cambridge University Press, 1987. 191–208.

Duff, William. *Letters on the Intellectual and Moral Character of Women.* Aberdeen, 1807.

Dunn, Richard. " 'Dreadful Idlers' in the Cane Fields: The Slave Labor Pattern on a Jamaican Sugar Estate, 1762–1831." In *British Capitalism and Caribbean Slavery: The Legacy of Eric Williams.* Ed. Barbara Solow and Stanley L. Engerman. New York: Cambridge University Press, 1987. 163–90.

Edgerton, Samuel Y., Jr. *The Renaissance Rediscovery of Linear Perspective.* New York: Basic Books, 1975.

Edwards, Bryan. *The History, Civil and Commercial, of the British West Indies.* 5 vols. 1796, 1819; New York: AMS Press, 1966.

Edwards, Phyllis I. "Company Sponsorship and the Beginnings of Indian Botany." In *A Selection of Late 18th and Early 19th Century Indian Botanical Paintings.* Pittsburgh: Hunt Institute for Botanical Documentation, 1980. 23–31.

Equiano, Olaudah. *The Interesting Narrative of the Life of Olaudah Equiano, or Gustavus Vassa, The African. Written by Himself.* Ed. Robert Allison. Boston: Bedford Books, 1995.

Eriksson, Gunnar. "Linnaeus the Botanist." In *Linnaeus: The Man and His Work.* Ed. Tore Frangsmyr. Berkeley: University of California Press, 1983.

Fabian, Johannes. *Time and the Other: How Anthropology Makes Its Object.* New York: Columbia University Press, 1983.

Feister, Lois M., and Bonnie Pulis. "Molly Brant: Her Domestic and Political Roles in Eighteenth-Century New York." In *Northeastern Indian Lives, 1632–1816.* Ed. Robert S. Grumet. Amherst: University of Massachusetts Press, 1996. 295–320.

Ferguson, Moira. *Subject to Others: British Women Writers and Colonial Slavery, 1670–1834.* New York: Routledge, 1992.

Flexner, James Thomas. *Mohawk Baronet: Sir William Johnson of New York.* New York: Harper, 1959.

Flint, Christopher. " 'The Family Piece': Oliver Goldsmith and the Politics of the Everyday in Eighteenth-Century Domestic Portraiture." *Eighteenth-Century Studies* 29 (1995–96): 127–52.

Fordyce, John. *Sermons to Young Women.* 1766; Philadelphia: Thomas Dodson, 1787.

Fosberg, F. R., and Marie-Hélène Sachet. "Plants of the Society Islands." In *Sydney Parkinson: Artist of Cooks' Endeavour Voyage.* Ed. D. J. Carr. Canberra: Australian National University Press, 1983. 76–127.

Foucault, Michel. *The Order of Things: An Archaeology of the Human Sciences.* 1966; New York: Vintage, 1973.

Fox-Genovese, Elizabeth. "The Ideological Bases of Domestic Economy: The Representation of Women and the Family in the Age of Expansion." In *The Fruits of Merchant Capital: Slavery and Bourgeois Property in the Rise and Expansion of Capitalism*. Ed. Elizabeth Fox-Genovese and Eugene D. Genovese. New York: Oxford University Press, 1983. 299–336.

Fryd, Vivien Green. *Art and Empire: The Politics of Ethnicity in the United States Capitol, 1815–1860*. New Haven: Yale University Press, 1992.

Fuss, Diana. "Freud's Fallen Women: Identification, Desire, and 'A Case of Homosexuality in a Woman.'" In *Fear of a Queer Planet: Queer Politics and Social Theory*. Ed. Michael Warner. Minneapolis: University of Minnesota Press, 1993. 42–68.

Galt, John. *The Life, Studies, and Works of Benjamin West, Esquire*. 1820; Gainesville, FL: Scholars' Facsimiles, 1960.

Garber, Marjorie. *Vested Interests: Cross-Dressing and Cultural Authority*. New York: Routledge, 1992.

Gascoigne, John. *Joseph Banks and the English Enlightenment: Useful Knowledge and Polite Culture*. Cambridge: Cambridge University Press, 1994.

Gaunt, William. *The Great Century of British Painting: Hogarth to Turner*. London: Phaidon, 1971.

Gilman, Sander. "Black Bodies, White Bodies: Toward an Iconography of Female Sexuality in Late Nineteenth-Century Art, Medicine, and Literature." In *"Race," Writing, and Difference*. Ed. by Henry Louis Gates Jr. Chicago: University of Chicago Press, 1986. 223–61.

Gilroy, Paul. *The Black Atlantic: Modernity and Double Consciousness*. Cambridge, MA: Harvard University Press, 1993.

Gipson, Lawrence Henry. *The British Empire before the America Revolution*. 13 vols. 1942; New York: Knopf, 1961.

Girouard, Mark. *Life in the English Country House*. New Haven: Yale University Press, 1978.

Goldsmith, Oliver. "The Deserted Village." In *Collected Works of Oliver Goldsmith*. Ed. Arthur Friedman. London: Oxford University Press, 1966. Vol. 4. 287–304.

Greenblatt, Stephen. *Marvelous Possessions: The Wonder of the New World*. Chicago: University of Chicago Press, 1991.

Gregory, John. *A Father's Legacy to His Daughters*. Ed. Gina Lurie. 1774; facsimile ed., New York: Garland Publishing Co., 1974.

Grewal, Inderpal. "Autobiographical Subjects and Diasporic Locations: *Meatless Days* and *Borderlands*." In *Scattered Hegemonies: Postmodernity and Transnational Feminist Practices*. Ed. Inderpal Grewal and Caren Kaplan. Minneapolis: University of Minnesota, 1994. 231–54.

Grewal, Inderpal, and Caren Kaplan. "Introduction: Transnational Feminist Practices and Questions of Postmodernity." In *Scattered Hegemonies: Postmodernity and Transnational Feminist Practices*. Ed. Inderpal Grewal and Caren Kaplan. Minneapolis: University of Minnesota Press, 1994. 1–33.

Grinde, Donald. *The Iroquois and the Founding of the American Nation.* San Francisco: Indian Historian Press, 1977.

Guest, Harriet. "Curiously Marked: Tattooing, Masculinity, and Nationality in Eighteenth-Century British Perceptions of the South Pacific." In *Painting and the Politics of Culture: New Essays on British Art, 1700–1850.* Ed. John Barrell. Oxford: Oxford University Press, 1992. 101–34.

———. "The Great Distinction: The Figures of the Exotic in the Work of William Hodges." *Oxford Art Journal* 12 (1989): 36–58.

Guha, Ranajit. "On Some Aspects of the Historiography of Colonial India." In *Selected Subaltern Studies.* Ed. Ranajit Guha and Gayatri Chakravorty Spivak. New York: Oxford University Press, 1988. 37–44.

———. "The Prose of Counter-Insurgency." In *Selected Subaltern Studies.* Ed. Ranajit Guha and Gayatri Chakravorty Spivak. New York: Oxford University Press, 1988. 45–86.

Hall, Stuart. "The Local and the Global: Globalization and Ethnicity." In *Culture, Globalization and the World-System: Contemporary Conditions for the Representation of Identity.* Ed. Anthony King. Binghamton: Department of Art and Art History, State University of New York, 1991. 19–39.

———. "Old and New Identities, Old and New Ethnicities." In *Culture, Globalization and the World-System: Contemporary Conditions for the Representation of Identity.* Ed. Anthony King. Binghamton: Department of Art and Art History, State University of New York at Binghamton, 1991. 41–68.

Hall, Stuart, and Tony Jefferson, eds. *Resistance through Rituals: Youth Subcultures in Post-War Britain.* New York: Holmes and Meier, 1976.

Hamilton, Milton. "Joseph Brant—'The Most Painted Indian.'" *New York History* 39 (1958): 119–32.

———. "Joseph Brant Painted by Rigaud." *New York History* 40 (1959): 247–54.

Hammond, J. L., and Barbara Hammond. *The Village Labourer.* London: Longmans, Green, and Co., 1927.

Harlow, Vincent T. *The Founding of the Second British Empire, 1763–1793.* 2 vols. London: Longmans and Green, 1964.

Harris, John. *The Artist and the Country House: A History of Country House and Garden View Painting in Britain, 1540–1870.* 1979; London: Sotheby's, 1985.

Headrick, Daniel R. *The Tentacles of Progress: Technology Transfer in the Age of Imperialism, 1850–1940.* New York: Oxford University Press, 1988.

Hebdige, Dick. *Subculture: The Meaning of Style.* London: Methuen, 1979.

Henderson, R. J. "Plants of Australia." In *Sydney Parkinson: Artist of Cooks' Endeavour Voyage.* Ed. D. J. Carr. Canberra: Australian National University Press, 1983. 128–177.

Henrey, Blanche. *British Botanical and Horticultural Literature before 1800.* 3 vols. London: Oxford University Press, 1975.

Hess, Thomas B., and Linda Nochlin, eds. *Women as Sex Objects: Studies in Erotic Art, 1730–1970.* New York: Newsweek, 1972.

The History of the County of Brant, Ontario. Warner, Beers, and Co., 1883.

Hodder, B. W. "Indigenous Cloth Trade and Marketing in Africa." In *Textiles of Africa.* Ed. Dale Idiens and K. G. Ponting. Bath, England: The Pasold Research Fund, 1980. 203–10.

Honour, Hugh. "Benjamin West's 'Indian Family.' " *Burlington Magazine* 125 (1983): 726–33.

———. *The Image of the Black in Western Art.* Vol. 4, part 1: *From the American Revolution to World War I: Slaves and Liberators.* Cambridge, MA: Harvard University Press, 1989.

———. *The New Golden Land: European Images of America from the Discoveries to the Present.* New York: Pantheon, 1975.

———. "Science and Exoticism: The European Artist and the Non-European World Before Johan Maurits." In *Johan Maurits van Nassau-Siegen, 1604–1679: A Humanist Prince in Europe and Brazil.* Ed. E. van den Boogaart. The Hague: Government Publishing Office, 1979.

Howse, Derek, ed. *Background to Discovery: Pacific Exploration from Dampier to Cook.* Berkeley: University of California Press, 1990.

Hulme, Peter. *Colonial Encounters: Europe and the Native Caribbean, 1492–1797.* London: Methuen, 1986.

Hulme, Peter, and Neil L. Whitehead, eds. *Wild Majesty: Encounters with Caribs from Columbus to the Present Day.* Oxford: Clarendon Press, 1992.

Huth, Hans. "Agostino Brunias, Romano." *Connoisseur* 151, no. 610 (1962): 265–69.

Irigaray, Luce. *This Sex Which Is Not One.* Ithaca, NY: Cornell University Press, 1985.

Ivins, William M., Jr. *On the Rationalization of Sight.* New York: Metropolitan Museum of Art, 1938.

Jaimes, M. Annette. Introduction to *Fantasies of the Master Race: Literature, Cinema and the Colonization of American Indians.* Monroe, ME: Common Courage Press, 1992. 1–4.

Jameson, Fredric. *Postmodernism, or, The Cultural Logic of Late Capitalism.* Durham, NC: Duke University Press, 1992.

Jay, Martin. "Scopic Regimes of Modernity." In *Vision and Visuality.* Ed. Hal Foster. Dia Art Foundation Discussions in Contemporary Culture, no. 2. Seattle: Bay Press, 1988. 3–23.

Jennings, Francis. *The Ambiguous Iroquois Empire: The Covenant Chain Confederation of Indian Tribes with English Colonies from Its beginnings to the Lancaster Treaty of 1744.* New York: Norton, 1984.

———. "Brother Minquon: Good Lord!" In *The World of William Penn.*

Ed. Richard S. Dunn and Mary Maples Dunn. Philadelphia: University of Pennsylvania Press, 1986. 195–214.

———. *Empire of Fortune: Crowns, Colonies, and Tribes in the Seven Years War in America.* New York: Norton, 1988.

———. *The Invasion of America: Indians, Colonialism, and the Cant of Conquest.* Chapel Hill: University of North Carolina Press, 1975.

———. " 'Pennsylvania Indians' and the Iroquois." In *Beyond the Covenant Chain: The Iroquois and Their Neighbors in Indian North America, 1600–1800.* Ed. Daniel K. Richter and James H. Merrell. Syracuse, NY: Syracuse University Press, 1987. 75–91.

Johnson, E. D. H. *Paintings of the British Social Scene from Hogarth to Sickert.* New York: Rizzoli, 1986.

Johnson, Michael. *American Woodland Indians.* London: Osprey, 1990.

Johnson, Samuel. *The History of Rasselas.* Oxford: Oxford University Press, 1990.

Joppien, Rudiger. "The Dutch Vision of Johan Maurits and His Artists." In *Johan Maurits van Nassau-Siegen, 1604–1679: A Humanist Prince in Europe and Brazil.* Ed. E. van den Boogaart. The Hague: Government Publishing Office, 1979. 297–376.

Joppien, Rudiger, and Bernard Smith. *The Art of Captain Cook's Voyages.* Vol. 1: *The Voyage of the Endeavour.* New Haven: Yale University Press, 1985.

———. *The Art of Captain Cook's Voyages.* Vol. 2: *The Voyage of the Resolution and Adventure, 1772–1775.* New Haven: Yale University Press, 1985.

Kame'eleihiwa, Lilikalā. *Native Land and Foreign Desires: Pehea La E Pono Ai?* Honolulu: Bishop Museum Press, 1992.

Kaul, Suvir. "Why Selima Drowns: Thomas Gray and the Domestication of the Imperial Ideal." *PMLA* 105 (March 1990): 223–32.

Kelsay, Isabel Thompson. *Joseph Brant, 1743–1807: Man of Two Worlds.* Syracuse, NY: Syracuse University Press, 1984.

Kepler, Angela Kay. *Hawaiian Heritage Plants.* Honolulu: Oriental Publishing Company, 1983.

Kirkpatrick, Kathryn. "Sermons and Strictures: Conduct Book Propriety and Property Relations in Late Eighteenth-Century England." In *History, Gender, and Eighteenth-Century Literature.* Ed. Beth Fowkes Tobin. Athens: University of Georgia Press, 1994. 198–226.

Koerner, Lisbet. "Purposes of Linnaean Travel: A Preliminary Research Report." In *Visions of Empire: Voyages, Botany, and Representations of Nature.* Ed. David Philip Miller and Peter Hanns Reill. Cambridge: Cambridge University Press, 1996. 117–52.

Kowaleski-Wallace, Beth. *Consuming Subjects: Women, Shopping, and Business in the Eighteenth Century.* New York: Columbia University Press, 1997.

———. "Home Economics: Domestic Ideology in Maria Edgeworth's *Belinda*." *The Eighteenth-Century: Theory and Interpretation* 29 (1988): 242–62.

———. "Tea, Gender, and Domesticity in Eighteenth-Century England." *Studies in Eighteenth-Century Culture* 23 (1993): 131–45.

———. *Their Fathers' Daughters: Hannah More, Maria Edgeworth, and Patriarchal Complicity.* New York: Oxford University Press, 1991.

———. "Women, China, and Consumer Culture in Eighteenth-Century England." *Eighteenth-Century Studies* 29 (1995–96): 153–67.

Landa, Louis. "Of Silkworms and Farthingales and the Will of God." In *Studies in the Eighteenth-Century.* Ed. R. F. Brissenden. Toronto: University of Toronto Press, 1973. 259–77.

———. "Pope's Belinda, the General Empories of the World, and the Wondrous Worm." *South Atlantic Quarterly* 70 (spring 1971): 215–35.

Latour, Bruno. "Opening One Eye While Closing the Other . . . a Note on Some Religious Paintings." In *Picturing Power: Visual Depiction and Social Relations.* Ed. Gordon Fyfe and John Law. *Sociological Review Monograph* 35. London: Routledge, 1988. 15–38.

———. *Science in Action: How to Follow Scientists and Engineers through Society.* Milton Keynes: Open University Press, 1987.

Lawson, Philip. *The East India Company: A History.* London: Longman, 1993.

LeGates, Marlene. "The Cult of Womanhood in Eighteenth-Century Thought." *Eighteenth-Century Studies* 10 (1976): 21–39.

Leppert, Richard. *Music and Image: Domesticity, Ideology and Socio-Cultural Formation in Eighteenth-Century England.* Cambridge: Cambridge University Press, 1988.

———. "Music, Domestic Life and Cultural Chauvinism: Images of British Subjects at Home in India." In *Music and Society: The Politics of Composition, Performance and Reception.* Ed. Richard Leppert and Susan McClary. Cambridge: Cambridge University Press, 1987. 63–104.

Lesch, John. "Systematics and the Geometrical Spirit." In *The Quantifying Spirit of the 18th Century.* Ed. Tore Frangsmyr, J. L. Heilbron, and Robin E. Rider. Berkeley: University of California Press, 1990. 73–111.

Lew, Joseph. "Lady Mary's Portable Seraglio." *Eighteenth-Century Studies* 24 (1991): 432–50.

Lewis, Matthew Gregory. *Journal of a West India Proprietor; Kept during a Residence in the Island of Jamaica.* 1834; New York: Negro Universities Press, 1969.

Lillo, George. *The London Merchant; or, The History of George Barnwell* (1731). In *British Dramatists from Dryden to Sheridan.* Ed. George H. Nettleton et al. Boston: Houghton Mifflin, 1969. 595–623.

Lovejoy, Arthur. *The Great Chain of Being.* Cambridge, MA: Harvard University Press, 1973.

Luffman, John. *A Brief Account of the Island of Antigua*. London, 1789.

Macaulay, Thomas Babington. *The Works of Lord Macaulay*. 12 vols. London, 1898.

MacCannell, Dean. *Empty Meeting Grounds: The Tourist Papers*. New York: Routledge, 1993.

Macherey, Pierre. *A Theory of Literary Production*. Trans. G. Wall. London: Routledge, 1978.

Mackay, David. *In the Wake of Captain Cook: Exploration, Science, and Empire, 1780–1801*. Wellington: Victoria University Press, 1986.

MacKenzie, John, ed. *Imperialism and the Natural World*. New York: St. Martin's Press, 1990.

———. *Orientalism: History, Theory and the Arts*. Manchester, UK: Manchester University Press, 1995.

MacLeod, Roy, and Philip F. Rehbock, eds. *Nature in Its Greatest Extent: Western Science in the Pacific*. Honolulu: University of Hawaii Press, 1988.

Mandeville, Bernard. *The Fable of the Bees*. 1714; New York: Penguin, 1970.

Marcus, George. "Ethnography in/of the World System: The Emergence of Multi-Sited Ethnography." *Annual Review of Anthropology* 24 (1995): 95–117.

Marshall, P. J. "The Whites of British India, 1780–1830: A Failed Colonial Society?" In *Trade and Conquest: Studies on the Rise of British Dominance in India*. Aldershot, UK: Variorum, 1993. 26–44.

Marx, Karl. *Capital*. 2 vols. Trans. Ben Fowkes. New York: Random House, 1977.

———. *The Grundrisse*. Trans. Martin Nicholas. New York: Random House, 1973.

May, Robin, and G. A. Embleton. *The British Army in North America, 1775–1783*. 1974; London: Osprey, 1989.

McClintock, Anne. "The Angel of Progress: Pitfalls of the Term 'Post-Colonialism.'" *Social Text* 31/32 (1992): 84–98.

———. *Imperial Leather: Race, Gender and Sexuality in the Colonial Contest*. New York: Routledge, 1995.

McConnell, Michael N. *A Country Between: The Upper Ohio Valley and Its Peoples, 1724–1774*. Lincoln: University of Nebraska Press, 1992.

———. "Peoples 'In Between': The Iroquois and the Ohio Indians, 1720–1768." In *Beyond the Covenant Chain: The Iroquois and Their Neighbors in Indian North America, 1600–1800*. Ed. Daniel K. Richter and James H. Merrell. Syracuse, NY: Syracuse University Press, 1987. 93–112.

McDonald, Roderick. *The Economy and Material Culture of Slaves: Goods and Chattels on the Sugar Plantations of Jamaica and Louisiana*. Baton Rouge: Louisiana State University, 1993.

McTigue, Bernard. *Nature Illustrated: Flowers, Plants, and Trees 1550–1900: From* the *Collections of the New York Public Library*. New York: Harry Abrams, 1989.

Miller, David Philip. "Joseph Banks, Empire, and 'Centers of Calculation' in Late Hanoverian England." In *Visions of Empire: Voyages, Botany, and Representations of Nature*. Ed. David Philip Miller and Peter Hanns Reill. Cambridge: Cambridge University Press, 1996. 21–37.

Miller, David Philip, and Peter Hanns Reill, eds. *Visions of Empire: Voyages, Botany, and Representations of Nature*. Cambridge: Cambridge University Press, 1996.

Mintz, Sidney W. "From Plantations to Peasantries in the Caribbean." In *Caribbean Contours*. Ed. Sidney W. Mintz and Sally Price. Baltimore: Johns Hopkins University Press, 1985. 127–54.

————. *Sweetness and Power: The Place of Sugar in Modern History*. New York: Penguin, 1986.

Mitchell, W. J. T. *Picture Theory*. Chicago: University of Chicago Press, 1994.

Moore-Gilbert, Bart. *Postcolonial Theory: Contexts, Practices, Politics*. London: Verso, 1997.

More, Hannah. *Practical Piety*. London, 1813.

————. *Strictures on the Modern System of Female Education* (1799). In *The Works of Hannah More*. 2 vols. New York: Harper, 1851. 1:311–415.

Morton, A. G. *History of Botanical Science: An Account of the Development of Botany from Ancient Times to the Present Day*. London: Academic Press, 1981.

Mukherjee, Ramkrishna. *The Rise and Fall of the East Indian Company: A Sociological Appraisal*. New York: Monthly Review Press, 1974.

Mullan, John. *Sentiment and Sociability: The Language of Feeling in the Eighteenth Century*. Oxford: Clarendon Press, 1988.

Myers, Mitzi. "Hannah More's Tracts for the Times: Social Fiction and Female Ideology." In *Fetter'd or Free? British Women Novelists, 1670–1815*. Ed. Mary Anne Schofield and Cecilia Macheski. Athens: Ohio University Press, 1986. 264–84.

————. "Impeccable Governesses, Rational Dames, and Moral Mothers: Mary Wollstonecraft and the Female Tradition in Georgian Children's Books." *Children's Literature* 14 (1986): 31–59.

————. "Reform or Ruin: 'A Revolution in Female Manners.'" *Studies in Eighteenth-Century Culture* 11 (1982): 199–216.

Nammack, Georgiana C. *Fraud, Politics, and the Dispossession of the Indians: The Iroquois Land Frontier in the Colonial Period*. Norman: University of Oklahoma Press, 1969.

Newby, Howard. *A Social History of Rural England*. London: Weidenfeld and Nicholson, 1987.

Newman, Gerald. *The Rise of English Nationalism, a Cultural History, 1740–1830*. New York: St. Martin's Press, 1987.

Nochlin, Linda. *The Politics of Vision: Essays on Nineteenth-Century Art and Society.* New York: Harper & Row, 1989.

———. *Women, Art, and Power: and Other Essays.* New York: Harper & Row, 1988.

Obeyesekere, Gananath. *The Apotheosis of Captain Cook: European Mythmaking in the Pacific.* Princeton, NJ: Princeton University Press, 1992.

O'Callaghan, Edmund, ed. *Documentary History of the State of New-York.* 4 vols. Albany: Weed, Parsons, 1849.

Pal, Pratapaditya, and Vidya Dehejia. *From Merchants to Emperors: British Artists and India, 1757–1930.* Ithaca, NY: Cornell University Press, 1986.

Palumbo, Anne Cannon. "Averting 'Present Commotions': History as Politics in 'Penn's Treaty.' " *American Art* 9 (1995): 29–55.

Parry, Benita. "Problems in Current Theories of Colonial Discourse." *Oxford Literary Review* 9 (1987): 27–58.

Parry, Ellwood. *The Image of the Indian and the Black Man in American Art, 1590–1900.* New York: George Braziller, 1974.

Patterson, Orlando. *The Sociology of Slavery: An Analysis of the Origins, Development and Structure of the Negro Slave Society in Jamaica.* London: MacGibbon and Kee, 1967.

Paulson, Ronald. *Emblem and Expression: Meaning in English Art of the Eighteenth Century.* Cambridge, MA: Harvard University Press, 1975.

———. *Hogarth.* 3 vols. New Brunswick, NJ: Rutgers University Press, 1991–93.

Perry, Ruth. "Colonizing the Breast: Sexuality and Maternity in Eighteenth-Century England." *Eighteenth-Century Life* 16 (1992): 185–213.

Petitjean, Patrick, et al. *Science and Empires: Historical Studies about Scientific Development and European Expansion.* Dordrecht: Kluwer, 1992.

Pevsner, Sir Nikolaus. *The Englishness of English Art.* Harmondsworth: Penguin, 1964.

Phelan, Peggy. *Unmarked: The Politics of Performance.* New York: Routledge, 1993.

Pocock, J. G. A. *The Machiavellian Moment: Florentine Political Thought and the Atlantic Republican Tradition.* Princeton, NJ: Princeton University Press, 1975.

Pointon, Marcia. *Hanging the Head: Portraiture and Social Formation in Eighteenth-Century England.* London: Yale University Press, 1993.

———. "Killing Pictures." In *Paintings and the Politics of Culture: New Essays on British Art, 1700–1850.* Ed. John Barrell. Oxford: Oxford University Press, 1992. 39–72.

Pollock, Griselda. *Vision and Difference: Femininity, Feminism, and Histories of Art.* New York: Routledge, 1988.

Pope, Alexander. "The Rape of the Lock." In *The Poems of Alexander Pope.* Ed. John Butt. London: Methuen, 1963.

Pratt, Mary Louise. *Imperial Eyes: Travel Writing and Transculturation.* New York: Routledge, 1992.

Prown, Jules David. "Benjamin West and the Use of Antiquity." *American Art* 10 (1996): 28–49.

Pulteney, Robert. *Historical and Biographical Sketches of the Progress of Botany in England from Its Origin to the Introduction of the Linnaean System.* 2 vols. London, 1790.

Regis, Pamela. *Describing Early America: Bartram, Jefferson, Crevecoeur, and the Rhetoric of Natural History.* Dekalb: Northern Illinois University Press, 1992.

Reid, Stuart, and Mike Chappell. *18th Century Highlanders.* Men-At-Arms Series. London: Osprey, 1993.

Reinhardt, Leslie. "British and Indian Identities in a Picture by Benjamin West." *Eighteenth-Century Studies* 31 (1998): 283–305.

Reynolds, Sir Joshua. *Discourses on Art.* Ed. Robert R. Wark. New Haven: Yale University Press, 1975.

Ribeiro, Aileen. *The Dress Worn at Masquerades in England, 1730 to 1790, and Its Relation to Fancy Dress in Portraiture.* New York: Garland Publishing, 1984.

Richardson, David. "The Slave Trade, Sugar, and British Economic Growth, 1748–1776." *British Capitalism and Caribbean Slavery: The Legacy of Eric Williams.* Ed. Barbara L. Solow and Stanley L. Engerman. New York: Cambridge University Press, 1987. 103–33.

Richter, David K. *The Ordeal of the Longhouse: The Peoples of the Iroquois League in the Era of European Colonization.* Chapel Hill: University of North Carolina Press, 1992.

Root, Deborah. *Cannibal Culture: Art, Appropriation, and the Commodification of Difference.* Boulder, CO: Westview Press, 1996.

Rousseau, G. S., and Roy Porter. *Exoticism in the Enlightenment.* New York: St. Martin's Press, 1990.

Said, Edward. *Culture and Imperialism.* New York: Knopf, 1993.

———. Foreword to *Selected Subaltern Studies.* Ed. Ranajit Guha and Gayatri Chakravorty Spivak. New York: Oxford University Press, 1988. v–x.

———. *Orientalism.* New York: Vintage, 1979.

Savigliano, Marta. *Tango and the Political Economy of Passion.* Boulder, CO: Westview Press, 1994.

Schaw, Janet. *Journal of a Lady of Quality; Being the Narrative of a Journey from Scotland to the West Indies, North Carolina, and Portugal, in the years 1774 to 1776.* Ed. Evangeline Walker Andrews. New Haven: Yale University Press, 1921.

Schein, Richard H. "Framing the Frontier: The New Military Tract Survey in Central New York." *New York History* 74 (1993): 5–28.

Schiebinger, Londa. *Nature's Body: Gender in the Making of Modern Science.* Boston: Beacon Press, 1993.

Sekora, John. *The Concept of Luxury in Western Thought, Eden to Smollett.* Baltimore: Johns Hopkins University Press, 1977.

Shephard, Charles. *An Historical Account of the Island of St. Vincent.* 1813; London: Cass, 1971.

Sharpe, Jenny. *Allegories of Empire: The Figure of Woman in the Colonial Text.* Minneapolis: University of Minnesota Press, 1993.

Shohat, Ella. "Notes on the 'Post-Colonial.' " *Social Text* 31/32 (1992): 99–113.

Shuffelton, Frank. Introduction to *A Mixed Race: Ethnicity in Early America.* Ed. Frank Shuffelton. New York: Oxford University Press, 1993. 1–16.

Simon, Robin. *The Portrait in Britain and America.* Boston: G. K. Hall, 1987.

Sitwell, Sacheverell. *Conversation Pieces: A Survey of English Domestic Portraits and Their Painters.* London: Batsford, 1936.

Smith, Bernard. *Imagining the Pacific: In the Wake of the Cook Voyages.* London: Yale University Press, 1992.

Soderlund, Jean R., ed. *William Penn and the Founding of Pennsylvania, 1680–1684, a Documentary History.* Philadelphia: University of Pennsylvania Press, 1983.

Solkin, David H. "Great Pictures or Great Men? Reynolds, Male Portraiture, and the Power of Art." *Oxford Art Journal* 9 (1986): 42–49.

———. *Painting for Money: The Visual Arts and the Public Sphere in Eighteenth-Century England.* London: Yale University Press, 1993.

Solow, Barbara, and Stanley L. Engerman, eds. *British Capitalism and Caribbean Slavery: The Legacy of Eric Williams.* New York: Cambridge University Press, 1987.

Sosin, Jack M. *Whitehall and the Wilderness: The Middle West in British Colonial Policy, 1760–1775.* Lincoln: University of Nebraska Press, 1961.

Spear, Percival. *The Nabobs: A Study of the Social Life of the English in Eighteenth-Century India.* 1932; London: Oxford University Press, 1963.

Spivak, Gayatri Chakravorty. "Can the Subaltern Speak?" In *Marxism and the Interpretation of Culture.* Ed. Cary Nelson and Lawrence Grossberg. Urbana: University of Illinois Press, 1988. 217–313.

———. "Subaltern Studies: Deconstructing Historiography." In *Selected Subaltern Studies.* Ed. Ranajit Guha and Gayatri Chakravorty Spivak. New York: Oxford University Press, 1988. 3–32.

Spivy, Mary, Joy Breslauer, and Ellen D'Oench. *Country Houses in Great Britain.* New Haven: Yale Center for British Art, 1980.

Spurr, David. *The Rhetoric of Empire: Colonial Discourse in Journalism, Travel*

Writing, and Imperial Administration. Durham, NC: Duke University Press, 1993.

Stafford, Barbara M. *Voyage into Substance: Art, Science, Nature, and the Illustrated Travel Account, 1760–1840.* Cambridge, MA: MIT Press, 1984.

Stafleu, Frans A. *Linnaeus and the Linnaeans: The Spreading of Their Ideas in Systematic Botany, 1735–1789.* Utrecht: Oosthoek's Uitgeversmaatschappij N.V., 1971.

Stearn, William Thomas. Introduction to *Species Plantarum and Cognate Botanical Works of Carl Linnaeus: A Facsimile of the First Edition 1753,* by Carl Linnaeus. 2 vols. London: The Ray Society, 1957. 1–176.

Steele, Richard. *The Conscious Lovers* (1722). In *British Dramatists from Dryden to Sheridan.* Ed. George H. Nettleton et al. 1939; New York: Houghton Mifflin, 1969. 435–69.

Stevens, Paul L. *A King's Colonel at Niagara, 1774–1776: Lt. Col. John Caldwell and the Beginnings of the American Revolution on the New York Frontier.* Youngstown, NY: Old Fort Niagara Association, 1987.

Stewart, David. *Sketches of the Highlanders of Scotland.* Edinburgh, 1822.

Stewart, Susan. *On Longing: Narratives of the Miniature, the Gigantic, the Souvenir, the Collection.* Durham, NC: Duke University Press, 1993.

Stoler, Ann Laura. *Race and the Education of Desire: Foucault's History of Sexuality and the Colonial Order of Things.* Durham, NC: Duke University Press, 1995.

———. "Rethinking Colonial Categories: European Communities and the Boundaries of Rule." In *Colonialism and Culture.* Ed. Nicholas B. Dirks. Ann Arbor: University of Michigan Press, 1992. 319–52.

Stone, Lawrence. *The Family, Sex and Marriage.* New York: Harper & Row, 1977.

Stone, William L. *The Life of Joseph Brant — Thayendanegea.* 2 vols. 1838; New York: Kraus Reprint Co., 1969.

Straub, Kristina. *Sexual Suspects: Eighteenth-Century Players and Sexual Ideology.* Princeton, NJ: Princeton University Press, 1992.

Swift, Jonathan. *Gulliver's Travels* (1726). Ed. Paul Turner. 1971; New York: Oxford University Press, 1990.

———. "A Letter to a Young Lady on Her Marriage" (1727). In *Satires and Personal Writings by Jonathan Swift.* Ed. William A. Eddy. London: Oxford University Press, 1973. 59–72.

Talman, James. Historical introduction to *The Journal of Major John Norton.* Ed. Carl F. Klinck and James J. Talman. Toronto: The Champlain Society, 1970. xcix–cxxiv.

Taussig, Michael. *Mimesis and Alterity: A Particular History of the Senses.* New York: Routledge, 1993.

Taylor, Ann. *Practical Hints to Young Females on the Duties of a Wife, a Mother, and a Mistress of a Family.* London, 1816.

Thomas, Nicholas. *Colonialism's Culture: Anthropology, Travel and Government.* Princeton, NJ: Princeton University Press, 1994.

———. "Johann Reinhold Forster and his *Observations.*" In *Observations Made during a Voyage round the World,* by Johann Reinhold Forster. Ed. Nicholas Thomas, Harriet Guest, and Michacl Dettelbach. Honolulu: University of Hawaii Press, 1996. xv–xxii.

———. "Licensed Curiosity: Cook's Pacific Voyages." In *The Culture of Collecting.* Ed. John Elsner and Roger Cardinal. Cambridge, MA: Harvard University Press, 1994. 116–36.

Thompson, E. P. *The Making of the English Working Class.* New York: Random House, 1964.

Thomson, James. *The Seasons and the Castle of Indolence.* Ed. James Sambrook. 1972; Oxford: Oxford University Press, 1987.

Thorton, Robert John. *The Temple of Flora: A New Illustration of the Sexual System of Linnaeus.* London, 1799, 1807.

Tobin, Beth Fowkes. *Superintending the Poor: Charitable Ladies and Paternal Landlords, 1770–1860.* New Haven: Yale University Press, 1993.

———. " 'The Tender Mother': The Social Construction of Motherhood in the *Lady's Magazine,* 1770–1837." *Women's Studies* 18 (1990): 205–21.

Todd, Janet. *Sensibility, an Introduction.* London: Methuen, 1986.

Tompkins, Jane. *The Popular Novel in England 1770–1800.* 1932; Lincoln: University of Nebraska Press, 1961.

Townsend, Joseph. *A Dissertation on the Poor Laws.* 1786; Berkeley: University of California Press, 1971.

Trevor-Roper, Hugh. "The Invention of Tradition: Highland Tradition of Scotland." In *The Invention of Tradition.* Ed. Eric Hobsbawm and Terence Ranger. 1983; Cambridge: University of Cambridge Press, 1993. 15–41.

Turrill, W. B. *The Royal Botanic Gardens, Kew, Past and Present.* London, 1959.

Viswanathan. Gauri. *The Masks of Conquest: Literary Study and British Rule in India.* New York: Columbia University Press, 1989.

———. "Raymond Williams and British Colonialism." *Yale Journal of Criticism* 4 (1991): 47–66.

von Erffa, Helmut, and Allen Staley. *The Paintings of Benjamin West.* New Haven: Yale University Press, 1986.

Wallerstein, Immanuel. *The Modern World-System.* 3 vols. New York: Academic Press, 1989.

Walvin, James. *Black Ivory: A History of the British Slave Trade.* London: Fontana Press, 1993.

————. *The Black Presence: A Documentary History of the Negro in England, 1555–1860*. London: Orbach and Chambers, 1971.

Waterhouse, Ellis. *Painting in Britain from 1530–1790*. 1953; Harmondsworth: Penguin Books, 1988.

Weinbrot, Howard D. *Augustus Caesar and "Augustan" England*. Princeton, NJ: Princeton University Press, 1978.

Welch, Stuart Cary. "A Confluence of East and West, of Art and Science." In *A Selection of Late 18th and Early 19th Century Indian Botanical Paintings*. Pittsburgh: Hunt Institute for Botanical Documentation, 1980. 8–19.

Wendorf, Richard. *Elements of Life: Biography and Portrait-Painting in Stuart and Georgian England*. Oxford: Clarendon, 1990.

White, Cynthia. *Women's Magazines, 1693–1968*. London: Michael Joseph, 1970.

White, John. *The Birth and Rebirth of Pictorial Space*. London: Faber and Faber, 1987.

White, Richard. *The Middle Ground: Indians, Empires, and Republics in the Great Lakes Region, 1650–1815*. New York: Cambridge University Press, 1991.

Williams, Eric. *Capitalism and Slavery*. 1944; Chapel Hill: University of North Carolina Press, 1994.

Williams, Raymond. *The Country and the City*. New York: Oxford University Press, 1973.

————. *Marxism and Literature*. Oxford: Oxford University Press, 1977.

Williamson, G. C. *English Conversation Pictures of the Eighteenth and Early Nineteenth Centuries*. 1931; New York: Hacker Art Books, 1975.

Wilton, Andrew. *The Swagger Portrait: Grand Manner Portraiture in Britain from Van Dyck to Augustus John*. London: Tate Gallery, 1992.

Wind, Edgar. *Hume and the Heroic Portrait: Studies in Eighteenth-Century Imagery*. Ed. Jaynie Anderson. Oxford: Clarendon Press, 1986.

Windsor, John. "Identity Parades." In *The Cultures of Collecting*. Ed. John Elsner and Roger Cardinal. Cambridge, MA: Harvard University Press, 1994. 49–67.

Wolff, Susan. *The Social Production of Art*. London: Macmillan, 1981.

Wollstonecraft, Mary. *Vindication of the Rights of Woman* (1792). 1975; New York: Norton, 1988.

Woodward, John. *The State of Physick, and of Diseases*. London, 1718.

Young, William, 2nd Bart. *An Account of the Black Charaibs in the Island of St Vincent*. London, 1795.

————. *Observations respecting the Conduct, the Accounts, and the Claims of the late Sir William Young, Bart. as Commissioner of Land*. London, 1793.

————. "Tour through the several Islands of Barbadoes, St. Vincent, Antigua, Tobago, and Grenada in the years 1791 and 1792." In *The History, Civil and Commercial, of the British West Indies.* Ed. Bryan Edwards. 5 vols. 1796, 1819; New York: AMS Press, 1966.

————, ed. *Contemplatio Philosophica,* by Brook Taylor. London, 1793.

Young, Virginia Heyer. *Becoming West Indian: Culture, Self, and Nation in St. Vincent.* Washington, DC: Smithsonian Institution Press, 1993.

Index

Abrams, Ann Uhry, 63, 79, 244 n.2, 275 n.7

Addison, Joseph, 34

African Caribbeans, free, 162–63, 165, 168

Algonquians, 5, 7, 18

Allan, David, 87

Alpers, Svetlana, 191

Ames, Ezra, 103

Anstey, Roger, 51

Anthropology, 4, 9–10, 15, 264 n.10

Antigua, 42

Apollo Belvedere, 84, 203, 205, 218, 220–24

Arber, Agnes, 190

Archer, Mildred, 3, 111, 115, 119, 129

Axtell, James, 10, 91

Bakhtin, Mikhail, 90

Banks, Sir Joseph, 24, 87, 174–78, 184–96, 271 n.36

Barrell, John, 14, 53, 211

Bayly, C. A., 117, 118, 119–20, 136

Beckles, Hilary, 11

Benevolence, 49, 50, 56, 62, 64, 76. *See also* Charity

Bentham, Jeremy, 50–51

Bentinck, William, 136–38

Berger, John, 265 n.18

Bergstrom, Ingvar, 191

Bhabha, Homi, 8, 9, 10, 15, 90, 101, 157, 257 n.44

Bigg, William: *A Lady and Her Children Relieving a Cottager*, 21, 46–55, 56

Bitterli, Urs, 61

Blackwell, Elizabeth, 182

Black Caribs, 43, 171, 237 n.39

Board of Trade, 71–78, 107, 214–17, 250 n.41, 251 n.45, 251 n.46

Bohls, Elizabeth, 209

Boldt, Menno, 61, 249 n.30, 250 n.42

Botany, 2, 24, 140, 145–47, 174–201, 212, 217

Brant, Joseph, 12, 15–16, 17, 19–20, 22, 81, 94–109

Brant, Molly, 94, 97, 256 n.28

Brindle, John, 180

Brockway, Lucille, 176

Brown, Laura, 33

Brunias, Agostino, 23–24, 139, 140, 144–45; *The Barbadoes Mulatto Girl*, 143; *French Mulatress Purchasing Fruit from a Negro Wench*, 169; *French Mulatresses and Negro Woman Bathing*, 140–50; *Linen Day, Roseau*, 170; *Linen Day, Roseau, Dominica—A Market Scene*, 160; *A West Indian Flower Girl*, 143, 170; and depiction of clothing, 146–47, 152, 156, 164, 172–73; and depiction of jewelry, 146, 161, 164, 172–73; and depiction of markets, 159, 160, 163–64, 170–71, 172–73; as an

Brunias, Agostino (*continued*)
ethnographic painter, 17, 19, 24, 139–47, 149–50, 158, 161, 173, 225
Bryson, Norman, 13, 191, 272 n.50
Burney, Frances, 30–32, 55
Butler, Judith, 15, 89, 90, 158

Calcutta artists, 12, 19, 24–25, 195–201, 225
Calcutta Botanic Garden, 19, 177, 195–96, 199
Caldwell, John (Lieutenant-Colonel), 84, 252 n.4
Caldwell, Sir John (5th Baronet), 3, 7, 22, 81, 84–91, 97, 108–9, 110, 252 n.4
Calloway, Colin, 85
Canasatego, 67–69
Carmichael, A. C. (Mrs.), 152–57, 162, 164–71
Carter, Paul, 187–88
Casteels, Pieter, 180
Catesby, Mark, 182
Cator, William, 120–21
Chakrabarty, Dipesh, 212
Charity, 47–55
Chatoyer, 171
Chrisman, Laura, 9
Churchill, Ward, 85, 91, 259 n.63
Clarkson, Thomas, 51
Cloth, 57–63, 97, 151–61, 257 n.35; in Africa, 160, 266 n.30; as a commodity, 57, 63, 65; cultural meanings of, 59–60; as fetish, 151, 161; as a gift, 65, 246 n.15
Clothing, 139, 140, 144, 145, 150; African Caribbean, 144, 151, 152, 158–61; African styles in, 158–61, 225; British, 81, 93, 96, 99, 102, 114, 136, 158, 161; children's, 47–48, 127, 240 n.57; classical, 209, 218; contemporary, 209, 220–21; exotic, 110–11; as finery, 59–60, 152–53, 156, 157; gala, 15, 152–53, 158; Highland, 104, 203, 221–24, 278 n.29; hybrid, 15, 19–20, 22, 84, 94, 96, 99, 105, 107; Indian (South-Asian), 115, 116, 126–28, 136, 262 n.42; military, 12, 19–20, 22, 81, 82, 93–102, 125, 220–22; Mughal, 7, 111, 114, 128; Native American, 7, 15, 19–20, 22, 57–61, 81–103 *passim*, 225;

Quaker, 58–60; semiotics of, 139, 157–61; slave, 19, 24, 151–62, 164, 166–67, 172–73, 225; as souvenirs, 84, 86, 87, 91; Van Dyck, 41–43, 46; women's love of, 59–60
Cohn, Bernard, 262 n.42
Colley, Linda, 54
Colonial discourse, 8, 13, 228 n.16, 243 n.76
Colonialism, 1–26, 202, 203, 207, 214, 224–26, definition of, 273 n.1; and knowledge, 211–17
Comaroff, John, and Jean Comaroff, 10, 264 n.10
Commerce, 28–30, 31–37, 57–65, 121, 144, 150, 171–72
Commodities, 168–70, 177; agricultural, 45; land as, 248 n.27; and luxury, 21, 27–29, 31–39; as trade goods, 57–63, 257 n.36
Conversation piece, 21, 39, 46, 111, 116, 120–25, 127, 235 n.27. *See also* Portraiture
Cook, James, 175, 185, 187–88, 214, 271 n.38
Copley, John Singleton, *Hugh Montgomerie*, 25, 202–7, 218–24
Cornwallis, Lord, 117–19, 128, 138
Costume. *See* Clothing
Craton, Michael, 10, 44, 45
Cross-dressing: cultural, 2, 12, 19, 22, 81, 82, 86–91, 108–9, 110–11, 139; definition of, 252 n.2; and drag, 88–90, 158
Cultural studies, 13, 15
Cumberland, Richard, 32

Dabydeen, David, 28, 37, 234 n.22
Davies, David, 50
Defoe, Daniel, 162–63
Delaware(s), 21, 22, 57, 59, 61–79, 93–94, 202
Desmond, Ray, 177
Devis, Arthur William, 23, 129–35, 262 n.37; *The Honorable William Monson and His Wife*, 130; *Lady Chambers*, 129; *Louisa Dent and Her Children*, 130–35; *Sir Robert Chambers*, 129; *William Dent with His Brother John*, 130–35

Dirks, Nicholas, 9, 228 n.16
Domesticity, 23, 25, 29–30, 41, 42, 45–55, 111–38 *passim. See also* Women
Dominica, 17, 40, 42, 43, 145, 152
Dress. *See* Clothing

East India Company, 4, 23, 24, 32, 117–21, 127–28, 136–38, 177, 195–96, 199
Edwards, Bryan, 145, 171–72
Edwards, Phyllis, 195–96
Ehret, Georg, 178
Elihu Yale, 2nd Duke of Devonshire, Lord Cavendish, Mr. Tunstal, and a Page, 38–39, 225
Enlightenment, 179, 189, 211
Equiano, Olaudah, 162–64
Eriksson, Gunnar, 184
Ethnographic art, 19, 24, 139–50, 158, 161, 164, 173, 214, 263 n.2
Ethnography (multi-sited), 7
Evelyn, John, 180
Exotic, 20–21, 27–30, 33–39, 54, 55, 57, 82, 85, 86, 107, 110, 114, 139, 140, 143, 185–87, 207, 220–23, 232 n.3, 257 n.36

Fabian, Johannes, 264 n.10
Fancy pictures, 140, 143. *See also* Genre paintings
Fanon, Frantz, 10
Ferguson, Moira, 52, 53, 233 n.6, 243 n.76
Fetish, 90, 266 n.32, 267 n.33
Fosberg, F. R., 194
Foucault, Michel, 15, 189
Franklin, Benjamin, 63, 75, 76, 79
Frontier, 6, 7, 65, 66, 71, 74–78, 96
Fryd, Vivien Green, 64
Fuss, Diana, 89, 255 n.20

Gainsborough, Thomas, 134–35; *The Morning Walk,* 134–35; *John Pamplin,* 135
Garber, Marjorie, 90
Gascoigne, John, 271 n.36
Genre paintings, 47, 140. *See also* Fancy pictures
Gilman, Sander, 39, 234 n.22
Gilroy, Paul, 14
Girouard, Mark, 21

Gorachaud, 196
Grewal, Inderpal, 9
Guest, Harriet, 14, 15, 85, 186
Guha, Ranajit, 9, 12

Hall, Stuart, 11, 15, 27, 230 n.25
Hamilton, Milton, 100
Harlow, Vincent, 5
Hastings, Warren, 4, 112, 113, 118, 126, 127, 128
Headrick, Daniel, 176
Hebdige, Dick, 15, 158, 160
Henrey, Blanche, 180
Hickey, Thomas, 116
Highland regiments, 203, 206–7, 221–22, 224
Hill, John, 95, 255 n.24
Historiography, colonialist, 10
History painting, 93, 96, 209, 221, 225
Hogarth, William, 142; *A Harlot's Progress,* 26–27, 36–37, 38, 39, 47, 55; *Marriage à la Mode,* 37, 38, 39, 47, 55
Hybridity, 20, 22, 96–97, 105, 107–8, 139, 225; in genres, 20–21, 205–6, 225

Illustration(s), 2, 139–40, 145, 146, 178–201, 208, 214, 225, 270 n.16
Imperialism, definition of, 273 n.1. *See also* Colonialism
Impey, Lady, 195
Impey, Sir Elijah, 126–28, 138
India, 4, 5, 19, 20, 23, 30–32, 50, 111–38
Indians (Native Americans). *See* specific tribes
Irigaray, Luce, 255 n.20
Iroquois, 18, 22, 64–79, 93, 95, 96, 101, 106

Jennings, Francis, 10, 66, 67, 70, 247 n.23, 248 n.28
Jewelry, 19, 57–60, 84, 97, 99, 103, 115, 139, 150, 158, 161
Johnson, E. D. H., 263 n.6
Johnson, Guy, 20, 81, 91–97, 99, 108–9, 110
Johnson, Samuel, 188–89, 208, 217, 218
Johnson, Sir John, 96
Johnson, Sir William, 6–7, 71–79, 94, 96–97, 216

Kew Gardens, 24, 175–77, 187, 201, 271
  n.37
Kneller, Sir Godfrey, 39

Landa, Louis, 33
La Pérouse, Jean François, 212–14
Latour, Bruno, 25, 211–18, 224, 277
  n.20
Lawson, Philip, 119
Lawson, William, 180
Leppert, Richard, 12, 14, 120–25, 235
  n.27, 239 n.52, 261 n.34
Lesch, John, 183–84
Lewis, Matthew, 151
Lillo, George, 34, 163
Linnaean botany. *See* Botany
Linné, Carl von, 175, 176, 178, 183–85,
  212, 271 n.46
Lovejoy, Arthur, 146–47
Luxury, 31, 35. *See also* Commodities

Mackenzie, Henry, 49–50
Mandeville, Bernard, 35
Marcus, George, 7
Marshall, P. J., 137, 138
Masquerade(s), 15, 16, 37, 41, 86–91,
  96, 104–5, 110, 254 n.12, 255 n.20
McClintock, Anne, 9, 90
McConnell, Michael, 248 n.28
McDonald, Roderick, 170
Merian, Maria Sibylla, 180–82
Mimicry, 12, 15, 19, 89–92, 101, 108,
  139, 157–58, 255 n.20, 257 n.44, 258
  n.48
Mitchell, W. J. T., 13
Mohawk(s), 15, 16, 67, 70, 81, 86,
  94–108
Montagu, Lady Mary Wortley, 110,
  253 n.11
Moore-Gilbert, Bart, 9
More, Hannah, 48, 52–53, 114–15
Morse, Robert, 121
Mulatto(es), 147–49, 169, 170

Nammack, Georgiana, 248 n.27, 249
  n.30, 249 n.33
Natural history, 17, 23, 24, 140, 144–
  47, 161, 174–75, 179, 190, 195, 199,
  212, 225
Natural history painting (Mughal),
  199–201

Nochlin, Linda, 3, 265 n.18, 275 n.8

Obeyesekere, Gananath, 10
Oneidas, 70, 86
Onondagas, 67, 70, 249 n.33

Pal, Pratapaditya, and Vidya Dehejia,
  262 n.42
Palmer, William, 112–14, 118
Parkinson, Sydney, 24–25, 140, 175–76,
  191–94, 201, 208, 214
Parody, 19, 88–90, 139, 157, 161, 255
  n.20
Parry, Benita, 8–9
Patterson, Orlando, 10, 158
Paulson, Ronald, 234 n.22, 235 n.23
Penn, Thomas, 57, 63–80, 216
Penn, William, 56–65, 75, 245–46 n.10
Phelan, Peggy, 15, 16, 103
Planters, sugar, 6, 19, 24, 32, 42–46.
  See also West Indies
Plantocracy. *See* Planters
Pocock, J. G. A., 33
Pointon, Marcia, 14, 231 n.30, 254 n.14
Pope, Alexander, 33
Portraiture, 205–6; country house,
  129, 131; dynamics of, 16, 219–20,
  231 n.37; family, 39–43, 45–46, 111–
  17, 121, 123–28; fancy dress, 41–43,
  46, 86–87; grand style in, 208–11,
  217–20; heroic, 218–24; of mis-
  tresses, 115–17; as performance, 16,
  103; state, 91, 99, 121; tourist, 87. *See
  also* Conversation piece
Postcolonial studies, 8, 9, 10
Postcolonial theory, 8–11, 13, 15
Pratt, Mary Louise, 9, 174–75
Pulteney, Robert, 183
Pye, Henry, 185

Quakers, 57–63, 94

Ramsey, James, 51
Regis, Pamela, 146
Renaldi, Francesco, 136; *Boulone,
  Bibi of Colonel Martin, Fishing with
  Martin's Adopted Son*, 116; *A Euro-
  pean with His Family*, 111–12, 114,
  116–17, 128; *Muslim Lady Seated
  with a Hookah*, 115; *The Palmer
  Family*, 112–17, 122, 123, 128

Reynolds, Sir Joshua, 188–89, 205, 208–12, 217–23
Richardson, David, 44
Richter, David, 10, 69
Rigaud, John Francis, 16–17, 22, 81, 99–101, 107
Romney, George, 99, 100
Roxburgh, William, 195–99

Sachet, Marie-Hélène, 194
Said, Edward, 8, 9, 12, 229 n.20
Sandby, Paul, 142
Schaw, Janet, 148, 166
Schiebinger, Londa, 182–83
Senecas, 67, 70, 75, 78, 86
Seven Years' War, 206
Sharpe, Jenny, 10
Shawnees, 70, 72, 75, 76, 78
Shohat, Ella, 9
Simon, Robin, 43
Sitwell, Sacheverell, 42, 43
Six Nations. See Iroquois
Slavery, 43–46, 52–53, 144–73 passim; abolition of, 51–54, 165, 242 n.72, 242 n.73, 243 n.76; defense of, 153, 165
Slave(s), 2, 52–53, 97, 140, 146–73
Slave trade, 31, 42, 43–46, 51, 54, 242 n.72, 242 n.73
Smith, Bernard, 3, 190–91, 232 n.3, 263 n.2, 271 n.38, 271 n.39
Solander, Daniel, 175–76, 191–94
Solkin, David, H., 14, 33, 49, 231 n.30, 235 n.23, 244 n.2, 274 n.2, 277 n.22
Sovereignty, 61, 80, 101, 105–7
Spear, Percival, 120
Spivak, Gayatri Chakravorty, 8, 9
Stafleu, Frans, 176, 184
Stearn, W. T., 183–84
Steele, Richard, 34
Stephens, Paul, 84
Stewart, Susan, 15, 86
Still life, 190–91, 201, 272 n.50
Stoler, Ann Laura, 4, 9, 260 n.12
Stone, William, 105
Stuart, Gilbert, 99, 100
St. Vincent, 17, 40, 42, 43, 145, 152, 171, 177
Subaltern Studies, 9, 10
Sugar Plantations. See West Indies

Sunday markets, 17, 152, 162–70
Swift, Jonathan, 34–35, 36, 37

Taussig, Michael, 15, 97–99, 157
Taxonomy, 139, 145–47, 183, 187–88, 189
Taylor, Ann, 49
Teedyuscung, 66, 76
Thistlewood, Thomas, 148, 151
Thomas, Nicholas, 9, 228 n.16, 264 n.10, 270 n.16
Thorton, Robert, 185–86
Tobago, 40, 42
Townsend, Joseph, 50–51, 53
Trade. See Commerce
Treaty of Fort Stanwix, 65, 251, n.45, 251 n.46

Valenti, Michael Bernard, 182
Vishnupersaud, 196
Viswanathan, Gauri, 9, 14

Walking Purchase, 65, 66, 68, 74, 75
Wallace, Tara Goshal, 30
Wallerstein, Immanuel, 273 n.1
Wallich, Nathaniel, 195
Walpole, Horace, 209
Walvin, James, 10, 148–49, 169–70
Weiditz, Hans, 190
Welch, Stuart Cary, 195
Wesley, John, 51
West, Benjamin, 205, 218, 244 n.2; Colonel Guy Johnson, 22, 91–97, 99, 101, 255 n.24; The Death of General Wolfe, 220–225; William Penn's Treaty with the Indians, 3, 12, 18, 21, 56–80 passim, 93–94, 96, 139, 225 and Banks, 87; and Native American dress, 57–61, 93, 95; in Rome, 223; and Thomas Penn, 21, 65
West Indies, 139–72 passim; history of, 10; planters, 42–46, 148–49, 151–57, 168, 169; sugar plantations in, 42–46, 144, 168, 238 n.51, 239 n.55. See also individual islands
Wheatley, Francis, 142
White, James, 180
White, Richard, 97, 257 n.36
Williams, Eric, 44–45
Williams, Raymond, 14, 25
Williamson, G. C., 40

Wilton, Andrew, 277 n.21
Wolff, Susan, 14
Wollstonecraft, Mary, 48, 241 n.63
Women: and charity, 49–55; and
    clothing, 59–61; and motherhood,
    47–49, 111–17, 122; and racial purity,
    119
Woodward, John, 35, 36

Young, Sir William (1st Baronet), 17,
    23, 40–46, 140, 145, 171, 236 n.34
Young, Sir William (2nd Baronet),
    40, 151, 152–53, 156, 157, 161–62, 164,
    167, 171–72

Zoffany, Johan, 127, 136; *Colonel Blair
    with his Family and an Ayah*, 123–25,
    133; *The Family of Sir William Young,
    Baronet*, 21, 23, 39–47, 55, 116–17,
    229; *The Impey Family*, 125–28, 135,
    195; *The Morse and Cator Families*,
    120–25, 127; *Sir Elijah Impey*, 91, 92,
    121

Beth Fowkes Tobin is Professor of English at the University of Hawai'i at Mānoa. She is the author of *History, Gender, and Eighteenth-Century Literature* and *Superintending the Poor: Charitable Ladies and Paternal Landlords in British Fiction, 1770–1860*.

Library of Congress Cataloging-in-Publication Data

Tobin, Beth Fowkes.
Picturing imperial power : colonial subjects in eighteenth-century
British painting / Beth Fowkes Tobin.
p. cm.
Includes bibliographical references and index.
ISBN 0-8223-2305-2 (cloth : alk. paper). — ISBN 0-8223-2338-9
(pbk. : alk. paper)
1. Painting, British—Themes, motives. 2. Painting, Modern—
18th century—Great Britain—Themes, motives. 3. Great
Britain—Colonies—In art. I. Title.
ND466.T59 1999
758'.9325341—dc21   98-38415